Kate.

MEMOIR

MY LIFE AND THEMES

MEMOIR

MY LIFE AND THEMES

CONOR CRUISE O'BRIEN

Cooper Square Press

Published by Cooper Square Press,
An Imprint of Rowman & Littlefield Publishers, Inc.
150 Fifth Avenue, Suite 911
New York, New York 10011

Distributed by National Book Network

Library of Congress Cataloging-in-Publication Data

O'Brien, Conor Cruise, 1917–
    Memoir : my life and themes / Conor Cruise O'Brien.— 1st Cooper Square Press ed.
        p. cm.
    Originally published : Dublin : Poolbeg, 1998.
    Includes index.
    ISBN 0-8154-1064-6 (cloth : alk. paper)
    1. O'Brien, Conor Cruise, 1917– 2. Authors, Irish—20th century—Biography.
    3. Diplomats—Ireland—Biography. 4. Scholars—Ireland—Biography. I. Title.

    PR6065.B67 Z47 2000
    808'.0092—dc21
    [B]   00-021774

DEDICATION

In loving memory
of dearest Kate:
Died 26 March 1998

PREFACE

FOR A GOOD MANY YEARS I HAD VAGUELY THOUGHT ABOUT WRITING MY memoirs, some day, but was in no hurry about it. Then, in July 1996 I suffered a stroke. With my wife's help, I made a very good recovery. But I had been made to realise that time was running out, and that if I was to complete my memoirs I had better start writing them.

My daughter Kate was by then Editorial Director of Poolbeg Press, Dublin. She encouraged the project and Poolbeg became my publishers, for the island of Ireland. She read the chapters, as I wrote them, liked them and encouraged me. By March 1998 most of the book was written and she told me she had written the publisher's material which she wanted to show me. We arranged to have luncheon together at a restaurant to discuss progress, and also to celebrate a little. I was to pick her up at her house and we would go to the restaurant, as we used to do from time to time. It was an occasion to which I greatly looked forward, as I drove to her house on March 25, 1998.

When I arrived at the house, Kate was stretched out on the floor, unconscious. Her son Alexander was with her and had just called for an ambulance. When the brain haemorrhage hit her she was on the phone to Penny Hoare of my London publishers, Christopher Sinclair-Stephenson,

1

about my book. The call was never completed. We got Kate to the hospital but she never recovered consciousness.

On the following morning, March 26, Kate was being kept alive on a respirator. Her husband Joe Kearney and son Alexander were with her, as were her mother, Christine, her sister Fedelma with Fedelma's husband Nicholas, my wife Máire and myself, and our Patrick. Her remaining family, my eldest son Donal with his wife Rita and my youngest daughter Margaret, were on their way from London. Around noon the doctors told us that she could be kept technically alive for some time on the respirator, but that all hope of recovery was over. They gently recommended that the respirator be switched off and that she be allowed to die. We knew that that is what she would have wished in the circumstances, and we agreed. She died in about half an hour. So far as we could tell, she did not suffer.

Her funeral was attended by a large number of friends and admirers, and we received many kind and moving letters which helped us greatly. One letter in particular put into words the thought which was already vaguely beginning to help me. The letter was from Susan Dunn, Professor of French at Williams College, Williamstown, Massachusetts. Susan had become a friend of Máire's and my own when I had been a Visiting Professor at Williams College and we had kept in touch ever since. In the course of her letter, Susan wrote: "Time helps to heal the acute pain we feel, but our loved ones always stay with us. I feel like Proust whom I taught the other day – my parents are never really gone from me. I can't see them or touch them, but they are with me, and their wonderful, generous, self-sacrificing love always remains. Our relationship evolves in its own way, and I find some peace."

As I read these words I thought not only about Kate, but also about my late friend, Vivian Mercier who – as it so happened – I had known for almost exactly the same time as had been given to me with Kate – fifty years in both cases. And since Vivian's death, I have never felt that he was finally gone from me. Faced with any difficult choice – and in particular when I felt I might be in some danger of fooling myself about my own motivation – I asked myself what Vivian would have said, and I knew him so well that I felt I knew exactly what he would have said. It would have been kind, but alert and a little sardonic. If I were inclined to kid myself, Vivian – for my own sake – would never allow me to do that.

And I could see, as I thought about Susan's letter, that I would have a continuing relationship with Kate, of a very similar kind, though not identical. I shall always consult her about any difficult choice, and I feel I know what she will have to tell me. There will be some irony too in her perceptions, but in both cases it is a kind and salutary irony. And the mild irony of intelligent people who love us, with all our failings, is one of the best things in the world.

As I finish this preface, only one section of these memoirs remains to be written. This is the section concerning Northern Ireland and the so-called "peace process" whose sinister evolution still continues, and so has to be left to the last. Kate's feelings and ideas about these matters were similar to mine, but not identical. So the silent dialogue with her will continue and help to heal. I know, to my deep consolation, that such a healing dialogue will continue on many topics. The words "a posthumous dialogue" came unbidden to my mind. And I know that dialogue will continue throughout whatever may remain to me of life.

Shortly after Kate's death, I asked Máire to write a poem about it, feeling that the poem would do me good. She wrote it, and it did help. The poem is as follows, first in the original Gaelic and then in translation:

"A Creature of Extremes . . ."
I ndilchuimhne ar Kate.

Do luaisc sí riamh ó rabharta go mallabhra,
Níorbh aithnid di leath-thaoide . . .
Ceileatram uirthi an Ghaoluinn –
Ach dá labhróinn as Béarla,
Ní sheasódh an croí.

Caoineann a cairde raidhse a hábaltachta
Agus a féile;
Caoineann a fear beanchéile thaodach chaoin,
An mac a mháthair . . .
Ach a máthair sise?
Agus a hathair?
Cé léifidh a ndólás?

Bearna san ál –
Na gearrcaigh eile claoite –
Cúlaím uaidh-sin . . .
Cuimhneoidh mé ar an ngearrchaile gleoite –
Faoi mar a gháir sí!
Sarar luigh ualach a buanna
Anuas ar a guailne.

In Loving Memory of Kate.

She swung ever between the tides of neap and spring;
Halftide was unknown to her –
The Irish disguises her,
But if I spoke in English,
Heart could not endure.

Her friends weep for the wealth of her ability
And for her generosity;
Her husband mourns his stormy, tender wife,
Her son his mother –
But what of *her* mother?
And of her father?
Who will read their grief?

The gap in the little brood –
The other nestlings prostrate –
I draw back from that . . .
I will remember the lovely little girl –
How she laughed!
Before her weight of talent
Descended on her shoulders.

Máire Mac an tSaoi

1

MY LIFE AND THEMES

THE FIRST SOUND I CAN REMEMBER IS A SERIES OF BOOMING NOISES WHICH woke me up. The cause of the noise was the bombardment of the Four Courts Dublin beginning at 4.07 a.m. on Wednesday, June 28, 1922. I was then four-and-a-half years old. That bombardment is generally considered to be the beginning of the Irish Civil War, which lasted throughout the remainder of my fifth year and into my sixth.

The background to the bombardment, and the political and military setting of my early life need to be told if the reader is to understand the rest of the story. These were as follows:

Up to December of 1918, all Ireland was still part of the United Kingdom, along with Great Britain. Representatives freely chosen by all the Irish constituencies sat in the parliament of the United Kingdom. My maternal grandfather, David Sheehy, was one of these representatives. He had started his active career as an organiser for the Irish Land League, the great agrarian combination that shattered the power of the Irish landlords in the 1880s. In consequence he was elected to Westminster as a member of the Irish Parliamentary Party, and sat there from 1885 to 1918. The policy of the IPP was to induce Britain, through parliamentary pressure, to grant Home Rule to Ireland. Home Rule did not mean independence; it meant autonomy within the British empire, a goal then generally accepted by most Irish people.

The goal seemed about to be achieved when, on May 9, 1912, the Third Home Rule Bill was carried in the House of Commons, an event that over the next two years was to take the whole of the United Kingdom to the verge of civil war. The Protestants of eastern Ulster – what is now Northern Ireland – pledged themselves to resist incorporation in a Home Rule Ireland, and armed themselves in proof of their determination to resist.

It soon became clear that eastern Ulster could not be included in Home Rule Ireland unless the British forced it in. The British government did not see how that could be done, and had no inclination to try to find out. So it would be Home Rule with partition; the nationalists (Catholics) could have Home Rule, which was what they wanted: the unionists (Protestants) could stay in the United Kingdom, since that was what they wanted. In retrospect this settlement, in its general character (though not in the precise form it was to take, in 1920), seems to me sound: respectful of the realities on the ground, and of the principle of the consent of the governed.

That, however, was very much not how it appeared to nationalists at the time (or since). Nationalists of every shade regarded partition as a betrayal, a capitulation to naked force. I don't think it ever occurred to any nationalist that the determination of a million Ulster Protestants to stay in the United Kingdom represented any kind of moral force whatever. Symmetrically, no unionist ever conceded that the desire of three million nationalists for Home Rule had any moral force whatever. In any case, each community had a low opinion of the general morals of the other, so the idea of the other as representing any kind of moral force was too outlandish to be entertained.

We can observe in many contexts that people bent on seceding from an established political entity are always outraged when someone else tries to secede from the political entity they are bent on establishing. We see this today in various parts of the former Soviet Union and the former Yugoslavia. It was strongly manifest in Ireland on the eve of the First World War. Nationalists held that they had a right to secede from the United Kingdom but that unionists did not have the right to secede from the entity the nationalists themselves sought to create: Home Rule Ireland.

Among those who held these opinions were my father and mother: nationalists of the mildest and most tolerant description and, of course, *constitutional* nationalists, as opposed to physical-force nationalists. Most Irish nationalists were constitutional before the First World War. My mother, born Kathleen Sheehy, was a teacher of Irish in a technical school; she is the original of Miss Ivors, the Gaelic-language enthusiast, in James Joyce's story "The Dead". My father, Francis Cruise O'Brien, was a journalist on two moderate nationalist newspapers; *The Freeman's Journal* and later *The Irish Independent*. He was an agnostic, and had produced an edition of WEH Lecky's history of the rise of nationalism in Europe. He had also written a tract intended to refute the unionist contention that "Home Rule means Rome Rule". Home Rule Ireland would, he thought, be quite a tolerant and secular sort of place. He was to find out, in the early years of the new state, that the "Rome Rule" gibe had a lot more substance to it than he had bargained for.

As a boy, of course, and also as a young man, I accepted my parents' interpretation of the Home Rule crisis of 1912-1914. I can no longer accept that, but I respect my parents' *feelings* about those transactions, quite independently of the validity of their interpretation of them. There could be no mistaking, in their faces and their voices, the depth of the personal anguish they both experienced as they contemplated that turning point in the history of Ireland (and of the United Kingdom).

The source of the anguish was not the "loss" of eastern Ulster – not by any means. Few Catholics and nationalists born in what is now the Republic of Ireland have ever cared all that much about what is now Northern Ireland, and my parents were no exception. The source of the anguish was the impact on *us* inside the Catholic and nationalist community (of what is now the Republic), of the tragic and unexpected flaw that became apparent at the very moment of the seeming triumph of the Home Rule cause. The totally unexpected partition of Ireland compromised the constitutional nationalists in the eyes of their own constituents. And the fact that partition had been conceded only after a show of force by unionists was seen, by an increasingly influential group, as legitimising recourse to force on the nationalist side. The creation and arming of the Irish Volunteers (Catholic nationalists) followed on the creation of the Ulster Volunteer Force (Protestant unionists).

Moderate nationalists and extreme ones interpreted the sequence of transactions in much the same way. As my father put it, speaking of Ulster Protestants, and unionists, "The Orangemen brought the gun back into Irish politics". Patrick Pearse, who was to provide the inspiration for the Easter Rising of 1916 (to which I shall come in a moment) expressed this thought with a significant difference, but the principle is the same. Pearse was replying to certain nationalists who were jeering at the Ulster Volunteers for their military posturing. Pearse said, "I think the Orangeman with the rifle a much less ridiculous figure than the nationalist without a rifle".

As I say, I shared, or rather inherited, my parents' feelings about the transactions of 1912-14 (as distinct from their intellectual interpretation of the source of their grief). I am their son, after all, and my grandfather's grandson. I have what Irish republicans (extreme nationalists) used to call "the bad parliamentary drop". The "drop" there is a drop of blood, meaning that republicans detected, in the families of members of the old Irish Parliamentary Party, a genetically transmitted inclination to be pro-British. They had a point of sorts. The members of the Irish Parliamentary Party, including my grandfather *were* pro-British by comparison with the Brit-hating republican tradition, from the Fenians to the modern IRA, and I, too, am pro-British in the same sense. When I listen to such republicans going on about the Brits, and quite often about me personally, I comfort myself by recalling the neat verdict on such as these pronounced by an unidentified wit: "He has a mind like an unripe gooseberry – small, bitter, fuzzy, and green."

When my father said that "the Orangemen brought the gun back into Irish politics" he was omitting the nationalist contribution. It was the nationalist insistence on including the Orangemen in a united Ireland *against their known and fervently declared wishes* that made the Orangemen "bring back the gun". But no nationalist, however constitutional, could ever manage to see it that way. I see it that way now because I have ceased to be an Irish nationalist.

When Imperial Germany's invasion of Belgium precipitated the entry of the United Kingdom into the First World War, the Irish Parliamentary Party, in the House of Commons, declared its support for the war effort. This might seem surprising in view of what nationalists generally regarded as a betrayal over partition. But most Irish Catholics still wanted Home Rule, even without eastern Ulster. There was at that time general (if grudging) acceptance in Ireland of the Irish Parliamentary Party's position, and Irish Catholics joined the armed forces in large numbers. Among those who did so were my mother's two brothers, Richard and Eugene Sheehy, and also Tom Kettle, the husband of my mother's sister Mary. (Mary, who was a great beauty, had been secretly admired by James Joyce, but didn't take him seriously. Tom was an MP, handsome and charming, and "brilliant" in more obvious ways than Joyce was.) My father was in favour of the war effort but not fit to serve; no recruiting sergeant would have looked at him twice. He had been a premature child and was small and thin to the verge of emaciation. But he was high-spirited and verbally aggressive, with a neat turn of phrase. He wanted to make recruiting speeches, but my mother put her foot down. She said that someone who could not fight on his own account should not go around telling other people it was their duty to fight. Fair enough – but I think there was more to it than that.

My mother was the youngest of the six Sheehy siblings. The eldest, and much the most forceful personality, was Hanna. Hanna was married to Francis Sheehy-Skeffington. Both Hanna and Frank were feminists (hence the hyphenated name), socialists, and pacifists. They were against the war effort, formally on socialist and pacifist grounds (with possibly a dash of feminism as well). But again I think there was more to it than that. Frank was very close, especially from 1914 to 1916, to James Connolly, who was to be joint leader, with Patrick Pearse, of the Easter Rising in Dublin. Connolly was the leading socialist in Ireland, and the initial bond between the two men was their common commitment to socialism. But from the outbreak of the First World War until his death in 1916, Connolly's real and passionate commitment was to revolutionary nationalism. As a recent biographer, Austen Morgan, says, "In August 1914 Connolly became a revolutionary nationalist". Skeffington went a long way, though not all the way, with Connolly in that direction. His pacifism had been subject to deviation even before the war. In March of 1914 his name appeared on a list of members of the "army council" of the Irish Citizen Army. He dropped out shortly afterward; he was clearly torn by conflicting feelings. In May of 1915 he wrote an "Open Letter to Thomas MacDonagh", reproaching him for having "boasted of being one of the creators of a new militarism in Ireland". MacDonagh – who, like Connolly, was executed for his share in the Easter Rising – was, in terms of the rhetoric still habitual to Connolly and Skeffington (though it was increasingly perfunctory in Connolly's case), a "bourgeois nationalist", which perhaps made his militarism more conspicuous that that of the "socialist" Connolly. Skeffington never addressed any such rebuke, or *any* known rebuke, to Connolly, whose newspaper, the *Workers' Republic* was becoming increasingly violent in its revolutionary nationalism at about the same time that Skeffington admonished MacDonagh about militarism.

Nine days after his open letter Skeffington was arrested and sentenced to six months imprisonment for his public attacks on British militarism. With characteristic courage and determination he went immediately on a hunger – and then a thirst – strike. Seeing that he was clearly prepared to die if not released, the British set him free after seven days. They were sufficiently unnerved to allow him to proceed to the neutral United States on a lecture tour, although the object of his journey was quite clearly to engage in propaganda against American support for the Allied cause. After his return to Ireland, Skeffington "reported his impressions of the new world" at a meeting chaired by Connolly. When a speaker proclaimed, according to the *Workers' Republic*, that she "did not want the war stopped until the British Empire was smashed", Skeffington countered by proposing a debate on "peace now". Yet the bloodthirsty speaker – Constance Markievicz, later sentenced to death (but not executed) for her share in the Easter Rising – was expressing Connolly's view. In the following month (on February 18, 1916) Markievicz, ably supported by Connolly, won the support of a Dublin meeting for the notion that Ireland could only benefit from a prolonged war. Skeffington was still a pacifist, but his loyalty to Connolly does not seem to have been shaken by Connolly's adoption of this extravagantly nationalist and militaristic position. Skeffington did criticize Connolly at subsequent rallies, but he continued to write for Connolly's *Workers' Republic*, at a time (March and April of 1916) when that paper was clearly on an insurrectionary course. And Skeffington retained Connolly's confidence to the end. Connolly had nominated Skeffington as his literary executor; he would not have taken this step had he not known that Skeffington, despite his pacifist scruples, was in full ideological sympathy with him. It seems that Skeffington's pacifism by this time had become limited to a personal determination not to commit any act of violence. But he risked his own life in a non-violent way, and lost it. Connolly, until the eve of his execution, did not know that his literary executor was already dead; shot by British troops in the course of the rising that Connolly and his friends had started. I shall come back to that.

The wartime conversion of pacifist (or near-pacifist) socialists into nationalists was a universal European phenomenon in 1914. But it generally involved support for the war effort. In Ireland, since Irish nationalism (in its intense forms) is anti-British, aroused nationalism took the form first of opposition to the British war effort and then, in 1916, of contributing to the war effort of the Central Powers.

At the beginning of the war Connolly had ostensibly been neutral. Across the front of his union's headquarters, at Liberty Hall in Dublin, was a banner reading "We serve neither king nor Kaiser but Ireland". But as the war went on, the causes of the Kaiser and Ireland began to coalesce. In October of 1915 the *Workers' Republic* identified Imperial Germany as (according to Austen Morgan) "a nation resisting dependency". By December of the same year the message was clearer and louder. Constance Markievicz presented a marching song to Connolly's Irish Citizen Army: "The Germans Are Winning the War, Me Boys." By January of 1916

Connolly had joined the military council of the Irish Republican Brotherhood, an organisation that, although it had nothing socialist about it, was preparing for an insurrection, for which it sought aid from Imperial Germany. The Proclamation of the Republic, in Easter week of 1916, referred to Ireland as supported "by her exiled children in America and by gallant allies in Europe". In the minds of the more politically sophisticated planners of the Rising, that event was to provide credentials for admission to the eventual peace conference, which was of course expected to be dominated by the Central Powers. At least two of those planners, Pearse and MacDonagh, intended that at that peace conference the Crown of Ireland should be offered to a German prince, whom they may have believed to be a member of a Roman Catholic branch of the house of Hohenzollern. The authors of that project – Joseph Mary Plunkett and Seán MacDermott – were to be two of the seven signatories, along with James Connolly, of the Proclamation of the Irish Republic.

All this was very far from the intellectual world which had normally been inhabited by Francis and Hanna Sheehy-Skeffington. But they were now near to it emotionally, through their association with James Connolly – an association not diminished by Connolly's mutation from a socialist into a revolutionary nationalist. Paradoxically, it was Frank's pacifism, even more than his socialism, that commended him to Connolly at this time. In theory pacifism was universal: opposed to all war efforts everywhere. In practice each pacifist lived in a particular country, and the activity of any particular pacifist damaged one particular war effort, and so benefited another one. An Irish pacifist impeded the British war effort, mainly by slowing up recruiting. Most Irish opponents of the British war effort were not pacifists: they were extreme nationalists. But the nationalists had a warm welcome for Irish pacifists, whom they saw as valuable allies, adding a humanitarian and cosmopolitan touch to the common cause. In those years pacifists were not welcome in the houses of most constitutional nationalists, who were committed to the war effort. The Sheehy-Skeffingtons kept up connections with their relatives "on the other side", but the conversation must have been restricted to items of family interest. Very few other pacifists were around, and those that were must have been worried about the Sheehy-Skeffingtons, especially when Frank's name appeared – however briefly – on the list of members of the army council of the Irish Citizen Army. Unionists hated pacifists, and in any case unionists and nationalists – of whatever description – did not mingle socially. So the only circle where the Sheehy-Skeffingtons were really welcome, having a sense of being on the same side on the things that mattered, was that of the extreme nationalists. It is not surprising that they should have taken on something of the tone and mind-set of the circle in which they were welcome. Just as exalted nationalism came to replace socialism in the case of James Connolly, so exalted nationalism came to replace both socialism and pacifism in the case of the Sheehy-Skeffingtons. In both cases something of the old vocabulary remained, but the uses to which it was put, and the feelings underlying it, had greatly changed.

The enormous chasm that had opened in the heart of Europe in the late summer of 1914 sent fissures, both large and small, first through the rest of Europe and then throughout the world, splitting people in every country. One tiny fissure of a fissure ran through our family, dividing supporters of the Allies from opponents of the Allied cause, who were thereby supporters of the Central Powers, objectively speaking.

The pro-Allies section was much the larger. My three uncles, Richard and Eugene Sheehy and Tom Kettle, were in British uniform. The other pro-Allies people were my grandfather, David Sheehy; my father; my aunt Mary, Tom's wife. (My mother, as we shall see, rather straddled the divide.) There were just two anti-Allies people: Frank and Hanna. But they were a formidable pair, and thoroughly convinced of the justice of their cause, although they were probably not conscious of how much that cause had changed since the outbreak of the war.

The constitutional nationalists never felt particularly comfortable with *their* cause: support for the British war effort. That went a bit against the grain for Irish nationalists of *any* description. My father, for instance, had been quite an advanced nationalist before the war. He had been lowered by a party of other advanced nationalists onto the organ at a conferring ceremony of the National University of Ireland, to prevent the playing of "God Save the King". (This protest had been far too advanced for my grandfather, because the Irish Parliamentary Party, hoping to achieve Home Rule through the support of the British Liberal Party, was opposed to gestures tending to alienate all sections of British opinion.) In wartime, gestures like that descent on the organ were the exclusive preserve of Frank and Hanna's friends, the extreme nationalists. My father and grandfather were now allied in condemning all such gestures for the duration of the war. But my father must have been a little ill at ease in his new-found respectability, and my mother would have sensed this, and worked on it.

My mother, through my father's known position, appeared as belonging to the "constitutional camp", and did not challenge this supposition. But she kept on close and friendly terms with the Sheehy-Skeffingtons. I used to be a bit puzzled at my mother's firmness in getting my father to drop his recruiting project. This seemed a bit out of character. In my experience as a boy, my mother always seemed to take her lead from my father. She was known as "the nicest" of the Sheehys, in favourable contrast to her formidable sisters, Hanna and Mary.

So I was a bit puzzled at the firmness. I ought not to have been, for I would not have come into existence without that underlying firmness. When my mother fell in love with my father, in the first decade of the century, her parents forbade her to marry him, for reasons that seemed obvious to them. My father had no money and poor prospects, was clearly in poor health, spoke with an unsuitably grand accent, and – to cap it all – claimed to be a more advanced nationalist than my grandfather. So David and Bessie put their feet down. My mother was looked on by her parents as the most loving and biddable of all the children, so she was expected to obey without question. Instead she defied her parents. They were strongly backed by my mother's brothers, Richard and Eugene, by her sister Mary, and by Tom Kettle. Of all my mother's siblings, only Hanna supported her marriage. Hanna was strongly supported by Frank.

It was a passionate and lacerating debate, and Frank's determination swung it. On one occasion, at my grandparents' home at 2, Belvedere Place, Dublin, Frank addressed my grandparents about their arrogant unkindness to their youngest daughter. Richard Sheehy, who was present, became outraged at Frank's disrespect to his father and mother. Frank, like my father, was a small man while Richard was hefty, and a rugby player. Richard picked Frank up bodily, carried him to the front door, threw him down two front steps into the street, and slammed the door. Frank picked himself up, and went back up the steps, and knocked on the door. Frank said: "Force solves nothing, Dick," walked past him into the house and resumed the dialogue that Richard had interrupted. This seems to have been the decisive moment that unnerved the Sheehys. At any rate, they gave in, and my existence followed.

My mother once said to me, "I give in on all the little things, but if a big one comes, I don't". I can now see, in distant retrospect, why the recruiting issue was one on which she had to make a stand. My mother's reasons were personal, not political. The Sheehy-Skeffingtons had been against the war from the beginning; Frank was soon to be engaging in anti-recruiting activities (which were to cost him his life). If my father were simultaneously engaging in *pro*-recruiting activities, he and Frank would be on a collision course. Frank was a pugnacious pacifist, and my father had the gift –

traditionally esteemed and feared in Ireland – of saying wounding things in a memorable manner. And a clash between Frank and my father would have meant a collision also between Hanna and my mother. For my mother this was an unbearable prospect. She loved and admired Hanna, and was deeply grateful, all her life, to both the Sheehy-Skeffingtons for the support they had given her at her moment of trial. So she induced my father to keep his opinions about the war to himself. In the light of later developments in Ireland in the course of that war, he must have been glad that he had done so.

The year before I was born, 1916, is remembered in European history (and also in Northern Ireland) as the year of the Battle of the Somme. In the rest of Ireland it is remembered as the year of the Easter Rising. There is something paradoxical about this, since Irishmen were killed in vastly greater numbers on the Somme than in Dublin during and after the rising. But those killed because of the rising – and especially the sixteen leaders executed after it – have about them, in retrospect, an aura of sacral and sacrificial nationalism, while those who were killed on the Somme came to be seen, in the version of nationalism that became official in Catholic Ireland in 1918, as having thrown their lives away for no good reason.

Two members of my family were killed that year: Francis Skeffington in the course of the Easter Rising, and Tom Kettle on the Somme, in the following September.

At the beginning of the rising many shop windows in Dublin's main thoroughfare, O'Connell Street, were shattered by the firing. Inevitably Dublin's poor (and probably a few others as well) started helping themselves. Frank Skeffington went downtown to try to stop the looting. In my youth I used to wonder why a socialist should be so anxious to stop the poor from benefiting. A socialist would not approve, of course, but why feel the urge to be a volunteer policeman?

Having pondered the relationship between Connolly and Skeffington, I now think that the role of looting-stopper was one assigned to Skeffington, probably implicitly rather than explicitly, by Connolly. The proclamation issued by the 1916 leaders, including Connolly, shows them to have been worried lest their cause be dishonoured by "cowardice, inhumanity or rapine". Looting was rapine. Patrick Pearse's second communiqué issued during the Easter Rising contained a specific reference linking the question of looting to the question of honour: "Such looting as has already occurred has been done by hangers-on of the British Army. Ireland must keep her new honour unsmirched." Connolly must have known that looters would emerge when windows got broken and the police were off the streets.

Connolly would have seen the looters as not only dishonouring the cause in general but also specifically dishonouring the working-class contribution to the cause, including his own contribution. The task of stopping the looting was a suitable one to assign (or leave) to a pacifist. Skeffington, who was committed to Connolly's cause but not to serving it in Connolly's way, must have been glad and proud to be allowed by Connolly to serve it in his own way. Connolly and Skeffington were drawn to their deaths by a common passionate commitment to the nation and its honour. As Marxists they were supposed to despise "the nation" as a bourgeois idea and "honour" as a feudal one. But their ideology did not govern their feelings.

Frank and Hanna both knew that Connolly and Pearse were headed toward insurrection, and their feelings on the subject diverged somewhat, Hanna's being perhaps somewhat more militant: "I think Connolly was right to go on once they got so far," she wrote to her son, Owen, many years later. She added that her husband "thought otherwise, feeling that any rising was foredoomed".

On Easter Monday, 1916, the day the rising broke out, Frank Skeffington and Hanna set out for the General Post Office, in O'Connell Street, Dublin, where they knew the rebels had established their headquarters. The police had abandoned O'Connell Street, and looters were everywhere, smashing shop windows and helping themselves. At the GPO Skeffington reported on the looting to Connolly who refused to intervene. Connolly sent Hanna off with food and dispatches to another rebel garrison, the College of Surgeons, in St Stephen's Green. On the following day, Tuesday, Skeffington was back in O'Connell Street, trying to organise a citizens' defence force to stop the looting.

It was of course very dangerous for *any* civilian to venture out in O'Connell Street, which was the main centre of hostilities during the Easter Rising. But it was especially dangerous for Frank Skeffington. He was unfavourably known to the British military in Dublin, probably most for his anti-recruiting activities and as a convict released before completion of sentence. And he was a conspicuous figure, bearded and wearing knickerbockers – in both respects like a miniature version of George Bernard Shaw.

Frank was picked up by a British patrol headed by Captain Bowen-Colthurst and taken to Portobello Barracks. (I tell this story in the form I remember hearing it from my mother.) On the way the patrol encountered a young civilian, whose name was Coade. Coade was carrying rosary beads in his hand. The sight of them infuriated Colthurst, who was a Protestant fundamentalist (and later found to be of unsound mind). He asked Coade what he was doing. Coade replied, "I'm coming from my devotions, sir".

(Rathmines Catholic Church is near Portobello Barracks). Roaring "Take that for your devotions!" Colthurst struck Coade on the head with the butt of his revolver, killing him instantly. Skeffington said, "I'll see you pay for this, Colthurst". Colthurst left Skeffington under guard at Portobello Baracks with instructions that he was to be executed if there was any further rebel firing. Pursuant to Colthurst's instructions, and as the rebel firing continued, Frank was shot by a firing squad in Portobello on Wednesday morning. All through Thursday, Hanna could learn nothing about what happened to her husband, or where he was. Leah Levenson and Jerry H Natterstad, the authors of her biography, *Hanna Sheehy-Skeffington, Irish Feminist* (1986) wrote: "On Friday morning Hanna's sisters, Margaret Culhane and Mary Kettle, decided to go to Portobello Barracks to see if they could obtain any information about Francis. There they talked with Captain Bowen-Colthurst, who denied any knowledge of their brother-in-law. Puzzled by the vehemence of his denial, they nevertheless accepted his story since they had no intimation then that a murder had been committed, let alone that he was the one who had ordered it.

"On the evening of the same day a British patrol led by Bowen-Colthurst raided the Skeffington home in quest of treasonable material. Hanna was at home, knowing of Frank's arrest but not of his murder. Her son, Owen, then aged seven, was with her. The raiders were noisy, brutal and destructive, as raiders usually are. Owen started crying. Hanna said in a cool clear voice: 'Don't worry. These are the defenders of women and children.'"

Shortly after Frank's murder Tom Kettle came home to Dublin on leave. When his daughter Betty (who had been staying with her aunt Hanna) saw him, she took fright at the sight of his uniform and ran away. Tom was distraught and considered resigning his commission, but decided instead to volunteer for active service. He was killed at Givenchy, Somme, five months after his brother-in-law had been murdered by soldiers of the army in which he was serving.

The circumstances of the Skeffington murder were embarrassing for the British government, then a Liberal-led coalition, headed by HH Asquith. Hanna was pressing for a public inquiry. In July she went to London to see Asquith about this. He offered her a large sum of money in compensation, and offered to pay for the education of her son at a first-rate school. The implicit proviso was that she drop her demand for the inquiry. Hanna refused. Asquith asked whether she had considered that her son might later reproach her for that decision. Hanna replied, "If my son were to grow up into a person who could reproach me for that, I would care nothing for anything he might say". Owen did not grow up into such a person.

I must have been about seven years old myself when I first heard, from my mother, the story of the deaths of Frank Skeffington and Tom Kettle. That would have been in 1924, in the immediate aftermath of the Irish Civil War. My mother told the story very carefully and deliberately. She strove for balance between Frank and Tom. Both were brave men doing their duty as they saw it, although they saw it in different ways. That much was obviously true. But the story itself – both as my mother told it to me and in its wider context, as I learned about it later – didn't make for balance. It strongly suggested that Frank had been right, and Tom wrong, in relation to the war effort. The Irish Parliamentary Party, which included Tom Kettle as well as my grandfather, had supported the war effort from the first day – a decision that was warmly welcomed in Parliament on that day and totally taken for granted thereafter. Regarding the most important event that occurred in Ireland – the Easter Rising – the passionately urged pleas of the party first to avert, and then to stop, the execution of the leaders of the rising went unheeded. Catholic and nationalist Ireland felt outraged by the executions. But the ones who felt most outraged were the constitutional nationalists, because they were the ones who had been let down and made fools of. Tom Kettle's personal outrage at the executions – a feeling shared by all Irish Catholics in British uniform at that time – was vastly magnified by the murder of his brother-in-law and, most poignantly, by the spectacle of his daughter Betty running away from the sight of his uniform. As my mother and Mary Kettle saw it, Tom Kettle died for a cause he could no longer whole-heartedly support. and his widow's bereavement was further darkened by her knowledge of that ultimate disillusion. Frank Skeffington was to be vindicated by the same events that disillusioned his brother-in-law. He had been opposed to the war effort from the very beginning, and the events of 1916 in Dublin seemed to have shown him to be right.

As my mother told the story, both men had laid down their lives for Ireland, and I should revere the memories of both of them. All the same, there was a difference. Tom's course was honourable but mistaken and he had come to know this. He had indeed fought for Ireland, as he believed, and he fully expected to die for it. But when he was facing death it was in the bitter knowledge that it was not, after all, death for Ireland. Frank, on the other hand had been clear-sighted in his course throughout.

In my adolescence, brooding over the parallel lives of Tom and Frank (and I have brooded over them at intervals throughout my life), I couldn't see why my mother seemed so sure that Frank had died for Ireland. Socialism and pacifism were his causes, and the occasion of his death. I couldn't see the link between the causes and the occasion, or between either and Ireland. It all seemed pretty incoherent. It doesn't seem that way any longer. As indicated earlier, socialism and pacifism had become recessive for Skeffington. What had become dominant was the exalted nationalism of Pearse and Connolly. Frank died defending the honour of Ireland – as conceived by Pearse and Connolly – against the looters. That is indeed dying for Ireland, by the most exigent standards.

Frank's story made far more impact on my imagination than Tom's. Tom died "out there", one of millions of casualties, in a land then unknown to me. But Frank's story was unique, vivid, dramatic – and it happened where I lived. Every Sunday my mother and I and Aunt Mary – Tom's widow – attended mass in Rathmines Church (neither my father nor Hanna went to mass). That was the church where young Coade had gone for his "devotions" before leaving, clutching his fatal rosary beads, for his rendezvous with Bowen-Colthurst and death.

At one level of my imagination the story of Frank Skeffington blended with the Passion and death of Jesus Christ. The image must have been suggested by the thought of the bearded pacifist being hustled through the streets by brutal soldiery to his death – a thought blended in my mind with the Stations of the Cross in Rathmines Church. The Dublin *Via Dolorosa* stretched south through O'Connell Street, then west for a bit along Dame Street, then south again through George's Street and Camden Street to Portobello Bridge, and over the bridge to Calvary in Portobello Barracks.

The Passion image should not mislead anyone into thinking that my feelings towards Frank Skeffington resembled those of a devout Christian towards Jesus Christ. Not at all. My attitude towards Jesus Christ was made up of puzzlement, discomfort and awe. My attitude towards Frank (whom, of course I never actually knew either) was closely similar. Frank, I was told, was a martyr. I agreed: he was a martyr in the most literal sense, in that he exposed himself to death in order to bear witness. I wanted to bear witness, all right – and have borne some – but I didn't want to die. There was a general assumption all round me (or almost all; my father didn't share in it, although he expressed this by having nothing to say on the matter) that to follow in the footsteps of Frank Skeffington was the finest course a young person could pursue. Considering where those footsteps had taken him, I didn't agree. And I didn't want to follow in Tom Kettle's footsteps either. Yet there was attraction there as well as repulsion; the combined result was a kind of wary fascination that has lasted all my life. Also, there was something distinguished about having a crucifixion in the family.

18

When I came to know more about the personalities of the two men who had died the year before I was born, I found that I would have liked Tom but not Frank. Tom in his heyday had been a most attractive human being: witty, humorous, and strikingly handsome, a notable talker, kind and companionable. He may have been "wrong" politically, but as a human being he was all right. But there seemed to me, from what I heard from my mother, to be something wrong with Frank as a human being. He was consistently priggish and occasionally cruel, and when the cruelty appeared, it took priggish forms. My mother told two relevant stories that shocked her greatly, though she admired him. My great-uncle, Father Eugene Sheehy, drank quite heavily in his old age for consolation. Frank, of course, disapproved. On one occasion Frank took Father Eugene's bottle of whiskey and poured it down the sink before the old priest's stricken eyes. The other story concerned Frank's son, Owen. Frank was a disciplinarian, but his principles forbade corporal punishment. So his way of punishing Owen was to lock him up for hours in a completely dark room. When I heard these stories, I decided I was glad that I had never had to contend with Uncle Frank. But I kept that opinion to myself. It was literally unspeakable in our family, belonging in the realm of blasphemy. Even today, as I write it, I shiver slightly.

The Easter Rising was unpopular in Dublin at the time, but a revulsion in favour of the rebels followed the execution of the sixteen leaders. The executions were spaced out over a period of weeks. The last man executed out of the sixteen was James Connolly. Wounded during the rising he had lost the use of his legs and as he faced the firing squad he was propped up against a wall on a chair – a detail, widely told, that increased the nationwide revulsion.

The revulsion was primarily against the British, but it also told against the Irish Parliamentary Party, with consequences that directly affected my family and its standing in the community. Rebel sympathizers spread the story that the party had cheered the news of the executions. One such sympathiser was Arthur Griffith, later to be President of the Irish Free State. One day he was telling this story to a Dublin crowd that happened to include my grandfather, David Sheehy. David mounted the platform, confronted Griffith, and shouted, "You lie! You lie and you know you lie!"

Grandfather was right. Griffith was lying and knew he was lying. The Irish Parliamentary party had vehemently opposed the executions and had demanded their cessation. All the same, the party's position with regard to them was uncomfortable. The Liberals, then in government, were the party's Home Rule allies, and the party's influence with its allies had been insufficient to avert the executions. (Actually the mainly Liberal government in this period probably did not have sufficient influence with the military to avert the executions, but the public was unaware of this factor.) And the party could not break with its allies over the executions, because the alliance represented its only hope of winning Home Rule at the end of the war. So my grandfather and his friends were in deep trouble. A government decision in April of 1918, at the time of the last great German offensive, to introduce conscription in Ireland drove them near to despair. The entire party withdrew from Westminster to mount a protest in Ireland. This tactic rebounded, because it was seen as an acknowledgment of the failure of parliamentary action, the policy to which the party had been committed since its foundation.

Conversely, the withdrawal of the Irish MPs was seen as confirming the validity of the principles of the Sinn Féin party, representing the ideals of the Easter Rising. Sinn Féin fought and won the elections of December, 1918. The Irish Parliamentary Party was wiped out.

I was just over a year old at the time of those elections, which had negative implications for the status of our family, and therefore for my own prospects in life. In the Ireland of before December, 1918, my grandfather had been a person of considerable consequence – one of the most senior members of the party, and the right-hand man of its last leader, John Dillon. The family sense of its own importance in the first decade of the century was ironically acknowledged by James Joyce in *Ulysses*, in the passage in which he recorded a conversation between my grandmother, the wife of "Mr David Sheehy, MP", and a Jesuit priest, Father Conmee.

"Father Conmee crossed to Mountjoy square. He thought, but not for long, of soldiers and sailors, whose legs had been shot off by cannonballs, ending their days in some pauper ward, and of Cardinal Wolsey's words: 'If I had served my God as I had served my king He would not have abandoned me in my old days.' He walked by the treeshade of sunnywinking leaves and towards him came the wife of Mr David Sheehy, MP.

"Very well, indeed, father. And you, father?

"Father Conmee was wonderfully well indeed. He would go to Buxton probably for the waters. And her boys, were they getting on well at Belvedere? Was that so? Father Conmee was very glad indeed to hear that. And Mr Sheehy himself? Still in London. The house was still sitting, to be sure it was. Beautiful weather it was, delightful indeed. Yes, it was very probable that Father Bernard Vaughan would come again to preach. O, yes: a very great success. A wonderful man really.

"Father Conmee was very glad to see the wife of Mr David Sheehy MP looking so well and he begged to be remembered to Mr David Sheehy MP. Yes, he would certainly call.

"Good afternoon, Mrs Sheehy.

"Father Conmee doffed his silk hat, as he took leave, at the jet beads of her mantilla inkshining in the sun. And smiled yet again in going. He had cleaned his teeth, he knew, with arecanut paste."

If Home Rule had been achieved by the parliamentary route, David Sheehy would certainly have had a seat in the Irish Cabinet. Our whole family would have been part of the establishment of the new Home Rule Ireland. As it was, we were out in the cold, superseded by a new republican elite. To be connected with the Irish Parliamentary Party had been an asset; it was now a liability.

The only member of our family who now had prestige was Hanna. Hanna had escaped from Ireland toward the end of 1916, dressed as a sailor (according to family tradition), and had reached America, where she had lectured in "British imperialism as I have known it". Her object was, of course, to try to keep America from entering the war on Britain's side. Her anti-British activities won her many friends and admirers in Sinn Féin, and she was part of the new Ireland in a sense that the rest of our family was not.

I am sure that Hanna, in that lecture, stuck to the literal truth of her terrible experience of Easter Week, 1916. The only distortion of her lecture was contextual, in the implication that this extraordinary episode was typical of British imperialism as Hanna had known it. Actually our family's relationship to British imperialism, up to, but not including, 1916, had been a fairly comfortable one. Hanna's father was still sitting in the Imperial Parliament at the time she was speaking. In the heyday of the Second British Empire, in the late 19th and early 20th centuries, the Irish had been among the ruling peoples of the Empire. The Irish Parliamentary Party had made and unmade governments of the Empire. Its importance was recognised by no less an imperialist than Cecil Rhodes, when he sent a large donation to Charles Stewart Parnell. Irish people were prominent in the Indian civil service and in the colonial service – and this at a time when neither India nor any other colony was represented in the Imperial Parliament. Hanna's brother Richard Sheehy had been a legal advisor to the governor of St Kitts, in the West Indies.

Most of the people who voted for Sinn Féin that December did not realise that what they were going to get was guerrilla war against the forces of the Crown. If they had realized that, they would probably not have voted for Sinn Féin. But Sinn Féin in its election campaign made it appear that its objective – sovereign independence for all Ireland – was obtainable by peaceful means.

It would appeal to the peace conference at Versailles, relying on President Woodrow Wilson's Fourteen Points, especially self-determination. The peace conference Sinn Féin had now to appeal to was, of course, that of the victorious Allied and Associated Powers. But those who had prepared the Proclamation of the Republic, in 1916, were thinking of an entirely different peace conference: one dominated by the Central Powers, the "gallant allies in Europe" referred to in the proclamation. The idea that the Peace Conference of the Allied and Associated Powers would even give a courteous hearing to people who thought of the defeated Central Powers as their gallant allies belonged in the world of fantasy. Sinn Féin non-fantastically knew that, but the electorate did not, and swallowed the bait.

Those who were elected in December – or, rather, as many of them as were not in prison – met in Dublin on January 21, 1919 as Dáil Eireann (the Parliament of Ireland). They declared the independence of Ireland and prepared to govern the country as if the British were not there. They did not explicitly declare war on Britain, but as it happened, the guerrilla war broke out on the day the Dáil met, when two policemen were shot dead by armed men who were (in theory) responsible to the Dáil.

There followed two and a half years of rebellion, repression, reprisal, and counter-reprisal, with plenty of atrocities on both sides. From March of 1920 to the summer of 1921 the British tried to stamp out the rebellion by the use of a force popularly known as the Black-and-Tans after their uniforms which were a mixture of police black and military khaki. This force was licensed to carry out collective reprisals and generally terrorise the population. My earliest memory is of an encounter – an entirely harmless one – with a Black-and-Tan. I was about three years old and my nursemaid, Sadie Franklin, was taking me for a walk on the Rathmines Road, in the middle-class south Dublin suburb where we lived. The Black-and-Tan was sitting on a gate. Sadie started when she noticed him and hurried me on past him. I looked at him. He was a small man with a rather sad expression, and he just sat there, slowly swinging a revolver up and down. But he had clearly frightened the wits out of Sadie without doing anything at all. As I myself was a bit frightened of Sadie this achievement made a strong impression on my infant mind.

During this period, popularly referred to as the Troubles, Hanna was serving as a judge in the Republican courts set up by the First Dáil. This is hard to reconcile with her pacifism. The violence that had Ireland in its grip in those days was the result of the Dáil's attempt to replace existing institutions with institutions of its own, including courts. Those courts in fact were an integral part of the rebellion. You may be sure that no one was ever brought before a Republican court for the murder of a policeman. If any republican was asked about that, the orthodox answer was (and still is) that the killing of a policeman who was in the service of the British Crown was not murder but a legitimate act of war. But that was not a distinction that a pacifist could explicitly acknowledge.

In my youth I thought that Hanna had been driven – understandably, by grief and anger at the murder of her husband – away from pacifism and into emotional nationalism and association with the republican war effort. In much later retrospect, and after giving more thought to the relationship between James Connolly and Frank Skeffington, I no longer see any inconsistency between Hanna's position and Frank's. *Both* powerfully felt the tug of emotional nationalism and insurrection. Both came to interpret pacifism in a minimalist manner, as requiring their own personal abstention from violence, but not precluding alliance with violent rebels in a civil capacity. Hanna's membership in the Republican court was entirely consistent with the role assigned (as I believe) to Frank Skeffington by James Connolly on the margin of the Easter Rising: keeping it from stain.

In July of 1919, at a public meeting in Dublin, Hanna declared, according to her biographers, that Ireland "was returning to the tradition of Wolfe Tone, of Robert Emmet, of the Manchester Martyrs, and of the leaders of the Easter Rising – all of whom had fought and died for that tradition". That tradition of physical force nationalism was of course altogether incompatible with the pacifism for which she and her husband had stood, up to the outbreak of the First World War.

These events and positions were important, and puzzling, to me as a boy. The strongest influence on me was that of my cousin Owen Skeffington. Owen saw himself as faithful to his father's causes: pacifism and socialism. He was in fact more faithful to these causes than his father had been; it is impossible to imagine Owen joining an "army council", even briefly. Owen was firmly and explicitly opposed to the republicanism of the IRA. His mother was ambiguous and reticent about this, but in fact gave support to the IRA throughout the '20s and '30s in a civilian capacity. Whenever an IRA-man was sent to jail, convicted of whatever crime, you could count on Hanna to be among those calling for "the release of republican prisoners." Owen neither joined in those calls nor criticised his mother for making them. The relationship between mother and son was affectionate but politically and philosophically fraught, heavily charged with mutual forbearance expressed through cryptic silences.

The rest of us – my father, my mother, Mary Kettle and me – were aware of the differences and the tension but never referred to them. It was a taboo zone. Like Owen, we all refrained from challenging Hanna's repeated calls for the release of republican prisoners. To that limited but real extent we were all under the spell of "the republican movement", which is the respectful way of referring to the IRA. I was over fifty before I was able to break that spell completely, and by that time both Hanna and Owen were dead.

Let us return now to the historical narrative, at the point where we left off: the summer of 1921. By this time both sides were getting tired of rebellion and repression. A truce was arrived at, which came into force on July 11, so that negotiations for a treaty could take place. On the British side, the foundation for a workable settlement had by then been laid, through the passage of the Government of Ireland Act in December of 1920. That act set up two political entities: "Northern Ireland" and "Southern Ireland". "Northern Ireland" was the entity that is still known by that name; "Southern Ireland" was the rest of the island, now known as the Republic of Ireland. The representatives of the majority in Northern Ireland accepted the act, and the parliament of Northern Ireland was opened by King George V on June 22, 1921, a few weeks before the opening of the treaty negotiations with the Sinn Féin leaders. These leaders all, of course, rejected the Government of Ireland Act. But it was the object of the British Prime Minister to get the Sinn Féin leaders and those who supported them to accept something that would be territorially identical, and in other ways similar, to the "Southern Ireland" of the act.

The Sinn Féin leaders, Eamon de Valera, Michael Collins and Arthur Griffith, all knew that what was obtainable through negotiation would be similar to "Southern Ireland" but with some improvement on it. The British were not about to hand over Northern Ireland whose parliament their King had just opened, and even if they wished to hand it over, they couldn't have delivered.

Both Collins and Griffith, who signed the treaty, and de Valera, who rejected it, knew that the Republic proclaimed in 1916 was not obtainable. De Valera's own version (Document No. 2) of what *should* have been obtained was so similar to the actual treaty that hardly anyone knew what he was talking about. But less complex minds among the rank-and-file saw the treaty as a betrayal of the Republic and no better than the Home Rule with partition that the Irish Parliamentary Party had been reviled for being willing to accept. If this was the outcome, all the sacrifices had been in vain. And there was much force in this argument.

The Dáil, however, by a small majority, and after an extremely bitter debate, ratified the treaty that set up the Irish Free State (territorially identical with "Southern Ireland") and a subsequent election returned a majority of supporters of the treaty. But these democratic transactions had no validity in the eyes of those who rejected the treaty. They were not to be governed by the outcome of any consultations restricted to the living. To them, the only mandate that counted was that of the Proclamation of Easter Monday, 1916, on behalf of a personified Ireland. *"In the name of God and of the dead generations from which she receives her old tradition of nationhood . . . The Irish Republic is entitled to, and hereby claims, the allegiance of every Irishman and Irishwoman."* This document was signed by seven men and has been felt by some Irish people in every generation since to be sanctified by their blood sacrifice, perpetually binding and above all man-made laws.

A party of men imbued with these convictions occupied and fortified the Four Courts, Dublin – the centre of the Irish legal system – on April 13, 1922. They were left in possession until after the post-treaty elections, which took place on June 16 and gave the pro-treaty party a majority. The new government, headed by Michael Collins, decided to tolerate no longer this armed challenge to its authority, and the bombardment of the Four Courts began on the morning of June 28.

When the guns woke me, just after 4 a.m., I was interested but not frightened. I was not frightened because my father was not frightened. I trusted him absolutely, and if he was not frightened, there was nothing to be frightened about. Nor was there. Our house was more than a mile away from the scene of the action, on the south side of the city, and the guns were pointed north, across the Liffey.

I was told later that when my mother started at one explosion, I reassured her: "Don't worry, Mammy, it's only an eighteen-pounder." Obviously I had learned this from my father. On consulting a textbook recently, I was pleased to find that his information had been accurate: the two field guns used for the retaking of the Four Courts were indeed eighteen-pounders. More significant to republicans than the calibre of the guns, however, was their source: they were on loan to the Free State government from the British Army. That became part of the Republican Black Legend of the Irish Civil War.

But the Black Legend did not prevent the Free State from winning the civil war a year later. Nor did it inhibit the leaders on the losing side, and most of their followers, five years later, from successfully working the democratic institutions they had once attempted to overthrow. The Republic of Ireland – as the former Irish Free State is now known – became a stable democracy. But few would have predicted that outcome at the time of the bombardment without which the outcome would not have been achieved.

All my life I have been both fascinated and puzzled by nationalism and religion; by the interaction of the two forces, sometimes in unison, sometimes antagonistic; and by the manifold ambiguities in all of this. But it wasn't until fairly recently that I began to realise that the relation of our family to this insurrection had been significantly different from what I imagined.

Thinking then in more literal terms than I can now, I had thought of Frank's pacifism, socialism and agnosticism as completely antithetical to the mystical, messianic Catholic nationalism of Patrick Pearse, identifying the Crucifixion and Resurrection of Jesus Christ with the crucifixion and resurrection of a personified Ireland. Owen saw his father's position as antithetical to that of Pearse, and I long saw Owen's father through Owen's eyes.

I now believe that the positions had *once* been antithetical, but that the antithesis had ceased to exist by Easter of 1916. It was James Connolly who had broken it down. As late as December of 1915 Connolly had mocked Pearse's mystical militarism and sacramental exaltation of "the red wine of the battlefields". But by 1916 Connolly had fallen under Pearse's spell – an expression that has to be taken almost literally in the circumstances. By February of 1916 the former Marxist was writing like a person hypnotised by Patrick Pearse:

"But deep in the heart of Ireland has sunk the sense of the degradation wrought upon its people – so deep and so humiliating that no agency less powerful than the red tide of war on Irish soil will ever be able to enable the Irish race to rediscover its self-respect . . . Without the slightest trace of irreverence but in all due humility and awe, we recognise that of us, as of mankind before Calvary, it may be truly said, 'without the shedding of Blood there is no Redemption'. [See C Desmond Greaves, *The Life and Times of James Connolly*, pp. 318-319.]

Frank was Connolly's disciple, as Connolly's choice of him as his literary executor makes clear. So when Connolly became Pearse's disciple, Skeffington became Pearse's disciple at second hand, though with reservations. He could not take arms along with Pearse and Connolly, or use the Pearsean language, which was so exotically at variance with that of his own ideologies. Connolly, as we have just seen, had already jumped a similar fence, with some panache. But the fences were only similar, not identical. Connolly had never been a pacifist. Skeffington must have winced, at least at first, at Connolly's new vocabulary. Yet he did not seriously demur. He was being pulled towards Pearse in the wake of Connolly.

In 1940, twenty-four years after the death of Pearse and Connolly and Frank Skeffington, I was on the Great Blasket Island, then Gaelic-speaking and now uninhabited. I heard a famous local storyteller, Peig, give her version of Frank Skeffington's death: how he was struck down by Bowen-Colthurst as he came out from mass with his rosary beads in his hand. The folk memory had conflated the figure of Skeffington with that of the boy, Coade. At the time I thought Peig's version absurd. I then still thought of Frank as Owen did: as a militant agnostic. He certainly *had* been that, but I don't think he was by Easter, 1916. The whole enterprise of the Easter Rising, which Frank served in his own peculiar way, was one of exalted Irish Catholic nationalism. James Connolly, who had once been an agnostic and a Marxist, was to be fortified by the last rites of the Church. And I think Frank might have gone the same way had Bowen-Colthurst permitted. So the folk intuition was not so far off.

Hanna Sheehy-Skeffington took part in the protests that turned into a riot on the fourth night of Seán O'Casey's *The Plough and The Stars* in the Abbey Theatre, Dublin. On the first night – February 8, 1926 – WB Yeats, the directing spirit of the Abbey Theatre since its foundation, made the occasion something of a political demonstration. This was less than three years after the end of the Irish Civil War. Yeats was a member of the Senate of the Irish Free State, having been nominated to it by the victors in the civil war, and he invited some of the luminaries of the Free State government to the performance and dinner. Gabriel Fallon, a close friend of O'Casey's suggested that Yeats hoped the play would "score over his republican enemies". This was an understatement. Yeats knew that the play would drive the republicans almost out of their minds. They would see it as both the hijacking and the defilement of the 1916 Rising, both sanctioned by the poet-senator who had betrayed his ideals. In the conditions of post-civil war Dublin violent protests were certain. Yeats had no objection to that. He enjoyed real-life theatre with the Abbey at the centre of the excitement. O'Casey, on the other hand (a little like Salman Rushdie later), seems to have had no idea of the fires he was kindling.

The first night, with a safe Free State audience, passed off without incident. As Hanna's biographers tell the story: "On the second night, there were some audience objections when the republican flag was brought into the pub in Act II and on the third night these protests were even more pronounced and seemed to be directed at the young prostitute." Gabriel

Fallon is described as having seen the protesters "as divided into two groups: those, like Hanna, who objected on nationalistic grounds, and others who found the play morally offensive". This is rather too neat and too cerebral. The whole protest was *both* nationalistic *and* religious (not moralistic). For Irish republicans the Easter Rising was (and still is, for those who are killing in its name) a sacred event – as Pearse intended it to be, timing it accordingly. *The Plough and The Stars* was felt as a desecration. *Both* the pub and the prostitute were part of the desecration, which occurs when the republican flag is brought into the pub and when Pearse's voice is heard proclaiming the Republic in that unhallowed context.

The second and third night of *Plough* were the warm-up. The big night was the fourth, Thursday, Hanna's night. Eamon de Valera – then seen as the heir of Pearse and Connolly – had appointed Hanna director of organisation of Sinn Féin, and I have no doubt that she organised the Thurday night demonstration. Her biographers wrote:

"All accounts agree that on Thursday night, disapproval climaxed in a republican demonstration: all seem to agree that Hanna led it . . . During the second act she arose and shouted that the play was 'traducing the men of 1916'. From that point on nobody could hear the dialogue on the stage and minor battles were breaking out in various parts of the theatre. Through it all, Hanna continued to orate. [Hanna's feminist biographers are uncomfortable with her passionate nationalism – CCO'B]. Before the fourth act began, Yeats brought in the police and the hall was cleared of protestors. Hanna, leaving the theatre under police escort made one last dramatic speech. 'I am one of the widows of Easter Week,' she said. 'It is no wonder you do not remember the men of Easter Week, because none of you fought on either side.'"

In Hanna's mind Frank had joined the executed leaders of the rising. And in spirit he did indeed belong with them.

The controversy continued in print, in *The Irish Independent*, between Hanna and O'Casey. There was one sentence in the exchange which I read with another of those shivers, when I came across it recently in Hanna's biography. Refering to the spirit of 1916, she wrote "That Mr O'Casey is blind to it does not necessarily prove that it is non-existent, but merely that his vision is defective."

O'Casey's vision already *was* defective, in the literal sense, and he was threatened with blindness. Hanna, being a civilised person, would never have deliberately alluded to a physical defect of an opponent. But the demon of nationalism, which had her in its grip, selected, through her unconscious mind, the metaphor that would hit the enemy at his weakest point.

At the end of the same letter, she took a swipe at Yeats: "'For they shall be remembered for ever' by the people if not by the Abbey directorate."

This was an allusion to the punch line of *Cathleen Ní Houlihan* which Yeats had written when he, like Hanna, was in the grip of manic nationalism, in his case through Maud Gonne, Hanna's friend and ally. Still, considering the heat of the circumstances, she dealt gently enough with Yeats, whose poetry she admired. But politics was more important for her than poetry, and she detested his politics. I remember a convesation with her shortly after Yeats's death. I wrote about it long after, in an essay about Yeats's politics:

"The day the news of Yeats's death reached Dublin I was lunching with my mother's sister Hanna Sheehy-Skeffington. Physically, Hanna looked a little like Queen Victoria and – a comparison that would have pleased her better – a little like Krupskaya. Mentally she was extremely and variously alert. Her conversation, when politics were not the theme, was relaxed, humorous and widely tolerant of human eccentricity; when politics were the theme she always spoke very quietly and economically, with a lethal wit and a cutting contempt for 'moderates' and compromisers. Hers was the kind of Irish mind which Yeats could call – when he felt it to be on his side – 'cold', 'detonating', 'Swiftian', or when, as in this case, it was not on his side, 'bitter', 'abstract', 'fanatical'.

"On this day I tried to tell her something of my generation's sense of loss by Yeats's death. I was genuinely moved, a little pompous, discussing a great literary event with my aunt, a well-read woman who loved poetry. Her large blue eyes became increasingly blank almost to the polar expression they took on in controversy. Then she relaxed a little: I was young and meant no harm. She almost audibly did not say several things that occurred to her. She wished, I know, to say something kind; she could not say anything she did not believe to be true. After a pause she spoke: 'Yes', she said, 'he was a link with the past.' I had been speaking of the poet; she was thinking of the politician."

Hanna did, however, know about good writing, and could appreciate it even coming from an ideological enemy. I owe a lifelong debt to her for that characteristic, for it was she who first introduced me to good writing, through the works of the great British imperialist, Rudyard Kipling. She gave me *The Jungle Book* for my ninth birthday. That was near the end of the year of *The Plough and The Stars*.

The climax of the O'Casey controversy took the form of a public debate between Hanna and O'Casey which, of course, Hanna won hands down. Her biographers wrote:

When O'Casey's turn came, he had to face an already hostile audience. His vision was bad, his glasses blurred, and he had great difficulty in deciphering his notes. After struggling for some five minutes, he said he could not go on and sat down. Hanna sympathised, sensing that, had he been an experienced public speaker like herself, he would have "had a lot more to say".

Possibly, as she watched O'Casey's performance, Hanna experienced some remorse for that metaphor of hers. Shortly after that grisly encounter O'Casey left Ireland for good. Having experienced, on more than one occasion over the years, brief touches of my aunt Hanna's cold and measured wrath, I can well understand O'Casey's flight after bearing the brunt of her all-out attack. Yet the odd thing is that although I was more than eight years old at the time of these stirring events, in which a leading member of our family was a protagonist, I have no personal memory of all this. I didn't read newspapers at the time, we didn't have a radio, and these matters were never discussed when our extended family met for the regular Sunday dinner at my mother's house. Divisive subjects were avoided there, in the presence of the young, and this was one such. My father, my mother and my Aunt Mary could not possibly approve of what Hanna was doing, but they were not going to argue with her on a subject that made Frank's ghost walk. Owen – who must have suffered intensely in those February days – did argue with his mother, to no avail, but did not say anything to me about any of this at the time.

About four or five years later, when I was better able to understand, Owen let me know, in a few careful words, that he did not share his mother's attitude toward O'Casey's play, and I was certainly glad of this. Owen was putting me quietly on my guard against the excesses of nationalism, notably the Irish kind, and I was to heed that warning, not immediately but increasingly in later life. Owen implied (and, I'm sure, believed) that his father, too, was opposed to nationalism, and I also believed that for a long time. Yet I can see now that Hanna was never more precisely faithful to her husband's ideas, in the shape those ideas had taken by Easter, 1916, than she showed herself in this episode over *The Plough and The Stars*. For the case against the play was that it desecrated the Easter Rising, by showing a group of Dubliners, including a whore, in a pub listening to Patrick Pearse proclaiming the Republic. This was nothing less than the dramatic and retrospective equivalent of the looting that Frank sacrificed his life in an attempt to stop. In the terminology of Pearse's communiqué, the rising was "besmirched". Both Frank and Hanna were committed, in heart and soul, to the defence of the immaculate conception of the Irish Republic. Both would have jibbed at that wording, wrongly scenting a sneer, but I have no doubt that it represents the underlying association of feelings, in their cases as in those of Pearse and Connolly.

2

BOYHOOD AND YOUTH, 1917-1937

FROM MY BIRTH IN 1917 TO MY SECOND YEAR IN TRINITY COLLEGE – 1937
– I lived at No 44 Leinster Road, Dublin. I lived there with my father and
mother up to my father's death in 1927, and thereafter with my mother
alone.

Leinster Road was then, and still is, a very pleasant residential road,
stretching from Rathmines Road to the south to Harold's Cross in the
north, the whole area being central to the suburb of Rathmines. Rathmines
had, since the turn of the century, been regarded as one of the classier parts
of the city. In my youth it was still so regarded, although by around 1920,
most of the wealthier residents had migrated to the east and south:
Ballsbridge, Foxrock, Glenageary. Still, Rathmines retained enough of its
old "privileged" character to number a much larger proportion of
Protestants and unionists – heavily overlapping descriptions – among its
inhabitants than was the case in the more populous central and northern
areas of the city. Politically, in my early boyhood, Rathmines was still, but
only just, unionist. Rathmines Urban District Council had a unionist
majority and unionist Lord Mayor until the late twenties, when my Aunt
Mary was elected Chairman.

My Aunt Mary was of course a nationalist – as all our family was – but a nationalist of a rather special kind, in the Ireland of the 1920s. Her husband, Tom Kettle, had fought and been killed in the British Army in 1916. So although she ran as a nationalist, she undoubtedly attracted a certain number of Protestant and unionist votes. In any case she won: a modest but satisfactory compensation for our family's loss of status in the national elections of 1918.

That mayoral election, when I was about ten, gave me my first personal experience of electoral politics. I was "canvassing" for my Aunt Mary; at least I thought of it as "canvassing" although I know now it was the more lowly activity of "leafleting". It might be thought that, after the rather grim trip I had had with my aunt on the day of my father's death, I would not wish to canvass, or even leaflet, for my aunt. But this was not at all the case. I knew that where the sacraments of the Church were concerned, my aunt was by no means to be trusted. In that area, the people to be relied on were the Skeffingtons. But this did not mean that I disliked or distrusted Aunt Mary in other areas where the sacraments were not directly involved. Like my grandfather, David Sheehy, Aunt Mary was deeply religious but strongly anti-clerical in political and social affairs. My grandfather, in his old age, used to attend six masses a day – one for each of his six children. He walked out of one of those masses when he found it was for the repose of the soul of Timothy Michael Healy, the most "clerical" of the members of the old Irish Parliamentary Party. Healy could look after the repose of his own soul, as far as my grandfather was concerned.

Similarly my aunt, around this time, had a ferocious – and indeed a fatal – run-in with our local parish priest, a certain Canon Hatton. Canon Hatton had opposed the admission of boys from across Portobello Bridge – poor boys – to Rathmines School in a middle-class area, which the Canon thought should be kept that way. My aunt thought this attitude was unchristian and called on the parish priest to tell him so. She had a fine line in righteous indignation – and looked splendid while engaged in it – and she gave Canon Hatton hell. The Canon died that night, which sent up Mary's status within the family considerably, not least with me.

So I had no bother about distributing political leaflets for my Aunt Mary, who was running against a candidate called Benson. But I did run into a bit of trouble while doing so. Proper canvassers and leaflet-distributors are of course supposed, where they find front gardens, to go up the garden path and return the same way. But I took short cuts, over garden fences. Mostly I got away with this, but in one case, in jumping over a fence I landed in a patch of begonias, and the lady who owned the begonias came angrily out:

"What are you doing?"

"Canvassing, Ma'am."

"Who for?"

"Benson, Ma'am."

When I reported this to my mother, and she told other members of the family, my status went up, just as my Aunt Mary's had done after the destruction of Canon Hatton.

* * *

In our road, while I was growing up, there were Catholics and Protestants, probably in about equal numbers. The two sets of people were always civil to one another, in a rather mournful manner. Both sets were a bit tired in the aftermath of the Troubles and the Civil war. And both sets – Protestant unionists and Catholic home rulers – had come down in the world. Neither set felt fully at ease either with the faction of Sinn Féin – now known as Cumann na nGaedheal – which had won the civil war and was now running the country – or with the faction, under Eamon de Valera, which had lost the civil war and was now working on a recovery. We were all glad that the Troubles were over – or seemed to be over – but most of us felt, in different ways, and degrees, uncomfortable about how they had turned out.

Most of the people who lived in Leinster Road at this time, and worked in the city of Dublin, to the north of us, used to go to and from the city by tram. When the tram arrived at the foot of Leinster Road, on the way back from the city, there was one tram conductor who always used to sing out "Rawth-mayons". This was a Dublin parody of the Protestant – and unionist – way of pronouncing Rathmines. It was a good-humoured parody and the passengers used to laugh. But I felt even then that there was something a bit rueful about the laugh. Rathmines was being reminded that it had come down in the world since 1914, 1916 and 1918. The reminder was addressed particularly to the Protestants. But it also affected the Catholic nationalists who had supported the British in the First World War: as most of my family had done.

Leinster Road, in my boyhood, had a much higher proportion of Protestants – a majority though a dwindling one – than any part of Dublin now has.

The most prominent residents on our road were both born Protestants. Lord Longford and Countess Markievicz. Lord Longford, the then head of the Pakenham family, was the owner of much the largest house on our road,

33

standing on its own grounds, quite near us but on the other side of the road. He was a patron of the arts and co-founder of the Gate Theatre in Dublin. He did a lot for the culture of the city, and got but little thanks for it. He and his wife were a striking and memorable pair. He was enormously fat, somewhere over the twenty-stone mark. She was tall, skinny to the point of emaciation, and resolutely plain. We never spoke to them.

With our other distinguished neighbour, Constance Countess Markievicz, there was some contact but not much. She was married to a Polish Count, Casimir Markievicz. That in itself didn't make her particularly grand, in Irish or English eyes at that time, but she was grand in her own right. Nee Constance Gore-Booth she was a member of a distinguished landed Sligo family. WB Yeats had written about her and her sister Eva when they were young:

Two girls in silk kimonos, both
Beautiful, one a gazelle.

Later, Constance became famous in her own right. She broke altogether with the "Ascendancy" traditions of her family and became a republican, probably under the influence of Yeats's *Cathleen Ní Houlihan* (1902). She headed a branch of *Cumann na mBan* ("Women's League", female branch of the IRA) and took part in the Easter Rising of 1916. She killed a policeman and was sentenced to death and later pardoned. She always remained a republican of strict observance and was in consequence a political friend of Maud Gonne's and of Aunt Hanna's. My mother and father, not being Irish republicans, had no standing in her eyes and had no direct contact with her, although her house was only a few doors away from ours on the same side of the street. However, we were much aware of her nearby presence and of her visitors. The most spectacular of these was Maud Gonne MacBride, whom I used to see from time to time as she passed our house on her way to and from a visit to "the countess" as everyone called Madame Markievicz. I wrote long afterwards about Maud Gonne as she looked when she walked past us in the late 1920s:

"When the husband, whom she loathed, was shot by a British firing-squad after the Easter Rising, Madame MacBride – as she now came to be known – attired herself from head to toe in the most spectacular set of widow's weeds ever seen in Dublin, to which she returned from Paris in 1917. Her mourning for Major John MacBride was so intense that it lasted all the remaining years of her life (nearly forty of them), as far as outward appearances were concerned. I still remember her as I first saw her in that garb, about ten years later in Leinster Road, Rathmines. With her great height and noble carriage, her pale beaked gaunt face, and large lustrous eyes, and gliding along in that great flapping cloud of black, she seemed like the Angel of Death: or more precisely, like the crow-like bird, the Morrigu, that heralds Death in the Gaelic sagas. That is how I think of that vision in retrospect; at the time I just thought: 'spooky'!"

The Countess did not visit us, but she did make use of us, or Hanna did on her behalf. The Countess was – quite rightly – an object of suspicion to the police of the then government, so her house was likely to be raided. Apparently she was afraid that a painting by her husband would be damaged in the course of one of these raids. So Hanna asked my mother to take in the painting which my mother duly did. It was an enormous painting which occupied one whole wall of our large drawing-room. It was called *The Polish Conscript*. It showed a young man seated between his parents at a table, on which there was a loaf. All were life-sized and all wore stricken expressions. The point was that the young man was likely to be killed for a cause in which he did not believe (probably that of Czarist Russia). This gloomy artifact seemed to dominate a large part of our house for some years or what felt like some years. I remember it as symbolizing what was the gloomiest period of my own life – though never one of unbroken gloom – after my father's death.

Our immediate neighbours on both sides were Protestants: on our right-hand side there was a prosperous family of auctioneers called Adams, their descendants are to this day pillars of the business community in Dublin. On our left-hand side were two sisters called Welsh, who had been missionaries in Africa, and who seemed to be quite poor in a genteel sort of way.

After my father's death, both sets of neighbours seemed disposed to befriend the orphan, but my mother coldly discouraged their efforts in that direction. The Welshes invited me in one day to look at their collection of Africana. I thought the Africana rather spooky, but I liked the Welshes. My mother, however, when she came to pick me up from their house was distinctly chilly towards them, quite unlike her usual friendly, rather genial, self. I got the message, and so did the Welshes. I was never asked back and never again conversed with them, except for formal greetings when we met in the street.

That episode was rather depressing, but quiet enough. The breaking off of relations with our neighbours on the other side – the Adamses – was rather more dramatic. After my father's death, my mother was desperately short of money and started to teach longer hours. This sometimes meant leaving me alone in the house, at night, when I was ten to eleven years old, and frightened of being left, perhaps, without any parent. On one such night, seeing the lights on in the Adams home, I made my way through the hedge to their door. They made me welcome, comforted me and fed me. Then my mother came home and found, to her consternation, that I had left the house and she didn't know where I was. Seeing the light in the Adams house, she went to find out whether they might have seen me. She found me comfortably ensconced at the Adams table, and she was furiously angry: angrier than I had ever seen her before or was ever to see her again. She removed me immediately, making known her displeasure and without thanking the Adamses. With them too, as before with the Welshes, all contact was henceforward broken off.

When we got home my mother threatened me: something she had never done before, and was never to do again. She said that if I ever did anything like that again she would have to send me "to Cabra". I understood Cabra to be an institution to which people sent unwanted or unmanageable boys. I didn't for a moment believe, even then, that my mother would do anything of the kind. I knew – even at this worst moment in our relationship – that she loved me, and that it was because she loved me that she was so upset. At the same time, the mere fact that she was so upset was in itself alarming, and somewhat mysterious.

My mother was normally a most considerate and civil person. Yet here she was, all of a sudden, freezing out our Protestant neighbours – on both sides – only for showing a friendly interest in me. I know my mother was not an anti-Protestant bigot. None of our family was that. My father, towards the end of his life, had had more Protestant friends than he had Catholic ones. My mother had not resented that and was about to send me to Sandford Park, a nominally non-denominational school of Protestant ethos by his decision and at considerable cost to herself. Years afterwards her closest friends, outside her own family, were Protestants: Vivian Mercier and his father. So why, at this time, this suspicion and rebuffing of friendly Protestant neighbours?

I have never, in years of thinking about the matter, intermittently, felt that I came close to an answer. But as I worked on this chapter of my book I think I may, at last, have hit upon it. I think this attitude on my mother's part may have been a reaction to an offer to adopt me, on the part of a distinguished Protestant family, who may have been distantly related to my father's family.

The offer came from the family of Lord Monteagle, whose own family name was Spring Rice, but who was closely related to the O Brien family of Foynes, Co Limerick. The spelling of the name was important. The Gaelic form of the name was O Briain, meaning descendant of Brian (that is Brian Boru, "Brian of the tribute", the 12th century king who defeated the Danes at the battle of Clontarf and became eponymous ancestor of all O Briens and O'Briens). Most O'Briens accepted the anglicized form with an apostrophe, as if it was a shortened form of "of". But the Foynes O Briens spelt their name without an apostrophe, which was felt to be more authentic, more Gaelic and grander.

* * *

The best known member of the family in the first quarter of the 20th century was Conor O Brien. Conor was a friend of my father's, and the two believed themselves to be related. However that may have been, Conor became my godfather, and it is after him that I am named. Conor O Brien was one of the most interesting people of the period and I should like to insert a digression about him before returning to my own attempted adoption by his relative Lord Monteagle.

Of all the Gaelic noble families, the O Briens had been the most loyal to the British monarchy. When Henry II came to Ireland at the end of the 12th century the Conor O Brien of the day is said to have been the first to do him homage, having come up at speed from North Munster for the purpose. Over many generations, the O Briens were steadily loyal to the Crown and prospered accordingly. When the Crown became permanently Protestant, under Queen Elizabeth, the then head of the family became Protestant too, and later became Baron Inchiquin. Inchiquin became the leading pillar of the British Crown in North Munster.

But this brilliant position did not make Inchiquin and his relations all that popular with the rest of the Protestant Establishment, or Protestant Ascendancy, as it soon came to be called. The O Briens were intensely proud of their ancient lineage, going back to the early middle ages. Most of the Protestant Ascendancy had acquired their lands from Cromwell in the mid-17th century, or from William III at the end of the same century. Before coming to Ireland most of them had been quite small people: "Cromwell's drummer boys" as I once heard my Aunt Hanna refer to them. The O Briens looked down on the new people and the new people resented the O Briens and distrusted them.

So in one sense the Munster O Briens were very much part of the Protestant Establishment, but in another sense – a more intimate one – they were not part of it all. By the mid 19th century a member of the family –

William Smith O Brien – headed a rising against the British in a late stage of the Famine, and was banished to Australia. His daughter Charlotte Grace O Brien became a well-known nationalist poet. It was to this nationalist O Brien tradition that Conor O Brien, my godfather, adhered in the early 20th century, on the eve of the First World War.

Shortly before I was born, Conor had played quite a prominent part in the Home Rule crisis of 1912-14. The Ulster Protestant unionists had run arms from Germany, in a demonstration of their willingness and capability to resist being included in an autonomous (and mainly Catholic) Irish State. When the British Government, understandably, flinched from the probable consequences of attempting to force the Protestant majority in Eastern Ulster into a Home Rule State which they resolutely rejected, nationalists of all descriptions – including all the members of my family – felt betrayed. It was felt that, if the Protestants were threatening the use of force to avert Home Rule, then nationalists must prepare to use force to secure Home Rule, incorporating the Northern Protestants irrespective of their wishes. The great majority of these nationalists were Catholics, but some southern Protestants were also Home Rule nationalists. Conor O Brien was one of those, as was Erskine Childers (later shot by other Irish nationalists during the civil war of 1922). Southern nationalists set up the Irish Volunteers, as a counterweight to the (Protestant) Ulster Volunteers and decided to import arms. O Brien and Childers, both experienced yachtsmen, successfully undertook the task of running the arms: Childers to Howth and O Brien to Kilcoole in Co Wicklow.

When the First World War broke out, Childers and (I think) O Brien also volunteered for service in the British Army but both remained Home Rule nationalists. In the period of the Troubles (1919-1922) Conor's most celebrated exploit was the horsewhipping of a journalist called Bretherton. Bretherton was a correspondent for the strongly unionist *Morning Post* and he wrote a piece in which he compared the (Catholic) Irish to monkeys. Conor horsewhipped him on the steps of the (upper-class unionist) Kildare Street Club in Dublin. I suspect there was a personal as well as political source for the ferocity of Conor's resentment. Conor had deep-set eyes, extremely thin lips and a barrel chest. I have never seen a human being who looked more like a gorilla.

Conor was also known for circumnavigating the globe in 1925 in a one-ton yawl called *Saoirse*. *Saoirse* means "freedom" in Gaelic, and I believe the yacht was named after the foundation of the Irish Free State in 1921-2. If so Conor, though a nationalist, had not followed Childers into the republican camp. (He didn't like Childers anyway, nor Childers him.)

There was a pageant, got up I believe mainly by the United Arts Club (and therefore partly by my father), to welcome Conor and *Saoirse* on their arrival at Dun Laoghaire that summer. In the pageant I was dressed in a little white sailor suit and played the part of Conor, after whom I was named; I was then eight years old. It ought to have been a happy occasion I suppose, but it wasn't for me. I was sitting in the front of a very large motorcar with my legs hanging down. It was the first time I had ever been in a motorcar. I could hear the engine, but not see it. I was afraid that if I slipped from my narrow rather bumpy seat, I would fall into the engine and be chewed up. So it was a pretty miserable ride.

Later I went out with Conor, just once, in the real *Saoirse*, and that was also a pretty miserable ride, in its way. Conor kept telling me to do this or that with "sheets". I couldn't for the life of me see any sheets, and he started shouting at me. I found out later that "sheets" meant ropes, but by then it was too late to repair the relationship.

* * *

Still, I think that despite my despicable obtuseness in maritime matters, Conor wanted to do something for me, after my father's death and for my father's sake. So I suspect that Conor was behind the offer to adopt me, made on behalf of Lord Monteagle, Conor's close relative, to my mother in the year after my father's death (1928).

The offer was conveyed by a woman called Dora Knox, who seemed to be a kind of confidential secretary to Lord Monteagle. My mother discussed the matter with Dora Knox at a Dublin restaurant called the Bonne Bouche. I was physically present, but at another table, with something to read, and I did not hear the conversation. Dora Knox ignored me, and I therefore did not like her. I could tell that my mother did not like her either. The conversation seemed to go on for a long time, more than an hour certainly. Dora Knox did most of the talking, with some earnestness. My mother's responses were brief.

After Dora Knox had gone, my mother and I walked home, a distance of about a mile and a half. My mother was crying, one of only three times I saw her cry. The first was the day of my father's death. This was the second. The third was about a year later, when I had diphtheria and she thought I was dying. When she had cried a bit on that evening in 1928, my mother gave me an account of what Dora Knox had said. Lord Monteagle was offering to adopt me. But if he did, I would have to go and live with him, and my mother would have to give me up completely. I understood – though I don't think my mother made that explicit – that if I was adopted I would be brought up as a Protestant. My mother had refused the offer. I understood that Dora Knox had criticized my mother, for selfish refusal of an offer whose acceptance would have greatly benefited me. I think it was above all this reproach – and my mother's recognition that there might be some truth in it – that made my mother cry.

Looking back on it now, I can see some symmetry between my mother's refusal of the Monteagle proposal and my Aunt Hanna's refusal of an offer from Prime Minister Asquith, over the schooling of her son Owen. Both offers would have been materially beneficial to the boys concerned, and both were refused without hesitation. My mother was generally a gentle and amiable person, but she could be resolute enough, where she felt there was a need for resolution.

For my part I was interested in the offer, but felt no inclination to criticize my mother for refusing it. It might have been nice to be adopted by Lord Monteagle, while continuing to live with my mother, but that was clearly not on.

As I look back on it now, while writing this, I think I can see a connection between this episode and my mother's uncharacteristically churlish reactions around the same time to our Protestant neighbours in Leinster Road. By carrying out my father's wish that I should be sent to Sandford Park, my mother had come under heavy pressure from the Catholic Church, including intimations that, by keeping me at that school, she might be prolonging my father's sufferings in purgatory. I think – I fear – that she half-believed these suggestions. She carried out my father's wishes, but in doing so she suffered greatly. She was suffering from the effects of my father's ecumenical tendencies, and she was not therefore, at this period feeling particularly ecumenical herself. Resenting as she did the attempted Monteagle takeover she also rejected – though unreasonably – the friendly overtures of our Protestant neighbours. By keeping me on at that "Protestant" school she was also cutting herself off, to some extent, from the Catholic community in which she had been brought up. I think she felt that she and I were being pulled farther in the direction of the Protestant community than she had bargained for, and was trying to check the drift, while still respecting my father's wishes about Sandford Park. A most difficult and lonely position.

* * *

The year 1928, immediately after my father's death on Christmas Day 1927, was the saddest and loneliest of my life to date. Up to that day in 1927, life had been a great deal of fun, due mainly to my father's lively good humour – despite his long illness – his keen intelligence and his loving attention to me. By the afternoon of Christmas Day, 1927, when I learned that my father was dead, life abruptly ceased to be fun. Fun did not return for more than a year, and then only slowly.

The disaster began at mid-morning when I went to my father's bedroom – to which he was confined by his illness – to receive his present: a bow and arrow. He greeted me with his usual cheerfulness, and sat up to bend the bow. As he bent it he suddenly turned deadly pale and fell back on the pillow. My mother must have known that he was dying, but I didn't. She sent me to fetch my Aunt Mary, who lived about a mile and a half away. I ran all the way and found Mary at her door, about to leave for mass. I asked her to come at once as my father was seriously ill. She was worried about missing mass but when I pressed her, she came. We walked in silence. When we arrived at the house, I learned that my father was dead. I also became aware that my mother and my aunt were preoccupied about what to do now. They sent me away while they talked. They talked for about fifteen minutes. Then my Aunt Mary left, in an aura of strong disapproval, and without taking leave of me.

No one ever told me what was said, in that discussion, but I can make a pretty good guess. Mary would have insisted that a priest should have been sent for, and should be sent for even then after my father's death. My mother knew that – whatever she personally might feel about the matter – my father, who took his agnosticism more seriously than other Irish agnostics did, did not want a priest to be sent for. My mother did not and would not send for a priest.

So Mary left, in high dudgeon. My mother then retired to her room, roaring crying, and remained there for the rest of that terrible afternoon. During those hours, my grief-stricken mother seemed entirely to have forgotten my own existence. It was as if I had lost both parents, not just one. I remember sitting in the dining-room contemplating the long, shiny mahogany table, and feeling that everything that made life worth living was gone forever. That afternoon was the worst part of my whole life to date.

The evening brought a considerable relief, with the arrival at 44 Leinster

41

Road of Hanna and Owen Sheehy-Skeffington. The Sheehy-Skeffingtons, being agnostics of strict observance, were supportive of my mother in her decision not to send for the priest, and they were aware of what that decision must have cost her, and determined to help. Also, they were aware of my own desolation and Owen, in particular, was determined to bring me such consolation and comfort as he could. All in all, after seventy years now, I remember that mercy mission with deep gratitude. If the conditions of that terrible afternoon had lasted much longer I believe I would have been psychologically impaired for life.

As it was, the Skeffingtons took us both back to their house. They sedated my mother – as I now think – and put her to bed. They fed me – I think my first meal of that day – and Owen put on a magic lantern show for me. I remember laughing, not because the show was particularly funny, but out of gratitude for being alive again, out of the chill of death.

I wasn't, as I soon found, quite out of the wood yet. On, I think, our third night at the Skeffingtons my Aunt Hanna called on me, in order to rebuke me, in an icy manner which she used occasionally and effectively. My misbehaviour, she said, was making things more difficult for my mother. Keeping the light on and reading in bed was part of the misbehaviour. She then turned the light off and closed the door, leaving me in the dark, feeling somewhat stunned.

Fortunately for me, this didn't last long. About five minutes later, the door opened again and Owen came in. Without comment he put the light on again. He said "good night" and closed the door. I waited to see whether Hanna would return. She did not. I now knew that I had a protector, and that he was the strongest personality in the family. I put out the light and slept well that night.

Years afterwards when I first heard of "the Enlightenment", I thought gratefully of Owen, turning on that light.

* * *

After a few days with the Skeffingtons, my mother and I returned to 44, Leinster Road, to pick up the pieces as best we could. We loved one another, always, but were desperately lonely together at this time, each in our own way.

Let me begin with my mother's end of it, as I dimly apprehended it at that time, and believe I understand it more clearly now. There was first of all an overwhelming sense of loss (by reason of my father's death). My father's portrait by FK (Frances Kelly) – a pupil of John B Yeats, father of

WB and Jack – hung at that time on the wall of her bedroom, and she used to kiss it every night before going to bed. That portrait hangs now in my home in Howth, Co Dublin.

If straightforward grief had been all, that might not have been too bad. But it wasn't all. There was guilt as well. A few days after my father's death, I noticed on the table beside my mother's bed, a Catholic devotional work, *In Heaven We Know Our Own* by a certain Father Blot, SJ. When I saw this, I knew it boded no good, either for my mother or for myself.

While my father had been around there had been no devotional literature in our house. It was understood that my mother went to mass, and would probably continue to do so indefinitely (as she did). It was also understood that I would go to mass along with her until I took my first communion. After that, I would continue to go to mass for as long as I considered appropriate. My father did not expect that that would be very long and neither did I. At one point – I think in the month before my father's death – a woman friend of my mother's brought me as a birthday present a Catholic missal. In thanking her I said – in a rather stilted diction acquired from my father – "It will relieve the tedium of the mass". My mother repeated this *mot* to my father, who was delighted with it.

That was then, when we were all quite light-hearted. Now, was quite another matter. I sensed that the presence in our house of *In Heaven We Know Our Own* was bad news. My mother was under pressure from the Catholic Church about me and about my father, and about the school I was going to attend. I underestimated my mother during this period and I thought she was about to give in to the pressure and send me to a Catholic school, in order to abridge or otherwise mitigate my father's time of suffering in purgatory.

I was wrong about how my mother would react to the pressure, but I was right about the nature of the pressure that was being applied to her. It was Owen who caught hold of what would be called at another place and time "the smoking gun". Owen gave me no warning of what he had found, but he addressed a family gathering about it. The formal word "addressed" about fits the tone in which Owen spoke to the family on this occasion.

In the period after my father's death our extended family – consisting then of my mother, my Aunt Hanna and Aunt Mary and their children, Owen, Betty Kettle and myself – used to meet regularly every Sunday evening for our evening meal at my mother's house. Generally the elders – mainly Hanna and Mary – did most of the talking and the children listened. Owen was a young adult rather than a child by now, but he

43

generally was not heard from. On this occasion, however, he had something he wanted to tell us, and there was dead silence among the listeners.

Owen told us that his close friend Christopher Gore-Grimes – "Christo" as he was generally called – had just been withdrawn from Sandford Park school which he had been attending along with Owen. Christo's father, like my own father, had been an agnostic (also of Catholic origin) and Christo had gone to Sandford Park by his father's decision, just as I had done. So why did his mother withdraw him? This was the point of the story, as we all could sense. Owen spoke very slowly and deliberately at this stage. Christo's mother – a Catholic, like mine – had withdrawn her son from Sandford Park because her confessor had told her that every day her son spent at that school was extending the period of her late husband's suffering in purgatory. Owen stopped right there: he had no need to say any more. And there was a long silence: the longest silence ever experienced around our family table.

During the silence, I looked around at the three grown-ups. My mother looked shaken but I thought a bit relieved as well, as if something had come into the open that had been bottled up too long. Mary looked flustered – unusual for her – and, I thought, a bit guilty. Hanna alone of the three looked completely calm, and even serene, something which she was good at, when she knew she was on a winner. Looking at her, and looking at Owen, I could tell that Hanna – unlike my mother and Mary – knew exactly what Owen was going to say, and had agreed to his saying it. I knew that Mary was being warned off the subject of my education. She was being told, implicitly, that the Skeffingtons believed that she had been abetting and thereby increasing the clerical pressure on my mother to remove me from Sandford Park. And I knew that a joint warning, from both Skeffingtons, was enough to resolve this matter. Mary was quite a strong character on her own, but she stood a bit in awe of Hanna. And she was altogether outgunned when Hanna and Owen were acting in concert, as on this occasion. Hanna and Owen didn't always agree – they didn't agree at all, for example, about the IRA. But over clerical interference with my education they were very much in agreement.

They were presenting Mary with an implicit ultimatum, with which I knew she would have to comply. So that was very much to the good, in this dark time. I would be educated in accordance with my father's wishes and my mother was not to be tormented about the matter, any longer.

I have often wondered since whether Mary had actually been a party to the clerical pressure on my mother. I would like to think not because I liked her, in spite of a few bad trips, and I remembered her spirited anticlerical performance, in the slaying of Canon Hatton. But that had been a clash over essentially secular matters, class and education. My father's fate in purgatory, as determined by the place of my education, was a different matter altogether. That was strictly theological, a matter of the *depositum fidei*, the deposit of the faith. The theologians *knew* what was happening out there and no good Catholic – however "anticlerical" on secular matters – could go against them.

So I believe Aunt Mary did put pressure on my mother, and did much to make her life a misery, in the period before Owen's intervention. She would have seen herself as actually *helping* my mother, by abridging the period of her separation from her husband and of her husbands' torment in purgatory and hastening on the blissful day of their reunion forever in heaven. Aunt Mary, poor thing, was doing what she believed to be right, until the Skeffingtons put a stop to that.

* * *

Things got a bit better between my mother and myself after the Skeffington intervention, but they were still quite fraught. As a matter of fact, they had become a bit fraught even during my father's lifetime. There had been a tiny incident lasting only a few seconds which seared me at the time, and whose memory has occasionally returned to haunt me even in my maturity and old age.

The little episode began as one of exceptional bliss which turned to horror in a second. I must have been about seven at the time and my father, who worked late on his newspaper, had returned from work a bit earlier than usual. When he turned in, I was in bed between my mother and father, something that had never happened before. I felt so happy and secure that I did a kind of a somersault in the air. Unfortunately as I did so, my nightshirt fell forward over my head, exposing my naked body. Apparently my mother found this spectacle revolting. She spoke to me with sharp disgust, a tone she had never used to me before, telling me to cover myself immediately. I felt as if I had been hit by an icy blast in a moment of joy and security. I cowered under the sheets. My father went on talking in a calm cheerful tone about some neutral matter. I was grateful to my father for changing the subject. But I wondered about my mother. Why should she make me miserable all of a sudden?

Years later, listening to my mother talk with her sisters – cheerfully enough – about their youthful convent experiences, I could understand the roots of her reaction. They had all been conditioned, in the convent, to a horror of exposure of the person as a probable occasion of mortal sin. My mother told a relevant story. As she walked down a corridor, a short-sighted elderly nun stopped her and peered at her chest. "Is that your person?" asked the nun, in a tone of horror.

"No, Mother," said my mother, "it's a slip".

"Slip" or "shift" were terms then used to designate a female undergarment. In Catholic and sexually-puritan Ireland these could be terms fraught with explosive emotions. It was the use of one of these terms that precipitated the riot in the Abbey Theatre, Dublin at an early performance of JM Synge's *Playboy of the Western World*. "The audience broke up in disorder at the word 'shift'." Lady Gregory cabled to Yeats. My mother's encounter with the elderly nun must have occurred very near the time of the *Playboy* riots (1906).

The term "slip" (as distinct from "shift") may have only recently come into use at the time, for the elderly nun doesn't seem to have understood the word as a reference to an undergarment.

"A slip?" said the nun. "Well, don't let it occur again".

Quite a funny story. But the conditioning it represented was not always funny in its consequences, as I found when my shirt fell over my head.

The faint mistrust of my mother which dated from that little episode deepened on the afternoon of the day on which my father died. During those hours, my mother seemed to have forgotten my existence. When we should have been trying to comfort one another, I thought, my mother was simply demented, leaving me with that awful table. But I didn't then understand that my mother wasn't just under the pressure of simple grief. There was also the pressure of guilt.

As I look back on it now, it seems to me that my mother's resistance to that emotional blackmail and terror, and her unbending compliance with her husband's wishes, constituted a notable example of heroic virtue and fortitude. But that was not how these matters looked to me that Christmas afternoon as I contemplated that table and felt, for several hours, that I had lost, not just one parent, but both.

* * *

As a new widow, my mother was not merely burdened by personal grief and clerical blackmail; she was also getting deep into debt. One day she handed me a letter addressed in her neat handwriting to The Sterling Finance Co.

No explanations passed between us, but I knew this was bad news. On my father's death, our family income had sharply declined, and my mother had been forced to borrow money from a firm of usurers at interest of 39 per cent. In her deep and multiple worries, my mother started smoking very heavily, around sixty cigarettes a day. Her health suffered and she was racked, once a week or so, by violent disabling headaches. She knew that I was emotionally dependent on her, and that I resented her frequent unavailability and glum preoccupations. But those were the conditions of her life with me; she was desperately busy seeing to it that I could live in physical comfort and be educated in accordance with my father's wishes. A grim enough time then, in 1927-29.

Yet not all grim, even then. My own material conditions of living actually improved after my father's death. My mother moved out of the room she had occupied along with my father, into a smaller room on the floor below. I now had their former bedroom. My new room was a room to cheer anyone up, even at a dark time. It was very large, and exceptionally bright with two big windows looking due south. Owen saw the possibilities of the room and had a full-size table-tennis table installed: seven feet by five. The room was large enough to give plenty of room for the run-back. Owen taught me the game there and I became quite proficient at it.

And although relations with my mother at this time were strained, they weren't all bad. They became better whenever we could get out of Dublin together for a while. While we were travelling together, she had more time for me and could be a bit more light-hearted. In the summers she would superintend the state examinations, in Irish, in various convent schools in the west of Ireland. On these visits, the nuns were kind to my mother and myself, and no awkward theological questions arose.

Good memories there. Even better was a trip I went on with my mother to London, in, I think, 1929. My mother had just completed an adaptation of Gregg shorthand for dictation in the Irish language, and she and I were honoured guests of the Gregg people at their annual conference in Marylebone that summer. Our host who chaired that conference was Irish and even extravagantly so. He rejoiced in the name of Roderick O'Conor-Ross (Roderick O'Conor was the last Gaelic king of Ireland). Roderick O'Conor-Ross made a speech of which the peroration ended in the words " . . . carrying the banner of Gregg shorthand down the ages". My mother thought this was rather funny, but I didn't. Since the banner of Gregg shorthand had flown benignly over our trip to London, I was all for its being carried down as many ages as possible. I liked that banner better than the Irish tricolour or the Union Jack, both of which were beginning to seem to me rather unpredictable and potentially oppressive.

* * *

The choice of my very earliest schooling, in two preparatory schools, bore the distinctive mark of my father's freethinking outlook and aversion from Catholic schooling. Both schools were Protestant in ethos, though not obtrusively so. I didn't worry about that. What did worry me a bit was that they were *British* in ethos (though again, not obtrusively so). At one of these schools, pictures of the signatories of Magna Carta occupied one whole wall. I wondered why. I knew enough – from my father – to know that Magna Carta was an exclusively English thing and that I was Irish, and that both my parents intended me to remain so. So what was I doing with Magna Carta?

This was my first brush against a phenomenon with which I was soon to grow very familiar: the tenacious, though often denied, connection between religion and political allegiance in Ireland. If you chose to cross the religious dividing line you were – willy-nilly – crossing the political dividing line as well and vice versa. My parents regarded themselves as nationalists, and so did I, for at least the next forty years of my life. I learned fairly early on that my nationalism was a bit suspect, in the eyes of my Catholic contemporaries. But it was only very much later that I came to realize that there were good grounds for that suspicion – from the point of view of those who held it – and to reconsider my position.

Towards the end of my eighth year, I was abruptly transferred to a radically different educational environment: a Dominican Convent school called Muckross Park, in Marlborough Road, Dublin. This transition was unexplained at the time but I soon learned the reason for it. It was that I should be prepared, in an acceptable environment, for my first communion, as a Catholic. It was, I think, the price paid to mother for agreeing that I should be sent, *after* my first communion to the non-sectarian, but essentially Protestant Sandford Park School, which my father had chosen for me.

I did not enjoy the change to the Catholic school. At my previous schools, teachers had explained subjects and encouraged you to understand them. At Muckross you were simply told things, and told to memorize them. If you failed to memorise them you were beaten. In my previous schools, no one was ever beaten, for anything. I remember one teacher at

Muckross with particular aversion; she was an ugly red-headed woman (lay not clerical) and if you weren't prompt or word-perfect with the memorization, she would rap you hard across the knuckles with a ruler. You knew she meant to hurt you and she always succeeded. Not everything was bad about Muckross Park. One nun in particular – Sister Stephanie – was always kind to me and I remember her with gratitude and affection. But the general atmosphere of the place was depressing, being based on the principle that pupils just did what they were told, without question and without discussion or explanation, and were physically punished for failure in any of those domains.

From Muckross Park I made my first confession and first communion, having answered a couple of easy questions, to which I had memorised the answers with the aid of the ruler. A kind nun told us, with some enthusiasm, that the Emperor Napoleon had said that his first communion had been the happiest day of his life. This was the source of the faint aversion which I have felt throughout my life for the Emperor Napoleon. My first communion was not the happiest day of my life, but all the same it was a relatively happy one. It was relatively happy because I rightly believed that once this grim requirement had been complied with my father would see to it that I was sent to another Protestant school, and would never be sent back to another Catholic one. And that was in fact how it turned out, after my father's death, at considerable cost to my mother.

I had some reservations about Protestant schools, but was all for the intellectual freedom which reigned in them, as compared with the only Catholic school I ever knew. All the same, my debut at Sandford Park was not a particularly happy one. In this period, right after my father's death, the life force was at a low ebb in me, and I allowed myself to be pushed around to a greater extent than at any other time before or since.

Two experiences of bullying are a bit instructive in that regard. While attending one of my early Protestant schools, I had my first experience of bullying, not from within the school but from outside. There was a boy, older and bigger than myself, who used to hang about outside my school and beat me up when I came out. I told my father. My father, though not physically strong, had survived in a tough environment: the very-lower-middle-class Christian Brothers School at Synge Street, Dublin. My father advised me that, on the next occasion when the bully approached me, I should kick him on the shin, as hard as I possibly could. I took this advice, with most gratifying results. The bully hopped about and howled and left me alone for ever afterwards.

My next experience of bullying was after my father's death, during my first year at Sandford Park School. The bully, a boy named Dugdale, was a pupil at Sandford Park and my way home from school partly coincided with his. He used to attack me on the way home, twisting my arm and so on. I feel quite sure – from later experience of him – that if I had again applied my father's advice in the case of the earlier assailant, and kicked Dugdale's shins hard I would have had no more trouble with him either. But in this, the immediate aftermath of my father's death, I didn't have the spirit to react in this way. I felt comprehensively let down and depressed and disposed passively to accept whatever punishment fate had in store for me.

Fortunately for me, this mood didn't last. I recovered confidence, saw off a couple of other bullies, and had no more trouble with Dugdale.

By my third year I was settling in reasonably well at Sandford Park. I was in the first third of my class and doing pretty well in all school subjects. I was doing particularly well at Latin, a subject then taught by the headmaster of the school, GSB Mack. My father had wished me to do both Latin and Greek. But the school insisted that Greek and Irish were alternative subjects; one or the other, not both. My mother insisted that it should be Irish, both because she herself loved the language, and because she thought – correctly – that it would be to my material advantage to know it. Owen, to my intense disappointment, agreed with my mother. Owen had no use for "dead languages": dead languages in his opinion ought to stay dead. Hanna and Mary agreed with Owen and my mother. So I was comprehensively overruled. Greek was out, to my lasting regret, accompanied by some resentment against all concerned.

Cutting my losses, I did well at least with Latin, and basked, for a couple of years in the favour of the headmaster. Mack, a former badminton champion, had a dashing and imperious style about him and the whole school stood in awe of him. Unfortunately, by the end of my third year at Sandford Park, Mack was riding for a fall. He had an extremely expensive lifestyle, dining and wining regularly at Jammet's, then by far the most expensive restaurant in Dublin. He was also – as later became clear – having an affair with a married woman, mother of two children then attending the school. Suddenly – I think near the beginning of my fourth year at Sandford Park – Mack eloped with the married woman and went to Canada leaving large debts unpaid at Jammet's and other establishments.

Mack was succeeded, as headmaster, by an elderly man called Steede. Steede had been headmaster of the Stephen's Green School, another Protestant school which had recently been amalgamated with Sandford

Park. The demand for Protestant schooling was shrinking in these the early years of the new and essentially Catholic state which Protestants were continuing to leave, and this led to the amalgamation. Stephen's Green was rather more militantly Protestant than Sandford Park and the amalgamation was always uneasy. On the day he took over as our headmaster, Steede addressed the school. He was extremely frank on the subject of his predecessor. Mack, he told us, had disgraced himself. He had behaved dishonourably, and we should forget about him.

In speaking in this way, Steede was expressing the opinion of most respectable people in the Dublin of the day. Nonetheless he was making a great mistake in expressing this opinion at that place and time. The Sandford Park boys had liked and admired Mack and did not like hearing him denounced by one who was vaguely felt to be an interloper. My own feelings were quite a lot stronger than that. As I listened to Steede, I decided that I hated him, and that I would do whatever in me lay to make his position as the headmaster of Sandford Park School untenable. This turned out to be quite a momentous decision both for the unfortunate Steede and for me. This was the first fully autonomous decision of my life. I consulted no one about it. I just made my own decision and set about carrying it out.

The first thing to do was to make it impossible for Steede to teach our class and that was the task I set about immediately. With the lucidity of concentrated hatred, I saw the weakness through which Steede could be destroyed. He was deaf – rather more than just slightly deaf – and he tried to conceal this liability. So I set to work on that. Whenever he put a question to me I would answer politely, but in a very low voice. When he asked me to repeat the answer I would speak in an equally low voice, but mimicking the action of someone speaking loudly and clearly. This tactic baffled Steede and it showed. As usually happens in a classroom or similar social context, an example of successful defiance speedily finds imitators. Soon half a dozen boys were pretending to raise their voices in order to be heard, and then pretending to be still unable to hear the responses.

If Steede had sent me away from the class at the beginning of the masked defiance, he could have been all right. But unfortunately for himself, he waited until I had imitators and then reacted with a *collective* insult. In this he ran counter (as I found much later) to a wise piece of advice offered by Guicciardini to Machiavelli some four hundred years earlier. "If you have the misfortune to need to insult somebody, take care that you do so in a matter that insults *only himself*. Do not use any insult that applies also to people of the same town, or religion or language, as the individual you need

51

to insult. If you make that mistake you are unintentionally multiplying the number of your personal enemies, and you are liable to suffer."

Steede broke Guicciardini's law by using a term of collective abuse, with both religious and racial overtones, to designate his classroom persecutors. He called us "Board School boys." This was a dangerously loaded term in the terminology of the early 20th century in Ireland. Board Schools were non-fee-paying schools and consequently held in low esteem by boys attending fee-paying schools such as Sandford Park. Board School boys were almost all Catholic, like most of the rest of the population. George Bernard Shaw was to recall the shame and humiliation he had felt, as a little Protestant, at being forced by family poverty to attend a mainly-Catholic Board School.

Steede's use of this collective insult precipitated a catastrophic decline in his control over the classroom. Catholic boys – about one third of the total – all hated Steede when they heard these words for they were heard as a Protestant insult to Catholic manners, which is how Steede undoubtedly intended the words, with me primarily (and understandably) in mind. The Protestant one-third was also alienated, by being lumped in with poor ill-mannered Catholics. The Jewish one-third did not in general care for insults based on religious affiliations and knew that, in Ireland at that time, a Protestant who insulted Catholics would be likely to be anti-semitic as well. (Just as, in another context, a Catholic who showed himself violently hostile to Protestants would be almost certain to hate Jews also).

So with the use of those three words, Steede had comprehensively alienated his whole class. It was a definitive demonstration of the correctness of Guicciardini's Law.

Backed now by the whole class (with the exception of the minority of Stephen's Green boys, who lay low) I led the driving out of Steede, which proceeded at a great rate. The more subtle proceedings of the earlier (pre-"Board School") period were now abandoned in favour of general uproar, sustained throughout the class. Steede collapsed. At one of his last classes, I heard him muttering repeatedly: "I can't go on! I can't go on!" I remember those words now with some pity, and even with some small degree of remorse. But at the time, I am afraid I felt nothing but a savage joy. I knew I had won.

The victory needed however to be exploited, in a spectacular demonstration that Steede – still the headmaster of the whole school – could not control his own class, and was therefore not a suitable headmaster. The final demonstration took a rather weird form. That sunny summer afternoon we all climbed on to a flat stretch on the roof of the school building. There we boiled kettles over spirit-lamps, held a picnic, shouted and sang. The whole school, as was intended, witnessed this performance. If Steede had been an ordinary master, he could have appealed to the headmaster to bring the situation under control. But he was himself the headmaster, and what we were conclusively demonstrating was his inability to control the situation. When the school met again, in the autumn of that year, we met under a new headmaster. The revolt had won, and everybody knew this.

* * *

When school resumed in the autumn of that year, Steede was gone, and the Stephen's Green boys along with him. The new headmaster was a man called FitzGerald, a jovial, florid man who had been a bosom companion of Mack's in his heyday, at Jammet's and elsewhere. So the Rule of the Saints was over, and good riddance, so most of us felt.

Not that FitzGerald inaugurated any reign of debauchery. It was, rather, a reign of Shakespeare. He was our English master as well as being headmaster (the latter rather briefly) and as English master, what he taught us was Shakespeare, exclusively. This would not have been possible, I believe, in any other school in Ireland in the period. All the others were tied to the state examination system, and to the curricular rigours that went with it. Sandford Park did not do the state examinations, mainly because the Irish language was compulsory in them, and most of the parents did not want their children to be required to learn Irish. Most of those who sat the state examinations went on to University College, the Catholic University in reality, though nominally secular. Those who went on from Sandford Park to university went to Trinity College (of which more anon) where Irish was not a required subject. I personally was learning Irish, quite hard, but preparing for Trinity College; a bit confusing, like much in my life at the time.

The advantage of not being tied to the state system was that bold innovations were possible, if someone happened to think of one. Much the boldest and happiest of the innovations that affected us was FitzGerald's decision to teach us Shakespeare, exclusively. He had been a Shakespearian actor, and he knew Shakespeare as a good actor knows him, which is very well indeed. Every English class became a rehearsal for a Shakespeare play, in which the pupils were assigned their parts. In this way, in the FitzGerald years, we worked our way happily through quite a lot of the canon. Where the meaning was not quite clear, FitzGerald would help out unobtrusively, as also where we got the emphasis wrong. Otherwise, he just let Shakespeare take over. It was the best educational experience of my life, and I am profoundly grateful to FitzGerald for it.

FitzGerald's appointment as headmaster had been a stop-gap one, I think and – while staying on as English master – he soon stepped down as headmaster in favour of AD Cordner, the geography master.

Cordner was a very large man, whose nickname was "the Bull". I don't know that he had much formal education, but he had a good fund of quiet authority, useful to a school which had been going through its time of troubles. He had been kind to me personally in my early, rather difficult, days at the school. I remember staying at the school for rugby practice on a day when there was no rugby practice, and Cordner was the only person around. Seeing how I was dressed, he asked whether I had come to play rugby. I replied "Such was my intention, sir". He looked at me steadily and, as it seemed, rather sadly. As I realised later, he understood from my way of speech that, as an only child, I had been spending most of my time with grown-ups, and would have some difficulty adjusting. He helped me to adjust, and I was grateful to him.

My own position in the school, after the fall of Steede, was a lot better than it had been before. Nobody ever referred to Steede after his departure, but his departure was universally felt to have been a good thing, and I was known to have played a considerable part in bringing it about. I had an entirely new weight within the school and I felt this like a liberation. I remember in particular one incident in the first post-Steede summer. It concerned Dugdale, my old enemy from my first year at Sandford Park. Dugdale had committed some offence – I forget what – against the ethos of the school, and for this he was sentenced to drag the heavy roller across the cricket pitch. I was among those deemed to have handed down the sentence, and who followed him on his journey. I felt no pity towards him, nor did I feel vindictive towards him. What I did feel – as I can now recognize – was smug. A few years back, I had been on the outside looking in. Now I was on the inside looking out. Only those who have experienced a similar transition in their own lives can understand fully what I felt.

No doubt fortunately for my future development, another incident shortly followed which lowered the smugness content. There was a new master called Good who had, I think, taken over the teaching of geography from Gardner, now headmaster. Good had been a senior police officer in the Malay States, and he was crisply competent, a factor which I underestimated. In class, I made some faintly disrespectful crack. Good was on to me immediately. "Will the boy who said that stand up?" he said quietly. He was looking straight at me and I stood up. He went on looking at me and said nothing for about a minute. I became conscious that I was not a particularly impressive figure. I was still quite small for my age at that time, and rather untidy in my dress. Finally, Good spoke again, still quietly. "I see," he said. "Sit down." I sat down.

Good never had any trouble from me again, nor did any of the other masters. The revolutionary period within my school days was at an end.

That little episode, and its consequences, apart, this was a happy time for me. After the fall of Steede, it was as if I had emerged from a long gloomy tunnel which I had been traversing since Christmas Day, 1927. I was breathing more comfortably, relaxing among my peers, and looking forward to still better things many of which were, in due course, to arrive.

Yet I was not left unscarred by the effects of the anti-Steede revolt. Before the entry of Steede on the scene, I had been quite good at mathematics by school standards: well up in the top third of the class. When I decided to devote maths class to the destruction of the maths master, my own knowledge of maths inevitably stood still and began to decay. But what long puzzled me in retrospect was that I never made any effort to make up for lost time, which should not have been too difficult to do. But I simply gave up and maths became and remained a disaster area within my education. Why should this be? As I look back on that time, I believe there was a factor of self-punishment at work. Part of me felt that I had treated Steede cruelly, and recognised that I should be punished for this. The appropriate punishment was that I should never again be competent in the subjects I had refused to allow Steede to teach me. That in any case was the effect which resulted, whatever the psychological mechanisms that may have led to it.

Apart from the blighted area of mathematics, relations with the teachers were now uniformly good, and the teachers were good. I remember two in particular: one was James Johnston Auchmuty. Auchmuty was a northern Protestant, and therefore a different being from the southern Protestants: the only kind of Protestants that I had known up to then. The southern Protestants – those who remained on after the Treaty – had adapted to being a small minority in a Catholic-majority State. This was something those who remained on absolutely had to do: there was no alternative. But northern Protestants, who had successfully opted out of the Catholic-majority State, tended to despise those who remained on.

One could detect this tendency in Auchmuty, but in him it was a somewhat qualified tendency. He had been educated at Trinity College among many southern Protestants and "bad Catholics". Among the latter was my cousin Owen, and Owen and Auchmuty became close friends. Auchmuty knew of the family connection and was consistently kind and helpful to me.

It was from Auchmuty that I learned an important fact about the island I lived in, which had hitherto been concealed from me, not by deliberate choice on anybody's part, but by the nature of the culture in which I lived. This fact was that Northern Ireland was part of the United Kingdom at the will of a majority of its population as expressed decisively at every single general election since Home Rule – envisaged as a qualified form of majority rule for all Ireland – was first mooted by Gladstone in 1886.

I must have been about sixteen when I first learned, from Auchmuty, this basic fact about the divided institutions of the island I lived in. This sustained ignorance on the part of an intelligent boy, belonging to a family with strong political interests, is in itself remarkable. How to account for the sustained ignorance?

The reasons lay deep in the nature and conditioning of the two cultures within which I more or less uneasily grew up. The two cultures were the nationalist one, to variants of which all my family adhered, and the post-1920 southern-Protestant culture within which I received most of my schooling.

From all the talk I heard within my nationalist family about the partition of Ireland, I never once learned that there was a genuine majority, in favour of partition, in Northern Ireland. I understood that the *apparent* majority in favour of partition was a result of gerrymandering. Nobody actually told me that this was the case, but this was the general impression one got from listening to nationalist discourse. It was only much later that I learned that, while there was indeed unionist gerrymandering in Northern Ireland – mainly in local elections and in Derry – there was also a solid and sustained unionist majority there, manifest in every general election since 1886.

My Catholic and nationalist family knew this quite well, but did not allow it to inflect the tenor of their discourse regarding the illegitimacy of Northern Ireland. What may seem a little odder was that I did not learn this basic fact from any of the Protestant boys with whom I went to school, or from any of my Protestant teachers; until the advent of the northern Auchmuty. The reasons for the silence of my schoolfellows and teachers are clear to me now, in retrospect. In the new, nationalist Ireland, those Protestants who "stayed on" had to be very careful what they said. Any sign of sympathy with the Protestant majority in Northern Ireland – who were manifestly anti-Catholic – could be dangerous for the small Protestant minority in the South. And any public acknowledgement of the undoubted fact, consistently ignored in the south, that there was a unionist majority in Northern Ireland, would be certain to be unfavourably construed in the South. So Southern Protestants consistently ignored – and thereby implicitly denied – the existence of such a majority. Instead they repeatedly condemned manifestations of bigotry – then, as now, frequent enough – among their co-religionists in the North. More than that, representatives of Southern Protestants repeatedly paid tribute to how well-treated they were in the south. Many Northern Protestants saw these tributes as implicitly extorted: the price of being let alone, and of respect for one's property rights.

I was grateful to Auchmuty for letting me know what the score really was about democracy in Northern Ireland. When I enquired, among Catholic and Protestant adults I found that the *fact* of the Protestant majority in Northern Ireland had never been in dispute among reasonably well-informed people, of any stripe. It was just a fact to which it was not customary to allude among citizens of the Free State, whether Catholics or Protestants, in the 1920s and for long after. These habits are not yet altogether shaken off.

I did not cease to be a nationalist until long after the Auchmuty revelation, but my nationalism had been dented a bit. Then an episode occurred centering on Auchmuty which put me off unionists a bit, for a while. Suddenly in the middle of class Auchmuty informed us that our Irish teacher, Donn Sigerson Piatt, was about to marry his maid. There was no point in this revelation other than to discredit Piatt and through him the Irish language; or rather the teaching of Irish to persons within the framework of a mainly-Protestant culture. I don't think any boy made any comment on this revelation. I think it made us all uncomfortable. It brought for a moment, into our normally ecumenical class-room context, a whiff of the savage sectarian political animosities and conflicts of the North. I didn't tell Owen about this curious and unpleasant incident. It would have caused a row between Owen and his friend Auchmuty and I didn't want to do that. Also, I wanted to put the whole disturbing episode behind me.

The other teacher who had an important impact on my life was my last Latin teacher, David Grene. David – who later became Professor of Classics at the University of Chicago – was at this time a very recent graduate from Trinity College, Dublin. Many people in his position would not have particularly enjoyed teaching Latin to schoolboys, but David did. He taught Latin with immense and infectious gusto: something habitual to him in every field, as I was to find later. I remember him teaching an Ode by Horace, about the attainment of peace under the Emperor Augustus. He came to the line *"tutus bos etenim rura perambulat:"* the ox in safety perambulates the countryside. David was a gifted amateur actor and when he read the line he marvellously mimicked the action of the ox perambulating the fields. To be taught Latin by David was both an entrancing and an enriching experience. Also I learned a lot of Latin. I had made a good start on the language under Mack, and my knowledge of the language flowered under David Grene. David knew that it needed to flower; I needed to get some kind of scholarship to get to Trinity College, and David knew my Latin needed to be good enough to compensate for my acquired deficiencies in the mathematical subjects. So he gave me private lessons, free of charge, and my Latin came on wonderfully.

I also worked hard on my French, Irish, History and Geography, before I sat the relevant Trinity College examinations in 1936. The exams were for Sizarship in Irish, and for Exhibitions (Entrance Exhibitions or Junior Exhibitions). Sizars were described on the statutes as students of limited means who have their commons [evening meals] free. Also sizars did not have to pay fees. So the sizarship was very useful, financially, but not particularly esteemed socially, because of the "limited means". In older times, sizars used to have to wait on the Gentlemen Commoners who were deemed to be of noble or quasi-noble status. All that was gone, long before the 20th century, but the associations tended to cling, in a faintly depressing manner.

The Exhibitions, being without a means test, carried higher general esteem. I had no hope of a full Exhibition, because of my long neglect of the mathematical subjects. Since these subjects were compulsory I got three out of a hundred in one mathematical subject (algebra, I think) and zero in each of the two others. So that immediately put me out of court for the full Entrance Exhibition. But my showing in all the other subjects was sufficient to win me – in spite of the miserable mathematics results – a Junior Exhibition, providing me with a limited amount of cash, supplementing the benefits of the Sizarship. Not a bad resurrection, I then thought and still think, for a mathematical suicide. So I prepared myself, with much inward rejoicing, for entry to Trinity College, Dublin, in the autumn of 1936.

3

TRINITY COLLEGE

AFTER I HAD ACHIEVED ENTRANCE TO TRINITY COLLEGE, WITH MY TWO modest but useful scholarships, I looked forward to an agreeable and fairly leisurely first year in College. But this was not to be. When he looked at my examination results, Owen proposed that I should sit for a Foundation Scholarship, aka Scholarship of the House, in my first year.

For those who are, in the witty phrase of one of Edmund Burke's biographers, "inspired by a stimulating ignorance of the conditions of academic distinction in Trinity College", a word of explanation is necessary here. The various scholarships and exhibitions available before entrance are very useful but do not carry any particular prestige. A Foundation Scholarship, competed for by undergraduates, is quite different. The academic performances of bright Trinity undergraduates tend to be rated by their performance at "Schol", and by how early they got it. Few undergraduates attempt Scholarship before their second year. To attempt Schol in one's first year is unusual, and to win it in that year very unusual.

In advising me to compete for Schol in my first year, Owen was influenced by my showing at Exhibition level which was – as a whole – considerably less than brilliant. I had been dragged down by my ridiculous showing in maths. But in Schol, I would not have to attempt any mathematical subject. You took Schol in the subjects in which you would eventually expect to graduate: in my case, French and Irish. I had had to work very hard at these subjects for my entrance examinations, to make up for the maths disaster, so I was as it were up and running in the contest for Schol.

In the autumn and winter of 1936 I worked very hard indeed to prepare for Schol. I worked so hard, in fact, that I attracted unfavourable attention from at least one of my seniors and competitors.

George Daniel Peter Allt was then in his second (senior Freshman) year. He was, several years later, to distinguish himself as a Yeats scholar: co-editor of the Variorum Edition of Yeats's poetry. But at this early stage in his career he was running for Schol and worried about how hard I was working. So he tried some nerve-warfare. He came up to me in Front Square and told me it was known that my mother was a charwoman and driving me on to attempt an exam in which I stood absolutely no chance. This wild attack, instead of worrying me, increased my confidence. If I had the competition rattled that badly, I must be in there with a good fighting chance.

In the event I got Schol quite easily. This was very agreeable. It also gave me a badly swelled head, an ailment which lasted throughout the rest of my college career (and, some would say, long after that). When you had Schol, you rated a Scholar's gown: a flowing affair, with long sleeves, identical with a graduate's gown, and very different from the ratty rag-like garment which most undergraduates were constrained to wear. To be the only member of your class entitled to wear a Scholar's gown was not conducive to humility, a quality of which I stood badly in need, though I was not aware of this.

I was very fortunate indeed that, at this crucial moment, I made a friend who was able and willing to take me down a badly-needed peg or two without giving me more than occasional, passing offence. The friend – who remained a friend until his death fifty years later – was Vivian Mercier (later well-known as a literary critic and authority on Irish literature).

When we first met, we took a dislike to one another. Vivian's schooling had been at Portora Royal School, Enniskillen, in Northern Ireland. Portora was a lot older and grander than Sandford Park, so I tended to regard it as a snob school; although I knew that many people in Dublin saw Sandford Park in precisely that light. Hearing my up-market "English" accent, inherited from my father, Vivian at first took me for a "Castle Catholic" which I was not; at least not then. When we got to know each other better, we both ceased to find such classifications at all relevant. We were both bright – the brightest in our year in our subjects – and, more important, we had senses of humour which were not identical but congruent, which is far better. Sometimes he could see the humour in something which at first escaped me, and sometimes it was the other way round.

After I got Schol, I became entitled to rooms in College, with priority and at half the normal rental. Vivian and I shared rooms, at No 4 TCD, in Regent's House, the large building in the Front Square, facing College Green, which was thought of by many Dubliners as "being" Trinity College. We shared those rooms for three years, the rest of our College career. The partnership was very beneficial to me. Vivian was a year younger than me, but he was in fact both more mature and more secure than I was. He was good at making remarks which were a little deflating, but not unkind, and I needed such remarks from time to time. He did not cure me of my swelled head – far from it – but he did teach me to be less obvious about it, and to realise at least part of the potential danger which the visible possession of a swelled head entails for the possessor.

During my second year in College, what was even more important than the relationship with Vivian was the warm relationship which sprang up – to me altogether unexpectedly – between Vivian and my mother, and between Vivian's father and my mother. Vivian wanted to meet my mother, and she invited him out to tea. Somewhat to my chagrin, she got on much better with Vivian than she did with me. The ice in our relationship which had been there ever since my father's death – and indeed a little before, as I have noted earlier – had never fully dissolved. With Vivian my mother relaxed, laughed and told stories. He liked her very much and she him. I was a little out of the picture.

A little later, no doubt at Vivian's suggestion, his father, Bill Mercier, invited my mother to stay with his family for a while at their home in Clara, Co Offaly. Bill was the manager of the Odlum jute works – Clara's biggest industry – and he was a devout Methodist. Like many Methodists, he did not share the negative feelings towards Catholics that were common among other Irish Protestants in those days (and still are in Northern Ireland). He was very kind to my mother, and she was delighted with him. Since my father's death, more than ten years before, she had never been asked to stay with anyone. I believe that week in Clara was her happiest for more than ten years, and the happiest she was ever to know.

* * *

For me also this period, at the start of my College year, was happier than anything I had known since my father's death. Success at College, and being able to live there, were part of this. But there had also been an agreeable loosening and lightening in the pattern of our family life. For about ten years after my father's death, the pattern of our not-very-extended family had been a bit oppressive, since this family consisted of three widows, each with just one child. The shadows of the First World War and of the Troubles lay over all this. The elders were greatly preoccupied with Irish politics but so divided with regard to these that the subject could only be discussed within elaborate conventions adapted to accommodate quite deep divisions. These conventions, though salutary in origin, began to feel a bit irksome, when one first realized that they were there, which in my case was when I was about sixteen (circa 1933).

But shortly after that, things began to brighten up a bit socially, with the appearance on the scene of family members who had hitherto kept themselves aloof, or been kept aloof. The first of these was my mother's brother, Eugene Sheehy. Eugene had been an officer in the British Army in the First World War. For that, Hanna could have forgiven him, as Tom Kettle had been posthumously forgiven. But Eugene had also served the first Free State government, as Judge Advocate General, in which capacity he had been responsible for the prosecution, conviction and execution of republicans charged with murder. From Hanna's point of view, this made Eugene himself a murderer. As in many families throughout the country at this time, a chasm appeared.

I don't know whether Mary retained any contact with Eugene during the post-Treaty period. She might have done. After all, her husband and Eugene had been comrades-in-arms and Mary had never been a republican. So she might have preserved contact, but I don't think she did. I am quite sure my mother did not. Basically, I think both my mother and my Aunt Mary would have been afraid to have to confront Hanna on a subject on which Hanna felt strongly and which was felt to be a sacred subject. It was the Seán O'Casey syndrome; I do not reproach any of those who fell victim to that syndrome, because I later fell victim to it myself in less excusable circumstances.

From 1932 on, the embers of the Irish Civil War began to cool. In that year Eamon de Valera, the person who was deemed to have been the leader of the losing side in that war, came to power in Dublin, through free and fair elections, organised by the party that had won the war and lost the elections. After this event, the atmosphere became somewhat more favourable to better relations between Irish nationalists of different stripes, through the gradual cooling of the old resentments. I believe that in the new and more favourable circumstances, both my mother and Aunt Mary got to work on Hanna and Eugene to resume relations with Eugene and his family.

In any case, relations did resume, in a way. One evening in, I think, 1934, the families dined together, by invitation at Eugene's house: Eugene and his wife, Carmel, Aunt Mary and Betty, Hanna and Owen, my mother and myself. It was not a particularly comfortable evening. The setting was wrong, to start with, much more stately than anything Eugene's guests were used to. Two large modern bathrooms, where the rest of us had each one poky one; paintings by Corot on the dining-room walls; even a butler, who doubled as my uncle's crier, wearing white gloves. Hanna looked all round wearing her most glacial expression. You could see that she was thinking: "This is how you can live, if you can sell your country out." You could also see that Eugene knew what Hanna was thinking, and bitterly resented it.

My mother and Mary and Carmel made valiant efforts at conversation. The children were not expected to contribute, and didn't. Hanna and Eugene said almost nothing, and nothing directly to one another. It was as if each was saying by demeanour only: "If you think my being here in the room with you means that I have anything whatever to apologize for, you have another guess coming".

No great success then. Still, with a Civil War, complete with murders and executions, in the background, the meeting represented a modest but real achievement. The two sides kept in contact, intermittently and in a rather melancholy way. Carmel took a liking to me, paid to have my teeth mended and listened to me boasting about cricket. (I was a member of possibly the most incompetent First Eleven in the British Isles). Hanna remained sore; I think her conscience smote her at having resumed relations with traitors and murderers. In Sheehy gatherings (without Eugene) Hanna was apt to drag in cutting comments about Eugene and Carmel, which embarrassed everyone else. Carmel's family, the Nearys, had made their money in the licensed trade, and this was held against her. As for Eugene, he had put on weight during the years, and this was held against him. A man, Hanna thought, ought to be made to wear a corset if he obviously needed one. Why should women be the only people made to wear corsets? This observation was made as if it were a feminist point, but (as often) of course it wasn't really. It was a republican point. Hanna would never have talked like that about a republican who was a bit overweight. Free Staters made good targets for feminist attacks. There was a lot of this kind of stuff going on within the culture at this time, as also in former times.

Other expanded inter-familial relations of the period were less complicated, and were simply cheerful. The first of these was the arrival on the scene of my first cousin, Pan Sheehy (who later played a significant part in Irish broadcasting as the principal assistant to by far the most successful Irish broadcaster, the phenomenal Gay Byrne). Pan's family and ours had become alienated not through politics, as with Hanna and Eugene, but as a result of the conflict, and the outcome of the conflict, over my mother's marriage, in the period before the First World War. During that conflict Cáit – Pan's mother – had been one of the most fervent champions of my mother's cause, of whom there were not many. But the trouble was that she couldn't quit being a champion. When, after the decisive Skeffington intervention my grandparents agreed to the marriage, my father and mother were happy to re-establish (or establish) friendly or (at worst) civil relations with the former opponents of the marriage.

Cáit, however, was of sterner stuff, and more thoroughly embattled. She thought it wretchedly feeble on my mother's part to resume relations with people who had treated her so abominably. My mother, very sensibly, thought that if she herself was prepared to forgive and forget, it was a bit absurd for a third party to insist that the war must continue. Cáit seems to have considered that this attitude on my mother's part was a poor requital for her own loyalty. So relations between my mother and Cáit were broken off, and seem never to have resumed. All that had happened before I was born.

Cáit's family were Moviddy Sheehys, Moviddy being a small town in Co Limerick. When a place-name was conjoined with a family name in this way, it was understood that the family in question was "landed" and therefore rather "grand", and this appears to have been the case with the Moviddy Sheehys. As with other Irish landed families, the Moviddy Sheehys were a bit odd, in an acrimonious kind of way, acrimony being, it appears, a kind of speciality with Cáit. It seems that Cáit and her husband – whose name I never learned – did not in their last years ever exchange a word. When one of them absolutely needed to communicate with the other over some practical matter, the would-be communicator would address the statement to the family dog. The required reply, if any, would be despatched through the same canine channel.

Despite this forbidding family background – or perhaps because of it, in a way – Pan grew up an absolutely marvellous person: a strong and courageous personality, but also kind and ingenious in her kindness. As soon as she was grown up, she left the family feud behind her, as if it had never been. She came to our house and soon made herself at home there, joining the family evenings as a member of the family. My mother soon became fond of her and she of my mother. She managed to get on with the formidable aunts without, however, being as impressed by either of them as I was accustomed to be. She made a point of taking me "out of myself" as the phrase then went. She organised long walks including me, with participation of both sexes – a novel feature as far as I was concerned, and a welcome one. So that was good.

The other welcome development around the same time was the arrival from Canada of my Aunt Margaret with two of her children, Garry and Ronan. Unlike her sisters, Margaret was not in the least interested in politics, Irish or other. She was interested in sex and – unusually for the time and place – cheerfully made no secret of the fact. She had been regarded as a great beauty. She was what was then said to be statuesque: that is to say, large and curvy. Her marital history was unusual. She had been an actress – a Shakespearean actress – and she attracted and married a wealthy feather-merchant called Frank Culhane. This was rated as a good match in the parlance of the day. The pair had four children: Garry, Patricia, Peggy and Frank. Then Frank Culhane suddenly up and died. Almost immediately, Margaret married again. The new husband, a man called Casey – I never knew his first name – was twenty years younger than herself and was actually her godson. Margaret left her four children in the care of the parents of her former husband, and departed with her new husband for Canada. In Canada there was one child by the new marriage: Ronan Casey.

Three of the deserted children accepted their fate, however bitterly. Patricia eventually became a nun; Frank a priest; only Peggy married. But Garry, then in his mid-teens, decided to rebel, and set about his rebellion with resolution and skill. He was aided by the fact that his grandfather was a man of regular habits who returned from his office to his home at a predictable hour in the evening. So Garry lay in wait for him on the third floor of the house. Garry had with him a volume of *Thom's Directory* (of Dublin), an exceedingly heavy tome. When Garry's grandfather, returning home, reached the top step and had his latch-key in his hand, Garry dropped *Thom's Directory* on him, with great precision, hitting him on the head and knocking him down. He had to have several stitches in his head and was treated for a number of contusions.

When Garry's grandfather was sufficiently recovered, he did exactly what Garry wanted him to do. He paid Garry's fare to Canada and shipped him off there, to take up residence with his mother and new step-father.

Margaret and the two of her sons who had been domiciled abroad returned to Ireland around 1936 and shook up our little society, greatly to my delight. They were all irreverent, cheerful and breezy and unimpressed by Irish institutions, especially the Church. Garry was the most impressive of them. He was a big, strong, handsome, powerful man. He had been a canoeing champion in Canada. He had also been a very militant trade union leader and (for a time) a Communist shop-steward which probably had something (though I don't know exactly what) to do with his having to leave Canada. He rode a powerful motor-bike on which he used to take me for long fast rides as a pillion-rider. I was a bit frightened at first but he soon convinced me that, with him in charge, nothing bad could happen. And, as it happened, nothing bad did happen. I was very fond of Garry and remained so until his death about fifty years later.

I didn't get to know Ronan so well. He was younger than me, but much more experienced. I was shocked, and in a way impressed, by his sophistication, when I stumbled on his possession of that attribute. One day when he visited my rooms in Trinity an acquaintance, a brother of a friend of mine, happened to come in. I shall call him JG. I knew him to be a homosexual, and I could see he was attracted to Ronan. I was a bit worried about this, seeing that it could lead to unpleasant repercussions for Ronan, and possibly also for me. When JG had left I started, rather awkwardly, to give Ronan some kind of warning, not quite knowing how to put it. Ronan cut me short. "You mean he's a homosexual," he said. "I know all about homosexuals. Maw used to keep one in the attic."

I could see that Ronan stood in no need of my protection. We remained friendly, in a cheerful but slightly distant way. For him I was a country cousin, agreeable enough, but a little retarded, socially speaking.

* * *

In the summer of my second year in Trinity, while I was living in rooms there, my mother died suddenly of a stroke. When I heard of her illness I ran from Trinity to the house in Rathmines. I later could see that a tram would have taken me there quicker. I think there was an unconscious desire to re-enact, in a way, my run on the morning of my father's death to my Aunt Mary's house in Ranelagh. When I arrived, my mother was unconscious, breathing very heavily, and she never recovered consciousness. I know I felt guilty because of my coldness towards her, since my father's death, and I think the guilt was reflected in the running. But the guilt was, and long remained, a little below the level of consciousness.

The funeral service for my mother was at the Catholic Church in Rathmines, her parish church, and she was buried in Glasnevin. I have just one distinct memory, each, of the service and of the burial. The memory of the service is of the most prominent person who attended it: Richard Mulcahy, who had been Minister for Defence in the first government of the Free State. I think Mulcahy and my mother had been friends as undergraduates in University College, Dublin in the days before the First World War and the associated national catastrophes in Ireland. I don't think my mother had seen him since the catastrophes. He was responsible for seventy-seven executions of republicans during the Civil War, and was in consequence, for republicans like my Aunt Hanna, the leading hate-figure in Ireland. I rather admired him for coming to that funeral, which he knew would be attended by Hanna and some of her friends, all of whom hated him.

My other memory, which concerns the burial, is more vivid. It is of my first cousin, Frank Culhane – Garry's brother the priest – who had come to the funeral from France, where he had been under treatment for tuberculosis. This was the first time I had ever met him. Frank was a very striking figures. He was extremely tall, thin and handsome, and in his black soutane – obligatory in those days for the French clergy, though not for the Irish – he made a very striking figure, a fact of which he was clearly aware. As the labourers were shovelling the earth on my mother's coffin, Frank took up his stand on a little knoll, just above the grave, as it was filled. So stationed, Frank was a figure to draw every gaze, as he clearly knew. As I looked at Frank, I silently hated him. This was MY mother's funeral, not his mother's, so what was he doing up there, hogging the limelight? That was the nature of the primitive feeling at work, though I wouldn't have put it that way to myself.

Many years later I came to know Frank quite well, in France, and grew to like him very much. I even came to understand what he had been up to by my mother's grave, and what he thought he was up to. He thought he was preparing for his own imminent death, and that was why he had come; I don't think he had ever even met my mother. His conscious intention was serious. But the passion of his life was the theatre, much more than the Church. Being in that situation before all those people, that *audience*, he simply couldn't resist hamming it up.

There was some falsity in his performance. But there was also some falsity in my reaction to his performance. In being angry at Frank for an apparent parade of grief, I was compensating for my own inner feeling of self-reproach, for not experiencing, then, as much grief as I felt I should, over my mother's death.

* * *

Problems connected with my mother's estate, such as it was, were handled by my Aunt Mary. I understood that the furniture of our house had to be sold, to meet the debts. All I retained was my father's portrait by Frances Baker, which I still have in my house in Howth. The Leinster Road house was let to new tenants. Fortunately for me, I had my rooms in Trinity College.

My uncle Eugene now offered to make me an allowance, for a period. This was decent of him, as he was in no way obliged to make such an offer. Unfortunately, however, that offer was accompanied by a stipulation: that I should leave Trinity College, and get a job in a bank. I don't know whether this condition was dictated by the religious factor – the Church's ban on Catholics attending TCD – or not. In any case I refused the stipulation, thereby forfeiting the allowance. I was in a position to do this because I had my rooms in Trinity – for a very small rent. I had my three scholarships, and while the cash income from these was small, one of them also entitled me to daily "Commons" – a substantial evening meal – free daily for the rest of my College career. I could lunch at the College buttery, on meat loaf, for sixpence. Because of my early Schol, I was in demand for private lessons from other students, which paid quite well. I soon became TCD correspondent for *The Irish Times*, whose then editor, Bertie Smyllie, had been a friend of my father's. This became my main source of cash income, and a good one. *The Irish Times* took a weekly article from me, for thirty shillings an article. This was good pay for the time; compare, above, the price of a meat loaf. So I was, all in all, in a position to defy any number of uncles, whether the Catholic Church was behind them or not. I thought it was, which made the situation more piquant.

The financial side was all right for the time being, but elsewhere there were clouds on the horizon. The one that troubled me most – though in ways of which I was not fully conscious at the time – was a distinct deterioration in my relations with my cousin Owen, which had been the emotional and moral mainstay of my boyhood since the day of my father's death. While I was a young boy, Owen's attitude had been wholly protective. But when I became an adolescent, he began to correct me, for my own good, as he seemed to think. I remember three little incidents in particular. The first was when I appeared wearing a handsome new blazer which my mother had bought for me. He told me that my mother could not afford to give me such presents, and that I ought to discourage her from making them. On that point, I now think he was right, but that was not how I felt at the time.

The second incident was a little more serious. Owen and Betty and I were together, and Owen asked me to leave as he had something serious to discuss with Betty. I was put out by this, as I was a bit jealous of Owen's attention to Betty, whom I did not trust. So I hung around the door, hoping to hear something of what was going on. Owen suddenly opened the door and hauled me in. He addressed me, for the first time, in a cold and menacing tone which reminded me of the tone in which his mother had addressed me, just after my father's death, on the subject of reading in bed. I felt sick at heart, especially because I knew Owen was in the right, and accepted that he could punish me with propriety. At least, my conscious mind accepted this.

The third incident was the most serious. We had been playing table tennis in my room, in the house in Leinster Road. At the end of the game, Owen picked up a book I had been reading, a collection of short stories. As boys sometimes do, I had given marks to the stories I had read. The story that got the highest marks was one by an English Catholic writer. Like other disgruntled Irish Catholics – Seán O'Faoláin for example – I was trying to find a way to a more agreeable kind of Catholicism than the Irish kind through the possibly more enlightened writings of Catholics in other countries. But Owen was clearly suspicious of the mark assigned, and of the writer who got the mark. Owen turned to the story I had approved, and started reading the passages I had marked. He read these passages in a heavily sarcastic tone. Again, I was reminded of his mother, in her worse moments. Then he commented on these passages, each in turn, again with heavy sarcasm. I don't remember making any reply: I just suffered in silence. Afterwards, reflecting on the scene, I reminded myself of all the kindness Owen had shown to me at the time of my father's death and after, when I was a boy. So I decided, consciously, to forget the incident. But in reality I did not forget it, and there was something in me determined to get my own back for the hurt inflicted.

Outwardly things continued on the same, mainly friendly, basis. I took Owen's advice over Schol and prospered because of it. But sadly, our relationship worsened because of the success he had prepared for me. I now became imbued with the conviction that I was more intelligent than Owen. I had got Schol in my first year while Owen had got Schol *only in his second year* . . . I never openly gave vent to this reflection, but it was always there at the back of my mind, and I suspect it was sometimes discernible in my bearing.

I attended Owen's lectures, regularly. His lectures dealt with the most modern period of French literature, and with writers then mostly living. After a while I found that I didn't think his lectures were much good. I don't think this opinion derived from the resentments which I was beginning to nourish against him. I think it was quite objective, though I might not have been able to frame it to myself, consciously, had it not been for the rift that had already begun to appear below the surface in our relationship.

As a teacher of French language and literature Owen's strength was in relation to the language. He knew and loved the French language and taught it – to me among others – with a skill derived from intimate knowledge. But his relation to the literature was always awkward, and somehow forced. He didn't really think literature was all that important, as compared with all-consuming politics. He didn't much care for Marcel Proust, whom I considered not only the greatest French writer of the 20th century, but one of the greatest writers of all time. Owen preferred Andre Gide. I thought Gide a mediocre writer, and his most ambitious work, *Les Faux-Monnayeurs*, seemed to me a pretentious fraud. But Owen liked Gide's politics, of the late thirties: left-wing but anti-communist. It seemed to me that because of the sympathetic politics, Owen was unconsciously magnifying the significance of Gide's contribution to literature.

I still think I was right on those matters, and Owen wrong. Yet I could and did still learn from him, even where I thought he was wrong. In my final year, I wrote a paper for him about Gide, expressing my negative view. He commented severely on the paper, and pointed out a number of mistakes in it. I realised that before I was examined *seriously* on this subject for Moderatorship – the Trinity Honours Degree – I had better be absolutely sure of my ground. I knew that Owen would not mark me down just for expressing opinions he personally did not hold or like. To that extent my old confidence in him was still like a rock. He gave me a very high mark for a piece of which he cannot have approved. But I also know that in expressing those opinions, at Moderatorship, I had marked out a deep intellectual divergence from him.

That was all right, and quite healthy, it seemed to me, at that stage of my life. But another aspect of the changing relationship soon came to light and appalls me in retrospect, for the cruelty it revealed on my side at a difficult and painful stage in Owen's life. Near the beginning of, I believe, my third year in Trinity Owen fell seriously ill. It was an onset of tuberculosis which was to necessitate an absence of a year in Davos, Switzerland, during which his French wife, Andree, temporarily took over his lectures. I called on Owen to convey sympathy, as I consciously thought. I found Owen in bed, lying on his front. Andree was applying heated tumblers with an internal vacuum, to his bare back: a French remedy, for any pulmonary disorder. It was a bizarre setting, and my own conduct was also bizarre. I had brought with me, as it seems with intent, a letter I had received from my old Latin teacher, David Grene, warning me against what he regarded as Owen's excessive influence over me. David didn't believe in Owen's causes – pacifism and socialism – and thought that this combination of causes was muddling me up. He admired Owen's character, but thought his ideology was a mess. "I have nothing against Owen personally, but a lot against his *Weltanschauung*" (world outlook). It was quite a sensible letter, and I would have done well to think about it seriously. But what I actually did now seems to me, in retrospect, almost inconceivably awful. I read this letter out to Owen as he lay there with those tumblers stuck to his back. Owen only laughed and did not comment. I think he took the reading of the letter as a kind of awkward declaration of intellectual independence, something of which he would have approved in principle, even if it was a bit painful in practice.

Looking back on it I wondered how I could have done such a thing, and I think I now understand. I had resented Owen's rebukes – especially Owen's reading of those marked passages in that Catholic book – much more fiercely than I was consciously aware. Something in me was biding its time to strike back. And, as in the case of my old headmaster Steede, in my schooldays (above, pp 50-53) I struck at a weakness: Steede's deafness, Owen's illness. But in Steede's case it had been a campaign sustained to the destruction of the adversary, whom I simply hated. In the case of Owen, this remained an isolated episode in a love-hate relationship, in which the love remained dominant, in most circumstances. When Owen came back, about a year later, the old friendship resumed, but with just a touch of wariness in it now on both sides. It was a wariness, I think, not just about one another, but of each one of us about something in ourselves. Each of us had a strong capacity for aggression, but as we became more aware of this, we were better able to control it. It never again seriously troubled our friendship, throughout the rest of Owen's life.

* * *

Over literature, I had shaken off Owen's influence quite early in my college career. Over politics, I did not shake off that influence for a very long time, and in some important ways never shook it off. Politics and religion, as often, were quite closely associated, and we both needed to dissociate them in our own personal lives. Specifically, it had become important to us to show that in choosing to be educated in schools of Protestant ethos, we had not thereby abjured the politics of our Catholic ancestors based on nationalism.

As it happened, the year I entered Trinity – 1936 – was the last full year in which the Irish Free State – as its designation then was – was officially and indubitably part of the British Commonwealth of which the Monarch was the head. For most Protestants this appurtenance was welcome and valued, for nostalgic reasons, preserving at least the semblance of the cherished past. For nationalists the link with the Crown was obnoxious: something to be broken as soon as possible. An opportunity seemed to present itself in 1936, with the divorce crisis and the abdication of Edward VIII. The allegiance the Free State had professed to the British Monarch, under George V and Edward VIII, need not extend to George VI, so republicans of the strict observance argued: mostly Sinn Féin-IRA but including my Aunt Hanna. De Valera's government, however, preferred to tiptoe legalistically away from the Empire, rather than break with it conspicuously, so de Valera was prepared to agree to the accession of George VI. Republicans therefore staged quite a large riot in Dublin that summer. In my first year in Trinity, I took part in that riot which was suppressed by the police without much difficulty. I sustained some bruises.

Trinity College, at this time, still toasted the King and sang (or heard), "God Save The King", on what were regarded as appropriate occasions. Owen and I thought it important to sit down on such occasions. This did not give rise to much unfavourable comment. Most unionists by this time glumly accepted that the Monarchy was a thing of the past as far as the Irish Free State was concerned.

Owen did not attempt to influence me directly as to how I should think about international politics, which in retrospect I can see was by far the most important subject of the time, this being the period of the rise and early expansion of Nazi power in Europe. Owen did not directly seek to influence me as to how I should view this, along with the many related issues. But he did refer me to a source which he suggested I could rely on for news and analysis of the international situation. The source he referred me to was the British weekly journal, the *New Statesman and Nation*.

The New Statesman was socialist, as Owen was, and I was, though more vaguely. Also, and much more pertinently, in the context of the time, the *New Statesman* was pacifist, not altogether in doctrine, but by strong inclination. This reflected what was then the mood of my generation in England, France and Ireland, which derived from the deep disillusion of our parents by the end of the First World War. And the disillusion had been deeper in Ireland than anywhere else. We were led to believe that after tens of thousands of our men-folk had been sacrificed in the war, British perfidy had then done us out of the Home Rule we had been promised, and refused the legitimate demands of the republican majority in the island of Ireland, represented by Sinn Féin, the winners of the 1918 election.

This retrospect left out quite a lot but variants of it made up the nationalist culture. Even more important than this nationalist component was the genuine horror at the thought of any new war which pervaded Ireland as well as England and France in the early and mid-thirties, and even later. The mood was "Never again. Not for any reason!" This mood pervaded the West and almost the whole of the youth of the West in this period.

Responsive to this mood, and the generally "progressive" outlook of its own readers, the policy of the *New Statesman* towards Nazi Germany was: opposition to the Nazis, but also opposition to British rearmament. As I can see in retrospect, the Nazis found this kind of opposition very much to their taste. If they could get on with their own rearmament while their enemies continued to disarm they could deal with all their problems in due course. In Nazi Germany, quite unlike the West, pacifism had no influence, or even any voice. The popular mood in Germany was for the reversal of the verdict of Versailles, preferably by peaceful means, but using the threat of war, seeing how effective it was with the all-too-peaceloving West.

The policy favoured by the *New Statesman* – and very influential in other quarters also – was intentionally hostile to the Nazis, but objectively helpful to them. This is how it seems to me now, but it is not how I saw it at the time. At the time I, along with millions of others in the West, saw such a policy as intellectually sound and morally responsible. And the reason we saw the thing in so false a light is that we were all blinded by fear. The thought of a Second World War was intrinsically so horrible, that we clung to a kind of nonsense that had the effect of seeming to lend dignity to the politics of fear. So the *New Statesman and Nation* seemed to have the answer.

In the period 1936-1939 Catholic Ireland was less preoccupied with the great question of the age – the rise of Nazi power – than with a relatively peripheral question: the war in Spain. This was a good religion-and-politics issue, with Catholicism in it, and so intrinsically interesting to Irish people in a way that the largely incomprehensible Nazis – neither Catholics nor Protestants – were not. The Catholic Church in Ireland was of course strongly on the side of Franco, and most of the media followed that lead. The de Valera government, like other democratic European governments, held to a policy of neutrality. The leading opposition party, now known as Fine Gael, saw this as an issue on which they could come back to power and became militantly pro-Franco, attacking Dev for letting Franco down. The Labour Party, to which I belonged, was, as often, split between a Catholic right wing, mainly rural, and an anti-clerical left wing confined to Dublin. The right wing was militantly pro-Franco, while the left wing approved de Valera's "neutral" stance and was emotionally anti-Franco.

I was a delegate from the Trinity College branch to the annual conference of the Labour Party in the autumn of 1936. I saw this as an opportunity for a blow at the political influence of the Catholic Church in Ireland, then at about its awesome peak. As readers of this narrative will understand, this was one of the causes nearest to my heart, and I duly struck the blow. I had spent the previous summer in France and had clipped a number of anti-Franco stories from the anti-clerical left-wing French press. As the historian I later became, I am mildly ashamed to say that I made no attempt to check on the authenticity of these stories. But I was then operating, not as a historian, but as a polemicist, and this was pretty good polemical material. There was one story in particular about Franco politicians doing lucrative deals with "white slavers" which made the delegates sit up.

The story of my intervention made some headlines in the Dublin press and it was claimed that I was "shouted down". This was not accurate. I was shouted at, but not down. Some of the delegates either really were, or purported to be, very angry.

But the chairman, the then leader of the Labour Party, William Norton, firmly defended my right to speak, and his ruling was obeyed. He was in favour, like Dev, of a neutral stance relating to the Spanish War and my intervention, while a bit overheated, at least offset the pressures for intervention on Franco's side. The little episode was not entirely without significance. I had got a hearing for a point of view which was anathema to the Irish Catholic Church. This would be commonplace today, but in the Ireland of 1936 it was not.

I don't, however, want to exaggerate the seriousness of my position on international politics at this time. There was a strong streak of frivolity there. This showed even over the Spanish War. I was Chairman of TCD Modern Language Society at this time, and an old school friend, Victor Craig, was Treasurer. The Society had amassed quite a healthy bank balance. I proposed that the bank balance be sent off as a contribution to the republican side in the Spanish War. Victor opposed this. I then, at a public meeting of the Society, proposed that the accumulated money be disposed of as follows: one half to go on a social outing, with free drink, and the other half to go to the Spanish republicans. I thought of this proposal as Machiavellian, ensuring majority support for a move that benefited the Spanish republicans. Actually I also quite liked the idea of the social outing with free drink. The motion was carried, but left furious resentment behind on the part of the more responsible undergraduates. At the party given on the proceeds, I was assaulted by Victor Craig's fiancee, a young woman called Joyce McGilligan. She was athletic and hit me quite hard across the shins with a large bench. The episode attracted some amused attention. A poem appeared about it in the college magazine, beginning with the following neat rime riche:

Oh the clash of literati
At that dreadful Mod Lang party!

I was reminded of this little episode in my past recently while re-reading Mary Renault's *The Last of The Wine*. I came upon the following passage:

"There was a long silence. Then a man in the far corner said:
'That is not only blasphemy. It is hubris.'
'It is more dangerous than that," Kritias said. 'It is frivolity.'"

* * *

Throughout my college career I worked quite a lot harder than my contemporaries. There was a special reason for this. It was a rather fiendish contrivance called the Hely-Hutchinson-Stewart Prize. It was a large prize – £300, if I remember rightly – awarded on the aggregate of the results of nine consecutive Term Honour examinations. All Honour students had to sit one examination a year, but if you were trying for the HHS you had to sit all three. I rather resented this burden at the time, but in retrospect I am grateful for it. I had a slightly loony tendency at this time, as I will explain, and the need to keep my nose to the grindstone kept that tendency within some bounds. Eventually, I won the prize. Vivian Mercier came second. I suspect he didn't try as hard as I did. He knew I needed the money, and he didn't.

Despite the sobering influence of the Prize, I did some pretty crazy things in those years. Some of these were fairly harmless. For example, I climbed on the roof of the Regent House and announced in a very loud voice across College Green: "This is the Provost of Trinity College! I am here to tell you there is no God!"

In a similar, but not identical vein, I scrawled "Lies and priestcraft (Blake)" on the bulletin board of the Divinity School.

The third episode was more dangerous to my career. I was at a bottle-party in the rooms of another undergraduate, Mark Mortimer (drink comes into most of these stories, but I think not so much as a cause as an excuse). As it happened these rooms looked out over the College Chapel. When I noticed this I opened the relevant window in the rooms and hurled six sherry bottles through the window of the College Chapel, justifying this action with the same slogan: "Lies and priestcraft".

The following morning Mark Mortimer came and told me he had been questioned about the episode by the Junior Dean, Kenneth Claud Bailey. Mark had not implicated me, but it was clear that it was up to me to confess responsibility. So I went to the Junior Dean and did so. Then, looking him straight in the eye, I said: "But I want you to know, sir, that I did not know it was the College Chapel." He in turn looked me straight in the eye and said: "I believe you, O'Brien."

In the course of my long life I have very seldom lied: indeed this is the only lie of mine I can recall. But I was bright enough to realise that if you are unfortunate enough to be required to lie, or risk serious punishment, the lie had better be a good, thumping one. If I had been believed to have *deliberately* attacked the College Chapel, I would have been sent down. As it was I got off with so slight a punishment that I no longer remember what it was.

Other episodes, potentially much more dangerous, involved Peter Allt, who had been my rival in my first year. We were now friends, in and around the College Historical Society, of which we were both Gold Medallists in Oratory. He got the Gold Medal before I did, and advised me as to how I might win it. He made the Machiavellian suggestion that to follow a pro-fascist line would attract attention. I rejected that suggestion because it would mean a break with Owen; otherwise I might have been tempted, though I believe I would eventually have rejected it. But I still, unwisely, continued to see a lot of Allt, which nearly got me into bad trouble, twice.

The first episode concerned a projected attempt on the life of the Vice-Provost, WA Goligher. Mr Goligher was unpopular, at the time, with the undergraduate body. There were rumours that he had sexual relations with some of the female undergraduates. I have no reason to believe that there was any basis in fact for this belief but the belief, whether real or feigned, was widespread among students at the time. Peter may really have believed it. I don't know. At any rate the professed belief became the basis for a project. On the evening in question, Peter and I had been drinking pretty heavily. I now think it possible that Peter had also taken some drugs. When the pubs shut, we adjourned to Peter's rooms. Peter then announced that he proposed to put an end to Goligher's wicked existence. Peter then got hold of a hammer and rather a large nail, as the instruments of the proposed deed. I was pretty drunk by this time and I thought this was some kind of fantastic joke. In any case, I accompanied Peter across the Front Square, to Goligher's rooms, to which we gained access through a window. We walked round Goligher's rooms and found he was not there. So this strange little episode ended without mishap.

Thinking the episode over, on the following day, I took it that Peter knew all along that Goligher was away so that the whole thing was a joke, though rather a weird one. But a subsequent experience – next to be narrated – led me to reject that theory. I now think that Peter was in no condition to know whether Goligher was there or not and that, in breaking into Goligher's rooms, Peter did intend to do him a mischief. In any case, whatever he may have intended, we would have been in terrible trouble if caught in illegal entry, armed with weapons, into the Vice-Provost's rooms. At the very least we would both have been sent down, without taking a degree. We would probably also have been prosecuted and have served a jail sentence. So it was as well that the Vice-Provost was not at home that evening.

Unlike the first episode, the second can be precisely dated. It was 29 September, 1938, the date of Neville Chamberlain's arrival in Munich. I don't remember now exactly what I felt about Munich, but I was certainly worried and apprehensive, like millions of other Europeans at the time. In my case, the worry manifested itself in a long, solitary pub-crawl; drinking was not unusual, but that solitary pub-crawl was, I believe, unique on my part. When the pubs closed, I returned to my rooms in Trinity where I found a strange scene before me.

Vivian was seated, looking very pale. With him were two large men, who, though in plain clothes, had the unmistakeable look of Dublin policemen. Vivian identified me as his room-mate. Then one of the policemen held up a sock. "Do you recognize this?" he asked. "I do," I said, "It's one of my socks." (I didn't have all that many.) The policeman relaxed slightly. He said: "It's as well you gave us that answer, Mr O'Brien. You see, the sock has your name stitched into it." And he showed me the label. Then he asked me where I had been and what I had been doing. Fortunately I was far from being drunk, and was able to give him a complete list of the pubs I had visited. The pubs had to form a credible pattern and would have accounted for the time. I never heard from the police on this matter again.

After the police had left, Vivian told me what had happened. About two hours before I came back, Peter had come to our rooms, with another undergraduate. Peter was in a state of high excitement, Vivian thought, probably drunk; I now think, probably drugged. He was carrying a large glass ashtray. He went into my bedroom and when he came back the ashtray was wrapped up in my sock. He then threw the loaded sock out the window. It was apparent immediately that he had hit somebody. He and his friend then fled, leaving Vivian to carry the can.

The police arrived in our rooms shortly afterwards. It turned out that the ashtray had hit and injured an old woman. Vivian told them what he had seen, but without identifying the culprit. He must have said he didn't recognise the person, but he would have felt bad about that lie and didn't acknowledge it. In any case we both agreed that there was no question of identifying Allt. To do so would have ended his college career, and probably also earned him a prison sentence. Vivian's reputation with the college authorities was unblemished up to that date and caused his story to be believed as concerned his own role; though he was probably suspected, rightly, of covering up for the culprit. As for me, my reputation was by no means as good as Vivian's, but my story held up.

We were in the clear as far as the police were concerned, but the college authorities felt that some kind of penalty was in order for our not-very-close relation to an event which had involved the authorities in considerable embarrassment. So we were both put on "night-roll" for three nights. This was not a fearsome punishment. It meant you had to cross the Front Square, at night, proceded by a porter carrying a lantern. The idea was that this ritual put you to shame, in the eyes of your contemporaries, but it didn't work like that. Nobody thought any the worse of you for being put on night-roll. There was even a slight touch of glamour in being singled out for this ritual.

Vivian made no protest at being put on night-roll. I think he felt that it was somehow a proper punishment for having lied to the police. But I, who had not been on the scene at all when the crime was committed and therefore had not had to lie, felt that I was in a position to be righteous and I went to the Junior Dean to complain about the sentence. He was not moved. He said, memorably: "You may not have thrown the ashtray out of the window yourself, O'Brien, but your friends are the kind of people who throw ashtrays out of windows."

And I had to reflect that I had, at least, one friend who had thrown an ashtray out of a window, and that I had helped him to escape punishment for doing so.

As for Allt, the last I heard about him, years afterwards, was that he had fallen under an underground train in London, thereby ending a most promising literary and scholarly career. I don't think he would have committed suicide, but I believe his fall must have been a drug-induced accident.

* * *

At this point the love-interest comes in. I had three love-affairs during my college years. The first two were quite short. The third was with Christine Foster, who later became my wife.

As it happens all three affairs had a bearing on that relationship between religion and nationalism which is one of the main themes of this book.

The first affair was with Patsy-Anne Drake. Patsy-Anne was English, with possibly some Anglo-Irish in her. She was tall and exceptionally beautiful, and she was also extremely amiable, with a nice sense of humour. I liked her a lot and wanted to fall in love with her. But there were signs of difficulty ahead. The fact that she was English was a drawback, in the eyes of a good Irish nationalist as I then was. She was also a Protestant, though that didn't matter to me, at least consciously. What did worry me a bit was the strength of her connections with the British Army. Her father, Captain Drake had been an officer in Britain's Indian Army. So also was her stepfather, Major Willoughby Weallens, whom Patsy detested. This military connection did not worry me enough to stop me being attracted to Patsy. We met on Achill Island in the summer of 1937. My mother, my Aunt Hanna and myself were on holiday there, staying at an hotel. Patsy's family had a nice holiday home in Dooagh, and Patsy and her mother were staying there. Patsy liked me and so did her mother. The mother was a formidable lady. She had once been a great beauty, and still looked pretty good. She was quite clever and talked well, with great assurance. Though English, she was in her way a sort of Irish nationalist, believing that England had treated the Irish badly and ought to make up to them in some way, she was not quite sure what. Even in those days I was rather suspicious of English people who believed themselves to be Irish nationalists: Maud Gonne, for example. But I thought (rightly, I still think) Mrs Weallens's Irish nationalism was no more than skin deep. In general, I enjoyed her conversation, and it sometimes opened up fascinating, if chimerical, perspectives. At one point she told me that if I were interested she could probably get me a commission in the Bengal Lancers, and I think she probably could have. For a few wild seconds I allowed myself to be tempted, and then reality closed in. If I joined the Bengal Lancers, not merely would both the Skeffingtons close their doors to me but – as I then felt – the whole Irish nation would reject me. I don't suppose the Irish nation would have given a tinker's curse, but I was certainly right about the Skeffingtons. So that idea was allowed to die. However, my friendship with the Weallens-Drakes continued to prosper, and one fine day this led to an invitation to my mother and my Aunt Hanna to have dinner with them at their house in Dooagh.

If I had had any sense, I would have seen that an encounter between my Aunt Hanna and a lady who was the widow of one British officer and the wife of another could only lead to disaster. If I was serious about Patsy – and I thought I was – I should have strained every nerve to avoid a meeting between the two. But I didn't. I let it happen: perhaps something in me wanted it to happen.

My mother and my aunt accepted the invitation and the doomed dinner engagement came into being. Hanna – as I should have known she would – took the earliest possible opportunity to break up the relationship between me and the scion of British militarism and imperialism. When Mrs

Weallens asked her whether she had ever visited India, Hanna sweetly acknowledged that she had not, but she did have a great friend who lived in India and who loved the country. Mrs Weallens asked for the name. "James Cousins." Mrs Weallens was puzzled.; the number of Britons living in India at that time was quite small, and they all knew each other, at least by repute. "Where does he live in India?" "Meirut." "I know Meirut a little but I don't think I have met him." Hanna went in for the kill. "No. You would not have met him. He is in prison in Meirut. He is in prison for what the British call treason. That is to say he wants India to be free from British rule."

And that was it. My mother did her best to save the proprieties, by desultory small-talk with Mrs Weallens, but the evening was dead on its feet, and so was my incipient love-affair with Patsy. We remained friends, in a rather wistful sort of way, but we could both see that marriage was out of the question, over such a gulf of belief-systems.

My next love-affair was so fleeting as scarcely to deserve the name. It was with a young woman named Maureen, whom I met – as I later thought, by design – at my Aunt Mary's house. She was pretty, though not as splendid as Patsy, and she was also amiable and good fun. She was, however, also Catholic; not ostentatiously so, but somehow solidly. My Aunt Mary was, too obviously, anxious to encourage the relationship. I soon saw what was in view: a Catholic marriage, with my own return to the bosom of Holy Mother Church. A happy ending, from Aunt Mary's point of view, but not from mine by any means. I broke off the relationship as soon as I saw which way the wind was blowing. I never saw Maureen again, and did not see Mary either, for quite a long time.

* * *

Those were fleeting relationships as it turned out. But in 1937 a relationship began which was to lead to marriage, in 1939. The marriage lasted for twenty-three years. There were three children of the marriage: Donal, Fedelma and Kathleen (Kate). In 1962 the marriage was dissolved, in Mexico, by mutual consent, on the statutory ground of *Assoluta Incompatabilitad.*

The children still love both their parents, as we, of course, love them. I do not wish to say anything that could hurt either the children or their mother. As the processes that lead to any divorce necessarily contain a good deal of hurtful matter, for both principal parties, and all their children, I do not wish to discuss these processes here. But I do wish to make one general point. It is customary to refer to such a marriage as a "failed marriage". But I do not regard a marriage that produced three splendid children, continuing to love their parents, as a failed marriage. It was something different: a marriage that worked well for a time, but ended in failure.

I do want to say something about the early stages of the marriage, when failure was undreamt of, because these have a signficant bearing on the subject of this memoir.

As soon as I met Christine – the year after I had put Schol behind me – I was attracted to her. She was very good-looking, bright and animated, with an exceptionally lively sense of humour, and she liked me: an important consideration. But I doubt if the relationship would have led to marriage had it not been for a disclosure made by her quite early on in our friendship. We were sitting in the Bailey Restaurant in Duke Street, Dublin, quite near to Trinity College, and much frequented by undergraduates. In the course of conversation, she revealed that Robert Lynd was her mother's brother. As she later reminded me, when she said this I turned round to her and said: "Let me look at you with new eyes." We both knew that from this moment on our relationship would be closer, and more serious.

Robert Lynd was a well-known essayist of the period on the liberal left. He wrote a weekly column, over the signature YY, in the *New Statesman* which I was reading regularly as I have said. All that was in his favour. But even more relevant was the fact that he had been a close friend, and strong admirer, of my uncle Tom Kettle, and a supporter of Home Rule. So it seemed that Christine's family tradition was nationalist, which was crucially important to me. The fact that I had left the Church made it doubly important to me not to leave the nation.

So Christine, as well as being a most attractive person, was also an eligible partner, or match.

And this was remarkably fortunate for me. My requirement for a partner – nationalist but not Catholic – fitted very few people in the island of Ireland. Almost all Catholics were nationalists and almost all Protestants were unionists (or, in the South reluctant and nostalgic ex-unionists; hardly more eligible from my then nationalist point of view). So from the moment I looked at Christine "with new eyes" I was set on marriage with her.

Yet, as I was soon to find, I had not got out of this eerie wood of religion and nationalism and it had still power to hurt both Christine and me. Christine's father and mother and other members of the family had indeed been nationalists, by the standards prevailing before 1916. That is to say, they had been Home Rulers; a very advanced position for any Protestants in the period and leading to friendships such as existed between Tom Kettle and Robert Lynd. Home Rulers were prepared to accept the link with the Crown, and a share in imperial defence, in exchange for limited self-government in Ireland. The great majority of Catholics before 1916 accepted all that and welcomed the few Protestants, like the Lynds, who also accepted it. Almost all of Catholic Ireland, in 1914, supported the war-effort and Catholics volunteered for the British war-effort in about the same proportions as Irish Protestants did.

But after the Rising of 1916, and the executions that followed, and amid the general disillusionment that accompanied the enormous casualties of the Great War, a great change occurred in the mood of Catholic Ireland. The politicians who had supported the British war-effort were now discredited. Those who had fought in British uniform were seen as dupes, and many of them accepted that this was indeed what they had been. As for Protestant Home Rulers, these were seen as irrelevant, surplus to requirements, and not much different from unionists. These were the positions of Sinn Féin which won the 1918 elections in all Catholic areas of what became the Irish Free State. And the two parties which derived from Sinn Féin dominated the politics of the Free State.

Like my father, I was a rather mild type of nationalist and the Home Rule connection sufficed for me. But it did not suffice for strong nationalists, part of the 1916 tradition, like my Aunt Hanna, and there were storms ahead in that quarter.

* * *

As my relationship with Christine developed I travelled to Belfast to meet her mother and father, and other members of her family. Her mother, born Annie Lynd, was gardening when I arrived and I shall never forget the warm, welcoming smile she gave me as I walked into the garden. Christine's father, Alec Foster, took a bit longer to get to know but very soon both became warm friends of mine, and remained so for the rest of their lives. In Alec's case, the friendship even survived the break-up of my marriage with Christine, twenty-five years later. (Annie was dead by then.)

I spent quite a lot of time in Belfast during this period. Alec Foster was headmaster of one of Belfast's principal schools – Belfast Royal Academy – and I taught there for some months. The society I was moving in in Belfast was very different from any I had hitherto known. All the people I met, without exception at that time, were Protestants. And they were not – as I had earlier fondly imagined they would be – Protestant nationalists. Some of them – including Alec and Annie – had been Home Rulers, and therefore nationalists of a mild description, in the years before the First World War. But now they were unionists, mostly of an equally mild description, and they all took it for granted that if Britain would be at war so would they be. They wished well to the Irish Free State (by now generally called Eire) but they had no wish whatever to be part of it, or even imagined that they could be.

Some of them were unionists of a rather fiercer description. One of these, Bill Lowry – married to Christine's Aunt Ina, nee Ina Lynd – was Minister for Home Affairs in Sir Basil Brooke's Unionist Government at that time. After war had broken out, Bill Lowry was at the centre of a political-religious rumpus. He had been asked to find a place where American soldiers, of the Catholic faith, could attend Mass. They were stationed in a Protestant area, where there were no Catholic churches, and Bill Lowry arranged for a state building to be made over to them, and adapted into a place of worship. In Stormont – then the seat of the Northern Ireland Parliament – some unionists, of what would be later known as a Paisleyite tendency, objected to this arrangement as constituting propitiation of Rome. Bill pointed out that this was only a temporary measure, and that, when the premises were no longer required by the Americans, they could revert to their former use. When the extremists continued to protest against the profanation, Bill added: "And we can always have the place fumigated."

In its context, this was not a bigoted remark, but a genial and humorous rebuke to bigotry. Nationalists knew this but it suited them to take the remark literally, not as a rebuke to bigotry but as an *expression* of bigotry. The Minister had publicly insulted the Catholic faith and the American Army, and he must resign. Bill didn't resign, and wasn't in the least fazed, but he did become for a time, a devil figure for Irish Catholic nationalists generally.

I dined in this period more than once at Bill's house and I liked him a lot. He was not a bigot, but he was certainly not an Irish nationalist, either. Neither did he conform to the Catholic and nationalist sterotype

– in which I had been brought up – of a Northern unionist. He was not sour and humourless or a teetotaller. He liked good food and wine, talked well and pungently, and had a strong and irreverent sense of humour. I could see that some of the stereotypes on which I had been brought up did not fit all the realities on the ground. This perception would ultimately carry me a long way.

Meanwhile in Dublin trouble was building up, in a rather complex way, as a result of an interaction between Owen and Hanna, concerning our marriage. Owen was favourable to the marriage. Hanna was deeply suspicious, and rightly by her standards, which were those of most Irish nationalists at this time. I had thought of the Fosters as nationalists, which they had been, but were now not any longer. At least the older ones were not. Christine could accept my own kind of milder nationalism, and I accepted her relatives – including her Uncle Bill – without consciously recognising what an adulteration of my own nationalism this was. I had subtly changed in that matter. But Hanna had not changed, and Christine and I would soon bear the brunt of her resentment.

When Christine and I were married we were soon in low financial water, as my scholarships dried up on graduation. I had a very good degree, but graduates in Modern Languages were not in great demand except in secondary teaching, a career I did not want. About the only really attractive jobs to be competed for in Ireland at this time were in the higher civil service, accessible through open competitive examination at the Junior Administrative grade. So I sat for the Junior Ad as it was called, and failed, the first time round, to my intense disappointment. I then decided to sit again, at the first available opportunity. In the meantime I would take a second honours degree – a supplemental, as it was called – this time in history and then have another go at the Junior Ad. In this I succeeded. After some superb private tuition by one of my seniors, RB McDowell – later a very distinguished historian – I got a first-class degree in history, finishing ahead of all the other competitors, all of whom had put in three more years of studying history than I had. And then I went on to sit the Junior Ad again and this time I got it.

All that was fine, but there was a price to be paid and it was paid mainly by Christine. In the run-up to my second degree I was intensely preoccupied by my studies to the extent of neglecting her. Also, money was tight. Her father paid us a small allowance that year, just enough to keep us going. Then Hanna offered us a flat in her house, at a low rent. She must have done so at Owen's request, and, grudgingly, I accepted. This was one of the worst decisions of my life.

I ought to have seen what was coming but I didn't, although there had been a clear sign of trouble to come. Just after the war had broken out – with Northern Ireland a belligerent as part of the United Kingdom, and the Republic of Ireland (Eire) neutral – Christine's mother came to Dublin on a visit. Hanna – no doubt again at Owen's instigation – asked her to tea and Annie accepted. The occasion fell short of a disaster, but it should have served as a warning. Hanna was polite and reserved: Annie chatted away in a relaxed manner. Then Annie used the word "we" in a context which clearly referred to Britain's war effort.

Hanna sat up very straight and said simply "We . . . " She spoke in a low voice and I think I was the only person there to realise the grim implications of that little "we": the great gulf between the Irish nation and its enemies. But then, even so warned, I had the folly to accept Hanna's invitation.

We had a rather poky flat in Hanna's house, not clearly demarcated, as a modern flat would be, from the rest of the house, but part of it. I was away most of most days in Trinity Library and Christine was in Hanna's house, and often in close proximity to Hanna. I should have taken care to find out how Christine was getting on with Hanna, but I didn't. I suspect now I was afraid of what I might find out. Christine never complained about Hanna, but I now know that Christine must have been having a most miserable time, in the shadow of that unrelenting, even if veiled, hostility.

I turned my mind away from all this as long as I could, but it was forced upon my attention by two episodes. The first involved Hanna at second hand, as it were. Christine was suffering from some form of blisters on her legs; they may well have been of psychosomatic origin. Medical attention was required and Hanna called in Dr Kathleen Lynn. Dr Lynn was a close associate of Hanna's, and thus a republican and feminist of strict observance. She would have known from Hanna that Christine fell short on both of these vital particulars. There was also another matter of irritation. Christine was beautiful, while Kathleen Lynn was middle-aged and plain. I was there when Dr Lynn examined Christine. She did so in a markedly hostile manner, without any expression of concern, or even formal politeness. When she bandaged the affected area she did so with a roughness that bordered on cruelty. Then she left with the air of a person who had carried out an unpleasant duty.

I should have discussed this ominous episode with Christine, and then I should have complained to Hanna about the awful doctor she had called in. I failed to do either of these things and I now know why: I was afraid of Hanna.

That fear manifested itself, even more horribly, in the second episode, involving Hanna directly. Our rather Spartan little bedroom was lit by gas. The gas-lamp was close to the window. The window was covered, rather inadequately, by a piece of muslin. One night, as we were preparing to go to bed, having left the window slightly open, the piece of muslin blew in and caught fire. It was a very brief flare-up of insubstantial fabric and did little material damage. But it brought Hanna on the scene, with appalling promptitude. She administered to Christine and myself – but I think more aimed at Christine than at me – one of her frightful cold quiet tongue-lashings. Christine said nothing; I think she expected me to say something. But I was incapable of utterance. I was in the grip, for the first and only time of my life, of the frightful phenomenon known as regression.

Twelve years before, in another room in that same house in Belgrave Road, three days after my father's death, I had been subjected to a similar tongue-lashing by the same woman. Owen had rescued me that time. But this time there was no Owen around; only the terrible Hanna. I was unmanned and struck dumb.

Years later, when I read of Hanna's shattering impact on Seán O'Casey, in the debate over *The Plough and the Stars*, I knew exactly how O'Casey felt. I had been unnerved, at a critical moment in my life, just as he had been unnerved.

Shortly after that grim encounter, I succeeded in the Junior Ad exam and was admitted to the Department of Finance. We were now reasonably well off and were able to rent a very pleasant flat in Fitzwilliam Square, Dublin. We both had the agreeable feeling of having made a fresh start in life, leaving the oppressive darkness of Belgrave Road well behind. Yet I could vaguely sense that something was still not quite right. There was a faint shadow of reserve in Christine's manner towards me which had not been there before the Belgrave Road episode. The shadow did not prevent our living together happily enough for a number of years, and bringing up three children, as a harmonious family. Still faint as it was, and unacknowledged, the little shadow would never quite go away.

It is the little rift within the lute
That slowly parting makes the music mute

Twenty years later, when the rift had widened to a separation and preparation for a divorce, I was in the Bailey Restaurant, Dublin, waiting for a friend. Then from a nearby room, invisible to me, I heard a laugh. I recognised it at once for Christine's laugh. It was a lovely laugh, hearty and with a little gurgle in it. And I realized then that she had not laughed quite like that, in my presence, for a great many years.

And I can now establish in my mind the precise moment when that laugh began to die. It died just after the gauze curtain blew in over the gas-light, when my aunt launched her attack, and I had been unable to speak. That was the little rift and twenty years later the music was mute.

4

INTERACTIONS OF NATIONALISM
AND RELIGION, 1939-1952

ON SEPTEMBER 2, 1939, VICTOR CRAIG DROVE ME OUT TO THE TOP OF THE
Hill of Howth to listen on his car radio to Neville Chamberlain announcing
that Britain would be at war with Germany on the following day, unless
Germany had by then withdrawn its invading troops from Poland. As it
happened, the place where Victor stopped his car on Howth Summit
looked out directly over the house which I acquired eleven years later and
in which I still live.

We had no clear idea what Chamberlain's declaration might mean for us
in Ireland. We suspected that if Irish neutrality – and particularly Irish
possession of the ports which Chamberlain had ceded to de Valera in 1938
– put Britain in danger from German submarine war, Britain would
reoccupy the ports and some form, or forms, of Irish armed resistance to the
British incursion would then ensue. But we hoped that Britain would
respect Irish neutrality – as in fact it did, throughout the war.

I think we assumed that Britain and France would probably win the war.
We gave no serious thought to what would happen if Nazi Germany won
the war. We assumed, as most Irish people did, that of course a victorious
Germany would accept the sovereign independence of an Ireland which had
been neutral during the war. What we failed entirely to see was that – if the

Nazis won the war in Europe, there would be only one sovereign independent power in Europe.

Many years later, in the course of a eulogy on the Irish writer, Seán O'Faoláin, then recently dead, and having praised his courage for speaking up in favour of the Jews during the Second World War, I mentioned that if Germany had won the war, Hitler would have demanded that the Jews resident in the Irish Republic – of whom there were slightly more than 4,000 – be handed over to him, and would have seen to it that they were handed over. Some of the Irish writers who had been present at the meeting where I had said this then published a statement denouncing me for what they took to be an insult to the memory of Eamon de Valera, the head of government throughout the war and for 14 years thereafter. But there was no insult given or intended. De Valera would certainly have wished to refuse Hitler's demand that the Jews be handed over, and he might well have actually refused. But had he done so, by then – on the hypothesis of a German victory – Nazi Germany, in full control of all of continental Europe and of Britain, would have certainly sent a task force to seize the Irish Jews and bring them to the gas-chambers. In a parallel operation the task-force would have seized and executed the members of the government responsible for any refusal – assuming there was one – and installed a suitably collaborationist government in their place. The collaborators might well have been rewarded by the incorporation of Northern Ireland – which had been part of the United Kingdom's belligerence against Nazi Germany – in a united Ireland. Some of the inhabitants of Northern Ireland would probably have resisted this project, but their resistance would speedily have been crushed by the overwhelming force of victorious Nazis.

A few of my potential readers – supporters of the modern IRA – will have found that quite an attractive picture. But I think most of my Irish readers will find the picture quite incredible – something out of science-fiction. And in a way they will be right. Nazi-occupied Europe, the world of genocide by gas-chamber, was more like the darkest sort of science-fiction than anything that had happened before in Europe. All the same it was part of the reality of the time, and it was a reality that would have come to Ireland after a Nazi victory, quite irrespective of Irish neutrality. We might have been neutral *then*, but we would not be allowed to be neutral *now*. We would be part of the New Order in Europe whether we liked it or not. Most of us would not have have liked it at all, but would have been cowed by overwhelming force. But some of us would have liked it very much – including some of the most vociferous patriots – and these would have run the country, according to the principles of their German masters.

I am not surprised that the critics of my Seán O'Faoláin speech missed the point of it. It is a point that I myself missed for a large part of my life. Irish nationalists *had* to miss it. Irish nationalists were conditioned to think of imperialism – primarily *British* imperialism – as the source of most of the evil in the world. The idea that Nazism differed from all previously known forms of imperialism as AIDS differs from the common cold was quite a new idea and unassimilable within our culture. And it apparently remains unassimilable in retrospect to several of our intellectuals; most of the rest of us simply don't think about it. Most of us don't know that the Irish Jews were on Hitler's list, and some of the few who do know seem to have missed the significance of the listing.

I learned for the first time about the 4,000 or so Irish Jews on Hitler's list in the 1980s when I was reading about the Holocaust for my book on Israel, *The Siege*. It was only when I considered the implications of that entry that I first began seriously to think about what would have happened to Ireland if the Nazis had won the war. Up to that time, I had assumed, as most Irish people did assume, that Ireland's independence would have been respected by the victorious Nazis, just as the victorious allies did in fact respect it. But that little entry about the Irish Jews was telling me something very different: the Nazis would not respect the independence of a country which harboured Jews. The Jews would be murdered, and the independence of a country that insisted on continuing to harbour them would be violated in order to have them murdered, and anyone who tried to protect them would also have been murdered.

It took me a little time to digest the full implications of that statistic from Hitler's list. When I had digested these general implications, I began to think about their particular implications for me and for Owen: Owen being the hinge. Had it not been for Owen, I might well have kept my head down, even had the Nazis come and taken the Irish Jews in order to murder them; kept my head down and tried to escape to America. But I knew Owen could not have kept his head down. He would have protested, even in the knowledge that protest meant certain death, and he would have died with the conviction that he was following the example set by his father at Easter, 1916.

But how about me? Would I have followed Owen's example, and met with Owen's fate? Or would I still have kept my head down, even after Owen had gone to his death?

I am not at all sure what I would have done, in those terrible circumstances. But I am quite sure that if I had kept my head down, I could not have survived him for much more than a year. I would have been killed by a mixture of grief, guilt and shame, probably working through a surfeit of whiskey.

* * *

In 1942, after succeeding in the Junior Administrative Officers examination, I was admitted to serve in the Department of Finance. This would not have been my first choice, which would have been the Department of External Affairs. But External Affairs was then not yet ready to receive me, for reasons which I will come to, and in any case the Department of Finance, which was in overall control of the Irish civil service, liked to steer new entrants to its own bosom, for at least a period of training and indoctrination in the principles of sound finance.

My debut at the Department of Finance was not a happy one. The Department ran a train-on-the-job situation; that is, the new entrant was left without guidance to sink or swim. I sank, on my first day. A new entrant was brought files on which he was supposed to make up his mind. All they told me was that when I was through with a given file I was to mark it either "PA" (for put away) or "BF" (for bring forward). In the latter case, one was supposed to indicate the date at which it was supposed to be brought forward.

I failed to reflect seriously on the reasons for such procedures. Worse, I failed to read the files brought to me with the close attention that was expected of me. I was accustomed to reading works of literature and of history with close attention. But the stuff now being brought to me seemed rather arid and petty and unworthy of the close attention of a first-class mind, such as I fancied myself to possess.

In this regrettable condition of mind, I failed to pay adequate attention to the files before me, and to one file in particular. This was a file about Statutory Rules and Orders and, finding it rather petty and boring, I marked it "PA" and it was duly put away. Unfortunately the Statutory Rules and Orders which it contained were due to be laid before both Houses of the Oireachtas (Parliament) before a given date. After that date had come and gone and the document had not been laid before anyone, having been Put Away, the Department of the Taoiseach enquired of the Department of Finance what reservations Finance had about these Statutory Rules and Orders in that it had failed to submit them before the due date. Enquiries were made and it was duly found that the file had been Put Away by a young junior administrative officer on his first day in the office. I was then summoned to appear before Arthur D Codling, Assistant Secretary of the Department of Finance.

This was quite an intimidating summons. My own immediate superior in the Department was an Assistant Principal Officer and his superior was a Principal Officer. The Assistant Secretary – there was only one in those distant days – came above Principal Officer. There was no one in the civil service above the Assistant Secretary except the Secretary, JJ McElligott.

Arthur D Codling was a Methodist, of Yorkshire origin. He was a holdover from the days when Ireland had been part of the United Kingdom. Under Article 10 of the Anglo-Irish Treaty of 1922, those who had formerly been British civil servants were encouraged to stay on, on favourable financial terms, in the service of the new state. People like Codling were anxious to see to it that the civil servants of the new state maintained the high standards bequeathed to them by their predecessors. My own treatment of the Statutory Rule and Order was a clear example of a lapse from those standards.

Codling asked gently for my explanation of what had happened. He listened to my explanation which was necessarily a pretty miserable one. Then he said: "I see. It's a mistake *almost* anyone might have made" and dismissed me.

I took the full force of that "almost". Not a promising start to a career in the Department of Finance. And it continued like that for a while.

My immediate superior in the service at this time, the Assistant Principal with whom I shared a room, was a man called Paddy O'Keefe. He was known as "Irish Paddy" to distinguish him from another Paddy O'Keeffe. Irish Paddy was a very remarkable man to whom I was to owe a great deal, as I only slowly came to realize much later. His father had been a farm labourer and he had entered the civil service at the age of fourteen as a Boy Clerk (Abstractor Class). From this lowly beginning he had made his way up through the ranks until he reached the officer class, with the rank of Assistant Principal. This was an exceedingly rare transition; indeed I know of no other example.

Paddy was ruggedly built with a memorably fierce red face. His manners were revolting to one delicately brought up, such as myself. He used to chew tobacco incessantly and would spit a lot, often for emphasis. For example, on reading the accounts of the Department of External Affairs, he would cry something like: "*Mothor-car* allowances!" and spit voluminously.

He belonged to that section of the working-class – with a rural background – which entertained a fierce hatred of the Soviet Union. "Here come the kulaks!" he would say. "Fetch the pole-axe!" Like many middle-class people in Europe and America at this time, I admired the fight the Soviet Union was putting up against Hitler, and was prepared to forget about Stalin's misdeeds. With Paddy it was the other way around; he forgot about Hitler's misdeeds and remembered Stalin's. And of course the Catholic thing was in there somewhere. Hitler had not persecuted the Catholics, but had concluded a Concordat with the Pope on the basis of shared anti-communism. Stalin (up to but not including the Second World War) tried to uproot all religions, including Catholicism.

Paddy and I were not made to be soulmates. Yet in his own way he cared for me and knew I would benefit from his knocking some of the rather copious nonsense out of me. I learned later that when he heard I was being assigned to his section, he said this would be like "harnessing Pegasus to a cart-horse": the cart-horse being himself. However that may have been, the harnessing was to do me quite a lot of good.

Under Paddy, I worked in my first year on the Law Charges Vote: items of miscellaneous expenditure related to the administration of justice; fees of expert witnesses and so on. This was very boring work and my threshold of boredom at this time was still very low. Paddy knew this and was waiting. In one report which I read quickly and carelessly there was a reference which I took to mean that a baby had been thrown out the window. This suggested to me a rare word, which interested me a lot more than the mere facts of the case. So in my minute to Paddy I included the words "the supposedly defenestrated baby". Paddy immediately exploded. He took me carefully through the relevant papers and showed me that I had completely misread them. No one had ever suggested any defenestration: I had simply got it all wrong, through sheer unpardonable carelessness.

This rebuke burned me up as Paddy knew it would. It hurt, first because I knew it was well-merited and second because it came from a man much less well-educated – in the academic sense – than I was, and on whom in consequence I had been looking down. And the searing rebuke had exactly the consequences Paddy hoped it would. I never again commented on any document without reading it slowly and carefully, and if necessary more than once, and without ever intruding a hypothesis of my own, unless it appeared to be justified by the facts at my disposal. So I owe a great intellectual debt to the man who had left school at the age of fourteen, and come up the hard way.

* * *

The time when I joined the Department of Finance was the first time, since my First Communion, that I found myself in a working environment which was mainly – indeed almost entirely – Catholic.

This was a somewhat eerie experience. The most conspicuous thing about me, in my new environment, was that I was a person of Catholic background, educated at Protestant institutions and married to a Protestant in a registry office, contrary to the specific and repeated instructions of the Catholic Church. In this matter I was, I believe, unique in the Irish civil service at this time. Formally there was no credal barrier, or test, concerning entry into the civil service. The requirement that all candidates admitted should be competent in the Irish language functioned, however, as a kind of rough-and-ready credal barrier also. All Catholic schools in the Republic taught Irish as a required subject. In most Protestant schools – such as my own – Irish was not a required subject, and was not often well taught. A young Protestant who wanted to enter the Irish civil service, and who took the trouble to acquire the necessary competence in the Irish language, was, in practice, regarded as a kind of candidate for inclusion in the Irish Catholic nation.

Such a person would be very likely soon to marry a Catholic – given the narrow and narrowing choice of Protestant matches in the Republic. Under the rules of the Catholic Church, the children of the marriage would have to be brought up as Catholics. Thus a Protestant, qualifying in Irish to join the Irish civil service, could be seen reasonably enough, as a Protestant about to turn into a Catholic.

Muslims speak of what they call the *Umma*: the Consensus of the Faithful. A Protestant, entering the Irish civil service, was also entering the Irish Catholic *Umma*, broadly conceived.

My case was, however, different. The few Protestants in the Irish civil service were drifting, almost insensibly, in the direction of the Catholic *Umma*. I had, however, once been *part* of the *Umma* – through baptism and First Communion – and had then deliberately and repeatedly broken with the *Umma*. To return to the *Umma* would require recantation and penance. Neither of which would be forthcoming.

Ireland was then – and for that matter still largely is – a country where people of different religions, when in contact with one another, not only avoid religion as a direct subject of conversation across the divide, but also avoid, almost instinctively, any of the many topics which are partly charged with religious implications, and so liable to lead to conflict, even of an insignificant kind. Thus none of my new colleagues ever alluded to my own unusual position in relation to the Church. But, as I found, there were different ways of avoiding the subject. Some colleagues avoided it in a friendly way, while being expansive on other subjects. Others made clear, without being directly rude, that they wanted as little to do with me as possible. And there were one or two who seemed friendly enough, but were really not.

At this time, as in my college years, I was still given to practical jokes – what my friend Brian Inglis used to call the Till Eulenspiegel side of my character. I think now that the practical jokes served much the same purposes as jokes serve in the Zen Buddhist system – that is that they were partly a means of exploring and assessing the immediate social environment.

The principal target of my practical jokes in this period was a government colleague called Michael Leo Skentelbery. Skentelbery had come first in the Junior Ad, when I had come third, and this of course did not endear him to me. Worse, he had got over 90% for English Essay where I had got 60%. The subject of the essay that year was "The Idea of a University", the famous title of a collection of essays by Cardinal Newman. I suspected that what Skentelbery had done was to paraphrase Cardinal Newman's work, thus signalling his orthodoxy to the Catholic examiner who had set the topic. The ignoring of Newman's essay, in my answer, sent the reverse message.

In one of my practical jokes the exploratory aspect was clearly predominant, and the result was revealing. I rang Skentelbery and pretended to be Dr Stafford Johnson, a rather eminent and controversial figure in the Dublin of that time. He was head of the Knights of Columbanus, an association of Catholic laymen set up as a counterweight to the Freemasons. Just as the Freemasons were supposed to be active in securing good jobs for their mainly Protestant members, the Knights were supposed to do the same thing for Catholics. As well as competing with Protestants, the Knights were also concerned about bad Catholics and excluding them from positions of influence. So I rang Skentelbery in the person of Dr Stafford Johnson, and the following dialogue ensued:

"Skentelbery, this is Dr Stafford Johnson speaking. Do you know who I am?"

"Yes indeed, Dr Stafford Johnson." (Reverential tone).

"Good. Then you also know of the organization of which I have the honour to be the present head?"

"Of course, Dr Stafford Johnson."

"We are considering you for possible membership of our organization. Would you be interested in that?"

"I would indeed, Dr Stafford Johnson."

"That's good. I hope you may be found to qualify. But first there's a period of probation. You would need to do one or two commissions for us, so that we may be satisfied as to your general suitability as well as your zeal in the common cause. Are you prepared to co-operate?"

"Certainly, Dr Stafford Johnson."

"Very well. Now there is one of your colleagues whose outlook and associations are giving us a certain amount of concern, in view of his present responsibilities and the higher responsibilities which may accrue to him. His name is Conor Cruise O'Brien. You know him, do you not?"

"I do indeed, Dr Stafford Johnson."

"Right. We know O'Brien to be a bad Catholic, which in itself should unfit him for a position of responsibility in a Catholic country. We also have reason to believe that he may possibly be a Communist. In short, a security risk. You must see him fairly often?"

"I do indeed, Dr Stafford Johnson."

"Fine. Then this is what I want you to do. Take as full notes as possible of every conversation you may have with him – however innocuous what he says may appear – and send us regular detailed reports. Are you willing to do this?"

"I am indeed, Dr Stafford Johnson."

"Excellent. The reports should be unsigned and sent to me personally at our offices in Ely Place. O'Brien should be indentified simply as 'subject'. That will be all for now. Make no attempt to contact me. I shall make the contact when I judge the time to be ripe."

I don't know whether any such reports were ever sent, or what happened to them if they were, nor was I particularly concerned about any of that. The Knights had been fairly influential under the first government of the Free State. But in the 1932 election they joined in the campaign against de Valera whom they depicted as soft on Communism or little better than soft. In consequence, their influence over the administration as a whole sharply declined after de Valera's election, though it lingered on for many years in a different kind of way, in certain administrative pockets, notably the Department of Justice and the Attorney-General's Office. But it was on the whole recessive in this period. I was not therefore alarmed by Skentelbery's side of the telephone conversation. But I did find his apparent willingness to become an informer faintly disturbing.

* * *

In my two years in the Department of Finance I made only one friend, but this was a friend for life. Patrick Lynch was a year senior to me in the service, and was more mature than I was. He was interested in some things I had written, and as we got to know one another we found we had a lot in common, intellectually speaking and – what was even more important – congruent senses of humour. Paddy's family background – in County Tipperary – was entirely Catholic, but he appeared to be evolving away from that background, albeit in a quieter way than I had been able to do. He has always been more discreet than I have been able to be, but this characteristic did not prevent him from rallying to my defence, in circumstances where such rallying would be likely to give offence to some powerful people in Ireland. In short, just one friend, out of that period, but that one a friend indeed.

In any case, my period in the Department of Finance was coming to an end. The Department of External Affairs, which would always have been my first choice, began to show an interest in me. I received an invitation to a dinner at which FH Boland, then Assistant Secretary of the Department of External Affairs, was a fellow guest (and also, I have no doubt, prompter of the invitation). Interestingly, the host was Joseph Hone, Yeats's biographer, and, like Yeats, of Protestant origins and rather eccentrically nationalist politics. By having Hone invite me, I believe Boland was obliquely signalling that my non-Catholic associations and inclinations would not be held against me in the Department of External Affairs, now preparing to face the post-war world, in which it was already clear that the United States and Britain would be the predominant Western powers.

Shortly afterwards, at a dinner in Boland's home, I met for the first time Máire MacEntee who was later to become a colleague in External Affairs and – much later still – my wife. I had no premonition of my future fate but I did like Máire very much indeed, even at that first meeting, and was very impressed by her conversation. Though five years younger than me, she was more mature and more secure than I was. No fissures of the kind that divided my family affected hers. Her father, Seán MacEntee, had taken part in the Easter Rising. Her mother, Margaret Browne, had in the same period carried to Liam Mellowes in Galway, for Patrick Pearse, an order that purported to countermand the order that Eoin Mac Neill, as head of the Irish Volunteers, had issued, itself countermanding the parade ordered for Easter Monday, 1916, which was destined to herald the Easter Rising. Her family was united by politics, not divided.

Shortly after these meetings, I was invited to leave the Department of Finance and join the Department of External Affairs, and I accepted the transfer.

Two questions arise: Why did I want to go there? And why did the Department accept me?

Let me begin with the second question. Anyone who knew the Department as it was in those days, and who knew me, would have thought it highly improbable that the Department would accept me. Joseph P Walshe, the secretary – that is, permanent head – of the department, was an exceptionally devout Catholic, even by the exacting standards of the Ireland of the first half of the 20th century. He had served thirteen years of the novitiate for the Jesuit order before being rejected on grounds of ill health. Rome, for Walshe, was still the centre of the civilized world. And not only papal Rome but also political Rome from the 1920s to the 1940s. Mussolini had been his hero, both as anti-communist champion and as restorer of the glories of Rome. A memo of Walshe's in June of 1940 reveals him as exhilarated by the victories of the Axis (as he saw it; they were of course really German) and implies that Irish neutrality should be revised in a pro-Axis sense. He hoped to see Ireland aligned, after the war, with Franco's Spain, Salazar's Portugal, and Mussolini's Italy, forming a stabilizing Catholic element within the New Order, which he expected would follow the victory of the Axis. By 1944, of course, this blissful vision was fading fast. But Walshe's outlook did not change. He remained an extreme-right-wing Catholic in his personal views. His official position was significantly different. I shall come to that.

To a person holding those views, my CV was necessarily repulsive. My secondary school, Sandford Park, in Dublin, educated the sons of liberal Protestants, liberal Jews, and dissident Catholics – roughly a third of each description. From Joe Walshe's point of view, this was the most disreputable and morally contagious connection and environment that one could find in Catholic Ireland, with one exception: Trinity College, Dublin, banned by the Catholic Church. From Sandford Park I went to Trinity College, without asking for a dispensation: a second large black mark in Walshe's book.

Others followed. In 1938, as a delegate from Trinity College to the annual conference of the Irish Labour Party, I made the anti-Franco speech which caused uproar among a section of other delegates, and therefore hitting the front pages of the Dublin newspapers. This defined me as being on the far left of the Irish Labour Party in those days. From the point of view of the Catholic far right, an anti-Franco activist was just as bad as a

Communist. The rumour spread that I actually *was* a Communist. Few people really believed this, but it clung to me vaguely, as an element in my reputation, and was revived occasionaly during my official career. It didn't do me nearly as much harm as it would have done an American. I was to have quite a good official career, ending up with ambassadorial rank after seventeen years of service. Most Irish people didn't really care much about Communism. They were against it when they thought about it, but they seldom thought about it. Catholicism, on the other hand, was something they did think quite a lot about, in one way or another, and it was my real relation to Catholicism, not my rumoured one to Communism, that was of most interest to people considering my case. That relation was an unusual one. There was nothing unusual, even then, about not believing in Catholicism. What was unusual then was to acknowledge publicly that you did not believe in Catholicism. There would be nothing unusual about that in the Ireland of the 1990s. It is common form. But fifty years ago it was quite rare. Apart from some of the IRA, after their excommunication in 1922-23, about the only people around who were behaving in that way in those days were my cousin Owen Sheehy-Skeffington and me. It is interesting that this did absolutely no harm to my public career around the mid- century – a time when the authority of a triumphant Catholic Church appeared to be overwhelmingly strong, in the media and in public life. But I think many educated people – including many in the public service – already resented that authority and, while being discreet about this themselves, had some respect for a person who publicly rejected it altogether.

However that may be, Joseph P Walshe, who was secretary of the Deprtment of External Affairs in 1944 (and remained in that position until he became Ireland's ambassador to the Holy See in 1946) had no respect whatever for such a person. So the question is, how did I get past Joe Walshe? This is not easy to account for. In 1939 I had filled up the cup of my iniquities, in Joe's eyes, by my marriage. My first wife, Christine Foster, belonged to a Belfast Presbyterian family. The marriage was in a registry office and was therefore no marriage in the eyes of the Catholic Church. So from Joe's point of view, I was up to my neck in mortal sin, and even living in the stuff. I was also politically unsound, to a high and heinous degree, owing to my public attack on Franco, and thus clearly no fit person to be a member of Catholic Ireland's Department of External Affairs. Yet I was duly appointed to the Department, which therefore was not Catholic Ireland's (only) or Joe Walshe's, as much as Joe would have liked it to be. Why?

The reason, I think, is that the decision was taken at a higher level.

Under God there was only one higher level. This consisted of Eamon de Valera, then Minister for External Affairs as well as Taoiseach. You may perhaps think it unlikely that so exalted a person should interest himself in a junior appointment: I entered his Department, after all, as a third secretary, the lowest form of diplomatic life. But Ireland is a small country, the Department of External Affairs was then a very small department, and Dev would certainly have been consulted about any proposed diplomatic appointment, even at entry level.

Although Joe and Dev were both believing and practicing Catholics, they were very different in their political and social outlooks. The matters that damned me in Joe's eyes would not have hurt me at all in Dev's. Dev would have regarded my religion as my own private affair, and no business of his. He had himself defied the authority of the Church in the matter of his rejection of the Anglo-Irish Treaty of 1921, and so incurred excommunication during the Irish Civil War (1922-1923). Nor would that anti-Franco speech have worried him. Catholic dictators left him cold. At the League of Nations he had supported sanctions against Joe's hero, Benito Mussolini, after the Italian invasion of Abyssinia, and his opponents had then played the "Catholic Italy" (betraying of) card against him. They later denounced him for failing to support the paladin of the Catholic faith, General Franciso Franco, in the Spanish Civil War. When Joe discussed me with Dev, he would have known better than to raise any such objections against me. After twelve years of serving under Dev, Joe knew his Taoiseach too well for that.

As it happened Joe Walshe had special reasons for minding his p's and q's where Dev was concerned. If my own past activities were worse than suspect in Joe's eyes, so were Joe's in Dev's. In 1932, the year in which de Valera's Fianna Fáil came into power for the first time, the Department of External Affairs, with Joe Walshe at its head, had been in charge during the general election of a subtle "anti-Communist" smear campaign directed against de Valera. This happened owing to circumstances surrounding the recent foundation of the state. Only a decade before, the state had been founded in civil war. After the war had been won, the winning side naturally had for a time a monopoly on public office at every level. The opponents of the winners, after all, were the enemies of the new state itself. There was no "loyal opposition" around (except for the small Labour Party), at least in the first five years. In 1927 the situation changed significantly when de Valera entered the Dáil (Parliament), thus recognizing the legitimacy of the new state, which he had formally denied in 1922, lending his prestige to the challenge of its armed enemies. But there were those who refused to credit Dev's apparent acceptance of the state. The intellectual head of this school of thought was Joseph P Walshe.

The general election of 1932 was an exceptionally dramatic and exciting affair, pitting as it did the adversaries in the civil war of a decade before against each other once more, this time in a purely democratic contest. That the contest was in general fairly conducted was demonstrated by the result, in that the governing party lost. But there are always some dirty tricks in any election campaign, and in this case the Department of External Affairs was the Department of Dirty Tricks. Under Walshe's personal supervision, the Department fed to the press (in suitably laundered form) a number of anti-Dev reports and articles. These did not depict Dev as a Communist (which would have been silly, as nobody would have believed it). They depicted him as a "Kerensky" – a person whose arrival in office would be a stage on the road to communism, because he would be incapable of countering its wiles or of resisting its rise.

This use of a government Department for party-political purposes was obviously highly improper, but Joe Walshe didn't think he had to worry about that. He and his friends were quite confident that "the long fellow", as they called him in those days, would lose. But they were wrong. The long fellow won.

I was fifteen in the year of that election, and I remember experiencing a certain sense of liberation at the result, ending as it did the rule of what I felt to be an oppressively clerical government. Joe Walshe's feelings about the same event must have been very different. Joe knew that Dev knew what he had been up to in the campaign, so Joe also knew that Dev was about to sack him unless he, Joe, could come up with something clever. And what Joe came up with, in those stimulating circumstances, was quite brilliant.

As the reader will have gathered, I am not in a general way an admirer of the late Joseph P Walshe. But I find it impossible to withhold a certain kind of admiration for the man's response to what was certainly the greatest challenge of his official career. He fended off the challenge with an eye for an opening and an uninhibited ruthlessness in exploiting it which would have earned full marks from the author of *The Prince*. "The Story of How Joe Walshe Saved the Department" was told to me shortly after I joined it. My informant was Michael Rynne, the legal adviser, and a close associate and admirer of Walshe's. He had been one of the team who had pumped out the "Kerensky" stuff, on Departmental time and with government money, during the 1932 elections. This team of civil-service politicians made up "the Department" that Joe saved, and save them he certainly did, along with his own skin. The political context was this: The Irish Free State was at this time still part of the British Empire, then evolving into the British Commonwealth. Its status was effectively that of a dominion, and like other dominions, it had a governor-general. That governor-general in 1932 was James McNeill, who had been appointed on the recommendation of the previous government. McNeill was therefore on the same side, politically, as Joe Walshe. Or rather, he was on the side that Joe Walshe had been on until he took on board the election returns of 1932.

For the government of a dominion to downgrade a governor-general was technically and legally impossible. The governor-general was appointed by the Crown, and an attempt to downgrade him without his consent would cause a crisis in Anglo-Irish relations and a constitutional crisis, alarming to Irish public opinion. De Valera wished to avoid this. This is where Joe Walshe saw his opportunity. He went to de Valera immediately after Dev's installation as Taoiseach and asked permission to call on the governor-general and advise him to resign. Permission was accorded and Joe Walshe duly obtained McNeill's resignation. De Valera was thus enabled to recommend a self-effacing successor, who effectively downgraded the office for him without any trouble, thus fulfilling a campaign promise that had been looking a bit dodgy.

Joe Walshe in this way succeeded in conveying two messages to his new Taoiseach. The first was that Joe could furnish valuable service with remarkable efficiency. The second was that he was prepared to sacrifice his former associates in the service of his new master. Successful politicians value servants of that type, even though they may not particularly esteem them. (Compare Napoleon's use of Talleyrand). So Joe stayed on, as secretary of the Department he had so deftly saved. He was to spend the next sixteen years in the faithful service of the disastrous "Kerensky" whose emergence he had fought so hard to avert.

In 1944 – which is where I came in – Walshe was still secretary, and still a force to be reckoned with. But his star was on the wane; the rising star was his deputy, Frederick Henry Boland, of whom more anon. This was because Joe was known to be pro-Axis – not the flavour of the year in 1944. It was to Freddie Boland, not to Joe, that the ambassadors who counted in that year – the American and British – would talk freely. It followed that it was Freddie, rather than Joe, who had de Valera's ear. This had a bearing on my own acceptance by the Department of External Affairs. I shall come to that. But first it is necessary to give a brief account of de Valera and Irish neutrality.

* * *

Dev was not a neutralist in principle. He had valued the League of Nations, provisionally. Ireland was a member of the League. The League's Covenant, if observed, offered protection to small countries. Dev therefore thought strict observance of the Covenant to be in Ireland's interests. For that reason he supported sanctions against Italy after Mussolini's invasion of Abyssinia. This was a courageous policy for an Irish leader: the opposition in the Dáil denounced Dev for "stabbing Catholic Italy in the back". If sanctions had been seriously applied – specifically, if Britain had closed the Suez Canal to Italian shipping – a League war might well have resulted. Ireland, having supported the sanctions, would have been part of that League war.

The same would have been true if war had broken out in 1938 as a result of France's adherence to its commitment to defend Czechoslovakia. That would have been a League war, too. But after Munich the League and its repeatedly violated Covenant no longer counted. Apart from the actual course of events, the document that started the Second World War was a unilateral British guarantee to Poland. To bring Ireland into war over a unilateral British guarantee to another country was never a possible option for de Valera. If he had tried to move in that direction, he would have had his own party against him, along with most of the rest of the country. So Ireland was neutral, by force, in part because of its history and in part because of the circumstances in which the war broke out. We couldn't just follow Britain into war. De Valera took care, however, to maintain good relations with Britain in so far as was possible in the circumstances. He assured the British that he would never allow Ireland to be used as a base for attack on Britain.

This meant clamping down on the IRA, which Dev did with a will, interning most of its members and hanging some. The IRA, in its efforts to help Nazis and get them "to help Ireland", was acting on Wolfe Tone's dictum "England's difficulty is Ireland's opportunity". Tone was the father of Irish republicanism, the ideology common to Dev and the IRA. But in governing Ireland, Dev ignored ideology and paid heed to circumstances and interests. This was a sound Burkean position, though Dev was not consciously a Burkean. Much later, after having had some experience of how Dev's mind worked, I once asked him whether he had been influenced by Burke. He looked shocked and said, "Of course not, Burke was *not a republican*". In spite of that non sequitur, his mind was more like Burke's than Tone's. This, of course, meant that I liked Dev.

Dev was never in danger of acting on Walshe's (implicit) advice and getting on the Axis bandwagon in the summer of 1940. Indeed, in May 1940, he publicly condemned the German invasion of the neutral Low Countries, which was about as far from that bandwagon as a fellow neutral could get. After Pearl Harbour, Dev interpreted neutrality in a consistently pro-Allied sense. For example, Allied airmen who crashed on Irish territory were allowed to return to their base, whereas German airmen were interned. The slant Dev gave to neutrality after Pearl Harbour attracted no public attention, which is how he wanted it. But a gesture of Dev's right at the end of the European war, early in May of 1945, attracted world-wide attention. Among the victorious Allies it excited universal execration. Dev had called on a bewildered German minister plenipotentiary in Dublin to convey, through him, his condolences to the German people on the death of their late head of state, Adolf Hitler. That was some bandwagon to be getting on at the end of the Second World War!

The usual explanation for this surrealist gesture is that Dev felt bound by pedantic adherence to diplomatic protocol. This doesn't fit. Dev could be pedantic, certainly, but only when it suited him. Why did it suit him in this peculiar instance? I believe that Dev was acting out of political calculation. With the war over, it was time to be thinking about a pending election. There was a presidential election due in the following month, and although the Irish presidency is mainly a ceremonial office, it was important to Dev at this point that his candidate, Seán T O Ceallaigh, should defeat his challengers. The triumph of Dev's candidate would set a seal of popular approval on Dev's conduct of neutrality throughout the war years.

Dev knew that that gesture would generate a great volume of abuse from the British against himself and neutrality, and that this could only do him good with the Irish electorate. It worked like a charm. Churchill himself rose to the bait. He delivered a scornful, scalding attack on De Valera and on Irish neutrality. Dev replied, over Irish radio, in a dignified, sweetly reasonable speech, with a gentle, almost subliminal, evocation of Ireland's past sufferings at the hands of the English, combined with an appreciative acknowledgment of Britain's respect for Irish neutrality in the Second World War. He was the Christian statesman to his crafty fingertips and his speech was hugely successful with the Irish public. With Churchill's help that May, Dev's candidate had no difficulty in winning the presidential election in June.

I spoke earlier of Dev's having no objection to those aspects of my life and education which were obnoxious to Joe Walshe. But there was a more positive side. Eamon de Valera had reason to be deeply grateful to a member of my family. My maternal great-uncle Father Eugene Sheehy had been his parish priest in Bruree, County Limerick, when Dev was a boy. Years later, in 1961, near the end of my career in External Affairs, Dev himself reminded me of this link. I was then about to leave Ireland, having been seconded by my Department to the United Nations, for service as Secretary-General Dag Hammarskjold's personal representative in the mineral-rich province of Katanga, then in unrecognised secession from the Republic of the Congo.

Dev had by now retired from active politics and was installed as (a largely ceremonial) President of Ireland. He sent for me to wish me well on my mission, which he knew to be difficult and perhaps dangerous. He spoke to me of his debt to Father Eugene. On a later occasion, after my Congo mission was over, Dev asked my second wife, Máire, and me to bring our adopted son Patrick, then aged three months, to see him. As he welcomed the three of us, Dev spoke again of Father Eugene, and this time he had a present for me: a 19th century daguerreotype of my great-uncle, with the inscription, in Dev's handwriting, "*Eisean a mhúin an tírghrá dhom*": "He taught me patriotism".

Later that afternoon, walking down a Dublin street, I met a friend, Alexis FitzGerald, a senator and a member of the anti-Dev party, Fine Gael. Proudly I showed Alexis that inscribed picture. Alexis commented, "If your great-uncle taught *that man* what *he* calls patriotism, then your great-uncle has a great deal to answer for!" (This sounds bitter, but was not so intended or taken. Alexis had a sense of humour and occasionally liked to parody the style of his more obtuse political associates.)

Father Eugene was indeed a militant patriot. In the great agrarian upheaval of the Land League (1878-1881), which overthrew the power of the Irish landlords, Father Eugene was known as "the Land League priest". I used to think this was because he was the only such priest, but he wasn't. He was the outstanding figure among a few such priests. Some Irish bishops had condemned the Land League, and Father Eugene was the most prominent of those who defied the ban. After being arrested, he led the Land League delegation to America in 1881, following upon the delegation headed by the Irish leader, Charles Stewart Parnell, in the previous year. Six years later Father Eugene went one better than defying the Irish bishops: he defied the Pope. The Pope had been induced to condemn the renewed agrarian movement, now known as "the Plan of Campaign". The Pope was at this time in self-imposed seclusion following the unification of Italy, and was known to his admirers as "the Prisoner of the Vatican". Father Eugene preached a famous sermon on this topic. My mother told me about it. She enjoyed it. So did I, and so did Owen, my fellow grand-nephew. The occasion was the annual collection known as Peter's Pence, a papal benefit. Father Eugene's sermon, in 1887, ran like this:

"Dearly beloved brethren:

"You will have heard our Holy Father described as "the Prisoner of the Vatican". I am afraid that must conjure a fearful picture to you. Many of you have friends or relations who are prisoners at this moment for having taken part in the Plan of Campaign, a morally lawful movement which the British misled the Pope into condemning. You know how those prisoners are treated. I visited my own brother in Tullamore Jail last week [this was David Sheehy, MP, my grandfather]. He was naked in his cell, in this freezing weather, because he rightly refuses to wear prison clothes, being no criminal. You may have pictured our Holy Father as enduring some such conditions. Let me relieve your anxieties. I visited the Pope in Rome last year. He lives in a splendid and spacious palace in which he is free to move around. He has whatever he likes to eat and drink. He has many servants. In no way does the Vatican resemble Tullamore Jail.

"You are not wealthy people. But you are to contribute whatever you feel you can afford to the support of the prisoner of the Vatican."

Not one penny reached the Vatican that year from the parish of Bruree according to most reports; one report says that sixpence was raised.

Towards the end of his life Father Eugene visited the General Post Office, Dublin, then the headquarters of the Easter Rising, and gave Holy Communion to members of the besieged garrison.

There is no doubt that Father Eugene did teach patriotism to the young de Valera. But he must also have been important to him in other ways, which the mature Dev would never talk about. Eamon de Valera must have been a very lonely boy in Bruree. He was born in New York, of a Cuban father and Irish mother. His father died during Eamon's infancy. When Eamon was two or three years old his mother sent him to Bruree to live with his uncle, Patrick Coll. Young Eamon must have felt rejected, and his foreign name can't have helped. In the circumstances, the friendly interest of his parish priest must have been a godsend. In rural Ireland in the 19th century (and, indeed, during most of the 20th century) the local parish priest was a greatly respected and powerful figure. His friendly interest conferred a degree of status and protection. So Eamon de Valera had more than one reason to feel warm toward Father Eugene Sheehy.

* * *

Father Sheehy, I believe, had something to do with my acceptance by External Affairs. But the immediate instrument of my acceptance was the interest of FH Boland, whom I mentioned earlier. Freddie Boland knew me, and thought I would be useful to the Department. The bad-Catholic bit didn't worry him. He was the type the French call *Catholique, mais pas enragé*. I believe that Joe Walshe, who was about as *enragé* as you can get, had blocked my assignment to External Affairs in 1942 – when I entered the Irish Civil Service – without reference to de Valera. But when the matter was formally raised by Boland, now the rising star and with easy access to Dev, Joe knew that the game was up in the matter of keeping this godless character out of his Department. Both Joe and Freddie knew about the Father Eugene factor. Both were of Tipperary origin, and the Sheehys – my mother's family – were a prominent Tipperary family. My grandfather and Father Eugene were especially well known: almost everyone in Tipperary seemed to know about that "Prisoner of the Vatican" sermon. Máire heard about it as a child from her Tipperary-born mother. Having made it their business to know about Dev, Freddie and Joe would know about the Dev-Sheehy connection, and thus, that Dev would not be in favour of turning down Father Eugene's properly qualified grand-nephew – certainly not on the grounds that mattered to Joe. So I was accepted.

Let me now turn to the other question: Why did I want to get into External Affairs in the first place? At the time, I never put that question to myself. I just knew that I wanted to get in. But as I consider the matter in retrospect, as part of this autobiographical exercise, I believe the answer is to be found in my education, and my cousin Owen's education, and the tensions and demands arising from these.

In a country where religion and nationality have gone together since the 16th century, being educated among Protestants raised questions about one's relation to the Irish nation. Owen and I, both children of Catholic families, were educated in places of unionist tradition, antagonistic to Irish nationalism. Protestant and unionist were generally synonymous in Ireland, as were Catholic and nationalist.

My aunt Hanna Sheehy-Skeffington was a passionate nationalist, so why did she send her son to be educated among unionists? She did so precisely *because* she was a passionate nationalist, a republican. The Catholic bishops had excommunicated the republican side in the civil war, so Owen would go to no Catholic school. The only alternatives were Protestant schools.

It is not surprising that my first two books grapple with Catholicism and Irish nationalism. The first, *Maria Cross* (1952), was an exploration of the Catholic imagination in literature. The second, *Parnell and His Party (1880-1890)* (1957), was a study of a phase of Irish nationalist history.

So when Owen and I went to those Protestant schools, were we then turning into unionists? "Certainly not!" was Owen's determined answer, fervently echoed by me. "Perish the thought!" Somewhere in there, at the levels of the psyche I am trying to explore, was the notion that religion and nationality were like lungs. One lung was gone; it might aptly be described as past praying for. If you lost the other one, you would be finished.

Fortunately for us, perhaps, there were rituals available through which we could bear witness to our continuing faith in the nation. Ireland (that is, the twenty-six county state) was still technically a dominion of the Crown, complete with a governor-general under the Anglo-Irish Treaty. Of course no proper nationalist would sing "God Save the King" or drink the loyal toast. But unionists (alias Protestants) were free to do so and did. At Trinity College, Owen sat down for "God Save the King" and the loyal toast. In due course I followed suit. The dons were less disapproving than I expected. Owen had broken the ice. The family penchant for sitting down at the wrong times had been established. Also we were in Protestant eyes Catholics by inheritance if not by theology, and therefore knew no better.

Owen, my role model, was a stronger character. Some things he conveyed to me by both precept and example. Of nationalism he never spoke, but conveyed the force of his commitment to it (at that time) by those symbolic acts. Nationalism must have been a most uncomfortable subject for him. Intellectually he resisted his mother's fanatical, mystical nationalism, but emotionally he could not escape being powerfully affected by it. That was the force that kept him glued to his seat on those symbolic occasions. And then it glued me, in my turn.

It was as if the ghosts of Patrick Pearse and James Connolly, the martyred heroes of the 1916 Easter Rising against British power, were reaching out to both of us through the magnetic medium of Owen's mother, my aunt Hanna.

That's a creepy thought, but creepy thoughts abound while I ponder my early motivations. Ghosts were beckoning. They were beckoning me quite specifically in the direction of the Department of External Affairs. I needed to represent Ireland, proving that one could reject Catholicism and still be accepted by Ireland. And I just made it past Joe Walshe. The year before I was born, 1916, was important, but so was the year after I was born, 1918. In that year my grandfather ceased to represent Ireland at Westminster, and our family came down in the world. By representing Ireland internationally I would be reversing that misfortune, and staging a family comeback.

Having discerned that pattern in my early life, I find it recurring in my middle years. After I resigned from External Affairs, in 1961 – in order to be free to write a book about the Katanga experience – I came to be, from 1965 on (after a spell as head of the University of Ghana), the holder of a cushy, congenial and tenured job as Albert Schweitzer Professor of the Humanities at New York University. I resigned that chair in 1969, in order to run – successfully – for election to the Dáil for Dublin North-East. This meant a considerable drop in income. But the pull of Ireland – and specifically of *representing* Ireland – was more than I could resist.

It is a bit disconcerting for me now to see how strong the pull of Irish nationalism has been throughout most of my life. Since 1971 – the begining of the Provisional IRA offensive – I have been known in Ireland, where I now live, as top anti-nationalist. I have addressed the Friends of the Union – the union, that is, of Great Britain and Northern Ireland. I am now a member of the United Kingdom Unionist Party. You can hardly get further away from Irish nationalism than that.

Yet I claim an underlying consistency and continuity. I was brought up to detest imperialism, epitomized in the manic and haunting figure of Captain Bowen-Colthurst, who murdered my uncle Frank Sheehy-Skeffington during the Easter Rising. As a servant of the United Nations, I combated a British imperialist enterprise in Central Africa in 1961 – the covert effort to sustain secession in Katanga in order to bolster the masked white supremacy of the then Central African Federation. From 1965 to 1969, in America, I took part in the protest against what I saw as an American imperialist enterprise: the war in Vietnam. And from 1971 until now I have been combating an Irish Catholic imperialist enterprise: the effort to force the Protestants of Northern Ireland, by a combination of paramilitary terror and political pressure, into a United Ireland they don't want. I addressed the Friends of the Union to show solidarity with that beleaguered community against the forces working against them within my own community. I joined the United Kingdom Unionists for the same reason. And I suppose my Protestant education has something to do with that solidarity.

Probably neither Hanna nor Father Eugene would have accepted that continuity. But Owen would. He died in 1969, before the Provisional IRA offensive began. But he had made known his uncompromising hostility to earlier IRA efforts in the same direction which he described as "crazy militarism". So when I first spoke out against the Provisional IRA and its accomplices, in the year the Provisional offensive began, two years after Owen's death, I had the inner certainty that we were at one on this. And that certainty still sustains me.

* * *

My new environment, in the Department of External Affairs, was far more congenial than Finance had been. It is true that it was, in a way, a more Catholic environment, as it contained fewer holdovers from before the foundation of the state, many of whom had been Protestants. But the quality of the Catholicity in External Affairs, as distinct from Finance, was a bit different. The younger officials, my own contemporaries, were – to use a vocabulary that later became familiar to me in South Africa – *verligte* rather than *verkrampte*: that is, relaxed and enlightened rather than stiff and suspicious. I think several of them rather admired me for the openness of my defiance of Church authority, and felt encouraged by the fact that I had got away with this, to the extent that I had. They had no need to follow suit – not being subjected to the same kind of pressures that I had been under – but they wished me well. Some of them became my friends for life: the poet Valentin Iremonger, later the archaeologist Eoin MacWhite, and the unclassifiable Tommy Woods.

Tommy was regarded, rightly I think, as the most brilliant of our number. But it was a brilliance which was of little use to him. Tommy, who never ceased to be a Catholic, was much more a victim of the Irish Catholic Church in its heyday than I ever was. He had attended a school run by the Patrician Brothers in Galway, an order similar to the Irish Christian Brothers. These Brothers actively discouraged their pupils from thinking for themselves: they were to accept what they were told, on authority. For many of the pupils, not particularly interested in thinking, this was no great hardship. But for Tommy's powerful and enquiring mind, to be discouraged from thinking was a misery. Things got a lot better for him at University College, Galway where he did brilliantly. All the same he never quite recovered from his early education. By the time I came to know him well in External Affairs he was drinking very heavily and neglecting his personal appearance, to the extent that he became known as "the dirtiest diplomat in the world". Early on in drink, he could still be great company, but later, and increasingly early, he lapsed into incoherence. He died young.

Some others were Catholics of a more decided stripe. There was Skentelbery, of course; but he didn't cut much ice. And there was Seán Mac

Reamoinn who kept on his desk a copy of the Catholic Missal and a small Irish Tricolour. Naturally, I at first regarded this flamboyant manifestation of Catholic nationalism with extreme aversion. But I later found that Seán was anything but a bigot. These symbols were a source of comfort to him, but he wasn't trying to force them down anyone else's throat. He was always personally friendly to me and good company. Later in life he attained some eminence as the most prominent liberal lay theologian in Ireland.

As in Finance, my work in External Affairs in the early years was routine. But it was as well for me that I had learned in Finance – the hard way – to do routine work methodically and accurately, for the Counsellor (equivalent to Principal Officer in a Home Department) for whom I worked was a notorious martinet called Nicholas Nolan, who never got an opportunity to rebuke me. This was fortunate, as rebuke was something of a speciality with him. He had exercised it to memorable effect on the Irish Ambassador to Paris, Seán Murphy. Murphy, as Ambassador, was senior in rank to Nolan as Counsellor. But Nolan at headquarters had the privilege of sending telegrams, signed with the Department's code-name "Estero". So when Murphy, writing to Nolan, complained that he was "at a loss to understand" how Nolan had failed to reply to letters about his housing, Nolan simply replied: "Subordinate officers should not be at a loss to understand. Estero." Which was universally acknowledged to be Nolan's round.

There was one apparent exception to my routine workload. In 1946 I was sent to Geneva to represent the Department at an International Conference on Refugees. I was rather pleased, at the time, about what I took to be a mark of confidence in me. In retrospect I can see clearly that in being represented at this Conference by a Third Secretary – the lowest form of diplomatic life – the Department was signalling its unwillingness to co-operate in any general policy of rehabilitating refugees. Joe Walshe, personally, was interested in one particular category of refugees: Catholics who had collaborated with the Nazis. There were a number of Croats, Flemings and Frenchmen who fell into that category. Walshe seems to have instructed the relevant diplomatic missions in Europe to encourage these people to seek refuge in Ireland. If so, he was losing his touch. Immigration to Ireland was then – and still is – controlled, not by the Department of External Affairs, but by the Department of Justice. A person could be in possession of a valid Irish passport issued by the Department of External Affairs and still be excluded from Ireland by the Department of Justice. The attitude of the Department of Justice towards would-be refugees might be described as one of non-ideological xenophobia. Foreigners might often be excluded as being possibly Communists, but even if they were not Communists – by any stretch of the imagination – they were excluded anyway. Years afterwards – during the Hungarian crisis of 1956 – I was in touch with the relevant official in Justice requesting the admission of a number of applicants from Hungary. "We don't accept applicants from Communist countries," said the Justice official. I pointed out that the people in question were all *anti*-Communists, and that was why they were refugees. "I don't care what kind of Communists they are," said the man from Justice. "We don't want them here."

Enthusiasm for the admission of former collaborators – provided they were Catholics – was pretty well confined to Joe Walshe. More pragmatic senior officials – such as Boland – didn't want to make our relations with the victorious allies even more complicated by the admission of some of the more obnoxious citizens of the defeated countries. As a kind of compromise between the positions of Walshe and Boland, the word was that the former collaborators were to be treated with sympathy – or an appearance of same – but informed that the decision was in the hands (as was the case) of the Department of Justice, which always refused to see members of the public in general, and would-be refugees in particular. Naturally enough senior officials of the Department of External Affairs did not wish to conduct such trying and unrewarding interviews, so this task was delegated to the Third Secretaries.

I conducted a few such interviews. I remember two in particular. The first was with a Belgian. From him, I learnt how one says, in French, "I was a collaborator during the war". The correct French expression for this is: "*Pendant la guerre, vous savez, j'ai fait une action anti-communiste.*" A more interesting interview was with the man known as "the officer in the Tower", Baillie Stewart. Imprisoned in the late 1930s for having supposedly given military information to the Germans, Baillie Stewart had been released just before the war and had gone to Nazi Germany to help the Nazis. He seemed to be a person of limited intelligence and he was soon in trouble with those he came to help. He told me the story. "I was accused of *Staatsfeindschaft*," ("hostility to the state") he said. This was just after the sinking of the German warship, the *Graf Spee* by the British in South American waters, near the beginning of the war. The German newspapers had published a story that the British navy had used poison gas against the *Graf Spee*. Baillie Stewart was asked by a reporter what he thought about this story. He was a political innocent, but not altogether without common sense, and he replied: "There would be no point in using poison gas against a navy ship. The stuff would just blow away, you know."

The poison gas story was one of Goebbels's inventions, and it was Goebbels who had Bailie Stewart imprisoned for *Staatsfeindschaft* for challenging it. But then Goering, who hated Goebbels – and also had a vein of robust common sense – had Baillie Stewart released, but not fully rehabilitated. Baillie Stewart eventually returned from Germany, even more confused than when he had first gone there. I don't know if he ever did settle in Ireland. If he did, he probably became even more confused than he already was.

This was all a prelude to my inglorious mission to Geneva, in 1946. My instructions were to keep a watching brief, say nothing, and report. All this I duly did. I was rather puzzled as to why I was sent, since all the other participants were of much higher rank. Only one of these showed any interest in me. This was the principal Vatican representative, whom I shall call Bishop Flaherty, a jovial, garrulous Irish-American prelate, who invited me to lunch. At lunch, the bishop's subject was the Jews. The Jews in the bishop's opinion, had done very well out of the war. He was referring to the minority of Jews who had survived the Holocaust, and who were still living in camps, though no longer ill-treated. They were all, according to the bishop, making fortunes on the black-market in scarce commodities such as razor-blades, and such international sympathy as went out to them was entirely misplaced. The bishop concluded, with a smile: "I'm not anti-semitic, you know. I just hate them."

Before the war, at Evian, an international conference mainly consisting of Western Europeans and Americans had decided not to admit the menaced Jews of Europe, in any substantial numbers, to their countries. At Geneva in 1946, the position adopted by the same countries (including Ireland) towards the survivors of the Holocaust was the same.

I wrote a quite long, and painfully objective account of the Geneva meeting and submitted it, as instructed, to the senior official in charge of refugee affairs, Leo T McCauley. I heard nothing further about the matter and some months later, moved by curiosity, I sent for the relevant file. I expected that McCauley would have made some comment – probably brief – on the report and sent it on to the Secretary. But no. The metal staples fastening the report had never been removed. McCauley had simply looked at the first page of the report and then marked the file "PA", more or less as I had done with another file on my first day in the Department of Finance.

I was a little crestfallen at this discovery, and also a bit puzzled. Why go to the expense of sending someone to attend an international conference, and then not bother to read his report? It was only years afterwards, when

I had acquired a lot more experience, that I could work out the outlines of an answer, as follows:

The Geneva Conference was certainly among the first international conferences to which Ireland was invited after the Second World War; perhaps it was *the* first. It might then be expected that the Department would put its best foot forward, and send a senior official to play a reasonably conspicuous role in the proceedings. But this would have been a simplistic expectation.

What Ireland needed, urgently, was to restore relations with both the principal victor powers – the United States and Britain – to what they were before they had deteriorated as a result of Ireland's neutrality. Now as it happened, by 1946 relations *between* the United States and Britain, were being strained, precisely by the subject matter which was at the centre of the Geneva discussions: the future of the European Jews.

Britain was still refusing to admit any of these to Palestine (still under the British Mandate). Britain's position was that the survivors of the Holocaust should stay in Europe, and make out as best they could. The US State Department fully sympathized with this position. But the State Department was no longer in full control of policy towards Palestine. Palestine had become an extremely hot issue in American internal politics, and that meant that the White House, and not the State Department, was increasingly in control. That in turn meant that Britain was under heavy pressure to admit at least some Jews to Palestine. And Britain, with Ernest Bevin in charge in Attlee's Government, was still strongly resisting that pressure.

All this made the subject matter of the Evian Conference about the hottest issue there was in international politics of the period. Boland, who understood such matters very well, felt it important not to be caught in the middle of the great Anglo-American controversy. And to be represented at Evian at senior level would risk some degree of involvement – not on the floor of the Conference where such matters were sedulously avoided – but off-stage, where the real issues would inevitably be raised. In such discussions a senior Irish representative might well become dangerously involved. For example, Truman's personal representative – not the State Department's – might well seek to involve a senior Irish representative in some kind of "mediation" which would incense the British. That was the sort of thing that Freddie Boland could sense coming a mile off. The remedy was to be represented at the conference at such a low level as to run no risk of being asked to mediate. The British and American ambassadors in Dublin – being on the same side in this matter – would have entirely approved. (American diplomatic representatives work for the State Department until the President reverses the State Department. That happened over Palestine in 1948, but in 1946 it hadn't yet happened.)

These things being so, Boland sagely decided to send an envoy so lowly as not to be consulted about anything, and therefore sure not to offend anyone. This meant a Third Secretary and the lot fell on me.

A chastening experience, but also an instructive one. The two categories often coincide.

* * *

My early years in the Department of External Affairs were intellectually undemanding, as my period in Finance had been. My intellect, however, could not stop working and found expression in my first two books. These books require some attention here, as it happens that they are extremely "thematic". The first has to do with Catholicism; the second with the workings of Irish nationalism, in the heyday of Charles Stewart Parnell.

My first book was entitled *Maria Cross: Imaginative Patterns in a Group of Modern Catholic Writers*. It was first published by Oxford University Press, New York and by Chatto and Windus, London in 1954. It was published under a pseudonym "Donat O'Donnell". This was prudential on my part. A colleague in the Department of Finance, John O'Donovan, had told me of a chilling experience he had had with a book of his on the cattle trade published under his own name. One of his superior officers had told him: "That book will be a millstone round your neck as long as you remain in the service." And indeed John O'Donovan did not remain in the service very long. He soon went into academic life and, years after that, he and I were to be rather cranky colleagues in the Irish Parliamentary Labour Party.

As I was dealing with what I wrongly assumed to be an even more thorny subject – Catholicism – I opted for the pseudonym. But the realities were other. In the course of John's book on the cattle trade he had attacked the dual purpose cow, then at the heart of official policy on the livestock industry, the mainspring of the Irish economy of the day. This was really hot stuff and kindled genuine passion. As compared with that, a book about Catholic writers was pretty marginal stuff. Most of the Irish people who would read it would be middle-class intellectuals, who would not be likely to be shocked, nor were they. A second edition of the book was brought out by the English Catholic publishers, Burns and Oates, in 1963 – after I had left the Irish service – under my own name, without arousing any passion.

One pleasing and unexpected by-product of the book was a warming of the reconcilation with Owen which had already set in. Owen had seen instalments of the book which had appeared in O'Faoláin's magazine, *The Bell,* and had asked to see the full typescript, which I sent to him. His comments were mostly friendly and approving, with one or two notes of dissent. Some things in the book were a bit much for him. In my essay "The Rhinegold of Paul Claudel" I had written: "His roots – to use a favourite metaphor of his – go down into things common to humanity, touch some essential all-underlying tufa."

Against that passage Owen had written: "Lemme out!"

Re-reading that pompous sentence, many years later, I find myself agreeing with Owen. But in general I was very happy with Owen's reaction. The episode of Owen's earlier readings from my comments on a Catholic writer was finally closed.

Yet the comments themselves remained relevant. I was still looking, in *Maria Cross,* as I had been as a boy reading that English Catholic writer, for a version of Catholicism that would be more worthy of respect, if not acceptance, than the version that had oppressed my mother and myself in Ireland after my father's death. In general, I have quite strong ecumenical leanings which have often got me into trouble, though not in this instance. As this book is of some importance in relation to some of the main "themes" of my life and writings, I propose to quote from it quite a lot here. The writers discussed are Francois Mauriac, Georges Bernanos, Seán O'Faoláin, Evelyn Waugh, Charles Peguy and Paul Claudel.

The one "Irish" essay, "The Parnellism of Seán O'Faoláin," was naturally of particular importance to me. It begins with a quote from Joyce's *A Portrait of the Artist* as a young man, and some commentary:

– *O he'll remember all this when he grows up," said Dante hotly – "the language he heard against God and religion and priests in his own home". –*

"Let him remember too," cried Mr Casey to her from across the table, "the language with which the priests and the priests' pawns broke Parnell's heart and hounded him into his grave. Let him remember that too when he grows up."

"There is for all of us a twilit zone of time, stretching back for a generation or two before we were born, which never quite belongs to the rest of history. Our elders have talked their memories into our memories until we come to possess some sense of a continuity exceeding and traversing our own individual being. The degree in which we possess that sense of continuity and the form it takes – national, religious, racial, or social – depend on our own imagination and on the personality, opinions, and talkativeness of our elder relatives. Children of small and vocal communities are likely to possess it to a high degree and, if they are imaginative, have the power of incorporating into their own lives a significant span of time before their individual births. Such a power has informed the greatest Irish writers: Yeats with his mysticism of tradition; Joyce, in whom the idea of a continuous flux of life broke down the conventional structure of language."

The weight of the Church behind characteristic Catholic father-figures in an O'Faoláin novel I discussed in another passage.

"He tries to bring up his children in the ways of righteousness, beats them, teaches them respect for their pastors and masters, and checks all manifestations of the sin of pride – as for the sin of lust, it knows better than to manifest itself in his presence. He is a worried and unimposing martinet, with no endearing qualities to make his methods and doctrines less unpalatable. But behind him, insignificant and insecure as he is, is something enormous and seemingly impregnable: the Catholic Church. The policeman and the builder, extremely pious men assisted by pious and submissive wives, are giving their children a sound Catholic education. The whole great weight of the Church is behind them and they appear less as individuals than as the points at which that weight presses down on the youth, Corney or Denis. In the family, the nightly rosary and, through the land, as far as sound can carry, the music of the church bells remind the mutinous adolescent that in revolting against his family he will be alone against a people, fighting a flagless war against a unanimous acceptance."

Some unspoken identification there between me and Corney/Denis. The passage continues:

"He finds, however, a natural ally in his grandfather and a flag in the traditions which his grandfather represents. The Irish rebels of the 19th century, so regularly condemned by the hierarchy, were inevitable heroes for the spirited son of a pious and 'loyal' family. Prometheus and Faust were remote and tenuous symbols, but the Fenian dead, to punish whom, in that treasured episcopal phrase, 'hell was not hot enough nor eternity long enough,' lived in the people's mind. In their names, revolt, which otherwise was doomed to futile isolation, found a way into the open, a fissure in the wall of acceptance. And even mightier than theirs was the name of Parnell, whose struggle not only against Church and State but directly against the power of sexual prohibition made him the essential hero of rebellious youth. The sort of conversation that Joyce remembered in *A Portrait of the Artist* and of which Mr O'Faoláin captures the echoes in *Bird Alone*, the skirmishings of grown-ups about Parnell and purity and the priests, must have been wildly exciting to hundreds of young minds. In young Corney's case, as no doubt in many others, such scenes helped, along with his grandfather's example, to establish a firm connection between the separate ideas of national, spiritual, and sexual emancipation. As one name will be needed for this triple association we shall call it "parnellism" (as distinct from political "Parnellism"). A good example of the inclusive nature of "parnellism" appears in a subordinate episode in *Bird Alone*. Corney, owing to the recklessness of one of his friends, is brought up in court on a political charge and has to exonerate himself by proving the truth, that he was "in the woods at midnight with Elsie Sherlock". Elsie's father, telling her that she has "disgraced her brother in Maynooth", forbids her to speak to Corney again, and, for the time, she obeys. Corney hates her weak submission, "the way she lets her family crucify her", and broods on it until "my contempt spread to so many people that I felt what had happened to me was an image of the far worse that had happened to . . . the Fenians, to the Land Leaguers, to Parnell".

The passage continued:

"The young rebel and the old, and their private rebellions, are merged in the national insurrection (in which their creator took part, at a later stage). They thus break out of their loneliness and recover through patriotism the unity with the people which they are unable to keep in religion. For them, and for almost all Mr O'Faoláin's central characters, this unity – perhaps because it is so difficult to achieve – is profoundly important, a condition of spiritual life, almost a religion in itself."

The last paragraph of the essay:

"It is probable that in a future novel Mr O'Faoláin will scrap the obsolete machinery that has confused and restricted so much of his writing. One cannot prophesy what will happen then. He might write an empty, meaningless novel about America, like the dreariest stretch of *Come Back to Erin*. He might develop the refusal further and abjure Ireland and religion together. But whatever he actually does, he will, by dropping the idolatries of 'parnellism', have a chance to turn his energies towards something of more than local significance. It is exceedingly difficult to be a Catholic writer in a Catholic country: the pressure of a community varies inversely with its size; ingrowing nationalism destroys a writer's scope. Mr O'Faoláin has been a living example of the truth and interrelation of these three propositions. He does not have to refute them all together in order to recover his direction as a writer. He may have to fly to the ends of the earth."

Well, not quite the ends of the earth. In a preface to the 1963 edition, I was able to add a footnote:

"In *A Summer in Italy* (1949), a travel book which appeared after the above essay was written, Mr O'Faoláin tells of his recent conversion to

Roman, as distinguished by him from Irish Catholicism. To myself I said: 'I have left a nation and joined an empire'".

Sean O'Faolain later wrote me a generous letter about a critique which would have irritated a lesser writer. He humorously imagined "the butter-tasters" down in [his native] Cork probing away at my prose.

The Catholic writer whom I admired the most is the French poet, Charles Peguy, partly because he is the least cerebral, and therefore the least open to refutation. My long essay on him – *The Temple of Memory: Peguy* – ends with the following passage on Peguy's idea of the Catholic Church.

"That idea is of something not abstract but embodied, historical, hereditary, and emotional. Peguy seldom speaks of Christianity (*christianisme*) but almost always of Christendom (*chretiente*). The difference between the two ideas, corresponding to a certain difference between Peguy's position and orthodoxy, is well shown in a dialogue in the first *Jeanne d'Arc*. Thomas de Courcelles, the famous Doctor of the Sorbonne who was the most intellectually eminent of all Joan's judges, gives her the definition of the Church:

Thomas: The Church is the communion of the faithful who follow the true religion instituted by Our Lord Jesus Christ under the authority of their legimate Pastors.

Joan: I don't understand everything that you say, Master.

Thomas: I don't think you could get a better explanation, Joan.

Joan: Then the Church, as you call it, is Christendom.

Thomas: No, Joan: the two words don't mean quite the same thing.

Joan: Then I don't understand.

In Peguy's view the essay continued:

The most important personal elements of Christendom are ordinary laymen (sinners) and the saints, and in Christendom spiritual loyalty and historical loyalties are inextricably mingled. God Himself, as we have seen, does not know whether patriotism should really be put below charity. Saint Joan, around whom the greater part of Peguy's work revolves, has the double character of saint and patriot and, as such, a doubly sacred vessel of faith and history. Peguy's dark and atavistic mind, contemptuous of any merely rational difficulties, assimilates and fuses into poetry all the great traditional beliefs of his friends and ancestors: Dreyfusard, nationalist, and Catholic. He felt the blood of kings and saints and revolutionaries to be one blood, one common passion. The Christian religion is the highest expression of this common passion which forms the essence of historic France and is the only element within which Peguy could live. One cannot imagine Peguy interesting himself in the work of English converts or subscribing to the African mission. What he believed in was the religion of his own people, the religion which once had covered them all, and to which, at least in a submerged part of themselves, they all still belonged."

I concluded by arguing that Peguy expressed the great latent community of emotion which exists in a nation or a Church, or nation and Church together, and which can so easily blow aside the reason of most rational peoples. The community, that mass of hereditary feeling, normally for the individual a distant sound, was in 1914 about to become a roaring, storm-tossed sea. It was Peguy's peculiar vocation to catch and turn to words the sound of that sea in its apparent peace and as it grew to anger. Like Victor Hugo, whom he venerated and whose oceanic speech he made his own, he became a 'sonorous echo' of history, but the sound he echoed came from a deeper level, more muffled and more ominous . . . Always he heard and made others hear: 'Ancestral voices prophesying war.'

The history that was present so intensely in the romantic Peguy certainly moved also, and not merely by external compulsion, those who died with him on the Marne. We may guess that his case was not the only one in which history took the form of a kind of poetry, touching the sunken faith, the fringe of darkness, and the sea.

On the brilliant and half-mad Leon Bloy:

> His thought is consistently "amphibological" – a favourite word of his, referring to the perception of the multiple supernatural symbolism of actual events and the supernatural repercussions of human language. In one of his best books, *L'Exégèse des lieux communs*, irony seems to find in 'amphibology' a new dimension: "When the midwife announces that "money doesn't give you happiness" and the tripe merchant knowingly replies "all the same it helps", these two augurs have the infallible presentiment that they have exchanged precious *secrets*, unveiling before each other's eyes the most inmost shrines of eternal life, and their attitudes correspond to the inexpressible importance of their transaction."

"Bloy does not add – he does not have to, if he has succeeded in involving the reader in his amphibiological net – that what the midwife 'really' said was, 'Christ crucified has nothing to do with comfort,' and that the tripe merchant replied: 'You can make yourself fairly comfortable by crucifying Christ'."

* * *

Parnell and his Party 1880-90, my second book, was published in 1957 by the Clarendon Press, Oxford. In this historical work also there is a bit of a puzzle and an effort at reconciliation. The book is dedicated: "In Memory of David Sheehy and Henry Harrison." David Sheehy was my grandfather, an anti-Parnellite. Henry Harrison, a friend of my father, whom I came to know and liked very much when I was working on the book, had been Parnell's last secretary and, as author of *Parnell Vindicated*, was dedicated, not altogether successfully, to the rehabilitation of his master.

For me as a boy the knowledge that my grandfather had been a leading *anti*-Parnellite had been rather a depressing puzzle. The Ireland in which I grew up was dominated, up to a point at least, by the historical retrospect of Patrick Pearse, a hero and a martyr in the eyes of both main nationalist traditiions. For Pearse, Parnell – betrayed by the British and let down by the weak Irish of his day and by the Catholic Church – was also a hero and martyr (though not of the first class, like the ones who got shot). In the Pearsean world-view, the parliamentarians who turned against Parnell did so because they had been corrupted by membership of the British parliament and had ceased to be proper Irishmen. Knowing my grandfather, I didn't believe a word of that, but didn't know how to answer it. I had always meant to look into it one day. And suddenly, just after I took my history degree, the opportunity to do so presented itself.

Just after my History degree results came in, Professor TW Moody, head of the History Department in Trinity College, asked me to come and see him. We met for about an hour, sitting in the sunshine in college park. He proposed that I should write a thesis, under his supervision, for a PhD. I told him this would take quite a long time, as I had a full-time job and the work would have to be done in my off-duty hours, mostly at night. [When I came to write it, it actually took more than ten years.] I accepted his proposal, by which I felt honoured, and offered as a subject "The Irish Parliamentary Party"; later narrowed, with his approval, to the ten years of Parnell's leadership of the party.

Then, still on that park bench, he gave me the most wonderful crash-course in historical methodology. Ironically – as it seems to me now – one of his principal messages was to be particularly distrustful of *memoirs*. Memoirs were written in the main for purposes of self-justification before posterity. The historian should use them, but with the greatest caution. He should always greatly prefer to them, if available, papers written with an immediate practical purpose in view, for the eyes of a limited number of associates, and without any thought of posterity.

I accept the modest historiographical place assigned to memoirs, and I accept also that self-justification enters into these. Mindful of the Moody warnings, however, I have tried to look as critically as is humanly possible at my own motivations and actions. In short, I have tried not to inhale.

The school of historiography into which I was now entering was headed by Moody himself and by Professor Robin Dudley Edwards of University College, Dublin. That is to say, it was a collaboration, most unusual for its day, between scholars formed in different and generally opposed traditions, Catholic and Protestant. Of that partnership, my friend Owen Dudley Edwards (Robin's son) wrote recently:

"Modern professional Irish historiography is customarily dated from 1938, when the Catholic Robin Dudley Edwards and the Protestant Theodore William Moody founded the academic journal *Irish Historical Studies*. They sought a discipline whose findings would be made and disclosed as impartially as human frailty permitted. They were guided by the pursuit of objectivity laid down (if not always successfully practised) by Acton and Ranke – and before them by William Robertson. More recently the term 'revisionist' has been applied to their philosophy: it is incorrectly employed, but most labels are. They were animated by their knowledge that history took lives in the worlds they came from, Edwards's Dublin and Moody's Belfast, notably in 1919-23 when they were boys between the ages of ten and fourteen. They wanted to shape schools of history, the products of which future generations could read with intellectual but not political profit, and above all without being driven to bloodshed by it."

I warmly fell in with the spirit and general orientation of *Irish Historical Studies,* and am still guided by it. But by the time my own thesis came to be completed, the Moody-Dudley Edwards relationship had begun to be somewhat undermined and was being affected by the normal relationship – generally pretty poisonous in this period – between Trinity College and University College. The deterioration was taking place mainly on the Edwards side. Ominously, Edwards had begun to keep a file entitled "Trinity PhDs", the purport of which tended to be that Trinity's academic standards were not all that might be expected. Apparently Moody was unaware of this development, for he invited Edwards to be the external examiner for my thesis. Edwards accepted.

Unexpectedly, as far as Moody and myself were concerned, the examination turned out to be quite a fraught affair. Edwards was there to make a point: that Trinity College's historiographical standards did not quite measure up to the rigorous requirements which prevailed in University College. With this objective in mind, Edwards largely ignored the body of my work but concentrated on the bibliography, where he had indeed found a juicy flaw which had escaped Theo's notice (and to which he had not apparently drawn Theo's attention prior to the meeting). The omission was the Gladstone Papers.

Now, the Gladstone Papers are not particularly important for my chosen subject, which centred on the internal workings of Parnell's party and movement. But they are important for the general political history of the period, and they ought to have had a mention in the bibliography. So the thesis had to be withdrawn for the moment and resubmitted after being amended in this particular. Very much Robin's round as against Theo.

I made the following amendment to the bibliography:

"Gladstone Papers (Aditional MSS 44086-44835) contain some material of interest in connexion with the Kilmainham treaty (Chapter II, p.77); Captain O'Shea's parliamentary ambitions (Chapter VI, p.169); the influence of the Irish party's parliamentary strength (and conjectures about its intentions) on Gladstone's course of action in 1886 (Chapter V1, p.160), and conversations with Parnell at Hawarden in 1888 and 1889 (Chapter VII1, pp 228 and 235). This vast collection contains much material relating to Gladstone's Irish policy but relatively little with a direct and significant bearing on the Irish Party and its leaders."

The last sentence appears in the bibliography of my book as published. It probably did not appear in the thesis when submitted.

Dudley's final report: "If the intern examiner recommends the award, I would for this reason be prepared to be associated with the recommendation. I would not be prepared to recommend the work as suitable for publication in its present form."

Moody's comment:

" . . . If Edwards tries to postpone publication by the methods by which he has delayed the award of your doctorate I am prepared to resist by all possible means. On your part there is no need to submit to any of his demands.

"My very sincere congratulations and kind regards."

Edwards had no personal animus against me; only against Moody and "Trinity PhD's". His stipulation against publication was ignored by the Clarendon Press, Oxford which published the book based on the thesis, without further amendments.

The above account is based in large part on my own personal impressions at the time, and may have been partly mistaken. Owen Dudley Edwards – Robin's son – having read this section along with the rest of the draft MS comments:

"I sat beside Father in a room in Cork where he was reading the thesis and he told me it was a work of overwhelming importance, that it was too good to be published by Faber and Faber as these usually were and that it would be published by Clarendon Press. He believed that with so vital a subject it was essential the best possible job be done and that the thesis would not be finished without investigating a potentially productive major source."

I am most happy to accept that this immediate reaction did reflect Robin Dudley Edwards's basic approach to this matter.

In the context of these memoirs, the most relevant parts of *Parnell and his Party* are those that concern the often fraught and strange relations between religion and nationalism. One episode will suffice to demonstrate both the complexities of the relationship and Parnell's mastery over the whole area (in the period before the divorce crisis). The episode concerned the agrarian combination known as the Plan of Campaign – involving the use of the boycott – launched (with Parnell's grudging assent) against some landlords and implicitly against the Tory Government in the aftermath of the defeat of Gladstone's first Home Rule Bill. The morality of the plan and boycotting in terms of Catholic theology, soon became an issue involving the intervention of the Pope himself.

The following section is the account of the core of this matter in *Parnell and his Party.*

"When the Plan of Campaign had first come into operation, the two most influential churchmen in Ireland had considered its morality and decided in its favour. Archbishop Walsh, indeed, had at first some qualms and 'privately conveyed to Land League organizer Harrington his apprehensions regarding its moral justification'. He found on examination, however, and informed the press, that the Plan was morally justifiable, in view of the 'dual ownership' which existed in Irish land 'since the Land Act of 1881'. At the same time he reminded his audience that the bishops were the custodians of the moral boundaries of the agitation, and a great latent political power: 'a single vigorous letter from the Archbishop of Cashel broke the back of the no-rent manifesto'. Dr Croke himself was not so queasy and thought it sufficient, in a letter to Dr Walsh, to justify the Plan on the ground that 'the so-called law as expounded by Irish judges and enforced by British bayonets is simply no law at all'. The other Irish bishops were less vocal, but the general impression was that most of them either favoured the Plan or had no views about it; those clergy – probably the majority – who were co-operating in the National League were usually also active in the plan.

"There were, however, a few churchmen who, from the start, strongly disapproved of the plan. Pre-eminent among these were Dr Healy, then coadjutor-Bishop of Clonfert, and Dr O'Dwyer, Bishop of Limerick, widely regarded as unionists or 'castle bishops'. When Archbishop Walsh had declared in favour of the Plan, Dr Healy wrote to Rome, to the Prefect of Propaganda, denouncing both the Plan and the archbishop and declaring that 'boycotting almost everywhere obtains, especially in the south and west and terrifies everybody, even the bishops themselves and the priests who hardly venture to absent themselves from the meetings of the National League.

"Moved apparently by such complaints, the Holy See decided to send a representative, Monsignor Persico, to investigate the situation in Ireland. His visit was embarrassing to nationalists, and especially to nationalist bishops, from the start. Archbishop Walsh had to deny a rumour that the mission had been abandoned because of his opposition. Knowing what he knew of the mission's object, he said, he could not possibly oppose it; the rumours had been put out 'to shake the confidence of the Irish people in their Chief Pastor'.

"Persico came in July 1887 and heard both sides. Archbishop Walsh gave him the nationalist point of view under four heads: the political movement was 'not revolutionary but thoroughly constitutional'; the land movement was 'not communistic' but in favour of fair rents; there was a complete absence of crime; these satisfactory aspects were 'the result mainly of guidance of the movement by the bishops and priests'. Persico, however, seems to have been more impressed by what he heard on the other side. Even during his mission a number of Irish priests were requested, at his instance, 'to act with the greatest caution and moderation' and to keep themselves outside the reach of the Crimes Act.

"Persico returned to Rome and a few months later the blow fell. The Congregation of the Holy Office addressed to the Irish bishops a circular, dated 20 April 1888, condemning both the Plan and boycotting: 'In disputes between letters and holders of farms in Ireland, is it lawful to have recourse to those means known as the Plan of Campaign and Boycotting? . . . their Eminences having long and maturely weighed the matter unanimously replied: In the negative. Our Holy Father confirmed and approved this reply on Wednesday the 18th of the present month. Your lordship will therefore prudently but effectively admonish the clergy and people in reference to this matter.'

"It was made known that this decision had been reached on three main grounds: that it was unlawful to break contracts freely entered into; that the land courts were available if rents were unfair; that the Plan funds were extorted by boycotting, a means contrary to justice and charity.

"The Roman circular threw many nationalists into consternation. True, it was not the first time that Rome had intervened against the sense of the Irish nationalist-agrarian movement, but this intervention was far more serious than the last. The so-called 'De Parnellio' letter, fruit of the Errington mission, [in 1885] had forbidden the clergy to participate in National League activities and in the Parnell tribute collection: matters not of vital importance. But the new circular was not a mere matter of ecclesiastical discipline: it was a pronouncement, approved by the Pope himself, in the sphere of morals, where every Catholic, lay or clerical, accepted the papal authority as final. And it struck not at some minor aspect of the Irish movement, but at the whole current organization of the agrarian sturggle – the Plan of Campaign – and at the one great principle, of the boycott, which gave the organized farmers all their power.

"The first, and natural, instinct of some important nationalists was to drop the Plan of Campaign. The *Freeman's Journal* editorial on the day the news was published is full of preparations for retreat. The Plan was 'a mere incident in the agitation . . . no part of the programme of the National League . . . always an open question . . . a moot point'. As for boycotting, it was 'diminishing'. However, it was for the bishops to give a lead: 'The Irish people will receive the decree of the Pope or the Propaganda with respect the most profound. They will await the propounding of it by the prelates whom they love and trust as ever heretofore with anxiety but with courage.' The editorial also expressed confidence in 'the great national movement led by Mr Parnell and his fellows of the Irish parliamentary party' and ended with some not very appropriate remarks about 'nailing colours to the mast'.

"The prelates whom the Irish people loved and trusted – and the *Freeman* was describing a class of prelates rather than referring to prelates, generally – differed in their initial reaction to the circular. Dr Walsh wrote to Dr Croke 'advising that it should be quietly accepted and that as far as possible all public discussions, especially in newspapers, should be avoided'. Dr Croke, however, seems to have been made of sterner stuff. William O'Brien has left an eye-witness description of that great archbishop at dinner – 'his purple-edged biretta planted as usual at the top of the massive brow, like a banner above a rampart' – receiving and reading out, to his guest (the chief exponent of the Plan) the Roman circular. O'Brien asked whether he should not leave. The bishop took a pinch of snuff. 'Mike,' he said with a solemnity worthy of the Day of General Judgment, 'Mike, kill another pig.' (Meaning 'open another bottle' and implying that O'Brien should stay, whatever about the Pope).

"The archbishop's ingenuity was as remarkable as his fortitude, for he now inspired a remarkable article, which undoubtedly saved the national movement a great deal of internal strife. This article which appeared in the Irish papers the day after the publication (on 30 April) of the text of the circular, looked to the bishops for 'an authentic interpretation of this highly technical document,' but drew the distinction between authority on doctrine and authority on fact: Irish Catholics would accept the decision if they could accept as correct the assumptions of fact which it contained; it did actually contain an incorrect assumption of fact because most land tenure in Ireland was not based on a simple relationship between letter and holder (*locator* and *conductor*) but on dual ownership, as established by the Act of 1881.

"So far, the lay leaders had made no public statement. Both O'Brien and Dillon, the leaders of the Plan, had, however, been in close touch with Dr Croke, and the line taken in the *Freeman* article was substantially agreed on in advance between Dillon and Dr Croke. Immediately after the publication of that article had formed a theological shelter belt, political leaders prepared to emerge. Dillon and Dr Kenny suggested to O'Brien that a meeting of the Catholic members of parliament should be convened by Sexton, then lord mayor of Dublin. Parnell agreed and the meeting was summoned for 17 May, at the Mansion House, Dublin.

"Parnell himself was not, of course, to be present at the Mansion House meeting, but it was very soon made known that he too intended to speak on the question of the hour. The *Freeman's Journal* on 4 May forecast that Parnell, at the dinner of the Eighty Club – an important gathering of the British Liberal elite at which he had been invited to speak – would make 'one of the most important pronouncements which the leader of the Irish parliamentary party and the Irish people has ever addressed to his sympathizers and followers'. 'We believe,' wrote a special correspondent, 'that it is Mr Parnell's opinion that the agrarian movement in Ireland may be conducted with sufficient effectiveness without collision with the religious feelings . . . of the Irish people.' The unionist *Irish Times* the next day added its unfriendly gloss: 'Mr Parnell was not the author of the plan . . . He has now an opportunity of throwing it over.' The Pope's decree, according to the writer, had 'forced the parliamentary party from the old and forbidden onto an entirely new and less startling track'.

"Parnell's speech, when it came, on 8 May, in London, was different in two important particulars from what friend and foe had expected. He did not bow in any way to the circular and he did not order the dropping of the Plan. Of the circular he said that it was bound to be 'a disastrous failure' but that it was not his business to interfere with any line which his Catholic colleagues might take on it. As far as the Plan was concerned, he pointed out that he had been very ill when it was started; he would have advised against it, because of its bad effects on English public opinion. By the beginning of 1887 when he could speak, Dillon and O'Brien had been under arrest and it was too late for him to disavow it. He had, however, stipulated that neither the league nor the party should be identified with it, that it should be restricted to the estates where it was then in operation, and that there should be moderation in speech and action. These conditions had been generally kept. He believed that the Plan would have to be gradually replaced by 'a method of agrarian organization' which he had for some time been engaged in maturing. 'But we shall now have to wait.' He concluded by advising his countrymen to rely for their release on 'the great liberal party of England . . . men who have never ultimately been beaten'.

"Parnell's speech to the Eighty Club was, in the literal sense, a masterly one. No leader who was not immensely sure of his own prestige could have made such a speech; the leader who could make it, and evoke no public protest, might be pardoned if he thought himself thereafter to be almost omnipotent. In the Parnellite movement, from the beginning, there had been a left wing, mainly agrarian in character, and a right wing, mainly clerical in composition and associations. For long, Parnell had had, as we have seen, to manoeuvre carefully between these two groups, assuring himself of the support of one before doing anything that could offend the other. He now, however, with consummate self-confidence, reached out and knocked their heads together, lightly but firmly. The coolness with which he treated the circular as a political irrelevancy was made the more effective by the criticisms of a purely political nature which he directed against the agrarian movement. No rhetoric against the circular could possibly have been so effective as his mild implication that, because of it, his decision to 'replace' the plan would have to be deferred. Conversely, no ecclesiastical denunciation of the Plan could have been so effective as the Irish leader's declaration against it on political grounds. The whole speech was a reminder to Irishmen that the grand object of their movement was Home Rule, and that he alone – and not agrarian agitators or ecclesiastical theorists – decided the strategy necessary to achieve that end. The setting in which he spoke – the Eighty Club – was a reminder of the victory which his strategy had achieved in 1886, and of the fact that the hope of final victory rested on the alliance which he then had won.

"A modern historian has claimed that in Parnell's last years his authority was slipping and that even without the divorce crisis he was about to be replaced by a committee of his colleagues. It is hard to reconcile this judgement with Parnell's masterly assertion of his authority over the entire Irish political system in May 1888 – just a year and a half before the opening of the divorce crisis. In fact, nothing short of the earthquake of the divorce crisis could have shaken Parnell's leadership.

After examining the course of the divorce crisis in great detail, *Parnell and his Party* concludes with the words:

"As for the leader, he survives most vividly not by the memory of his constructive acts, but by the mark which his romantic image in the last struggle made, and continues to make on young imaginations. The young saw him as Samson pulling down the pillars of the temple – and forgot that it was a temple he himself had planned and built for his own people. For the boy James Joyce, Parnell was the murdered Caesar: 'Et tu, Healy!' written when Joyce was nine, is his first known work, and Parnell is present in all his major books. In Yeats's old age the image of Parnell pulled down by the mob was an aristocratic symbol:

> 'But Popular rage,
> Hysterica passio, *dragged this quarry down.*
> *None shared our guilt; nor did we play a part*
> *Upon a painted stage when we devoured his heart.'*

"The image of the stage, repelled though it is, is significant, as is the poem's opening line:

> *Under the Great Comedian's tomb, the crowd . . .*

"One thinks of Healy's admiring gibe – 'a splendid comedian' – and reflects that Parnell had, at least, a great curtain. 'The split' was a natural drama, with a nation participating in it most intensely. It seized certain strong imaginations – I think of Mr Seán O'Faoláin – with a grip that has never loosened, and it is still capable of capturing young minds: 'The class,' wrote a Harvard professor who had lectured on Irish patriots, 'were Parnellites to a man.' Did this collective emotional explosion of 1890 help to set free the imaginative forces which, for a time in the early 1900s made Dublin – the Parnellite city – an important centre of world literature? One cannot prove it to be so, but one does sense in that literature the Parnellite shock. Those who feel – as does the present writer – that the Parnell of the split deviated from politics into literature, may reflect that, in that second field as in the first, he made his power felt:

> *And here's a final reason,*
> *He was of such a kind*
> *Every man that sings a song*
> *Keeps Parnell in his mind.*

After the publication of *Maria Cross*, Ivor Richards, who liked the book, and whom I did not yet know, invited me to have dinner with him at Pratt's in London. I was delighted at the invitation as I had long been an admirer of Richards's contributions to literary criticism and semantic theory, especially his own *Practical Criticism* and the formidable *Meaning of Meaning*, co-authored with CK Ogden. I was not surprised that Ogden was a member of the party in my honour. But I was a bit surprised, at first, to find that the remaining member of the party was Alfred Munnings, then extremely celebrated for his paintings of horses. I had stupidly assumed that Munnings must be a low-brow, but from the company he kept he obviously wasn't. It was a most enjoyable and intellectually exciting dinner, and often very funny.

Ivor and his wife Dorothea became friends of Máire's and mine and when years afterwards I became Vice-Chancellor of the University of Ghana I asked Ivor to come as a Visiting Professor for a term. His lectures – often conducted in the format of a Socratic dialogue – were hugely popular and well attended and he found them, as he told me, uniquely stimulating.

While he was with me I received a letter from William Empson, a critic whom we both admired very much, his most celebrated work then being *Seven Types of Ambiguity*. I had sent him a copy of a long and controversial essay I had written on the politics of WB Yeats, in which I had dwelt on Yeats's intermittently pro-fascist writings. Empson's comments on this reached me one morning at breakfast-time while Ivor was staying with me. Empson described my essay as "sordid" and this of course infuriated me.

I brought the letter with me down to the breakfast-table, where I found Ivor eating a pineapple, a favourite Ghanaian delicacy. Furious, I showed Ivor Empson's letter hoping for some moral support. Ivor read the letter, and his prominent and expressive eyes widened as he did so, fastening on the key word. Then he said, thoughtfully:

"Sordid . . . *Sordid* . . . do you suppose Bill Empson means that as a term of *praise?*"

At that blessed word, all my irritation vanished and was replaced by exultation. I was able to write to Empson a letter of reasonable and amicable remonstrance, and we remained friends.

So much so indeed that after Empson's death, his widow, Hetta, invited me to deliver the eulogy at his funeral. By that time Empson's celebrated essay, *Milton's God*, a fierce attack on historic Christianity, had appeared. So the funeral proceedings in the Orangerie on Hampstead Heath were resolutely secular. To prepare myself for the momentous event I read (mostly re-read) everything that Empson had written. As I did so, I realized how inexpressibly funny Empson could be in the midst of often subtle and abstruse reasonings. This aspect seemed to have escaped the notice of his critics, as they grappled with what was serious. So I decided – rather audaciously – that I would devote my eulogy exclusively to the funny side, which I illustrated copiously from his writings. Fortunately for me this proceeding was hugely successful. The roars of laughter coming from that packed funeral service must have been heard for a considerable distance across Hampstead Heath.

I know Ivor Richards would have been pleased and I also feel sure that Empson himself would have wished it that way.

5

SERVICE UNDER SEÁN MacBRIDE,
1948-1951

IN 1948, THERE CAME ABOUT THE GREATEST CHANGE IN THE POLITICAL LIFE OF the new state since Fianna Fáil's victory in 1932. Fianna Fáil by 1945 had held power continuously for sixteen years. Fianna Fáil was now replaced by a coalition made up of Fine Gael (the party which had concluded the Anglo-Irish Treaty), Labour, the Farmers' Party (Clann na Talmhan), and a new party, Clann na Poblachta, "The Children of the Republic", headed by Seán MacBride. Seán MacBride now became Minister for External Affairs, undoubtedly the post he had stipulated for himself. This represented an important change in the lives of all of us at Iveagh House. Throughout the de Valera years, de Valera had always been Minister for External Affairs, as well as Taoiseach, and worked in the Taoiseach's office in Merrion Row. He had been advised on political matters by a very small, tightly-knit confidential group of officials of the Department: the Secretary, Joseph Walshe; Assistant Secretary, FH Boland; Legal Adviser, Michael Rynne; and Archivist, Sheila Murphy.

These four *were* the Department at headquarters, under de Valera, for all those years. The rest of us were out of the loop, as far as matters considered of importance were concerned. But now we were to have a Minister all to ourselves, with an office at Iveagh House, and considerable power within the new government, which could not survive without him. For many of us – outside the narrow circle which had advised de Valera – this appeared at first as a welcome change. I shall shortly be considering how the change affected me personally. But first of all a word about Seán MacBride and Clann na Poblachta.

Seán MacBride had been a very young man at the time of the Irish civil war, when he fought on the republican side. When the IRA, having lost the civil war, laid down their arms, a small number of irreconcilables kept a kind of paramilitary nucleus in being, and Seán MacBride had the title of Chief of Staff within this nucleus. These people do not appear to have had any significant military role at this time, but they did vigorously denounce, not merely Fine Gael but also de Valera, for "betraying the Republic". De Valera and his colleagues never forgave MacBride for this phase in his activities, though MacBride himself seems to have clung to a hope that he could exert sufficient clout to force de Valera to come to terms.

Evidence is only fragmentary but it seems that, after the Second World War, MacBride succeeded in getting IRA support for a "New Departure" that would put de Valera out of power. The IRA now hated de Valera for having suppressed them during the Second World War even more than they hated Fine Gael for much earlier misdeeds. So the way was now open for a new coalition motivated by hatred, or at least dislike, of de Valera, for a variety of sometimes conflicting reasons.

With this objective in mind MacBride had founded Clann na Poblachta ("Children of the Republic") with the tacit but valuable support of the IRA. The support had to be tacit because it would have frightened off the voters if it was explicit, raising the spectre of renewed "war" with Britain. The trick was to sound more nationalist (or "national") than de Valera but less nationalist than the IRA. The IRA seemed to see the sense in this recipe for the victory of a coalition, which would include a group over which they could expect to exert great influence and which would exclude those whom they most yearned to punish. On MacBride's side, he seems to have seen himself as weaning the IRA away from violence and steering them into the peaceful paths of parliamentary politics. In this he was anticipating, with some prescience, the reasoning of a later generation of "peace processors", led by John Hume, more than forty years afterwards. But the problem about weaning away terrorists from violence is that you have to make concessions to them first, in the hope of weaning them. They, for their part, are likely to see these concessions as extorted by the threat of renewed violence: a threat which, if maintained, might extort further concessions. These things being so, when the concessions appear to be exhausted, the violence will resume, and only be broken off again, for a time, on receipt of some new concessions, with promises of more on the way. And when the new concessions, in turn, run out, the violence can again be resumed. This system became perfected only in the last two decades of the 20th century, the Hume-Adams period. But the 1950s, under Seán MacBride saw the first tentative exploration of the potential of such a system.

* * *

I have quite a vivid memory of the arrival of Seán MacBride at Iveagh House to assume his new duties as Minister for External Affairs. The diplomatic staff were summoned to his presence. Or rather, I don't exactly know who was summoned, but the people who came were the middle and low-ranking diplomatists. Those who had advised de Valera on policy, most notably the Secretary and Assistant Secretary, were not there. There was the feeling of a silent changing of the guard, as regards policy-making, and this was naturally a matter of considerable interest to the younger members of the Department, including myself.

MacBride was affable to us all, with an air of putting us at our ease. He smiled and beamed a good deal. I was later to be reminded of a phrase used by the great Swedish journalist Herbert Tingsten about Dag Hammarskjold: "He has a humourless twinkle in his eye". MacBride made a short affable speech, with no overt political content, looking forward to working with us all and so on. But he ended on a wrong note, of excessive cordiality. "Don't you think," he asked, "it may be rather fun?"

Some of us, including myself, did indeed think – and not altogether mistakenly – that it might be rather fun. But things were in those days organised on strictly hierarchical lines. Nobody was entitled to reply except the most senior member of our group. The most senior member happened to be a dour counsellor from Derry called Brian Gallagher. He was a devout Catholic and (I think) a silent Fianna Fáil supporter (as most senior civil servants were by this time, after sixteen years of Fianna Fáil control over senior appointments). Brian said nothing and also looked unsmilingly at his boots. After a short pause, MacBride dismissed us, with an air of well-controlled displeasure.

As a result of this encounter, MacBride had to know that although all of his diplomatic staff would be obedient to his instructions, many would be so in a spirit of recalcitrance verging on obstruction. He was not in a postion to make sweeping changes because the new Taoiseach, John A

Costello – who did not trust MacBride very far – would not sanction sweeping changes. The Department's personnel would mostly stay intact, as under de Valera. But he could seek authority for expanded activities requiring additional personnel. Costello – who needed MacBride just as MacBride needed him – would consent to new appointments within reason and MacBride would be in control of the new appointments. And, as it happened, the principal new appointment was coming my way.

When MacBride became Minister he had the right to bring to the Department with him a personal assistant, in his political confidence. The assistant was Louie O'Brien, a discreet and capable young woman, who (officially) handled party-political matters for him, and also (unoffically) advised him on matters of personnel. He had also, by tradition, the right to choose his own private secretary, from within the Department. On Louie's advice (I believe) MacBride chose Valentin Iremonger. Earlier, while a junior civil servant, Iremonger had been mildly active in radical left politics, which in Ireland tended to involve sympathy with Sinn Féin, and that is how he seems to have come in contact with Louie O'Brien. On Iremonger's advice (I believe) MacBride appointed me as head of a new Information Section at Iveagh House, with the rank of First Secretary. "Information", of course, meant propaganda. As MacBride took a keen – indeed inordinate – interest in this aspect of his Department's work this meant that henceforward – until shortly before the fall of the first Inter-Party Government, three years later – I would be in close daily contact with MacBride, to whom I reported directly on information matters, and from whom alone I received instructions.

* * *

This seems an appropriate moment to say more – and more than I knew at the time I served him – about the strange and in many ways exotic personality with whom I had suddenly become so closely associated.

Seán MacBride was the son of Maud Gonne and Major John MacBride. Seán was born in Paris (in January 1904), but his mother brought him to Ireland to be baptised. (John O'Leary was to be the godfather, but the priest refused to let him, because O'Leary was a known Fenian.) The marriage broke up in a particularly grisly manner, shortly after Seán was born. Maud and her children soon returned to France, where Seán was brought up. Maud did not want to bring Seán back to Ireland in case MacBride laid claim to him. The break-up of the MacBride marriage began in October,

1904, when Seán was less than a year old. The separation was complete, after an appeal, by January 1908. Maud wrote to Yeats:

"The monthly visits which Seagan [Seán] was to have paid to his father each year when he was six years old have been suppressed and the visits which MacBride, by the first verdict, had a right to receive twice a week have been reduced to once a week but my request that they should take place at my house or at the house of the doctor has been refused. This is a very great cause for upset and anxiety for it facilitates MacBride stealing the child and I shall have great worry and expense making things quite safe. However for the last eighteen months MacBride has not once asked to see the child and as he is not likely to live in Paris I hope these visits will be a dead letter. Still they are always a nuisance and will prevent me living in Ireland for the present".

There is a portrait of Seán, by his mother, done in the same year in which that letter was written. It is an arresting and disturbing portrait. The child's expression is not that of a child but of an ageless being: tense and brooding and apparently confronting dark forces. Seán's arms are folded on his chest.

In the context of that letter, written in the same year, this looks to me like the picture of a little boy who has been told he is in danger of being kidnapped by his wicked father.

Maud's anxiety that John MacBride might somehow get hold of Seán continued up to as late as 1915, when Seán was eleven. But then came 1916: Major John MacBride, as a prominent participant in the rebellion, was executed on May 5.

On May 11, Maud wrote to Yeats: "Major MacBride by his death has left a name for Seagan [Seán] to be proud of. Those who die for Ireland are sacred." Later, speaking of all the executed leaders she quoted Yeats's *Cathleen Ní Houlihan*: "The deaths of those leaders are full of beauty and romance. They will be speaking for ever, the people shall hear them for ever."

For Seán, then aged twelve, the birth of Yeats's "terrible beauty" must have been especially wrenching and poignant. The father whom he had never known, and towards whom he must have entertained feelings of aversion and apprehension (at best) was now metamorphosed into a sacred being in the eyes of his mother, who had loathed his father for as long as Seán's memories could go back. Yet he must have instantly recognised the legitimacy of the totally unexpected metamorphosis for he had been brought up, by his mother, on a peculiarly intense mystical-nationalist form of the cult of those who died for Ireland.

In November, 1915 – five months before the Easter Rising – Maud Gonne wrote to Yeats of a vision she had had about "the Souls of the Dead".

She had seen the spirits of Irish soldiers killed in the World War, and of these she writes with respect and sympathy, but not with any reverence, and then she goes on to those who died for Ireland:

"Others have died with a definite idea of sacrifice to an ideal, they were held by the stronger and deeper rhythms of the chants, leading in wonderful patterns to a deeper peace, the peace of the Crucified, which is above the currents of nationalities and storms, but for all that they will not be separated from Ireland for as an entity she has followed the path of Sacrifice and has tasted of the Grail and the strength they will bring her is greater."

Maud saw that vision a little over a month before Pearse delivered his message of Christmas Day, 1915, about "the power of the ghosts of a nation". Seán MacBride was brought up under that power, and it had been strengthened by the addition of his formerly alienated father to the number of the ghosts in question. (See *Ancestral Voices* [1994], section on "Son of Maud Gonne".)

I found MacBride a courteous and considerate person to work with, except that he expected you to be available at all hours, whenever required, like a member of a revolutionary organisation. (He, apparently, had similar expectations of his entire staff.) There were always distant semi-revolutionary overtones when he was around: a rather somnambulistic obeisance to the Pearsean call.

You could sense the presence of ghosts all right; MacBride's face, when in repose, had a perpetually haunted expression like his mother's. Indeed his features, in middle age, had an uncanny resemblance to his mother's in old age: the large and lustrous eyes, the hollow cheeks, the pallor, and the salience of the skull beneath the skin. He looked, in Yeats's words, like a being who "took a mess of shadows for its meat".

He didn't, though; appearances were deceptive in that respect; he must have had a marvellous metabolism. He was a notable gourmet and connoisseur of wine. He also liked women, and pursued them even at an advanced age, in the course of the international career which was to bring, to the former Chief of Staff of the IRA, both the Nobel Peace Prize and the Lenin Peace Prize. At that stage, his combination of an amorous disposition with what was by then a spectacularly sepulchral appearance earned him a nickname among the female members of the international press corps (as I learned much later from one of them). The nickname was "Death Takes a Holiday".

Looking back on it, I have an impression that Seán had managed to strike a kind of bargain with those ghosts: that, if he would always do what they required of him in Irish politics – by always helping the IRA – they would let him alone in every other respect. This was a bad bargain as far as Irish politics was concerned. But one can hardly blame Seán for striking it, when one thinks of the circumstances of his childhood and boyhood. In dealing with ghosts, practice makes perfect. Like her son, Maud Gonne lived to an advanced age in a perennially funereal manner.

Combining with the revolutionary pull, in a weird sort of way, was an ecumenical urge. MacBride never ceased to seek accommodation with the two most powerful forces in the Ireland of his day: the Catholic Church and the Fianna Fáil party. Both the Church and Fianna Fáil continued to distrust him and hold him at arm's length, but he never ceased to cling to the hope that one day . . .

There was not much he could do about reconciliation with Fianna Fáil for the time being. The coalition in which he was a Minister had been formed for the express purpose of putting Fianna Fáil out and keeping it out. Also the most significant section of his own core-support – Sinn Féin-IRA – had helped to found Clann na Poblachta also for the express purpose of putting Fianna Fáil out and keeping it out. So reconciliation with Fianna Fáil would have to be deferred for some time, but MacBride never ceased to hope for it.

Full reconciliation with the Church must have seemed more immediately feasible, and it was in this area that MacBride showed the greatest originality. Since Parnell's day, and also in the civil war period, the Irish radical left, the broad-based constituency to which Clann na Poblachta belonged, had been the most anti-clerical section in Irish politics. MacBride saw such a position as inimical to the growth and influence of his party and he set out to change it.

However the young radicals in the party may have felt, Clann na Poblachta policy, as presented to the public, was Catholic-nationalist, very much in line with the Irish Ireland of the early part of the century. The Clann was bent on resisting "the alien, artificial and unchristian concepts of life": DP Moran's programme exactly. Seán MacBride as leader of Clann na Poblachta and Minister for External Affairs of the Republic was at some pains to emphasise his personal Catholicism. When there was work to be done on a Sunday – as often happened – he would show up at Iveagh House clutching his missal. As Honor Tracy wrote, about this time, "Ireland is a country where Seán MacBride goes to Mass".

The new inter-party government, with Clann na Poblachta in it, sent to the Vatican from its first Cabinet meeting the most effusively Catholic message ever sent by any Government of the Irish state, since its foundation in 1921. Their telegram desired "to repose at the feet of your Holiness the assurance of our filial loyalty and of our devotion to your August Person, as well as our firm resolve to be guided in all our work by the teaching of Christ, and to strive for the attainment of a social order in Ireland based on Christian principles". This was a Catholic-nationalist government with an unusually strong and explicit emphasis on the "Catholic". It was also the first government, since the state was founded, to be strongly influenced by the post-Treaty IRA. The first, but not the last.

As was disclosed only recently, MacBride carried his policy of appeasing the Catholic Church to extraordinary lengths.

Abortion was then, as now, illegal in Ireland and, also then as now, women who wanted abortions went to England. The Church was supposed to deplore this safety-valve, but actually had little to say about it. MacBride, however, now wrote to John Charles McQuaid, Archbishop of Dublin, to suggest the possibility of making it illegal for pregnant women in Ireland to leave the jurisdiction, thus making legal abortion impossible in Ireland while illegal abortion inside the jurisdiction remained difficult and dangerous in practice, instead of safely available outside the jurisdiction. The Archbishop wrote in reply a curt letter showing no interest in the idea. This may in part have been due to distrust of MacBride – a sentiment widely cherished by churchmen as well as by laymen – but probably much more important was the prudent recognition of the utility of the safety valve. The ban on abortion recognised Ireland's peculiar holiness, but the "lower standards" of "pagan England" were a convenient resource in practice. And this still remains the case.

If I had known at the time of MacBride's letter to the Archbishop I would have been revolted by it, and would have felt much less personal regard for MacBride than I had at the time. But I would not for that reason, at that time, been likely (I think) to have broken off a relationship that was so beneficial to my official career. However, I neither knew of the offer, or even guessed at any such possibility, so never suffered whatever qualms I might have experienced had I known more.

* * *

The start to the new phase of my career as Head of Information was busy, but not particularly dramatic. I started a Weekly Bulletin of the Department, in the early issues of which MacBride showed a keen interest. I ran a poster campaign advertising Ireland's alleged devotion to the cause of European Unity. I engaged for a rather short time in rather mild anti-partition activities including a contribution under my pseudonym "Donat O'Donnell" to the (Catholic up-market) *Revue Generale Belge*. I also produced a lavishly-illustrated pamphlet celebrating Ireland. This gave rise to the only really memorable episode occurring during the early months of my new phase. The pamphlet contained a very dramatic picture of Maud Gonne as she was at that time: gaunt cheeks, huge luminous eyes and a complex geometry of deep wrinkles. The Irish High Commissioner in London, John Dulanty, sent a copy of the publication to Bernard Shaw, apparently drawing his attention to the dramatic photograph. Shaw was then himself extremely old and had known Maud Gonne in the days when she had been a great beauty. He sent the High Commissioner one of his famous post-cards: "Tell that young man [MacBride] not to be a bloody fool."

Shortly after this, the conduct of Ireland's international affairs became a more serious matter and propaganda concerning it also began, to a great extent, to be taken out of MacBride's hands and therefore out of mine. MacBride induced the new government to pass the Republic of Ireland Act [1949]. This Act made very little difference in practice. By observing neutrality, while all the rest of the former Empire was at war, de Valera had established the independence of the Irish state more convincingly than tinkering with any document could have asserted it. The Republic of Ireland Act took Ireland (Éire) out of the Commonwealth of which the head had been the Crown. But Commonwealth members in practice now went their individual ways. Apart from the rather minor matter of Commonwealth membership and the new title "Republic of Ireland", the new Act changed nothing.

The territorial jurisdiction of the Republic remained the same as that of the old Free State, as ambiguously amended in de Valera's 1937 Constitution, which remained in full force after 1950, as before.

All the same, the move was – or at least seemed at the time – politically astute. De Valera had always called himself a republican, but had never actually declared a Republic, though he could have done so. Hardline republicans (i.e., the IRA) could not possibly be satisfied by the Costello-MacBride Republic: the old Irish Free State under a new name. But they were ready to welcome the new name as a step in the right direction, achieved by their friends in office and not achieved by Fianna Fáil. It did not suit them to crab a claimed national achievment of a coalition with Seán MacBride in it.

De Valera's government had got very rough with republicans. They knew that a goverment depending on Seán MacBride for its existence could never move in that direction. So the more clout MacBride had in the coalition the better. The Republic of Ireland Act demonstrated MacBride's clout, and so was not to be despised.

There was another factor working to endear that Republic to the IRA. Costello's argument in favour of it was that it would "take the gun out of politics". The IRA had their own ideas about how the gun might eventually be taken out of politics. But as a tendency on the part of the government, a policy of "taking the gun out of politics" by manifestations of deference towards the feelings of the IRA, had much to be said for it. It was vastly preferable to de Valera's wartime formula for taking the gun out of politics, through internment, executions, and letting hunger-strikers die. So on the whole, the IRA was in favour of giving the Costello-MacBride coalition an easy ride. In any case, the IRA itself, in the aftermath of the Second World War, was in some need of repose and reorganisation after its gruelling wartime experiences at the hands of the de Valera government.

In the retrospect of nearly half a century later, we can see that the Costello government's "taking the gun out of politics" by enacting the Republic was an early manifestation of the sort of thinking that has given us "the peace process" from 1993 on. That is to say, you give the IRA a bit of what they want in the hope that they will be so pleased with the bit that they will stop, without holding out for the whole. In other contexts such a policy has been known as appeasement. It does not have an impressive international track record.

However, the British reaction to the Republic of Ireland Act was stronger than expected. The move away from the Commonwealth gave the new Republic's claim to Northern Ireland – already present in Articles 2 and 3 of the Constitution – greater salience than it had before. And Northern Ireland had then great and fresh claims to Britain's gratitude. It had been part of the British war effort, while what was now the Republic of Ireland had been neutral. So the British government passed the Ireland Act, reaffirming Northern Ireland's status as a part of the United Kingdom.

Taken together, the Republic of Ireland Act and the Ireland Act made no substantial change in either of the two polities into which the British Isles were divided. But a lot of stuff from the past had been stirred up by the Irish move which would have been better left unstirred. The British move was an inevitable response to the Republic of Ireland Act, and the Irish nationalist response to the British move was equally inevitable: a storm of protest, supported by all nationalist parties, and followed by a long outpouring of propaganda, all vociferously challenging the legitimacy of Northern Ireland's existence. De Valera was visibly unenthusiastic about all this, but felt constrained, by his own past commitments since 1925, by his own Constitution, and by the popular mood, to give the campaign his nominal support.

* * *

At first I thought that the new situation would enormously increase the importance and change the function of my Information Section: a matter about which I had mixed feelings. I found the nationalist uproar about the Ireland Act personally uncongenial but I would not, at that time, have refused a role within it, had one been assigned to me. But fortunately for me (as I now see things) anti-partition propaganda now assumed such importance as to take it out of the hands of any government Department.

Faced with the enormity – as it seemed to all nationalists – of the Ireland Act the political parties of the Republic set up an all-party committee to deal with a matter which was felt to transcend differences which had hitherto divided nationalists. I suspect that the impetus behind the all-party committee came from MacBride and that there was an ulterior motive behind it. While the Republic of Ireland Act had been intended to steal de Valera's clothes, the Ireland Act may have seemed to offer an opportunity for reconciliation with de Valera. Fianna Fáil and Clann na Poblachta were both republican parties, with a common history of rejecting the Anglo-Irish Treaty of 1921. After that, de Valera had diverged from the other republicans, and MacBride had gone along with Sinn Féin-IRA. But might not the new great national crisis – as what was otherwise a storm in a teacup was built up to appear – lead to the reintegration of the two wings of the republican movement? In that case might not MacBride eventually succeed de Valera in the leadership of the reunited republican movement? I cannot prove that such ideas were in MacBride's mind, but I did know that he wished to re-open lines of communication with de Valera and I believe that he saw the Ireland Act crisis as the great opportunity to move decisively in that direction.

In any case, he now made a remarkable move. He took responsibility for anti-partition propaganda – at that time the hottest political property in town – altogether out of the hands of the government to which he belonged. He could do so because the government had actually left it in his own hands. He handed it over nominally to the all-party committee but in reality to de Valera. On MacBride's initiative, the main responsibility for anti-partition propaganda was taken away from External

Affairs and given to a group headed by the late Frank Gallagher, for many years Dev's principal assistant in press and propaganda affairs, and the animating spirit behind Dev's newspaper, *The Irish Press*. This group met in the Mansion House, putatively under the authority of the all-party committee but in reality under authority delegated to de Valera, courtesy of Seán MacBride. I attended the first meeting of the all-party committee, along with Seán MacBride.

Thirteen years afterwards, when I was being seconded to UN service and about to leave for Katanga, de Valera, then President of the country, sent for me. The first thing he talked about was his memory of that meeting.

"It was at a time . . . when we were not in office . . . "

Slight pause there, as if drawing a veil over a period of dubious legitimacy in Irish history. Dev went on: "Mr MacBride was Minister for External Affairs. You were there with him. Mr MacBride addressed the meeting. He spoke for some considerable time. I noticed that while he was speaking you were not watching him. You were watching me. And I said to myself: 'That young man is . . . interested in politics.'" He realised that this surprised me, for he went on: "I know you thought I couldn't see you for I was supposed to be blind. So I was, very nearly, but at that time I still had what they called peripheral vision . . . That is to say I could see out of the corner of my eye." Dev then produced his famous smile, which had been likened (by an opponent) to "moonlight on a tombstone", but which was really rather shy and pleasant.

If, as I believe, the move through the all-party committee was an act of political courtship from MacBride to de Valera it was never reciprocated. De Valera knew the close connections between MacBride's party, Clann na Poblachta, and Sinn Féin-IRA. He knew therefore that if he took MacBride's party on board with Fianna Fáil, he would thereby be entering into an unavowed but close association with the modern Sinn Féin-IRA. More scrupulous by now, in relation to political violence, than some of his latterday successors, de Valera was determined to enter no such association. MacBride was soon in internal difficulties with his own party. And as a result of these difficulties I was soon to acquire new responsibilities.

* * *

One of MacBride's weaknesses as a political leader in a democracy arose from his connections in the recent past with a revolutionary organisation, the IRA. He expected from his political associates the same implicit and total obedience which he had been accustomed to receive from IRA members when he had been Chief of Staff. But no open political party, even one with unavowed and deniable links with Sinn Féin-IRA, can function quite like that. MacBride was soon in trouble with one of his subordinates, an able but angry and bitter lawyer, Noel Hartnett.

Hartnett had been sent, during the rumpus over the Ireland Act, on a mission to the United States to make known the unparalleled insult which had been offered by Britain in that Act to Ireland. It is clear that Hartnett was greatly enjoying both his mission – in which he fervently believed – and the sheer pleasure of touring the United States. And then, not long after arrival in New York and when he was about to leave for San Francisco, he received a telegram from MacBride summoning him home. As Hartnett's travelling expenses would have been cut off if he had not obeyed the summons, he returned home. But the man who came home was different from the man who had gone out. The man who had gone out had been a loyal supporter of MacBride's. The man who came back, humiliated, was McBride's bitter enemy.

Now MacBride had a plan, in which Hartnett had been intended to play a central role. The plan was for the establishment of an Irish News Agency. Hartnett was intended to be managing director and had apparently agreed. That was before the frustrated American tour. But now, just on the eve of the announcement of the formation of the Agency, Hartnett told MacBride that he would not accept the post of managing director, though he would accept a seat on the board.

I had been intended to be an ordinary member of the board, which would not have entailed any great expenditure of time or energy. But MacBride now told me that he wanted me to be the managing director.

My first inclination was to refuse. I knew that MacBride intended the Agency to be another implement of anti-partition propaganda, although there was nothing about that in the instrument establishing the Agency. It was supposed to be a *bona fide* news agency, but MacBride's original choice for managing director – Noel Hartnett, a dedicated republican propagandist – had sent a clear signal as to what was to be expected of the Agency.

I did not, at this stage, want to fill that role. Anti-partition propaganda – in a mild version of which I had been willingly involved early in the MacBride period – had become repulsive to me when it became hyper-excited and stridently anti-British, after the Ireland Act. The formation of the all-party committee had relieved me of direct responsibility for the major tasks of anti-partition propaganda. By then I had become quite closely involved with MacBride in the presentation of Irish foreign policy, as shaped by him. The foreign policy, so shaped, was rather a weird affair. It had two aspects: an anti-British one and a "pro-Western" one. The anti-British aspect consisted mainly of long explanations of the iniquity of the Ireland Act. The general lines of the explanations were dictated by MacBride. MacBride's argument – designed for American consumption and Irish-American consumption in particular – was that Ireland could not enter NATO as long as part of Ireland's territory, Northern Ireland, was "occupied" by a leading NATO member, Britain. The fact that the alleged "occupation" was sustained by the will and the votes of a majority of the inhabitants of the territory in question was totally ignored, as was customary in anti-partition propaganda at the time (and is still frequent). MacBride claimed – sometimes in statements drafted for him by me – that Britain's "occupation" of Northern Ireland was identical in iniquity with the real occupation of Eastern Europe by the Soviet Union. No doubt in an effort to extenuate the obvious absurdity of this position, I managed to include in one of the drafts the formula that that was how it looked "from where we sit". When I read over that speech of MacBride's these four words contributed by me stuck in my gullet where they still remain, nearly fifty years later.

The "pro-Western" aspect of MacBride's foreign policy consisted in maintaining that Ireland was passionately committed to European unity, while Britain – as well as "occupying" Northern Ireland – was not merely dragging its feet on European union, but also sabotaging movement in that direction in various perfidious ways. I travelled to Europe at this time in the capacity of MacBride's press officer and was involved in the peddling of this stuff at press conferences. We found no takers. At this period, when the Soviet Union was consolidating its grip on Eastern Europe, and appeared to threaten Western Europe, attacks on a founder member of NATO as insufficiently "European", coming from a country which refused to join NATO, could only arouse bewilderment mingled with contempt.

By the time MacBride invited me to become managing director of the Irish News Agency, I was weary of all this stuff, and begining to feel more than a little sick about my own position with regard to it. Relations with MacBride, though still cordial on the surface, were beginning to show some signs of strain. One little episode I remember as significant. MacBride had just come back from the United States and called me into his office to show me a pamphlet which had just been issued by the American League for an Undivided Ireland about perfidious British monetary policy. It contained what I already thought of as the usual anti-partition rubbish. When I had read it, MacBride asked me what I thought of it. I replied: "I think you wrote it." He said: "How do you make that out?" I said: "It refers throughout to 'the sterling'. You are the only person in the English-speaking world who calls sterling 'the sterling'." This was one of several gallicisms *(le sterling)* which used to creep into MacBride's English: he had grown up in France and his first language was French. MacBride looked at me with unusual attention. I think he was detecting signs of incipient rebellion. He was already seeing quite a lot of such signs, within his own party.

I knew McBride intended the Agency to be another outlet for anti-partition propaganda, and by now I hated the idea of any further immersion in all that. So I refused. At this MacBride became extremely angry: the first and only time when he manifested anger towards me. I now had to think quite rapidly about the implications of all this for my own career, never a matter of indifference to me at this time. To fall into disgrace with MacBride would expose me both to punishment from pro-MacBride people and – more formidable within the service – reprisals from anti-MacBride people who resented my previous advancement under MacBride. I could not be dismissed or reduced in rank, but I could be given some uncomfortable foreign posting, knowing that I would be left to rot there, both under MacBride and any probable successor to MacBride. To have been favoured by MacBride and then be dropped by him was not a promising career option. So I accepted the post of managing director of the Irish News Agency and MacBride relaxed. But I accepted with the intention of taking literally MacBride's public assurances that the agency would be independent of government, and ignoring what I knew to be his dissimulated intention that it should be a journalistic vehicle for anti-partition propaganda.

* * *

Early in 1950, the board of the Irish News Agency held its first meeting. The board consisted of Roger Greene (chairman) myself (managing director) and three ordinary members: Noel Hartnett, Robert Brennan, and Peadar O'Curry. Roger Greene was probably recommended by the Taoiseach and MacBride's acceptance of him was probably an effort to keep the coalition solid behind the agency, which was in fact an idea of MacBride's own. Roger was a very successful lawyer and businessman, whose attitude to MacBride was politely suspicious. Knowing my official closeness to MacBride, he was initially suspicious of me also but when he found that I wasn't trying to impose MacBride's ideas on the agency we became close friends and allies.

Apart from the chairman and managing director, the most significant other member of the Board was Noel Hartnett. Noel was still formally a member of MacBride's party but was in fact at this stage MacBride's deadly enemy; however, very few people were aware of that enmity at this time. Among those not in the know were the two remaining members of the Board: Peadar O'Curry and Robert Brennan. O'Curry was editor of the Catholic weekly paper *The Standard.* Brennan had been Minister Plenipotentiary in Washington – the age of ambassadors everywhere had not yet dawned – and was known to have the confidence of Eamon de Valera. Together, O'Curry and Brennan represented MacBride's by now rather wistful yearning to be reconciled with the two most powerful forces in Ireland: the Catholic Church and Fianna Fáil.

At its first meeting, with no argument and very little discussion, the board took the decision that the INA should be a *bona fide* news agency, and not either a features agency or a propaganda instrument. The motion that this was to be the basic policy was proposed by Roger Greene and seconded by myself. It was immediately and fully supported by Noel Hartnett. Noel, had he been chairman, as originally intended, and on good terms with MacBride, would have run INA as a propaganda outfit. But by now Hartnett was devoting himself heart and soul to thwarting and tormenting Seán MacBride, and turning INA into something its creator had not intended it to be seemed to be a promising move in the thwarting and tormenting business.

Seeing our motion supported by Hartnett, and not knowing of the MacBride-Hartnett rift, O'Curry and Brennan supposed that our motion was known to and approved by MacBride. They therefore saw no difficulty in making the decision to run a *bona fide* news agency a unanimous one.

When the decision was announced, I was expecting a call from MacBride, followed by a difficult interview, but neither materialised. I think this was probably mainly due to Clann na Poblachta's internal troubles. MacBride knew Hartnett was spoiling for a fight and interference by MacBride with the first decision – and a unanimous one – by a board which MacBride himself had just appointed would have provided Hartnett with ideal ground on which to challenge MacBride. So MacBride did not react, nor did he ever afterwards make any attempt to influence the decisions of the agency. In fact, he distanced himself from the agency, to our great relief.

As a result of my role with the agency – which in the foundation period was to take up most of my time – I had in fact by now largely escaped MacBride's control. I was still in charge of the Information Section at headquarters, but anti-partition propaganda was now defined and controlled by Frank Gallagher, Dev's propaganda agent, and our role in External Affairs was now confined to the distribution of the Gallagher product – sending "bundles of booklets to Bootle" as I later defined our share of the operation. This business neither required nor received much of my personal attention. So to a great extent I was already emancipated from MacBride's personal control. And this was exceedingly refreshing, by the stage now reached.

* * *

Roger and I were determined to run a genuine news agency. We knew this would prove a difficult task, but it proved even more difficult than we had anticipated. The most formidable difficulties were structural. All the other European countries had their own national news agencies. Ireland didn't. Why? When we looked into that, we soon found the disconcerting answer. Ireland didn't have a news agency of its own, because all the Irish newspapers already belonged to a news agency which was based in London: the Press Association. This was a survival from a previous historical period, outlived in most other respects. Throughout most of the 19th century, and the opening part of the 20th – the period of the United Kingdom of Great Britain and Ireland – the Press Association had been in effect the national news agency of that United Kingdom. It gathered news from all over the United Kingdom and circulated the news to all the papers of the United Kingdom. Reuter's – closely linked to the Press Association members and also drawing on the Press Association services – distributed throughout the world such news from the United Kingdom as it thought would interest readers overseas and also supplied world news to British (including Irish) newspapers.

All that was routine, when Ireland was part of the United Kingdom of Great Britain and Ireland. What is rather remarkable is that when nationalist Ireland – first as the Irish Free State and then as the Republic of Ireland – left the United Kingdom, the newspapers of the new state continued, as before, to be part of the Press Association. The relationship held, even after de Valera's 1937 Constitution weakened many other relations with the United Kingdom almost to vanishing point. The press relationship survived even the strain of Irish neutrality during the Second World War, and the pressures of Irish wartime censorship. And finally the relationship survived both the Declaration of the Republic in 1947 and the nationalist outpourings that followed it. Most of the newspapers joined in the howls of anti-British rage that followed the Ireland Act, but they quietly chose to remain in the Press Association dominated by the national oppressor.

Membership of the Press Association in fact represented one aspect of the national ambivalence towards Britain. On the one hand, we felt betrayed and oppressed by Britain; on the other hand we felt both comfortable and rather proud to be still part of a great national British institution. Habit came into it too, and trust. At least we knew where we were with the Press Association. But where might we be with a new Irish national news agency, especially one founded by Seán MacBride?

Before launching the Irish News Agency, Seán MacBride had tried to overcome the resistance of the proprietors of the Irish newspapers to the idea of a national news agency on European continental lines. But he had altogether failed to sell the idea, and went ahead with the rather forlorn hope of an Irish News Agency, established by governmental fiat and without the active support of the Irish national press. The Irish newspapers did not oppose the Irish News Agency – after all, it gave employment to Irish journalists – but neither did they rally around it. They agreed to take the INA's news service – once established – and to pay by the line for any material used, but from there on we were on our own.

During the early months of the INA's existence, Roger and I travelled quite a lot, meeting news agency people in Western Europe and the United States. We fairly soon found that business opportunities for the agency were very limited: indeed that they narrowed down to just one serious opportunity, as we shall see. But we enjoyed the exploration and we enjoyed one another's company. I remember in particular, early on, a visit to Rome, quite unproductive from a business point of view, but memorable for other reasons.

In Rome we were welcomed with surprising warmth by Joe Walshe. MacBride had made Joe Ambassador to the Vatican, partly because Joe's past record had caused him to be distrusted by republicans but partly also in the hope that Joe's presence in Rome and his connections there might facilitate MacBride's pet project of reconciling republicanism and Catholicism. To me personally, Joe was most agreeable when he met us in Rome: something which had never been the case before. I soon found the rather disconcerting but diverting reason. Joe had disliked me partly because he thought I might be a communist. He still thought so, but this had now actually become a point in my favour, as a result of a distressing Roman experience which had hit Joe quite unexpectedly.

The experience was as follows: Joe's ambassadorial residence in Rome was a rather splendid palazzo, the Villa Spada, atop the Janiculan Hill. The Villa Spada had a swimming-pool: important to Joe because he had a heart condition, for which regular swimming was considered beneficial. But alas!

Joe soon found he could make no use of his pool. The reason for this was that a convent beside the Villa Spada was being used by the nuns as an asylum for fallen women. The windows of the convent looked out over Joe's swimming-pool, and Joe was tormented by the thought that fallen women might be looking on his near-nakedness. So he retreated into the sombre interior of the Villa Spada to brood over his condition.

He tried to use his Vatican connections to get the fallen women accommodated somewhere else, but the nuns seemed to have a lot more real influence than he did. But then he found an altogether unexpected ally: the Italian Communist Party. The Villa Spada had been occupied by Garibaldi's forces about a hundred years before, during the *risorgimento*. Now the Italian communists regarded themselves as the spiritual heirs of the *risorgimento*, just as the French communists regarded themselves as the heirs to the French Revolution. So the Italian communists decided to denounce the presence of fallen women in the vicinity of the Villa Spada, as a Catholic profanation of one of the holy places of the *risorgimento*. In those days, shortly after the end of the Second World War, the Communist Party still had a good deal of clout in Italy, and the Church was alarmed by the party's use against the Church of Italian nationalism under the historic war-cry of the *risorgimento*.

Joe had been greatly cheered up by the emergence of this unexpected ally, and he radically revised his opinion of Italian communists, and indeed of communists in general. Communists, he now thought, were really patriots, misguided indeed in some particulars, but patriots, with sounder values than those awful nuns – and even perhaps than the modern Vatican which had condoned the obscene intrusion sanctioned by the awful nuns. So to me Joe Walshe, once so suspicious, was now cordial.

Roger Greene, like myself, had a Till Eulenspiegel side to his character and this came out during that Roman visit. Roger, though still well capable of getting around, was already seriously ill with an illness which was to kill him a few years later. An infection from drinking contaminated milk had left him with a gaping hole in his side, requiring regular dressing. In Rome he went to a local hospital and I went with him for moral support and some linguistic assistance. Roger was always impeccably dressed and he had an impressive demeanour. Partly as a result of this, a mistake occurred. The hospital, it turned out, was expecting an inspection team from the World Health Organization, and they took the two of us for the inspectors. When the case of mistaken identity became clear to us, Roger decided to defer his dreary dressing and find some amusement instead. He winked at me, I took the drift of his wink and we became the WHO inspection team. And a rigorous inspection team we were. Roger's long experience of hospitals provided him with a good stock of questions to ask, and his resentment of the medical profession supplied him with adequate motivation for being dissatisfied with the answers. At the end he informed the ashen-faced medical team that we would be reporting to WHO that recognition and facilities should be withdrawn from their hospital, pending reorganisation and radical changes of personnel. It must have been a great relief for the unfortunate doctors when the real WHO inspection team showed up, as no doubt they did later that day. But by that time Roger and I had gone on to another hospital, this time for straightforward medical attention to Roger's wound.

In the plane returning to Ireland from that trip, we were threatened with disaster. Five minutes from take-off, the plane filled up with smoke and the pilot announced that we were returning to Ciampino airport, which we had just left. Roger asked me: "Are you frightened, Conor?" "Of course I am," I said. "I'm afraid of being killed. How about you?" "I'm not any more frightened than usual," replied the sick man. "This is about how I feel every hour of every day. Death doesn't feel any nearer at this moment than it usually does."

The plane landed safely.

* * *

After about a year's work, the agency project was beginning to take shape, and both the possibilities and limitations had become fairly clear. We had recruited a highly competent journalistic staff including, as editor, Douglas Gageby, who later became editor of the *Evening Press* and who still later became the most successful editor of the *Irish Times* in the second half of the 20th century. We were well advanced in negotiations with United Press International, one of the major American wire services. The deal beginning to take shape was that the INA would buy the UPI service and distribute it in Ireland, and that the UPI would normally rely solely on the INA for coverage of Ireland. We felt we had achieved the only kind of breakthrough that was actually possible. If indeed – as Arthur Griffith and other nationalists believed – there had been a "paper wall" distorting world coverage of Irish news, that wall had now been breached. Though this was not what Seán Mac Bride had really intended, we believed that he would be happy to claim it as a personal victory and ratify our deal with UPI.

Unfortunately in this respect the days during which Seán MacBride would be in a position to ratify anything were already numbered. The Costello-MacBride government was about to crash in a major crisis over Church-State relations: the greatest such crisis to occur in Ireland since the fall of Charles Stewart Parnell in 1891.

The man who was at the centre of the Church-State storm was the Minister for Health, Dr Noel Browne. Noel Browne was the only member of Clann na Poblachta besides MacBride to be a member of the coalition government.

Dr Browne was a person of passionate social concern, and he was determined to use his position in the coalition to help the poor and disadvantaged. His contribution to the fight against tuberculosis was generally admired, and he followed this up with a Mother-and-Child health scheme, without a means test. This was an expensive measure, and unpopular with the medical profession. For both these reasons, it was also unpopular with the Fine Gael party, much the most important partner in the then government, numerically speaking.

John A Costello, the head of the coalition government, in an effort to quash Browne's scheme, called in the help of the Catholic Church. He must have known, through the doctors, that churchmen had at least serious doubts about the scheme. In Ireland, senior Catholic members of the medical profession have very close relations with the Catholic clergy. This is a country in which theology and obstetrics overlap, and consequently one in which it is both eschatologically and professionally beneficial for doctors – especially but not exclusively, gynaecologists – to be known to be on good terms with the Church. This connection is often rewarding for both sides. On this occasion, it was rewarding to the doctors, but less so to the Church.

As Owen Dudley Edwards has pointed out to me, it was also important that the hospitals be protected from non-Catholic interference. Reverend Mothers ran most of the hospitals.

Costello announced that, in his concern over whether the measure proposed to his government was morally sound, he had consulted the Catholic Archbishop of Dublin, John Charles McQuaid. Dr McQuaid had advised him that a Mother-and-Child health scheme without a means test was "contrary to the moral teaching of the Church." Costello made it known that for him, as a faithful son of the Church, it was unthinkable that he could be responsible for recommending such a measure to the Dáil. He had therefore asked the responsible Minister, Dr Browne, to amend his scheme in such a manner as to bring it into line with the moral teaching of the Church. Seán MacBride, the leader of Dr Browne's party, backed

Costello, and the Clann na Poblachta parliamentary party backed MacBride. (See *Ancestral Voices*, pp 140-141).

In the uproar that followed MacBride was blamed for cynically forsaking his idealistic colleague in order to cling to office at any price. This was a misreading. MacBride's abandonment of Noel Browne was disastrous – for both of them – but it was part and parcel of a policy which MacBride followed steadily throughout his meteoric political career. This was a policy of reconciling the Church and the republican movement: religion and nationalism. Those republicans who followed MacBride's political lead – with whatever theological reservations – believed that the republican cause had suffered at least as much as the Church from past confrontations between the two great forces. That must sedulously be avoided for the future. Thus one of the first public statements of the Costello-MacBride government had been one of grovelling submission to the authority of the Catholic Church, and the coalition government now followed through consistently on that statement. Nobody should have been surprised, although a lot of people were.

So Dr Browne was on his own. He later recalled the harsh questioning to which he had been subjected by strong republicans in the party. The main thing was that the Costello-MacBride government was satisfactory to the republican movement, in its narrow sense, of which the core is always the IRA. Dr Browne was caught in a pincers: religion and nationalism converging.

Dr Browne's leader, Seán MacBride, ordered Dr Browne to comply with the Taoiseach's directive. On Dr Browne's refusal to do so, MacBride demanded and obtained Dr Browne's resignation.

A stormy Dáil debate ensued. On the government side there were fervent assurances of unconditional loyalty to the teachings of the Church. Even Noel Browne professed obedience to "the moral teaching of the Church" but claimed that this had not come explicitly into play.

The only politician to emerge from the whole affair with credit was Eamon de Valera. After the contributions from Fine Gael, and a bitter exchange between MacBride and Browne, de Valera rose in his place and pronounced four words: "We have heard enough". He thereupon led his party silently out of the chamber. His political flair and his profound understanding of Church-State relations in Ireland was never so clearly demonstrated. Most Irish people, whether themselves devout or not, distrusted public professions of devotion coming from politicians. Churchmen themselves were annoyed at being dragged into noisy public debate, over advice privately tendered. The general feeling was that de Valera had demonstrated a maturity and sureness of touch in which the government side and especially MacBride's party was alarmingly lacking.

The government fell, and in the ensuing elections the main loser was MacBride's Clann na Poblachta party. It was reduced from ten seats to two: MacBride himself and Jack McQuillan. The party lingered on for awhile, but petered out completely in the late 1950s. It was clear that MacBride, himself a republican romantic, had grossly overestimated the electoral strength of the republican component, as distinct from the vaguely progressive and faintly anti-clerical component, in the electoral support for his party. The republicans would have to find other channels and they eventually did.

The episode was atypical, in its blatancy. Issues were aired which were, and are, normally discussed behind closed doors. To outsiders, it looked like a case of the Church dictating to the state. It was actually a case of a politician asking for a *public* intervention by the Church, for political reasons, and spectacularly bungling the whole business. This is not the way the culture works and those who went against the grain of the culture paid the penalty. Both the Church and the republican movement operate most successfully by indirection: saying one thing, while implying another, and meaning, perhaps, a third. By the late 20th century, religion and nationalism, the two great forces in the culture, had achieved a highly sophisticated form of intercommunication and interaction along those lines. MacBride, foreign in so many ways, had failed to understand the sophisticated and cryptic aspects of the relationship.

As for Dr Browne, he remained, after the Mother-and-Child debacle, a greatly respected but politically-isolated figure, opposed as he now found himself to be both to the political influence of the Catholic Church and to the republican movement. As the old Fenian John O'Leary had told the young WB Yeats: "In this country a man must have either the Church or the Fenians on his side . . . " Dr Browne, after his Mother-and-Child ordeal, had neither. For an Irish Catholic, a collision with the institutional Catholic Church in the mid-20th century was no light matter. But the other rejection perhaps hurt more. Dr Browne's repudiation at the hands of his own leader and his republican colleagues had been peculiarly painful to him. Long afterwards, in 1969-70, he and I, being then members of the Parliamentary Labour Party, shared an office in Leinster House with two other Labour Party TDs. One day in the summer of 1970 I was sitting in that office, writing something about the ominous forces then taking shape in and around Northern Ireland, when Noel Browne came in. Noel and I already had our political differences (not relevant here) but I was aware that we had one important thing in common: both of us had felt constrained to ignore John O'Leary's politic and weighty advice. On an impulse, I put to Noel the question:

"Noel, if you were obliged to choose between Holy Mother Church and Cathleen Ní Houlihan, which of the two would you prefer?"

Without an instant's hesitation, Noel Browne replied: "Holy Mother Church, every time!"

Me too.

* * *

Shortly after MacBride's fall, I wrote a comment on his career which appeared anonymously in a local periodical *The Leader* which I insert here:

When he laughs, which he does often, his skin, of very good quality parchment, cackles into a complex system of fine folds; the remarkable eyes, prominent and yet recessed, like those of some mad monk of romance, flicker with the persuasions of gaiety: the chuckle of that exotic uvula conspires with the bandit eyebrows, giving a touch of *diablerie* to what you may be very sure is a most harmless witticism. The total effect is rather impressive and not at all amusing. You do not feel as if you had taken part in an exchange of pleasantries: you feel more as if you had been exposed to the action of an unknown ray.

In repose, or in that expression of utter desolation which takes the place of reposes, the face is more attractive, if not more reassuring. The great tragic eyes shine out from a skull in which they seem the only living things: the rest of the almost fleshless face with its high forehead and cheekbones, its thin curved nose, is such that you feel in the presence of an apparition. It is as if one of those death-masks, of Tone or of Emmett, which are to be found in glass cases in certain patriotic houses, were to open its eyes and look out at you.

The contrast between the two faces is, in the strict sense, dramatic: these are the masks of Comedy and Tragedy, and the man who carries them both with such an air could, one imagines, have been a great actor. There are those who say that this is no hypothesis, that he is in fact constantly acting a part: poseur, they say, and, most inappropriately, "playboy". This gibe, although it often merely voices the envy of the inarticulate and drab, is not altogether unjust. The professions of law, politics and diplomacy are not conducive to unconditional sincerity. One who brings to these professions, in addition, something of the actor's temperament, and a foreign accent,

The Sheehy family cicra 1895. Front row: the author's mother, Kathleen, and grandmother Bessie. Middle row: his great-uncle Eugene, aunt Hanna, grandfather David, aunt Margaret, and aunt Mary. Back row: his uncles Eugene and Richard.

Conor's mother, before he was born.

Tom Kettle.

Conor O Brien (left) with my father, on the eve of Conor O Brien's round
the world voyage on the *Saoirse* (June 1923).

Joseph Walshe, Secretary of the Department of External Affairs leaving Government
Buildings, Dublin ahead of (from right): Prime Minister de Valera and Cardinal Lauri.

Roger Greene and CCO'B, outside St Peter's, Rome.

CCO'B with Kate, then aged about three.

Son Donal, with his daughter Sarah, at Cape Cod.

Kate (left) and Fedelma, in a boat on the Seine at La Frette.

Daughter Fedelma, on her graduation.

Conor and Máire, wedding picture.

Left to right: George Ivan Smith, Máire, Conor and Ralph Bunche.

Left to right: CCO'B, Margaret Mac Entee, Máire, Seán Mac Entee: outside our home in Howth (Whitewater) just after our marriage in New York.

may be expected to fall occasionally a little short of rugged candour. Mr MacBride is hardly so often amused, or so affectionate towards his interlocutor, as outward appearances suggest. "Switching on the charm," say his critics sourly, to which his friends might reply – indeed the remark has been attributed to Mr Con Lehane – that it would be a pity for one who controls so much candle-power not to let the light of his countenance be seen from time to time. Yet, if the Comic mask, with its whole range of social expressions, is assumed, the same is certainly not true of the face in sadness: that is, in reality, not a mask at all, but the face itself. The relevant myth is not that of the Actor, who plays any part at will, but that of the Clown. On a superficial view this comparison seems wild: there is not the faintest suggestion of buffonery about this distinguished ex-Foreign Minister, on whom the adjective "suave" has been stamped in indelible printer's ink. Yet – apart from the stereotype of the clown who laughs while his heart is breaking – acute observers, who know him well, have seen in that drawn and humourless face an extraordinary resemblance to Charlie Chaplin. Mr MacBride, like Charlie, looks wistfully at the world: he is full of unrequited loves – for the Six Counties, for journalists, for the Fianna Fáil party, for the constituency of Dublin South-West. He often, especially in the Dáil, pleads his case, not like the lawyer that he is, but like the tramp, bowler-hatted, twisty-footed, before the circus giant or the haughty maiden. Some of his speeches would indeed have been better if, like Charlie's, they had been confided to the medium of the silent screen. No matter, he implores, he entreats, bankers to break the link with sterling, Orangemen the link with Crown. The maiden turns her back, the giant lumbers threateningly, the hero breaks into a run. Confronted with bulky grim realities, Charlie is often a sad figure. But there is also a dream-world – O Salon de l'Horloge, O Palais de la Muette! – in which he is a brilliantly successful statesman, elegant, eloquent, strolling with the leaders of Europe; what he is doing is not very clear, but with what distinction he does it! Now he is addressing the Congress of the United States: the representatives of the greatest nation on earth are on their feet denouncing the Partition of Ireland, the television cameras are whirring, it is an unheard-of scene, he is being carried shoulder high by the nine Justices of the Supreme Court along the road to Lincoln's tomb, he has saved his country! The tramp stirs uneasily on his bench and awakes to the cold winds of Crumlin.

The dream was not, of course, all a dream, nor did the hero always run before the giant; the myth of the Clown does not explain the whole character, but it gives an essential clue. Yet there are many, both friends and enemies, who would find it absurdly irrelevant. Dr Noel Browne, for instance, who gave prolonged and anxious study to the character, could find nothing pathetic or romantic in it. He saw it, certainly, as "two-faced," and eventually informed the public of the fact, but the two faces which he saw are not those which we have here described, the tragic Clown, with and without his mask. He saw, instead, that figure of melodrama, the cold and deliberate hypocrite, the Machiavellian who assumes a mask of idealism. Politicians have long accused each other of Machiavellism; this is a cliché of invective rather than a contribution to political psychology. But when Dr Browne said, as he did in his letter of resignation from the Inter-Party Government, that he had had "a bitter experience" of Mr MacBride's "cruel and authoritarian mind," his words had a more exact ring. They accord, it must be admitted, but ill with the Chaplinesque conception of Mr MacBride's character, and they fit certain known elements in his career. It is more than plausible that the underground commander, the aggressive cross-examination lawyer, the politician who insists on being known as "the Leader," should be authoritarian and perhaps even apparently cruel. This thin-lipped fanatic whose very laughter is somewhat chilling, who is to his immediate following almost a god, how could we have seen him as a Clown? We may say that we can conceive of a cruel Clown, one who laughs while other peoples' hearts break, that even an authoritarian Chaplin is not quite unimaginable, when one has seen *The Great Dictator*.

The word is like a knell; at any rate it has been so for Mr MacBride. It was the accusation of dictatorial methods – with the implication that he was aiming at an actual dictatorship – which split and ruined his party and overthrew the Government to which he belonged. "It is my fervent hope," wrote Dr Browne in his best-known contribution to English prose, "that the destiny of this country will never be fully placed in your hands because it would, in my view, mean the destruction of all those ideals which are part and parcel of Christian democracy." Leaving aside the philosophical question of whether one can destroy ideals – and whether Mr MacBride is more efficacious than the gates of Hell – we may say, with Antony, that if it were so, it were a grievous fault. But is it so? There is probably something in the accusation of dictatorial methods. Mr MacBride was not, as Dr Browne reminded us, used to democratic politics; it was said of him, probably with justice, that he treated his Civil Servants as if they were members of his party, and the members of his party as if they were Civil Servants. Even this, exasperating though it must have been to all concerned, was probably not so much a "method" as an effect of temperament. Mr MacBride's charismatic radiations do not affect a wide field, but within a restricted danger area – the danger is to the wits – they are exceedingly intense; most of the people around him were inclined to do what he told them, should the sky fall, which it did. There were, as the world knows, those who revolted. Of Mr

Noel Hartnett it would be too weak to say that he shook off the yoke; he bolted with the yoke between his teeth. Such exploits do not disprove the existence of a dictatorial spirit in Mr MacBride. True, Captain Cowan did not meet the fate of Captain Roehm, but then Mr MacBride did not have the power, even if he had the will, to constitute himself, like Hitler, as the Supreme Court of the nation. Certainly the new, purged, party follows its leader with uncritical devotion, unsupported by either talent or numbers. Before the war, the National Socialist Party of Germany published a very glossy book containing portraits of the principal Nazis, with such captions as "a constructive organizer", "the great orator", "the hero of the youth", and so on. Under one portrait, however – that of Hess – the caption read simply "Distinguished by his dog-like fidelity to the Fuehrer". If Clann na Poblachta were so unwise as to publish such a portrait-gallery it would, at least, be saved the expense of having to print more than one caption.

Many good democrats have been dictatorial in their own circle, however, and there is no real evidence that Mr MacBride wishes anything but well to our democratic state. His main achievement – apart from giving the Fianna Fáil Government a short holiday – was to get the Commonwealth party to take Ireland out of the Commonwealth. The value of that achievement, as Mr Costello explained, was that it "took the gun out of politics". That is to say that it weakened, and was intended to weaken the power of the IRA which, if Mr MacBride was a conspirator, was the only organisation which could have enabled him to seize power. Certainly the organisation which he weakened would have been more use to a plotter than the organisation which he did so much to build up: the Department of External Affairs. One senses somehow that on the Night of the Long Knives, the inhabitants of Iveagh House will manage to be among those who neither knife nor – above all – are knifed. True, he managed, with the aid of General Marshall, to induce these gentlemen to put their fingers into the pies of various other Departments – pies from which they were hastily withdrawn when Mr Lemass and Mr MacEntee came riding back – and he got Mr Blowick to plant a great deal of Sithca Spruce. He also – and it was not an inconsiderable achievement – got the money for Dr Browne to build his hospitals, and he seems to have given Dr Browne a good deal of advice, not all of it on photographic and ecclesiastical subjects. In the sphere of justice – and notoriously the main interest of the plotter – his interventions were aimed at saving men from the gallows. It is reliably told that, at one of the last Cabinet meeting before the election which led to the fall of the Inter-party Government, Mr MacBride spent many hours of Government time struggling for the reprieve of a man who had been condemned to death. The young Nero, of course, is said to have wept as he signed a death sentence, but then he did sign it, whereas Mr MacBride, on this occasion, as so often before, got his man off.

Mr MacBride is much more like Jan Masaryk than he is like Nero or Hitler or any of those apocalyptic tyrants. He is not a dictator, he is, at worst, one of those through whom dictatorships occur. In such a man the danger to democracy lies not in his strength but in his weakness, and his over-confidence. He thinks he is bridging gulfs that are unbridgeable; he thinks that hard work is a substitute for sound judgement; he thinks he is using people who are really using him. These were the gifts that led to the *debacle*, when he and his young rival, locked in a death-struggle, like Holmes and Dr Moriarty, rolled together into the political abyss.

What symbol for so complex a man? One thinks, even more than of Chaplin, of Don Quixote. (And, incidentally, how fine it would be to have a film in which Chaplin would be both Quixote and Sancho Panza.) "Quixote" is a term of abuse among the marxists – worse than "lackey" but better than "bandit" – but we use "Quixote" rightly in a spirit of kindly criticism. The gaunt knight, wistful yet severe, in the dilapidated La Mancha of Roebuck, has been reading tales of chivalry, from Standish O'Grady to Patrick Pearse. He will rescue the fair lady Cathleen Ní Houlihan from the castle Discrimination, where the British giant, Gerrymandering, holds her thrall. The ogre Sterling bars the way with his famous Link, which will have snapped. The good fairies from America will help to accomplish this. (They have all been expelled from the State Department, but Quixote does not know this.) He saddles his spavined mare, Poblaclante, and gallops down the drive. But something is missing. He calls aloud for Sancho Panza. But Sancho will never come again. Sancho has locked himself into the lodge.

I was rather pleased with this little piece at the time. Looking back on the occasion, and knowing more about MacBride's terrible family history. I am a bit ashamed of my piece, which did not come well from a person whose career had profited greatly from serving MacBride, in pursuit of obsessions which I came to regard as absurd, but which I served for a time even after I came to see them in that light. MacBride had been like Don Quixote, nobly pursuing fantastic obsessions. But I had been like Sancho Panza hoping that in serving his master in his wild career, he might attain the governorship of an island. But unlike Sancho Panza I not merely obtained from my master the civil service equivalent of the governorship of an island, but retained that prize after my master's fall. So it ill became me to laugh at my master when at last he crashed down, while I remained safely in possession of what I had gained through him.

6

INTERLUDE: FRANK AIKEN TO
LIAM COSGROVE, 1950-1955

THE MACBRIDE YEARS LEFT FEW IMMEDIATELY PERCEPTIBLE TRACES IN IRISH
politics, although MacBride's tacit alliance with Sinn Féin-IRA did provide
a tentative precedent for more momentous transactions of similar tendency
more than a quarter of a century later. But there was one significant and
permanent change within the administration, which had a bearing on my
own life and career. Fianna Fáil, on returning to office, did not go back to
the old system whereby the Taoiseach ran External Affairs, along with his
own Department, from Merrion Street. Whatever else MacBride may have
done, he had made the Department of External Affairs bulk larger in the
national consciousness than it had done before, and Fianna Fáil, on
returning to office, decided that the Department should have a minister all
of its own.

The new minister was Frank Aiken who – along with Seán Lemass – was
one of de Valera's two most trusted senior associates. Frank Aiken had
become Chief of Staff of the post-Treaty IRA, after the death of Liam
Lynch, at a time when the republican side was clearly losing the civil war of
1922-3. Immediately after becoming Chief of Staff, Aiken had ordered the
IRA to dump their arms, thus ending the civil war. It was known that this
order had the full approval of Eamon de Valera and the order was

immediately carried out, though a minority of republicans, including Seán MacBride, protested against the decision.

I think many of my colleagues assumed that, once Aiken took office, I – who had been so close to MacBride, deeply distrusted by Fianna Fáil – would be transferred out of Information to some less sensitive and more obscure responsibilities. But this did not happen.

Very shortly after becoming Minister, Aiken summoned me to his office where we had what was, for me, a most enjoyable and heartening conversation. Aiken had just read my book, *Parnell and His Party*. He liked it very much and told me so. He made it clear that he wanted me to carry on as Head of Information and to work as closely to him as formerly I had worked for MacBride. But the spirit of my instructions would be very different. There would be no more of what his colleague Seán MacEntee called the "sore thumb", always going on against the British about the injustice of partition and generally making trouble for them. He didn't want to attack partition, as such, but he did want to expose the undemocratic disabilities under which the nationalist population of Northern Ireland then suffered. These disabilities were limited but real, consisting mainly of discrimination against them in housing and allocation of local government jobs, and of electoral discrimination in some areas. Aiken believed that if these abuses were exposed in a film, this would put pressure on the British to get rid of the abuses in question. He wanted me to go to Derry and produce a film showing up the abuses.

This idea seemed to make a lot more sense than the kind of thing MacBride had been up to, but I could still see a snag. I said that if I went to Derry for that purpose, the local unionists would soon become aware of what I was up to, and then I would be likely to be flung into the River Foyle.

At this Aiken laughed heartily and told me the following anecdote: at the height of the "Troubles", probably late in 1920, Aiken and two other IRA volunteers, Dan Breen and Oscar Traynor, had carried out some operation in Co Louth and then had to escape in a side-car travelling at a high speed over bad, mountainous roads. During their flight, Dan Breen fell out of the side-car onto the rocky road. He was apparently unconscious. Aiken and Traynor got out and had a look at him.

"I think poor Dan is finished," said Aiken.

"He is," said Traynor, "Very sad . . . but why don't we take him a few miles North, across the Border, put a few bullets into him, and make it an enemy atrocity?"

162

At this point, Dan Breen sat up in the middle of the road and said: "I wouldn't put it past ye, ye pair of bastards ye!"

By the period of his life when I knew him, Aiken had become virtually a pacifist, but all the same this reminiscence of his bellicose youth seemed somehow to cheer him up.

In the event, Aiken did not go ahead with the film about Northern Ireland. I think Seán Lemass, who was already contemplating the kind of rapprochement with Ulster unionism that was to be attempted in 1965 with Terence O'Neill, objected to any kind of anti-unionist propaganda. Freddie Boland, as Secretary of External Affairs, would have quietly discouraged such ideas and would have kept Lemass discreetly informed about any tendencies in that direction.

Frank Aiken did, however, make use of my services in Northern Ireland in two ways: to bring foreign journalists into contact with Northern nationalists, and to carry his advice to Northern nationalists as to their relations with Northern unionists.

The first form of activity was relatively straightforward.

In practice at this time – when the interest of the media in all aspects of Ireland was languid – it was not unusual for a foreign journalist to come to Belfast, to get "Northern Ireland's side" and then come to Dublin for "the Republic's side". In Dublin the journalist would see me and if I found, as I usually did, that his contacts in Belfast had been exclusively Protestant and unionist, and if it seemed sufficiently important, I would take him to meet Catholic and nationalist leaders, usually in Belfast, Derry, Armagh and Omagh – renewing my own contacts there at the same time.

I remember in particular, from one journey (in 1952 I think) various epiphanies. I was acting as guide to an English Jesuit, Father Wingfield-Digby, who was carrying out an enquiry for his Order into the condition of Catholics in Northern Ireland.

In Armagh, Senator JG Lennon showed us the electoral map of the city, providing the necessary key of religious denominations by area, and touring the city boundary. What he showed us was a classical gerrymander, thorough to the point of pedantry: at one point the city boundary, following the line of a certain terrace, suddenly skipped behind the back-gardens of three houses, homes of Catholics. Gerry Lennon explained these things, with controlled indignation, but at the same time a faint touch of local pride: it was not everywhere you could see the like of this abomination. But Father Wingfield-Digby was simply disgusted by such an example of rustic bigotry. "Good Heavens!" he exclaimed. "How perfectly stupid!" Gerry Lennon looked sourly at the Jesuit. "In the name of God," he asked, "what's *stupid* about it?"

Later that day, in Derry, I brought Father Wingfield-Digby to see Mr Eddie McAteer, MP, and some of his friends. The Jesuit was already a bit worried at this stage about the tendency for politics and religion to run together when they should, he thought, be separate. He wanted to know, in the case of Derry, for example, how many Catholic unionists there were, and how many Protestant nationalists.

Mr McAteer and his friends looked at one another: the Jesuit might have been enquiring as to the prevalence of unicorns in the vicinity. But they applied their minds to the question. There had been a Catholic unionist – and they named him – but the Protestants snubbed him of course, and the Catholics boycotted him, and he gave up. Protestant nationalists? Well. Such indeed there might well be. Professor – , for example, at Magee College, a thoroughly decent man: "He must be a nationalist really, but of course he calls himself a communist. It's safer, you see." This was at the height of the McCarthy period in America.

From Derry we drove back to Dublin. When we crossed the border, the Jesuit sighed with satisfaction. "It feels like coming home," he said. It was an odd remark, since he was leaving the United Kingdom, to which he belonged, and entering a foreign country. Yet he was a very English Englishman, and I had the impression from him that he didn't mean that the Republic was like home because it was Catholic, and so home for Jesuits. I think he meant that the Republic was more English than Northern Ireland.

Crossing Monaghan the Jesuit looked at his notes. He still seemed troubled. He said what fine people Mr Lennon, Mr McAteer and their friends were. I agreed. "Just one thing," said Father Wingfield-Digby. "Can you be quite sure they're . . . well . . . loyal?"

I could have said they were as loyal as 16th century English Jesuits, or 20th century western communists: that is, fanatically loyal to something other than the state in which they lived. But it hardly seemed worthwhile.

I never learned what Father Wingfield-Digby reported. I expect it was to the effect that the disabilities of the Northern Catholics were real, but due, not to their religious faith, but to their misplaced political allegiance. No action. (See my *States of Ireland* [1972]).

The second aspect of my mission to Northern Ireland was more strictly political. Its results were almost entirely negative but it brought me into contact with some aspects of Catholic life in Northern Ireland which were not well understood in the South.

I remember one discouraging Northern journey, taken on the instructions of Frank Aiken. The object was to convey to various nationalist/anti-unionist/Catholic leaders and publicists the wish of Mr Aiken and the Dublin Government that they should take a more active part in public life, cease to boycott local official ceremonies, and associate with Protestants to a greater extent. Most of them heard me with resignation, but without manifest assent. A typical comment I heard from Eddie McAteer was that, although Frank Aiken had been born in Armagh, he had been away from it a long time. There was one man, however, a local chieftain in a remote village in a desolate hilly part of South Armagh who made no reply at all to my message. He was sitting in front of his little shop and looking out across the glen in the stillness of the summer evening. Uneasily, to break the long silence which followed my remarks, I asked him whether there were many Protestants in the district. Then he spoke, quietly: "There's only one Protestant in this townland. And with the help of God, we'll have him out of it by Christmas."

As a result of my frequent and close contacts with Frank Aiken, I conceived a great respect for him, which was to increase at a later stage, when I worked with him even more closely at the United Nations. He made some mistakes, but he was a very serious and thoughtful man, profoundly ecumenical by disposition, bordering on pacifism, and always aware, even in those relatively peaceful days, of the explosive potential of sectarian-political relations in Northern Ireland.

I had one disappointment with Aiken, and this concerned the future of the Irish News Agency. When the new government took over in June 1959, headed by Seán Lemass, the draft contract between INA and United Press International was due to be signed. I explained to Aiken what was involved. Aiken thought for a while and then said: "Take a chance on it." So we did, and the contract was signed. Then the Lemass government, to which Aiken belonged, decided to wind up the agency (while compensating UPI for the termination of the contract). For a fairly short time I was quite bitter against Aiken for – as it seemed to me – letting me down. I came to see later that this was quite unjust. I have no doubt that Aiken did make a case in cabinet. But the INA was the brainchild of Seán MacBride, and – after the Mother-and-Child debacle – MacBride was the most unpopular politician in the country, leader of a party about to be extinguished altogether at the next following election. So, with MacBride politically gone, his brain-child could not be expected to survive very long.

This occurred at a difficult time in my life, for my marriage with Christine was on the verge of breaking up. It was held together indeed at this point only by concern for the feelings and future of our three children, whom we both loved. Might it be possible somehow to hold the marriage together? We both convinced ourselves morosely enough that somehow it might. The end of the news agency seemed to offer an opportunity for a clear break. Despite the difficult row over the news agency, I was still in high favour with Aiken, and knew I could get a good foreign posting if I applied for one. Around this time the post of Counsellor in the Embassy at Paris – regarded as one of the cushiest jobs in the Irish Foreign Service – fell vacant. With Christine's agreement I applied for this posting and got it. Thus began the most miserable fifteen months of my life to date.

*　*　*

In my sad preoccupations of this period I had not given sufficient attention to the fact that the Irish Ambassador in Paris – my boss to be – was William P Fay. Now this Fay, though a decent enough man at least in his motivations, was a martyr to what is known as the *morbus diplomaticus*, the diplomatic disease. The *morbus diplomaticus* is pomposity. Even at home in Dublin – not very propitious territory for manifestations of the *morbus* – Fay had shown alarming symptoms of this propensity. There had been a memorable visit to Dublin, shortly after the war, by Anthony Eden, recently Foreign Secretary of the United Kingdom. The visit sent Fay into a tizzy. He was Chief of Protocol at the time and he called in all the Third Secretaries for what turned out to be a sartorial inspection. We had to be prepared, said Fay, to appear before the best-dressed diplomatist in Europe. Some of us were wearing fountain pens in our breast-pockets, a petty-bourgeois manifestation sternly suppressed by Fay. Skentelbery, who was wearing a fairly bright yellow suit, was sent home to change into something suitably dark. Then when Sir Anthony duly arrived, he was found to be wearing a yellow suit, of a shade several shades brighter than poor Skentelbery's. This cheered everybody up, except Fay.

In Dublin, Fay was generally regarded as preposterous and was the subject of mild jokes, one being a play on his name: "Willie Pee or won't he?" But when he became Ambassador in Paris, the *morbus* flourished oppressively, as I found in my first meeting with him, shortly after my arrival there. He invited me to a dinner he was giving – giving dinners was his principal preoccupation. I excused myself because of a previous engagement. Bill's complexion changed from its usual puce to a darker shade of purple. After a pause he said: "I am the personal representative of the President of Ireland in this country. I could say that an invitation from me is the equivalent of a Presidential Command." He paused and looked at me. I said nothing. Then he said, with a magnanimous air, "But I won't say that," and dismissed me.

But although pompous, Bill was not a man to bear a grudge. It was his wife Lillian's pomposity that had a bitter strain. She became my enemy, and made life unpleasant for me in a variety of little ways. All in all, a bad start to a trying period.

There was, however, some light relief, and occasional benign intervals. Much of the light relief was provided by Bill's use of the French language, colliding as it did with the susceptibilities of the titled French guests whom it was his principal pleasure to entertain. Bill assumed that being a model European gentleman, he must speak French perfectly. But as he had never taken the trouble to learn the language properly he was constantly administering shocks, without being aware of this. Normally, small shocks. Thus when confiding a newly-arrived lady guest to the care of one of his servants, Bill would say loudly: *"Déshabillez Madame!"* meaning "Strip, Madame!", in place of the current French formula, *"Débarassez Madam,"* meaning, "Take Madame's coat."

One of Bill's errors was of more epic proportions. Bill was describing, with sentimental enthusiasm, a visit by then President René Coty to some small French town where a little girl had presented the President with a bouquet. Bill's account of this little episode ended with the words: *"Et quand le Président a baisé la petite fille, les applaudissements étaient énormes!"*

The dinner guests looked at one another in horror, not realising that Bill had made an elementary linguistic mistake. In French *baiser*, the noun, means a kiss. But *baiser* the verb, means something quite different. So what Bill's stunned guests were hearing him say was: "And when the President fucked the little girl, the applause was enormous!"

Listening to one's Ambassador making a fool of himself was occasionally diverting but in the long run only added to the general depression. But there was one unexpected moment of relief, in the shape of a visit from Seán MacBride, who had now become Secretary General of the International Commission of Jurists. The Ambassador entertained

MacBride to dinner at his residence and had me along as the only other guest; I had an idea Fay didn't want too many people to know that he had entertained MacBride, who was out of favour with the government at home. The dinner itself was extremely tedious. Fay did almost all the talking and there were only two topics. One consisted of anecdotes about Bill's titled friends in Paris. The anecdotes were all pointless in themselves, serving only as vehicles for the introduction of the titles. The other topic consisted of accounts of Bill's charitable work as a member of the Irish Catholic Society of St Vincent de Paul, among the poor of Paris. He went on quite a lot about a visit he had paid to a poor, old, female invalid and how grateful she had been for his attention. Understandably, MacBride stood up to leave as soon as he decently could. I drove him to the airport.

As we drove, both of us were silent for a while. Then MacBride suddenly spoke, slowly and in a sepulchral tone. He said "Conor . . . can you imagine anything worse . . . than being old . . . and poor . . . and sick . . . and visited by Bill Fay?"

I said at once that I could indeed imagine nothing worse than such a visit in such circumstances. I was cheered and pleased by MacBride's remark, and by the ready convergence of our views of Ambassador Fay. Pleased, but also surprised. This was the first time I had ever heard MacBride make a fully spontaneous remark. All our many long conversations in Dublin had been set to a political agenda, and motivated by a political purpose. Looking back on it now, I can see that MacBride, as Minister in Dublin, had been doomed to appease ghosts, following the agenda prescribed by Patrick Pearse in *Christmas Day, 1915*: "There is only one way to appease a ghost. You must do the thing it asks you. The ghosts of a nation sometimes ask very big things and they must be appeased, whatever the cost."

Throughout his period in office in Dublin, MacBride had been appeasing the ghosts of a nation, at a high cost to himself as a person. But by driving him from office and into exile, the Irish people had set MacBride free for a time at least from the ghost-appeasing business. He was now free to be his natural, humorous and pleasant self. It was a real pleasure to meet him, without the attendant ghosts, and it consoled me for many things.

In any case, the sad period of my Parisian exile was now drawing to an end. Ireland had been kept out of the United Nations from its foundation by a Soviet veto – for having being neutral in the Second World War after the Soviet Union ceased to be – but was admitted to the UN under a package deal in 1955. I was brought home from Paris and put in charge of a reconstructed political section at headquarters, with responsibility for relations with the United Nations. I was greatly pleased by the change. I saw myself as having challenging work ahead of me, and the opportunity of starting something new.

My personal life was still in quite a bad way, but had at least assumed a clearer and more stable shape. In Paris, we had both been miserable in separate ways and we were both glad that chapter was ending. For a time we would share the outward semblance of a marriage for the sake of the children, but in reality we would go our separate ways. All this was painful, but the worst of the pain was behind us, along with the uncertainty and the false and fading hopes. As I went home, I felt more grown-up than I had been when I had gone out. I also felt that I had left behind the most miserable long period of my life (there had been an even more miserable *short* period, right after my father's death). And indeed, in the more than fifty years that have passed since then, I never again experienced anything nearly as bad in my personal life, until the bereavement of 1998.

7

UNITED NATIONS ONE, 1957

IRELAND HAD BEEN FORMALLY ADMITTED TO THE UN IN 1956 BUT A FULL Irish delegation first took its seat in the General Assembly in the autumn of 1957. As it happened Ireland's entry coincided with a major double crisis in world history. This was caused almost simultaneously by the dissimulated attack on Egypt by Britain, France and Israel, and by Hungary's attempt to leave the Soviet alliance system, followed, after brief hesitation, by Soviet military intervention and the forcible reintegration of Hungary into the Soviet-dominated structures of the Warsaw Pact.

First of all it is necessary to look a little more closely at the structures and working of the UN, and in particular of the General Assembly, as these stood in the period of the dual crisis.

Formally, and according to the declared intentions of the leading founders of the UN – the United States and the Soviet Union – the General Assembly to which all member states belonged from the moment of their admission occupied quite a lowly place in the structures of the UN. The structures were designed to put all major decisions nominally under the control of the Security Council (with limited membership) but in reality under the control of the Five Permanent Members of the Security Council: Britain, China, France, the Soviet Union and the United States. Under the

170

Charter, each of the Permanent Members had the right to a veto in the Security Council, so that no decision could be taken contrary to the declared wishes of any permanent member.

Practice, however led at first to gradual modification, and then to drastic erosion of this position. The process of modification and erosion was led by the Americans. It worked like this: of the five permanent members, Britain and France, being allied to the United States, normally (though not invariably) voted with the United States. After the Chinese revolution, from 1950 on, China's seat at the United Nations was held, not by the people actually in control of the Chinese mainland, but by refugees from the mainland, in control of the island of Taiwan, under the protection of the American Navy. Thus China's vote on the Security Council was in fact controlled by the United States. So, in one way or another, the United States could generally count on the votes of three out of the other four Permanent Members of the Security Council. In this way the Soviet Union, in defence of its own perceived interests, was isolated and so had frequent recourse to the power of veto which it possessed under the Charter.

In the American media this situation came to be habitually referred to as "the Soviet veto" and perceived as a main weakness of the United Nations. The American Right came to see "the Soviet veto" as a result of treachery on the part of communists within the Democratic Party. Around this time – though a little later – I found myself in conversation with a woman in Boston who fervently supported the Republican Party. I began a sentence with the words "the trouble with the UN". The republican cut in magisterially: "The trouble with the United Nations is the veto that the traitor Alger Hiss sold to the Russians at Yalta." Most American republicans saw matters more or less in that light and many Democrats agreed with them.

It was a general American perception, across the political board, that the Security Council was "paralyzed by the Soviet veto". As a result of this perception, American interest in the United Nations had come to concentrate on the General Assembly. In the General Assembly, the Soviets had no veto, and the Americans had (up to 1958) always the necessary two-thirds majority, made up in the main of Latin American and some other delegations, whose votes the United States was in a position to control, through economic and other leverage.

In this condition of affairs, roughly from 1950-1958 – and thus including the period of the dual crisis – many American writers and speakers came to refer to the General Assembly as "the moral conscience of mankind" (in contrast with the Soviet-polluted Security Council). It was a considerable comfort to any American Government, at this stage, to know that it was securely in control of "the moral conscience of mankind" and that it could count on the approval of that organ for any decision it might find it expedient to make.

From 1950 on, "the moral conscience of mankind" had also acquired, through the use of American political power, a kind of political authority not foreseen by the framers of the Charter. In that year Stalin – apparently led by unguarded American rhetoric to believe that the United States had written off Korea – invaded that country. The United States, however, did decide to intervene and – as a result of Soviet carelessness – was able to make its intervention appear as a UN initiative. The Soviet Union was boycotting the Security Council, in protest against what it saw as a bypassing of the Security Council's authority by the Americans. But the Soviet boycott gave the Americans a golden opportunity to bypass "the Soviet veto" and turn the decision already taken by the Americans – to fight against the Russians in Korea – into a UN decision. The fact that the war could now be fought under a blue flag and wearing blue helmets was a political plus for the Americans. America was visibly acting as the world's policeman and upholding world order, and potential critics at home were mostly silenced.

Realising its mistake, the Soviet Union returned to the Security Council and henceforward no further legitimation for America's war against Russia would be forthcoming from that body. But the damage was already done, the blue flags and blue helmets were already in place, and a psychological barrier had been broken. Under American impulsion the General Assembly – with its safe two-thirds – passed the "Uniting for Peace" Resolution, sanctioning the continuation of the war, under United Nations auspices. It is more than doubtful whether the General Assembly possesssed the authority under the Charter to do this. But this hardly mattered by now. By now the blood of the belligerents was up. Maybe the "Uniting for Peace Resolution" involved a de facto modification of the Charter, but if so well and good. The Soviet veto had been bypassed, and it was high time, in an American view in which America's allies acquiesced, though without much enthusiasm.

The "Uniting for Peace Resolution", enacted by a majority of the General Assembly, became, from the point of view of the Western allies, a document with no less authority than the Charter itself, and one to which the Americans could have recourse against the Soviet veto whenever the American government chose to do so. It could have done so, over the Soviet intervention in Hungary, but – for reasons which I shall soon be considering – it chose not to do so.

* * *

Freddy Boland was now Ireland's Permanent Representative at the UN and as a result he normally took the Irish seat on the more important of the two Committees dealing with political affairs: appropriately known as the First Committee. As the second person on the official delegation, I took the seat on the second relevant body, the Special Political Committee. The Special was generally and rightly known as "the crocks' committee". To it were assigned – in order to keep the hands of the First reasonably free – those disputes for which no agreed solution could reasonably be expected. Pre-eminent among these was the Arab-Israel dispute, inscribed on the Special's agenda under the decorous and neutral rubric "The Question of the Palestine Refugees". Historically and habitually, this was the "hottest" debate at the United Nations, as well as the most sterile. By fortune of the alphabet, I found myself in a seat which appeared particularly "hot" – between Israel and Iraq. As a matter of fact this seat did not turn out, when I first took it, to be at all hot. Both my neighbours greeted me in a friendly manner. I soon realised that my arrival, and alphabetic qualification, had the benign effect of relieving both of them from a most uncomfortable neighbour.

I still remember my first intervention on that committee. My only instructions were to avoid giving offence to either of my neighbours. In pursuit of this objective I urged Israel to accept some of the refugees back, subject to security clearance. I advised the Arabs to agree to this, as a basis for agreement and to make peace with Israel on that basis. In retrospect, I regard this, with no great pride, as a pretty typical "Western moderate" UN speech.

As I came out into the corridor I ran into a journalist whom I knew, from the Hearst press. She asked me how my speech had gone? Rather pleased with myself, at the moment, I reported that as a matter of fact I had been congratulated on it, by both my neighbours, the delegates of Iraq and Israel. "Jesus," she replied. "Was it as bad as *that*?" I'm afraid it was.

The Middle Eastern end of the dual crisis did not present much difficulty, or cause much controversy within the UN. In the Security Council a resolution condemning the tripartite attack on Egypt was vetoed by Britain and France and the debate was immediately transferred to the General Assembly where there was a huge and noisy majority against the aggressors. As had never happened before at the UN on a contentious matter, the United States and the Soviet Union found themselves on the same side. The Soviet Union was extremely noisy on the subject of the aggression against Egypt, in order to distract attention from its own aggressive posture in relation to Hungary. The United States was not noisy, but its steady determination to stop the tripartite aggression in its tracks was much more alarming to the aggressors than the railing of the Soviets could be.

There was a personal element in this, on President Eisenhower's part. In timing their intervention in Egypt, and drawing Israel in on their side, the British and French governments calculated that, since a presidential election was imminent in the United States, Eisenhower would not dare to take any stance with regard to Israel which would alienate Jewish voters and so the intervention on Egypt could proceed unimpeded.

This was the kind of silly-clever interpretation of the American scene to which European politicians are sometimes prone. The Jewish pro-Israel lobby is indeed powerful in the United States, when circumstances are right. But this does not cover a military intervention by Israel which appears as hostile to the general interests of the United States. In such circumstances, the lobby in question does not exert pressure on the United States to leave Israel alone. Quite to the contrary, it adds weightily to the general pressure on Israel to pull back. Which is precisely what happened on this occasion. When – after the British and French had begun their retreat from Egypt – Ben-Gurion tried to hang on to the Sinai Desert, the fruits of Israel's brilliant military victory, he immediately became the target of the most intense pressure that Israel, in all its history, has experienced from the United States. When the Soviets threatened Israel with rocket attacks unless it immediately withdrew from Sinai, United States representatives coolly informed the government of Israel that, if the Soviets attacked Israel for keeping its forces in Sinai after the United States had asked Israel to withdraw these forces, then Israel would be on its own if attacked by the Soviet Union. In these circumstances, Ben-Gurion capitulated and the process of evacuation began.

This was not at all how the British and French imagined the world to be when they began their attack on Egypt, under the fond illusion that the involvement of Israel, and the Jewish factor in the impending elections, would neutralise the American government over the attack on Egypt and hand the attackers an almost bloodless victory.

Ireland, being only a tiny component in the enormous and vociferous majority against the aggression in Egypt, had little to say in the one-sided debate on this subject. Most of what little was said was delivered, felicitously, by Boland in the First Committee. But there was one intervention of my own which I believe may have had a significant effect on my future career, if on little else. At one point, after Britain and France had announced their intention of withdrawing their forces from Egypt, Boland was away and I occupied the Irish seat on the First Committee. I heard Commander Noble, the senior British delegate, announce that he "could not condone" Israel's attack on Egypt. This was too much for me and I made an impromptu intervention, in which the key words were:

"Far be it from my Delegation to be less censorious about an attack on Egypt than the distinguished delegate of the United Kingdom judges it appropriate to be . . . "

That was the nearest thing to a kind word that the delegation of Israel heard in the course of that debate. My relations with my Israeli neighbour on the First Committee, Michael Comay, improved and flourished. He began to offer me the fruits of his deep and hard-won expertise on the workings of the UN. On one occasion, I had criticised what I considered to be an unworkable proposal offered by the Italian delegation. It was unworkable all right, but that was no reason to oppose it, under the prevailing conditions. "Leave it alone and let it wither away" was much wiser. When I had finished my little speech, Comay pushed over to me a little verse, of his own composition:

> Every new boy in this school
> Should learn at once the Golden Rule:
> It is advisable not to knock
> Proposals by the Latin Block.

Good advice, by which I abided. Good advice, and also a good and wise friend for the future.

* * *

The Middle Eastern imbroglio of the autumn of 1957 was a relatively straightforward issue as it presented itself at the United Nations. It was otherwise with the other main subject of concern: the Soviet pressure on Hungary. Within a few days of taking my seat on the Committee, I was contacted on this subject by one of those whom I was later to come to know, only too well, as the American "arm-twisters" on my Committee at the UN.

To digress on the subject of "arm-twisters": this was a term very little heard in public discussions of the UN, and little used in academic examinations of the workings of the world body. But the concept was absolutely central from about 1948 to 1958 to the actual workings of the

UN. Arm-twisters, of which there was invariably at least one on each of the seven main committees, were American delegates, usually of middle rank, whose function was to influence crucial votes, and make sure the United States got the necessary two-thirds support for whatever proposition might appear, at any given moment, required by American interests. The *modus operandi* of the arm-twister varied according to circumstances. Often, in the case of delegates who had been through the mill, a mere recital of what the United States wanted would do the trick. But the main function of the arm-twister was to smell out possible recalcitrance, and deal with it. "Dealing with it" could include bribery or blackmail or both together. If these techniques failed, in relation to an individual delegate, they would sometimes be employed directly on governments which were weak, dependant on American subsidies, or corrupt. Most of the world's governments fell into at least one, if not all, of these categories.

The heyday of the arm-twister and the most virulent period of his activity had come in 1948, when the United States government, after considerable hesitation, had thrown its weight behind the recognition of the state of Israel, and needed to have this recognition rubber-stamped by the General Assembly. I was not there at the time of course, but I have heard from old-stagers hair-raising tales of the pressures employed, both on delegates and on governments in this period. Some delegates were bribed, some of those who could not be bribed personally were recalled by their bribed or intimidated governments and replaced by suitably-instructed people. The necessary number of "unsuitable" delegates was replaced by an equal number of "suitable" ones. Several careers were ended and several new ones were promoted. In the end the General Assembly passed the required resolution and the United States could bask once more, for a time, in the approval of the "moral conscience of mankind".

That particular exercise (of 1948) was so drastic and scandalous as to excite a certain amount of media attention and for a time thereafter the United States government was inclined to rein in the arm-twisters. But by the late 1950s the arm-twisters were beginning to come into their own again. The Arab delegations, cultivated by the State Department but unable to bring about basic change in the generally pro-Israel policies of the White House, were beginning to show signs of getting out of control. The new situation over Hungary would require delicate handling. The old exuberant rough stuff of *circa* 1950 would no longer serve.

To come back to my own particular arm-twister, of the autumn of 1957. He offered no bribes, nor did he use any threats. He simply offered me an analysis of the situation in Hungary in this brief period, when Imre Nagy was apparently seeking to extricate his country from the Warsaw Pact and trying to enlist the support of the United States. My arm-twister told me that Imre Nagy deserved absolutely no support or encouragement from any democratic country. He was as bad a communist as any other. Whether he was left in charge or replaced by some other communist would make absolutely no difference to anyone.

I was quite surprised by this discussion. Virtually the entire western press was highly supportive of Nagy, at this time, and wished him well in his efforts to liberate his country from the communist yoke. Nobody in the west was anything but supportive of Imre Nagy *in public*. But my little arm-twister was telling me something different and what he was telling me was correct in that it reflected the substance, as distinct from the style, of United States policy at this point.

The attempt of the Hungarian government, under Imre Nagy, to break away from the Warsaw Pact and Soviet dominance in general had placed the American government in a most difficult and anomalous position. In one sense, though not the most important one, this was the breakthrough in Eastern Europe for which the American Republicans, in particular, had been working for years. "Rolling back the Iron Curtain" had been the theme, and the principal roller-back had been John Foster Dulles, Eisenhower's Secretary of State. Two clandestine radio stations, controlled by the Americans, sent out the message hour-by-hour: the peoples behind the Iron Curtain were to revolt against their oppressors, and it was strongly implied that if they did so, they would have the full backing of the United States. It was never I think explicitly stated that this would be *military* backing, but many listeners got the impression that it would. Most East Europeans were a bit suspicious about the message: the Poles, for example, felt they had been incited to revolt by the Americans, in the past, and then let down. But in Hungary, Imre Nagy and his government believed the broadcasts, understood them as pledging American support if Hungary made its bid for freedom, and they went ahead with precisely such a bid.

That any of the Iron Curtain countries might actually be inspired by the broadcasts to revolt against their leaders does not seem to have seriously occurred to those who organized the broadcasts and paid for them. I once asked C Northcote Parkinson, the celebrated political aphorist who formulated "Parkinson's Law", to give an aphorism which would convey the real meaning of international political propaganda. He responded with the formula: "All propaganda begins, and ends, at home." And I believe this is precisely how it was with Republicans and "rolling back the Iron Curtain". The Republicans did not really expect to roll back any part of it. But they did want to give the impression that the republicans, unlike the Democrats, had a policy for ending communist rule and were actively engaged in promoting it. This message would be highly congenial to many Americans of Eastern European origins, and more vaguely agreeable to many other Americans. In other words, it was a foreign policy for *internal* consumption. But unfortunately it had been consumed *externally* and a reckoning had now to be paid for the frightening degree of success unexpectedly attained by the policy of "rolling back".

Eisenhower seems to have decided very early on that no material encouragement was to be given to the Hungarians. Whatever those broadcasts might have encouraged them to hope, their hopes must now be dashed. Eisenhower, the most experienced soldier-politician in the world, seems to have taken this decision on strictly military grounds, which were indeed cogent. He didn't mind *sounding* belligerent, but he didn't want America to be caught in any more wars. He had ended the Korean War – which Truman had helped to start – with a compromise settlement based on restored partition and he was determined not to have to send American troops to support the Hungarians. To fight the Russians in Central Europe would involve the Americans in vastly greater casualties than even the Korean War had entailed. Eisenhower had no intention of going down that road, and there is no question but that Eisenhower was right. All the Western European countries supported that line, and dreaded any suggestion of American commitment to "rolling back the Iron Curtain" if the rolling back were to take the form of military intervention.

Eisenhower's basic policy for the avoidance of war in Central Europe was sound. Unfortunately this policy also involved reneging on past promises of "rolling back" and it meant leaving in the lurch those who had believed in these promises, and acted on their beliefs.

Letting down the Hungarians was a tricky business, in the light of previous propaganda, but the letting-down was accomplished in stages with considerable skill. While the fate of Imre Nagy and his colleagues remained in doubt, the United States government professed to see the situation as troubling but unclear. Privately and to friendly governments, the message was the same as that conveyed by my own arm-twister: Nagy, not to be trusted, as bad a communist as any of them. Reading the American signals correctly, the Russians decided on military intervention in Hungary, in the well-founded belief that the American reactions would be political, not military.

Eisenhower, though rejecting any military reaction, was under pressure to find forms of reaction which would be showy and moralistic, but safe. And these are among the kinds of reaction that the machinery of the UN is designed to accommodate and has accommodated many times.

To suggestions that the United States should intervene in Eastern Europe after the Russian intervention, Eisenhower's spokesmen replied that the United States, unlike the Soviet Union, was a law-abiding power, bound to act only under the constraints of the Charter of the UN. In fact, as those who talked in those terms well knew, there are no such constraints. The Charter allows a power which feels threatened by the actions of another power, to act in legitimate self-defence: as the United States had been prepared to do over Korea, whatever the UN might have done. Still the picture of the United States as constrained to inaction by the UN Charter lent dignity to a policy of inaction and was highly congenial to the popular mood, both in the United States and Western Europe.

At the UN the appropriate rituals were observed, and other rituals felt by the Americans to be inappropriate were eschewed. The matter was first brought before the Security Council and a resolution ordering the Soviet Union to withdraw its forces from Hungary was duly vetoed by the Soviet Union. Western spokesmen then spoke of the parlous condition of the UN "paralysed by the Soviet veto" and this was much healthier, from the point of view of the United States, than a public discussion of the position *of the United States* could have been.

Then the matter was brought to the General Assembly for debate. If the United States had been bent on war over Hungary it would have submitted a "Uniting for Peace" resolution allowing the United States to wage war on the Soviet Union, as had been done in 1950 over Korea. The resolution would probably have carried with it the support of Latin American and other countries which would have had no intention of taking part in the operation for which they voted. But there was no talk at all now of "Uniting for Peace"; it was as if no such procedure had ever been invented. Speaker after speaker in the General Assembly roundly condemned the Soviet intervention and a resolution condemning it was passed, but without any suggestion of consequential action. The United States congratulated the General Assembly for its forthright stand against aggression. But it deplored the failure of the Security Council to bring the aggression to an end. The Security Council had been "paralysed by the Soviet veto" and there was vague talk about the need to bring about "Charter revision".

The point of the whole exercise was, of course, to shift the blame for letting down the Hungarians away from the United States and on to the UN, which has in reality no material power to take any action at all. The UN can function, and often does, as a convenient scapegoat, and its availability as a scapegoat when one is required is a principal reason for its long survival. Western countries all regarded the general outcome of the crisis – the avoidance of a terrible war in Europe – as eminently satisfactory. Along with this but a lot less vocal was a rather widespread sense of guilt and shame over the sacrifice of the Hungarians, and the shabby and dishonest series of transactions directed by the Americans but supported by the Europeans through which the sacrifice of the Hungarians had been achieved.

* * *

Around this time I was beginning to be aware of certain strains which I had never expected within the Irish Delegation to the UN. At home I had been on friendly terms with both Boland and Kennedy and with Boland, in particular, I had friendly and open discussions in which he enjoyed analysing international situations, often acutely. But in New York, during the dual crises, there was nothing of that. Analysis was not required or accepted. I was given to understand that the Permanent Mission – in effect Boland and Kennedy – understood the realities of the situation and that I, as an outsider and newcomer, could not. I was therefore to take my cue from them, without discussion or explanation. Naturally, I did not find this congenial, and at first I did not understand the situation.

With further experience, however, light began to dawn. The kind of thing that was silently beginning to divide our delegation was also affecting other western delegations, perhaps all of them. In each delegation, during the three-month meetings of the General Assembly, there was a division of roles, and in part, of interests, between the Permanent Missions and the delegates who came out from home for the General Assembly only.

The permanent delegates saw themselves as equipped by their long-term presence in New York to understand the situation better than their comparatively unsophisticated colleagues out from home, and there was something in that. But there was also a difference of interests as well as of knowledge. The obvious jobs in the gift of the UN – chairmanships of committees, rapporteurships, the presidency of the General Assembly itself – never went to the members of the floating population out for the Assembly. They always went to the members of the Permanent Missions. And they were in practice in the gift of the Americans, who dominated all aspects of the workings of the UN. Members of the Permanent Missions of the western countries and of many other countries also were seen as on probation, in terms of reliable and unquestioning service to the United States, as defined at any given time by the government of the United States. Those who passed the probation tests got clearance for UN jobs. Those who did not pass those tests got nothing, and were encouraged to pursue their careers elsewhere.

These conditions applied across the board and tended, within each delegation, to divide a "Permanent" elite from the comparative peasants who came out from home for the three months of the Assembly. In the particular case of the Irish delegation, Freddie Boland and Eamon Kennedy were by now in the best books of the Americans, meeting their most exigent standards. They could therefore hope for, and eventually did obtain, their reward. Kennedy was to obtain his in being elected to the Rapporteurship of the Fourth (Trustee) Committee, a most delicate post, requiring inconspicuous but reliable support for the Americans in gradually acquiring preponderant influence in an area in which America's allies, France and Britain, still wished *their* influence to be preponderant.

Freddie Boland at this time was already aiming at acquiring the presidency of the General Assemby, a position not attainable by anyone but a discreet but understanding supporter of American policy on all important matters.

I am not suggesting that either of these officials did anything he believed to be wrong. They both genuinely believed that the United States was the unquestioned leader of the Free World, and deserved the unflinching support of all other countries within the Free World. And if they should be well rewarded for that unflinching support was that not in the nature of things and so altogether acceptable?

But these considerations could not of their nature be frankly discussed with the lesser breeds who came out only for the General Assembly, and could not understand the fine points. So communications between the Permanent Missions and those who were there only for the Assembly tended to become clouded in most of the delegations to the Assembly, not excluding the Irish.

The Druses of the Middle East have a relevant policy, as part of their religion, governing when they are required to tell the truth and when not. According to the Commandments of Hamza, their founder, Druses are required to tell the truth, the whole truth and nothing but the truth to other Druses (or those of them who are sufficiently competent and well-informed to understand the truth). In dealing with non-Druses, however, Druses are at liberty to administer such mixtures of the truth and falsity as may best serve the common interests of the Druses, as understood by their elites.

Rather similarly at the UN, those members of other delegations, who understood the paramount necessity of always serving the United States, could speak candidly to one another, but not ever to the members of their own delegations who had as yet failed to grasp that paramount necessity.

All of this was always in the background during that first year. But it came near to the surface once. This was during the course of preparation for the General Debate, which closes each session of the General Assembly and in which each delegation is expected to give a general exposition of its understanding of the major international issues involved. Boland asked me to draft the speech, and I supplied a draft. When I had submitted it he called me into his office, where he had Eamon Kennedy with him. Boland said he would like me to have another look at the draft. Kennedy, as if unable to help himself, added that the draft was "too donnish". He said this with what I regarded as an odious little smirk, and I knew that he and I were to be enemies henceforward: as was indeed to be luxuriantly established in the following year, under new conditions.

I knew well that the expression "donnish" came from Freddie himself, and not from Kennedy. I had heard it used by Freddie with reference to the distinguished Cambridge historian, DW Brogan, who appeared to have irritated Freddie in some way (perhaps by criticising a paper of his). Freddie was contemptuous of Brogan's habit of basing his books and papers on dated reference-cards: a practice then universal among all working historians, though Boland did not appear to understand this. In any case, Boland, without any unpleasant language in my presence, indicated broadly the nature of the changes required: making it more explicitly pro-American and less abstract. I was used, as a civil servant, to amending drafts in such ways, having had to make far more trying changes under Seán MacBride and I quickly submitted a revised draft, which Boland accepted *in toto*, without any comment from Kennedy.

The speech was to be delivered by the Minister for Foreign Affairs, Liam Cosgrave. I rather liked Cosgrave. When he was a Parliamentary Secretary and I was waiting in the civil servants' corridor for Ministers and Secretaries to emerge from a session of the Dáil, I heard him asked by one of his officials about what was going on inside. "So-and-so was speaking," he said, referring to a Fianna Fáil deputy. "What was he saying?" asked the official.

"Oh, dying for Ireland, as usual," said Cosgrave, thus unwittingly endearing himself to me.

Cosgrave was without experience in international affairs at this time, and I believe his only instructions from his government were to place himself entirely in the experienced and trusted hands of Freddie Boland. So he accepted without reservation the draft composed by me and recommended by Boland. At the last moment, however, Cosgrave decided to add one sentence of his own right at the end. This was a recommendation to Jews and Arabs "to solve their differences on Christian principles". The Minister told Freddie of this decision in the Assembly Chamber, just as the speech was due to be delivered. Freddie, who was seated between the Minister and myself, passed the draft addition to me with a little smile, for comment. I pointed out that the great majority of Palestine Arabs were Muslims, and that it might perhaps be a little out of place to appeal to Jews and Muslims to settle their differences on the basis of a religion in which neither of them believed.

Freddie with a straight face passed these observations on to the Minister, who rather sheepishly indicated that that was still the note on which he was determined to conclude. Turning to me, and with his back to the Minister, Freddie said in a low voice: "It may not be all that appropriate for the Middle East, but the Minister feels it will go down well in Dun Laoghaire-Rathdown" – Cosgrave's overwhelmingly Roman-Catholic electoral constituency in Greater Dublin.

* * *

The speech went down very well with those whom it was designed to please: the Americans and their regular supporters. One of the most outstanding of these was Victor Belaunde, the Permanent Representative of Peru. Belaunde was a notable orator himself and a connoisseur of similar oratory in others. Coming out of the Assembly after Cosgrave had delivered the speech Belaunde pronounced the speech to be of phenomenal transcendence, *de una transcendencia fenomenal.* I knew exactly what he meant, because I had heard Belaunde speak himself. He used to soar to great heights of philosophical and benevolent generalisation, before reaching a conclusion which was precisely tailored to meet the current requirements of the United States. This was one falcon who could always hear the falconer with no difficulty at all.

Yet Belaunde was no fool. Though a notable orator himself – or perhaps for that reason – he distrusted oratory. In private he liked to say, "The freedom of the speech is the enemy of the freedom of the thought". In any case Belaunde's encomium meant that the speech had hit its mark: it had gone down very well with the supporters of the United States, whose general reactions Belaunde always reliably summed up. I had reservations about all this, but these were outweighed for the moment by the satisfaction I felt at having carried out my task successfully within the parameters allotted to me.

And I needn't have worried about the embarrassing peroration concerning the Jews and the Muslims. Nobody minded about a little bit of obvious nonsense, provided it didn't have some dangerous political tendency. In any case, I later found there was a perfect American precedent for Liam Cosgrave's intervention. Years before, Warren Austin of Texas, addressing the UN, had also appealed to Jews and Muslims to resolve their differences on Christian principles. Austin was an intelligent and well-informed man and he knew this was total nonsense in relation to the Middle East. But he didn't care about the Middle East. Like Liam Cosgrave he was thinking about what would go down well with his public at home. Just as C Northcote Parkinson had said: "All propaganda begins and ends at home."

As for me, my standing was notably enhanced – for the time being – within the delegation by the speech and its success. Freddie Boland now showed a cordiality towards me which had been lacking in the earlier part of the session. I had shown a capacity to take guidance and then deliver the goods. As for Kennedy, he was clearly miffed, but I found Kennedy less obnoxious in a miffed condition than in his earlier triumphalist phase.

On my way home I was reasonably satisfied about how that particular session had turned out. But I wondered a lot about the future. At the 1957 session our role – successfully sustained with my assistance – had been that of an approving chorus to policies dictated by the Americans. Would it be like that again in 1958? And if so, how much of that could I stand?

As it turned out, I didn't have to worry. There were indeed – unknown to me – troubles ahead for 1958. But those troubles were not to derive from excessive Irish subservience to the dictates of the United States. Quite the contrary. And much more stimulating and interesting.

8

UNITED NATIONS TWO, 1958-1960

BETWEEN THE 1957 SESSION OF THE GENERAL ASSEMBLY AND THAT OF 1958, there was a change in the government of Ireland, which had quite drastic consequences in the little matter of Ireland's relations to the politics of the UN.

The Fine-Gael-led government in which Liam Cosgrave had been Minister for Foreign Affairs fell and was replaced by a Fianna Fáil government in which Frank Aiken was once again Foreign Minister. Shortly after he resumed office, Aiken summoned me for a discussion of Ireland's policy at the UN, a matter which he clearly regarded as of considerable importance. He had followed the 1956 session with close attention, and with much better understanding than most observers. He referred respectfully, but in a somewhat guarded manner, to Cosgrave's intervention in the general debate and I took it that he was aware that I had written the speech, though under guidance. Then he got down to business.

He told me that, as he saw things, Ireland's position in the 1957 session had been too subservient to the position of the United States. For the future he wanted Ireland to follow a more independent position, generally supportive of the authority of the Secretary-General, even when this authority was exercised in a manner resented by some of the Western

185

powers. (Hammarskjold had annoyed the French, in particular, by his support for policies which had helped to bring about the independence, first of Morocco, and then of Tunisia, with further shocks ahead in relation to France's determination to hold on to Algeria.)

When he had finished his brief but decisive statement, Aiken paused and seemed to be waiting for me to say something. I very much liked the general tenor of what he had said. I knew there would be quite a lot of trouble ahead – both inside and around the Irish delegation – if he held to the line he proposed. But I saw that kind of trouble as vastly preferable to the peace secured in 1957 by a mindless servitude to policies framed and enforced by the United States.

It was not for me, however, to express approval, or disapproval, of a policy-orientation defined by the Minister. What he needed from me was advice on how to pursue that policy-line to the greatest effect. And even my rather brief direct experience of the workings of the UN had imbued me with quite clear ideas as to how this might best be done.

I told the Minister that if any delegation at the General Assembly wished to be accepted as following an independent line, the test was the annual vote on the question of the representation of China. Because of differences in the positions of Britain and the United States in relation to this matter, the question of the representation of China at the UN had attained a condition of Byzantine complexity. If it came to a straight choice between seating Peking or Taiwan, Britain would have to choose Peking; not because it liked Peking, but because it had to recognise Peking or run the risk of having the Chinese re-occupy Hong Kong, many years before Hong Kong was due, under treaties, to revert to China. The American government understood the British position, but not to the point of agreeing to recognise China. So a compromise was worked out. The General Assembly would be allowed to debate the question, each year, but would then vote, not on the substance, but on the question of whether or not to discuss the question which had already been discussed at length: whether Taiwan should continue to be seated as representative of China, or whether a delegation appointed by Peking should take its place.

Now, the position of the United States government on this matter was adopted for internal political reasons, having to do with international "face", and in particular, (under Eisenhower) republican face. No well-informed delegate, among America's allies, was prepared to defend the substance of the position of the United States on this matter. The line was simply that the United States would probably come around on this issue some day, but that, until it did so, western solidarity required support for the Leader of the Free World, however misguided the Leader's position might appear to be on this particular matter.

On a free vote, there would have been a majority in the General Assembly for seating Peking. As it was, the United States (with Britain) could still muster two-thirds for the nonsense of not discussing a proposition which had already been discussed *ad nauseam*. This question was therefore central to the matter which was preoccupying Frank Aiken: how to establish Ireland's position as a genuinely independent country. No country which voted in favour of the Anglo-American "compromise" aimed at continuing to exclude Peking would be accepted as representing a genuinely independent position in the Assembly. The minority of countries who voted against the "compromise" would certainly regard any country which voted for it as not being genuinely independent. But even the countries which voted *for* the compromise – such as the Latin American countries – knew that their own votes in favour were constrained votes, and would assume that anyone else who voted "for" was also operating under constraint.

I explained all this to Aiken; much of it he knew, or at least sensed, already, but I was able to fill in a lot of details, and what I said made sense to him. In the end he simply said: "Very well, we shall vote against the compromise, and in favour of a straight vote on the question of which delegation should represent China in the General Assembly. We had better begin to prepare other relevant delegations for a change in Ireland's voting position on this matter."

I knew that this decision, if Aiken could sustain it, would make a big change in my life. I heartily approved the assumption by Ireland of a more independent position. But I was also aware, in a less disinterested way, that the new Irish line, if sustained, would make quite a big difference to my own life, and be to the immediate benefit of my influence and career. Aiken had accepted my guidance on the fundamental choice facing him in relation to the UN and I sensed that he was likely to continue to rely on me as his closest advisor in relation to these matters. I was thus turning from a rather wan and peripheral figure in the Irish delegation to a person at the centre of things. And I found this, in itself, highly congenial.

I could also sense plenty of trouble ahead in relations with the Permanent Mission. In 1957, Freddie Boland had been, in effect, in sole charge of the Irish delegation. Liam Cosgrave, a novice in foreign affairs, had been instructed by his government to be guided in all things by Boland

and was in fact so guided. Boland's policy was to follow the American line in all matters of importance, and he did so. But Aiken was a strong minister, of great experience, and carrying great weight with the Fianna Fáil party and government. If he could sustain the position he had indicated on the China vote, that meant that Boland's policy had been reversed, and that the United States could no longer rely on automatic support from Ireland. And this was a much more important consideration in those days than it later became. The United States still, just, held that two-thirds majority in the General Assembly which could be represented as "the moral conscience of mankind" and this was a valuable property in rallying public opinion in the United States to the foreign policies of the United States government. But the two-thirds was slipping and might soon be out of reach. In the circumstances, Ireland's coming defection was quite a serious blow to America's position at the UN, and the United States would certainly exert strong pressure on the Irish government to deflect Frank Aiken from the position he proposed to adopt.

As well as the overall political considerations, there were personal factors involved for the two leading figures in the Permanent Mission which lent a keener edge to the emerging controversy. Both Boland and Kennedy sincerely believed in the policy of unflinching support to the Leader of the Free World and were bound to resent the abandonment of that policy. But they had also to know that that abandonment – if sustained – would put their career prospects within the UN at risk. To put it bluntly, they might not be of much use to the United States any more. Freddie had been counting on United States support for the future Presidency of the General Assembly. Kennedy had been counting on the same for the rapporteurship of the Fourth Committee. But if these individuals were seen not to be in a position to avert an undesirable shift in the policy of their own delegation, then the United States might switch its support to more effective candidates from other delegations.

All in all, I could see plenty of trouble ahead. But I liked the prospect of trouble better than the deathly Pax Americana which had prevailed in 1957.

* * *

I am sure that, once the intention to change "the China vote" was made known to the United States government, pressure was applied from Washington on the Irish government to reverse its policy. It is clear that the pressure failed. I think that this was largely because of the great weight which Frank Aiken carried within the Fianna Fáil party and government. But I think it was also due to the character of the subject matter, inherently repellent to Seán Lemass's plain and powerful mind. If Aiken had proposed to vote *for the seating of communist China*, Lemass would have stopped him. But all Aiken was proposing was that a vote on the question of representation of China should be taken, instead of a vote for not discussing a subject which had already been discussed. I believe that once Lemass found that that was all that was in question he would have felt that there were other matters more worthy of his attention than whether or not to discuss things that had already been discussed.

I think the decisive battle on this issue had already been fought – involving Frank Aiken, the American Ambassador and Lemass – before our delegation set out to attend the new session of the UN. Aiken did not tell me about these discussions, which would only have been relevant if they had led to a reversal of the new policy which he had laid down. But there was some trouble awaiting us in New York, as I knew there would be, and it broke immediately on our arrival.

The flight from Ireland to America could take quite a long time in those days, and it took us about eighteen hours. Freddie Boland met us at the airport, together with Seán Leydon. Leydon was head of Seán Lemass's Department of Industry and Commerce and his most trusted advisor. Leydon was also a particularly devout Catholic, even by the exacting standards of those days. It was a Sunday morning when we arrived, and Leydon said he assumed we would wish to attend mass at the airport before going on to the policy discussion at the Permanent Mission. Aiken said we were rather tired after the long flight and would rather go straight ahead with whatever discussions were necessary. At this Leydon became quite agitated and said that, if we failed to attend mass, "the American public would not understand". How the American public would come to know about it, and why it would care, Leydon did not say. But Aiken seemed to understand what way the wind was blowing, and we all duly attended mass.

Then there was a lengthy and exceedingly fraught discussion at the Permanent Mission. Freddie did almost all the talking, with Aiken responding calmly and monosyllabically. I thought Freddie was not at his persuasive best on this occasion. He was clearly very angry, and yielded to the temptation to talk down to his Minister. He even – contrary to his usual wont – threw in a number of not-particularly apposite Latin tags, as if to remind the company that Aiken had left school at an early age, and should defer to better-educated persons. For the rest, Boland gave us a *tour d'horizon* of the grave world situation and the need to stand up for the Leader of the Free World. As for the particular question of "the China vote", there were indeed some anomalies there, but the anomalies could be left for the Americans to sort out for themselves in the fullness of time without any need for new initiatives on our part, which could only encourage the communists and divide the West.

Having heard Freddie out, Aiken thanked him for his advice, and told him that the question of how to speak and vote on the China question was one to which he had devoted considerable thought, and his decision stood. He would *not* vote "not to discuss" what had already been discussed. He would vote for a discussion of the substance.

After that, the meeting broke up, altogether frigidly on the part of the Permanent Mission. Much of the frigidity was aimed at me. Both Freddie and Kennedy knew where the identification of "the China vote" as the key to the adoption of a non-aligned position had come from. Both of them identified me as what they call in Ghana "the paleface in the woodpile". Boland came, a couple of years later, to reject this assessment, and even to see how the new independent stance could be turned to his advantage, as we shall see later. Kennedy, less capable of adaptation, always remained my enemy, though for the moment without the power to inflict serious damage.

As the crucial vote in the General Assembly loomed nearer and the Aiken line remained unchanged, the controversy assumed a theopolitical form, just as Seán Leydon had already hinted that it might. Cabot Lodge, the American Permanent Representative sent Irene Dunn to see Cardinal Spellman. Irene Dunn was a "twofer" on the American delegation – a woman and a Catholic – the latter being the relevant qualification for this particular mission. Irene seems to have told the Cardinal that Aiken was about "to vote for Red China" and asked him to do what he could to avert this disaster. The Cardinal's secretary rang the delegation at the UN itself. It is significant, I think, that he is not known to have rung the Permanent Mission. I infer that the Permanent Mission already knew what the Cardinal's office was doing, and approved. Máire MacEntee – by now a member of the delegation – took the call. She was a strong supporter of "the Aiken Line". The Cardinal's secretary said the Cardinal had been invited to a reception by the Irish delegation. He would have liked to attend, but he had just learned, what he could hardly believe, that the Irish Delegation was about "to vote for Red China". Máire explained that this was not exactly the case. Ireland was about to vote for discussion of the representation of China at the UN – not the same thing. The Cardinal's representative couldn't see much difference and reiterated that it would be difficult for the Cardinal to attend the Irish reception, unless he could be assured that the Irish government would continue to oppose "the seating of Red China." Máire said, "the Cardinal must do as he thinks fit". The Cardinal's representative chose to interpret this as a discourteous response, and hung up.

The outcome of the Cardinal's move must have been deeply disappointing to those who had encouraged that move. The diocesan organ, *The Brooklyn Tablet*, completely under the Cardinal's control, ran a couple of articles denouncing the Irish move. But, even among American Catholics, outside the controlled press of the Archdiocese of New York there was little tendency to be alarmed at the Irish move. Spellman himself had been a warm supporter of Joe McCarthy, in that demogogue's unscrupulous and exuberant heyday, and had in consequence suffered from McCarthy's disgrace at the hands of the US Army. Most Catholics were Democrats, and Democrats – having been copiously smeared by Spellman and McCarthy in that grim period – had no time at all for Spellman. After the "China vote" our delegation received a number of invitations to address societies in Catholic universities. Máire MacEntee and I, both strong supporters of the new line, were delegated to accept such invitations, which led to a number of quite agreeable encounters. The Permanent Mission was not drawn into what would, for them, have been a most distasteful form of activity.

At home in Ireland, also, "the China vote" as an issue proved to be something of a damp squib. Spellman tried to get the Irish Catholic hierarchy to denounce the Aiken line, but the most that this effort produced was a few faint rumblings from individual churchmen. Lemass could not be drawn to denounce a senior and trusted member of his government. Shaken by the repercussions of its intervention in relation to Noel Browne, the hierarchy was not attracted to a new Church-and-State controversy. And certainly not with Fianna Fáil. Those who were now the Fianna Fáil leadership had all been excommunicated in 1922-3 for supporting the republican side in the Irish civil war. But ten years later, the excommunicated leaders headed the largest party in Ireland and were returned to power, frequently and for long periods.

The Catholic Church and Fianna Fáil were the two most powerful institutions in Ireland, and were warily respectful of one another. The relationship recalled what Gorki described as Tolstoy's to God: Maxim. "With God he maintains very suspicious relations. They are like two bears in one den." But mutual suspicion usually entails a considerable degree of mutual respect, and so it was with the Catholic Church and Fianna Fáil. They were certainly not to be drawn into a clash which could be seriously damaging to both of them, by anything so nebulous and remote from Ireland as "the China vote". The calculations of Cardinal Spellman and Cabot Lodge were almost ludicrously remote from Irish realities. Aiken duly cast his China vote, explained it, and remained unshaken as Foreign Minister and head of the delegation to the UN.

Indeed he not merely survived this little ordeal, but emerged strengthened from it. For a delegation which had formally been totally aligned with the United States to break away from it, on a matter then seen as of great importance to it, and then get away with that, was a most unusual event. A minister who had made such a break and survived attracted a good deal of interest and respect, not least from those who would have dearly liked to make such a break but did not dare. Frank Aiken had now become a significant figure at the UN. And I too was beginning to attract some attention. This was due to behind-the-scenes efforts of Boland and Kennedy who portrayed me as the sinister figure who had lured an ignorant minister into forsaking the Western camp. Not all of those who listened to this interpretation thought any the worse of me for it.

* * *

In any case the global context of all this was beginning to change, and in such a manner as to undermine the role of the General Assembly portrayed by the United States as "the moral conscience of the world".

The most fateful of the changes that led to this outcome were occurring in the Middle East. For some years the United States had been trying to construct a system of alliances in the Middle East which would correspond to NATO in the west, and operate as a barrier to the extension of Soviet power. The Iraq of Nuri Said had been central to this concept, as the designation of the alliance – "the Baghdad Pact" – showed. Unfortunately, on July 14, 1958, a revolution occurred in Baghdad. Nuri and all his associates were murdered. The successor regime was violently anti-West and – for a time – appeared to be communist-orientated.

The western powers panicked. The United States and Britain sent military forces to prop up Lebanon and Jordan, seen as threatened by the new Iraq. Israel – long kept out in the cold by the Baghdad Pact – was able to come in again by allowing the allies to overfly Israel territory in order to come to the rescue of Jordan.

The United States – fairly confident still in the possession of that two-thirds – had the General Assembly convened in August 1958 to give moral approval to the United States interventions in Lebanon and Jordan. The manoeuvre failed. The Arab countries opposed to the intervention were able to mobilize "a blocking third", so defeating the United States proposal. From that moment on, the "the moral conscience of mankind" formula, as applied to the General Assembly, vanished altogether from political usage. Also, since efforts to influence voters in the General Assembly now involved quite a high risk of failure, the United States became much more sparing in its efforts along that line, and more tolerant of delegations which would sometimes, but not always, vote with the United States. All of which had the effect of making life at the UN quite a lot easier for Aiken's delegation.

We were also reminded by our neighbour on our right – now post-Nuri Iraq – that the fact that a given country was resistant to United States control did not necessarily make it an agreeable neighbour. When the General Assembly resumed, after the coup in Iraq, the old Iraqi delegation of Nuri people had of course been mostly replaced. I had been on friendly terms with the previous Iraqi delegate on the Special Political Committee, so – rather naively – I asked my new neighbour whether he had any news of his predecessor. Looking straight ahead he replied with a monosyllable: "Hanged!" We were to sit beside one another for another two years and that was the only word he ever addressed to me. However, my other neighbour – Israel – kept me well supplied with stimulating and instructive conversation.

The Irish delegation now became unexpectedly involved – for about a year – with the affairs of a country which was not a member of the UN at all – Tibet. Curiously, this involvement was a kind of mirror-image of the politics that had led to the Anglo-American formula over the China vote. Chinese forces had intervened in Tibet, which they claimed as an integral part of their national territory. Britain did not dispute that claim, again because it had to think about Hong Kong. The United States, again, did not want even an implicit clash with Britain – which had just given it military support over Lebanon and Jordan – but neither did it wish to deny a victim of communist aggression the right of appeal to the UN. It didn't want to back Tibet openly, or even to allow one of its usual surrogates (such as an amenable Latin-American country) to do so. In these circumstances, somebody – I suspect Freddie Boland – had a bright idea: why not get

Ireland involved? After the China vote, nobody was likely to accuse Ireland of acting as an American catspaw. Aiken's reputation as a maverick was now well-attested. And a reputation as a maverick can become, in certain circumstances, quite a desirable property.

Aiken could see quite clearly, of course that he was being offered a way in from the cold of American displeasure over the China vote. But he didn't shrink from the way in, any more than he had flinched from the cold. He saw Tibet as a small nation, under attack from a more powerful neighbour. Aiken's leader, Eamon de Valera, had intervened in the League of Nations, and joined in pressure for sanctions, against fascist Italy after Mussolini had invaded Abyssinia (although the opposition in Ireland had supported "Catholic Italy" at that time). Aiken wanted to do his best for the Tibetans, as Dev had done for the Abyssinians, and was not deterred, but pleased, by the thought that he was also thereby doing himself some political good and confounding his adversaries.

Aiken left a lot of the direct dealings with the Tibetans to me. I liked them and came to appreciate them as allies. Indeed I got on better with them than Aiken did, because he tended to lecture them on the political line they ought to pursue for their own good. To these representations they invariably replied "Quite right, Excellency". I soon found that "Quite right, Excellency" was a Tibetan formula for "no way" when addressing a respected ally.

One of the delegation, a younger brother of the Dalai Lama, was himself a minor emanation of the Buddha. He had become engaged to an American Episcopalian lady, and declared his willingness to become an Episcopalian himself in order to marry her. He was questioned by the Episcopalian adherents about his Tibetan faith, and then told he must renounce his role as a minor emanation of the Buddha. He said that he could not renounce it, because it was an inescapeable condition of his existence. He could no more renounce it than a living person could renounce his body. He could accept, in good faith, every article of the Protestant religion, but that could have no effect on his existential status as an emanation of the Buddha. Alas! I do not know how the story ended.

I had many long conversations with the Tibetans, during which I sometimes got a little tired of their relentless Buddhist piety. One of them told me proudly that there is no word in the Tibetan language for "victory". I asked him how would he then refer to the outcome of a conflict in which the Tibetan side had decidedly the best of it? He smiled broadly. "Oh, *that*!" he said. "We call *that* 'Very Excellent Best Peace.'"

They had with them a very formidable "minder", Hugh Richardson, the former British High Commissioner in Lhasa. He also ran into trouble with Tibetan linguistic conventions. When he questioned some figures produced by a senior member of the delegation who had been at one time Minister for Finance, he was told politely that they represented "an average". I can remember him cursing loudly and saying, "When I was in Lhasa it was part of my job to 'strike an average' in order to ascertain what proportion of Tibetan postal charges should be borne by HMG. I was politely informed by that very fellow there that the concept of an average was foreign to Tibetan thought!"

Tibetans didn't expect much from the UN and of course they got very little. But they did get – mainly through us – a hearing of their case at the UN and thus established for themselves a certain real, if very limited, nuisance value. On that understanding we parted from the Tibetans, still good friends. Their leader, Diallo Thondup, the Dalai Lama's "Chinese brother", presented us, on my second marriage, with a beautiful Tibetan rug – subsequently stolen from us, in a Chinese dry cleaner's, when we were living in New York.

* * *

Towards the end of my period with the General Assembly, there was a second clash with the Americans, of which the focus was my own committee: the Special Political Committee. Austria had appealed to the UN in protest against what it regarded as the ill-treatment of the Austrians remaining in South Tyrol by the Italian government. This complaint was registered at the UN as "The Problem of Bolzano/Bozen". As Italy was an ally of the United States, and Austria was not, Italy looked to the Americans to ensure that Austria's claim was rejected as contemptuously as possible, so that it might never be renewed before the General Assembly.

This looked quite feasible. This was the year – 1960 – of a large number of admissions of newly-independent African states. When the Americans took soundings with the new entry they found that the African states were disposed to be neutral concerning what they regarded as a purely inter-European dispute. If the Africans stayed out, the Americans – though they could no longer be certain of an automatic two-thirds of those who voted – had a good chance of seeing off the Austrian complaint. Austria's friends were few, and NATO's many.

Bruno Kreisky, then Chancellor of Austria, came out to address the

General Assembly on the Austrian resolution and met with a rather frigid response. Then Kurt Waldheim, Permanent Representative of Austria, approached me on the subject of the Austrian resolution. This was a simple proposition calling for a "friendly, just and neighbourly solution of the dispute," a formula used when the Assembly did not wish, or was not able, to take sides with either party. Austria's hope was to avert the humiliation of a simple and curt rejection of the Austrian case – a rejection which the Italians, backed by the Americans, were seeking.

Waldheim wanted me to speak in favour of the Austrian proposition. He knew that the Republic of Ireland would be likely to want to be helpful in such a case. At any time, some development in Northern Ireland might lead the Republic to wish to raise that matter in the General Assembly. And the idea that a non-member of NATO should be precluded from raising an issue because the country appealed against was a member of NATO was inherently uncongenial to Ireland, since it did not belong to NATO.

I told Waldheim that there seemed to be a good *prima facie* case for an Irish intervention and that I would raise the matter at the next meeting of my delegation. When I did so I confidently expected Frank Aiken's support and I got it. This was an occasion on which Ireland's capacity to resist American pressure could again be demonstrated. This seemed to be needful. Ireland's support for the Tibetans could be interpreted as an attempt to creep back into the American fold, and this was never Aiken's intention. Also, this time around, Aiken's position in relation to the Austrian case could not possibly be interpreted as pro-communist, and would readily be understood at home.

There was nothing unexpected about that. What did surprise me was that Freddie Boland did not oppose the idea, and even implicitly supported it. On consideration, I could see why. Freddie still needed American support to become President of the General Assembly. But – with the expanded membership – American support would no longer be enough. The new African intake were all non-aligned and a reassertion of Ireland's non-aligned position and demonstration of Ireland's clout among the non-aligned would not come amiss. A President of the General Assembly who was known to be *personally* committed to the United States, but whose delegation's credentials as "non-aligned" were accepted in the Third World, might be just what the United States was looking for, in its difficult dual quest for a president who would be both amenable and electable. Privately, in conversation with the Americans, Freddie could deplore Ireland's stand in the Special Political Committee as due to my malign influence, and

Aiken's stupidity. But at the same time, Freddie could reap the benefits of a demonstration of Ireland's influence over the non-aligned. And this Freddie duly did when he was elected President in 1960.

With the full support of all who now counted in our delegation, I intervened in the debate with some confidence.

The case I made was this: I understood that many of the countries which had just become members of the UN were disposed not to vote in what they regarded as a purely inter-European dispute. This was an understandable position, generally speaking, but I thought I could show that it was a mistaken one, in the actual circumstances of the present case. The distinguishing feature of the dispute before the committee was not that it was a dispute between Europeans, but that it was a dispute between a member and a non-member of NATO. In calling for no more than "a peaceful just and neighbourly solution" we were obviously not asking members to take sides in the dispute. But we were asking members not to humiliate a country which, not being a member of NATO, had dared to make a case against a NATO member. To vote for the very moderate Austrian resolution was not a matter of sentiment for non-aligned countries, but one affecting their vital interests. Any non-NATO country, at any time, might have a grievance against a NATO country which they would wish to raise in the General Assembly. The American-Italian position, against the Austrian resolution, was designed precisely to deny that right of appeal. It was in the common interest of all non-aligned countries – including Ireland as well as African countries – to ensure that that right of appeal was kept firmly open.

The African countries got the message more fully and quickly than even I had hoped. Delegation after delegation announced that they would vote for the Austrian resolution, for African reasons, which had now become clear to them. I learned about the impact of all this on the Italians from a colleague who was a member of our representation on the First Committee. One of the Italian representatives on the Special arrived to report to his colleagues on the First what was going on following my intervention. By reason of alphabetical proximity, my Irish colleague was able to hear what the Italians were saying. The Italian from the Special reported to his colleagues, "It is Caporetto!" He was referring to the rout of the Italians by the Austrians towards the end of 1916. In any case the American-Italian resolution was heavily defeated in the Special Committee, and the right of members to appeal to the Assembly was decisively vindicated.

Not long after this, I was invited to lunch by the senior American arm-twister on my committee. At the lunch, I found that arm-twisting had become a much more sophisticated art-form than it had been in 1957. My American colleague simply reminded me that not all international differences lent themselves to resolution by peaceful means. I agreed that, philosophically, this was so. But the difference we were talking about had not in fact led to war. By avoiding the humiliation of one of the parties to the difference, we were making conflict less likely. The American and I did not agree but parted amicably.

* * *

Long afterwards, Kurt Waldheim was charged with complicity in genocide while he had been an intelligence officer in the German army, then in occupation of Yugoslavia. Waldheim said that he had not known of the mass-arrest and deportation of Jews which had been taking place all round him. On that point, I was quite certain that Waldheim was lying.

During our brief but rather intense period of UN collaboration, I had got to know Waldheim fairly well. I never cared for him personally: he was a very cold fish indeed. But I came to have a high regard for his professional competence. As we worked together on the *pointages* – the computations of how different delegates were likely to vote – I found him extremely well-informed and competent. In relation to such calculations, cold-bloodedness can be a distinct advantage. And of one thing I was quite certain: if mass deportations, destined for mass-murder, were going on in Kurt Waldheim's vicinity, when he was working as an intelligence officer, Waldheim knew all about it. When he said afterwards he did not know about it, he was lying. The lie was as cold-blooded as the original awareness had been.

* * *

In November 1960, a major change came over the United States, and therefore over the UN. The Republicans were defeated in the American elections and John Kennedy became President of the United States.

Kennedy, when in opposition, had adopted a distinctly "anti-colonial" position, especially in atacking the French over Algeria. As Ireland had held a similar position, Ireland's relations with America benefited from Kennedy's victory. Ireland's difficulties with the American delegation in the past were now seen as having been difficulties with the Republicans, and no subject for American recrimination, under the Democrats. And of course

Kennedy, as the first person of Irish Catholic origin to become President of the United States, was immensely popular in Catholic Ireland and highly responsive to his popularity in the land of his ancestors.

So things got a little easier, all of a sudden, especially for Frank Aiken. No one any longer would reproach him for that old "China vote": a challenge to the Republicans, not to the Democrats. Yet American policy on China had not yet changed. The new American Permanent Representative at the UN, Adlai Stevenson, changed the appearance, but not the substance, of American policy over China. China would no longer be excluded from the UN simply on principle. It *could* be admitted, if it accepted the resolutions of the Security Council *and the General Assembly*. This was the device of a clever lawyer, not of an international statesman. China could conceivably have accepted the resolutions *of the Security Council* since – because of the Soviet veto and the long alignment of the two communist powers – these contained nothing basically offensive to the Chinese. But the resolutions *of the General Assembly*, so long under the control of the United States when the Assembly represented "the moral conscience of mankind", were quite a different matter. In resolution after resolution, the General Assembly had condemned the Chinese government in unbridled language, for all sorts of crimes, some of which it had actually committed, and some of which it had not. Stevenson, in offering his purported "olive branch", must have known that the Chinese would reject it angrily and would appear in the wrong, before American opinion, when it did that. Our delegation did not challenge this cynical American move, or anything else that the Kennedy administration did. We just accepted that they were better than their Republican predecessors, and hoped for the best from them. Hoped; but with increasing uneasiness, as far as I was concerned.

The next important matter, of particular concern to the Americans, that came before the General Assembly was the American intervention in Castro's Cuba, the incident known in history as "the Bay of Pigs". Adlai Stevenson addressed the General Assembly in a very long speech. Adlai's international reputation had been very high. He had shown himself to be an elegant and witty speaker in a liberal vein, and had been a target of McCarthy's abuse – "Alger, I mean Adlai" – during McCarthy's heyday. I had admired Stevenson in those days and some of the admiration had even survived that "clever lawyer" performance over inviting China. But Adlai's performance over the Bay of Pigs blew his reputation completely in the eyes of many of his former admirers, including myself.

He began with a long and totally mendacious statement, denying any American involvement in what had been, from covert beginning to ignominious end, a totally American operation. As Adlai read out his long speech, it soon appeared that he was speaking, not from a draft of his own composition, but from a text supplied to him by officials of the administration with an interest in the cover-up. Furthermore, he seemed to be signalling to us, almost desperately, that this was not his own speech. He kept stumbling over words in a most uncharacteristic way. This was manifest throughout his speech, but especially in its peroration, which began: "I have spoken about Fidel Castro's crimes against man. But there's worse to come. I now come to Castro's *crimes against God*".

I could sense that many of Adlai's auditors were groaning inwardly, because that is what I was doing myself.

Adlai went on: "Fidel Castro . . . " pause. "Fidel Castro has . . . " Adlai turned a leaf of that awful text . . . "Fidel Castro has circumcised the freedom of the Catholics of Cuba."

My neighbour Gideon Rafael, of the Israel delegation, had been doodling quietly away during most of Adlai's speech. Where the subject matter is not the Middle East, Israel always casts its vote – usually a silent vote – with the United States. But at that unexpected word Gideon sat up suddenly. He turned to me and said: "*Circumcised!* . . . I always knew, Conor, *we* should be blamed for all this too, some day."

9

UNITED NATIONS THREE: KATANGA

IT WAS IN MARCH 1961 THAT SECRETARY-GENERAL DAG HAMMARSKJOLD asked my Government to release me for service with the United Nations Secretariat. He subsequently appointed me as his personal representative in the breakaway Congo province of Katanga. This was by far the "hottest" post in the UN at this time. My tenure of this post, for less than a year, was to alter the course of the rest of my life.

I need at this point to give a brief account of the turbulent history of the former Belgian Congo and especially of Katanga, since the Congo became independent on June 30, 1960. This phase of this account deals with matters in the public record. Other aspects will be considered later.

The granting of independence to the Congo followed the Congo's first elections, as a result of which Joseph Kasavubu became president of the Congo, and Patrice Lumumba, prime minister. It is clear that the Belgian government intended that the independence of the Congo should be strictly nominal. The armed forces of the Congo – the Force Publique – were under exclusively white officers. The commander of the force – General Janssens – gave a lecture on the eve of independence to the black NCOs. He wrote on the blackboard the words: "*After* Independence = *Before* Independence."

That was what was intended. But it didn't work out that way. Baudouin, King of the Belgians, blew the whole thing when he came out to the Congo to address the new parliament on Independence Day. The King told the parliament how much the Congolese owed to its "benefactors" at the head of whom Baudouin placed Leopold II, whom literate Congolese, like most other people familiar with the history of the Congo, regarded as an odious tyrant.

It seems that Lumumba had intended to make a conciliatory address, stressing continuity. But when he heard the King's speech, Lumumba threw aside his draft, and made an inflammatory speech, dwelling on the crimes of Leopold II which provided him with plenty of material.

This was more than a mere speech; it was a major political event. For the black Congolese soldiers this was the proof that "after independence" was not the same as "before independence". In the whole history of the Congo no black man had ever addressed a white man in such a manner as that in which Patrice Lumumba addressed King Baudouin. Under the impact of that speech, the black soldiery mutinied against their white officers and most of the Congo collapsed in anarchy.

Lumumba and Kasavubu appealed to President Eisenhower for aid and Eisenhower referred the request to the UN which agreed, without being at all sure what it was agreeing to.

Before the UN forces could be mobilised, however, the Belgian government decided to intervene in by far the most valuable part of the Congo; the mineral-rich province of Katanga. Belgian paratroops landed in Elizabethville, capital of Katanga, on July 10, 1960. On the following day, the provisional president of Katanga, Moise Tshombe, in the presence of the Belgian paratroop commander, declared Katanga an independent state. Katangan independence was never formally recognised by any state – not even Belgium – but it received de facto support, in "disavowable" forms, from France and Britain as well as Belgium.

Lumumba then appealed to the UN to intervene to end the secession of Katanga. Hammarskjold agreed to deploy United Nations troops to Katanga, as to the rest of the Congo, but he did not agree to end the secession. Lumumba then appealed to the Soviet Union for aid, and he did receive some military equipment. From that moment the United States was committed to eliminating Lumumba from the political life of the Congo, and was successful in this. The nature of the role of the United States, and of the UN in the elimination of Lumumba will be considered later. At this stage it is enough to note that Lumumba was in fact eliminated. His

Congolese enemies were enabled to ship him off to Elizabethville on January 17, 1961.

On February 13, Godefroid Munongo, Tshombe's Minister for the Interior, announced that Lumumba had escaped from custody and had been killed by some villagers. This announcement, which hardly anyone even affected to believe, was singularly ill-timed from the point of view of Tshombe and his leaders. A new administration – that of John F Kennedy – was now in power in the United States and wished to improve relations with African and Asian countries. Further appeasement of Katanga, after Lumumba's murder, was rightly judged to be incompatible with that objective. The United States government now became committed to a policy of real pressure, through the UN, to induce Katanga to abandon secession. And the realities of life at the UN meant that a major shift by the United States also automatically entailed a major shift in the position of the United Nations.

I shall be examining the nature and extent of that shift, and also the fluctuations within it. But first let me look at the nature and extent of the Irish involvement and my own originally limited personal involvement in the affairs of the Congo, in the period between the Congo's independence/collapse and the news of the murder of Patrice Lumumba.

* * *

Less than two weeks after the collapse of the Congo into anarchy, the Security Council passed a resolution "to authorise the Secretary-General to take the necessary steps, in consultation with the government of the Republic of the Congo, to provide the government with such military assistance as may be necessary until the relevant security forces may be able, in the opinion of the Government, to meet fully their task". (July 13, 1961.)

Under the authority of this resolution, Hammarskjold invited a number of mainly small neutral nations to contribute to the "military assistance" authorised. Ireland was among the countries invited. In accordance with his policy of support for the United Nations in general, and for the Secretary General in particular, Aiken persuaded the Irish government to authorise the despatch of one battalion – later increased to two – to the Congo as part of the UN force.

A week later, on July 20, Hammarskjold made an important statement on his own responsibility to the Security Council. He affirmed that

Belgium's obligation to withdraw from the Congo included Katanga but affirmed also "that the UN force could not become a party to an internal conflict and that its presence in Katanga would not be used to settle the constitutional issue".

It may be assumed that this statement was at least cleared with the Americans in advance, if not, as is more probable, prompted by them. Eisenhower relied for guidance on the area of "the powers who know Africa". These powers included Britain, France and Belgium. They did not include any Africans. During the remaining months of the Eisenhower administration UN policy for the Congo was dominated by a consensus between the United States and the European colonial powers. In terms of that consensus, the status quo in Katanga did not appear to be seriously threatened.

Hammarskjold was now able – no doubt with British and French support – to secure the consent of the Tshombe regime to the deployment of UN troops in Katanga. But it was a consent with a significant qualification. The troops deployed were to be Europeans only – no Africans. Hammarskjold flew to Elisabethville on August 12 and issued a joint communique with Tshombe announcing that the participants "took note of the principle of non-intervention in internal affairs which applies to UN forces as the Security Council has explicitly stated in its resolution of August 9". This agreement was loudly trumpeted and embellished by the Tshombe regime over Radio Katanga, which could be heard throughout the Congo.

Humiliated and discredited by the Hammarskjold-Tshombe agreement, Lumumba had denounced the United States and United Nations and appealed to the Soviet Union which supplied *some* aid: "one hundred and twenty-nine Ilyushion transport planes together with 200 technicians." This degree of aid was by no means sufficient to save Lumumba, but it was sufficient to sink him. It was then that the Americans decided to destroy Lumumba, with the help of the UN. How they set about that is a matter which will be examined shortly, in the light of information not available to me at the time.

The Secretary General at this time had an advisory committee consisting of representatives of the countries contributing forces to ONUC. I sat on this committee in late 1960. We received briefings from the Secretary General. The briefings were anodyne and uninformative in the extreme. They told us nothing of what the UN was actually doing in the Congo at the time – which was undermining and destroying Patrice Lumumba as we shall see. As I found later when as a member of the Secretariat I had access to the telegrams from the Congo, the actual role of the UN in the Congo had been far more dynamic than the advisory committee had been allowed to suspect. As for the Congo Advisory Committee, "advising" the Secretary-General on the basis of the information with which the Secretary-General saw fit to supply it, it seemed, in the light of the telegrams, much less like an advisory body than like a group of innocent outsiders being taken for a guided tour.

Still, even at this stage, I did get an occasional whiff of the disconcerting realities on the ground. One such whiff came after an incident in Nyemba, North Katanga, in January 1961. Nine Irish soldiers had been killed in a bow-and-arrow ambush by Baluba tribesmen. Aiken, deeply distressed by this episode, summoned the two Irish battalion commanders then in Katanga to meet him in New York and brief him on what exactly had happened. I was with Aiken at the briefing, over lunch for four. The two officers were Colonel Bunworth and Colonel Buckley. Colonel Bunworth sported a large RAF moustache, and possibly had been in the RAF during the war. The soldiers who were killed had been under his command, so he was first to speak. He told us that there was no way the attack could have been anticipated. There was no knowing what was going on behind those black faces. They had seemed to be quite friendly and then suddenly they attacked – for no reason!

Then Colonel Buckley was called in to deliver his opinion. He was a Kerryman, considerably older than Bunworth. He sympathised with Bunworth on the loss of his men but did not agree with Bunworth's interpretation. He said the soldiers, under orders, had been repairing a bridge which the local natives had destroyed. The local natives – Baluba of North Katanga – were loyal to the central government; the Tshombe government had tried to coerce them into accepting the jurisdiction of Katanga. A small-scale civil war had been going on in the area for months. Tshombe's forces had used the bridge to gain access to the refractory area and punish it by burning villages. The Baluba had accordingly destroyed the bridge. When they found the UN party engaged in repairing the bridge, they saw the UN as abetting their enemies and helping them to reinvade their home territory. So they attacked the party engaged in mending the bridge.

"It's very sad," concluded Colonel Buckley, "but as a Kerryman, I can't see anything mysterious about it." He was clearly referring to Kerry's experiences during the last stages of the Irish civil war of 1922-23.

I found Colonel Buckley's interpretation wholly convincing, and it sowed in my mind the first serious doubts about the conduct to date of the UN operation in the Congo. Tshombe's forces were in revolt against the Congo central government, whose authority was accepted both by the UN (at least in theory) and by the Baluba majority in North Katanga. So what were UN forces doing in helping a government it did not recognise to assert its illegitimate authority over people who wished to live under the legitimate authority of the central government?

In September, the United States and the UN, acting in concert, moved to destroy the political authority, and in consequence the physical existence, of the prime minister who had invited the UN into the Congo. The hinge of this combined effort was Andrew Cordier, the senior American representative at the UN, and UN representative in the Congo in September.

Because of the constant American preponderance at the UN, the senior American representative in the Secretariat is in practice more powerful than the Secretary General, and nobody knew this better than Cordier. Cordier used all the resources of the UN to crush Lumumba and encourage his enemies. He did this with a rather perfunctory show of impartiality. Thus, when President Kasavubu, under US influence, declared Lumumba dismissed, Andrew Cordier used UN forces (Ghanaians) to close down Radio Leopoldville to both contenders. But Kasavubu could still be heard throughout the Congo on the powerful, and to him friendly, Brazzaville Radio, and Tshombe could also be heard, of course, on the no-less powerful Radio Elizabethville. Cordier also closed the airports to "non-UN traffic", while apparently classifying Lumumba's enemies as "UN traffic".

I did not know of these transactions at the time, but I learned of what had happened later, while serving in the Congo myself, and was disturbed by the story. But I comforted myself with the thought that Hammerskjold may not have been aware of what was going on. Having noted the relevant transactions referred to above, I wrote in a footnote in *To Katanga and Back*: "It was generally believed in the UN at the time that Hammerskjold was dismayed by Cordier's action but felt he had no alternative but to cover it."

Hammerskjold himself did nothing to discourage this "general belief" but as I found years after I had left the Congo, and written *To Katanga and Back*, the belief is without foundation. Catherine Hoskyns, in *The Congo Since Independence* (Oxford University Press, 1965), was the first to tell the story in scholarly detail. Hammerskjold played a key role in relation not merely to the downfall, but also in the death of Patrice Lumumba. After Lumumba's political downfall, he was offered physical protection by the

UN at his villa in Leopoldville. But the physical protection was guaranteed only while Lumumba remained at his residence, politically immobile, and cut off from his supporters.

Lumumba decided to leave Leopoldville and try to reach Stanleyville, which was controlled by his supporters, a decision that cost him first his liberty and then his life. Hammarskjold personally instructed UN forces in the Congo *"not to intervene between Mr Lumumba and his official pursuers"* [my italics – CCO'B]. The "official pursuers", using helicopters supplied to them, caught Lumumba and took him to the Leopoldville Airport, then fully controlled by UN forces. Pursuant to Hammarskjold's express instructions cited above, the UN forces looked on while Lumumba was savagely assaulted on the tarmac and forcibly fed with wads of paper supposed to contain his own speeches. From Leopoldville Airport, Lumumba was flown to Elisabethville Airport where he was again beaten and tormented, again under the passive and disciplined scrutiny of UN troops and again covered by the cameras. Then Lumumba was removed under the custody of Godefroid Munongo and never seen alive again.

Around the time I read the grim revelations in the Hoskyns book, I had also been reading *Markings*, Hammarskjold's spiritual diary in which he sees himself as a persecuted Christlike figure. The two books together had a weird effect on me. I had a dream in which I thought I had come into possession of a kind of political analogue to the spiritual *Markings*: a diary in which Hammarskjold candidly examined the nature of his political decisions and the reasons for them. The dream was an extremely vivid one and during it I was delighted with the discovery of the political diary. When I woke up and found that there was, in reality, no such document, my sense of loss was acute. I decided that I myself must fill the gap by writing a play, setting out the interaction between Hammarskjold's spiritual aspirations and his Machiavellian course in practical political decisions. I started to write the play, which became *Murderous Angels*, at four in the morning on which I awoke from the dream. (For the fate of *Murderous Angels*, see below, *Flights of Angels*).

* * *

Lumumba had been duly destroyed, and those who had laid the political base for his destruction were about to punish those who had physically destroyed him for the consequences of the crime for which the UN had itself prepared the way.

As I contemplate this sequence of events now, I am reminded of an analogous sequence of events which took place in India in the late eighteenth century. Philip Francis, briefly enjoying the leadership of the new Bengal Council, encouraged a prominent Brahmin, Nuncomar, to bring charges of corruption against Warren Hastings, Governor-General of Bengal. But the charges backfired. The Chief Justice of Bengal, Elijah Impey, was a friend and ally of Hastings. Impey had Nuncomar taken up on a charge of felony, committed and thrown into the common jail. Nuncomar appealed to Francis to come to his aid. But Francis, realising that he was now himself in deadly danger from the Hastings-Impey combination, sent Nuncomar's appeal to be burned by the common hangman and allowed it to be known that he had done so. Nuncomar was duly hanged. But subsequently Francis, by an extraordinary mental reversal of reality, saw himself as Nuncomar's avenger. Francis wrote, on his own return to England: "Nuncomar is returned and like Caesar's ghost with Ate by his side, is now ranging for revenge."

There are some resemblances there with Hammarskjold's position in relation to Lumumba. Hammarskjold had played a major role in seeing to it that Lumumba was handed over to the Katangans who promptly murdered him, as could have been predicted. But once Lumumba was safely murdered, Hammarskjold took a leading part in the international pressure designed to bring an end to the secessionist regime that had murdered Lumumba. In that sense, Caesar's ghost was now ranging for revenge.

The session of the Security Council that followed the announcement of Patrice Lumumba's death was the stormiest in the history of the United Nations. Large numbers of young blacks, furious at what they regarded as the betrayal and murder of Lumumba, filled the auditorium and chanted slogans. When security guards tried to eject some of them the guards were overwhelmed. Young women wielding shoes with stiletto heels were particularly effective. The imperative case for a change of course was dramatically demonstrated.

Against this dramatic background the Security Council, with the necessary agreement of all five Permanent Members, carried its Resolution of February 21, 1961, of which the cutting edge was contained in Paragraphs A1 and A2, running as follows:

A1: "Urges that the United Nations take immediately all appropriate measures to prevent the occurrence of civil war in the Congo, including arrangements for ceasefires, the halting of all military operations, the prevention of clashes and the use of force, if necessary in the last resort;

A2: "Urges that measures be taken for the immediate withdrawal and evacuation from the Congo of all Belgian and other foreign military paramilitary personnel and political advisers not under United Nations command, and mercenaries."

In retrospect I can see, much more clearly than I did at the time, that the British reservation regarding this Resolution – expressed in the debate after which they voted *for* the Resolution – was hardly of less political significance than the Resolution itself. Having referred to Paragraph A1 and some other paragraphs, the UK Representative, Sir Patrick Dean, on behalf of the British government, said that "each of these paragraphs taken in isolation could, it seems to me, mean that the United Nations would take action in the Congo by force without appropriate consultation with the representatives of the Congolese people. This interpretation would be, in the opinion of my delegation, extremely dangerous".

After the dire and then still recent experience of its Suez venture, when Britain had attempted to defy the United States, and failed miserably, Britain was not again about to challenge the United States, *openly*. A vote "for", combined with an express reservation, was as near as Britain could come to saying right out "Hands Off Katanga", but that is what Sir Patrick Dean's reservation meant.

I noted the British reservation, of course, at the time. But I did not then even come near to understanding the full force of the motivation behind it. The British government at that time was still strongly committed to the creation of a Central African Federation, and their attempted Federation was identical in its governing concept with Tshombe's Katanga. In both cases the governing concept was to protect the reality of continuing white rule behind a facade of black authority. And as well as that, the territories concerned were contiguous. The proposed Central African Federation was to consist of Northern and Southern Rhodesia and Nyasaland (later, Malawi). Northern Rhodesia and Katanga had a common border and the white inhabitants of the two territories had an acute and passionate community of interest.

In short, the British government, together with the white Rhodesians, had a far greater political and emotional commitment to the status quo in Katanga than any other power had to changing that status quo. That was the rock which I was about to hit.

* * *

My three predecessors representing the UN in Katanga had, as their unspoken mandate, not to rock the secessionist boat. They could and did advise Tshombe from time to time to rejoin the Congo. When he refrained from taking that advice, as he invariably did, matters rested there. After Lumumba's murder this would no longer do. Pressure was to be exerted, and Hammarskjold, in nominating me as his Special Representative in Katanga, was relying on me to exert that pressure directly on Elizabethville.

For some time before the crisis of January 1961, Hammarskjold had been taking some interest in me. That interest seems to have been first aroused by reading my book *Maria Cross*, since Hammarskjold shared my interest in the interplay of religion and the literary imagination. But Hammarskjold had also taken some interest in my activity at the UN. His closest adviser and friend here was George Ivan Smith, the Australian who handled press relations, and who later became a close friend of mine in rather peculiar conditions in Katanga itself, as I shall explain. George was of Irish descent – the "Ivan" sounds Russian but is in fact an Australian abbreviation of Sullivan. George had taken quite a close interest in my contributions to the debates at the UN and Hammarskjold himself had also taken some interest in these. The interest was, even then, not entirely academic. Hammarskjold realised that at some time I might turn out to be useful. An Irish representative could be expected to be more "anti-colonial" than other Europeans, but he could see that I was more "anti-colonial" – for example in supporting the Algerians against the French – than some other Irish representatives were, and certainly than most other European diplomats were. So when he wanted to send a representative to Katanga who would push Tshombe into accepting the February resolution the choice rather rapidly narrowed down to me. Tshombe would not have accepted an African or Asian, and white diplomatists with good "anti-colonial" credentials were not, at that time, thick on the ground. So my government agreed to release me and I was appointed.

Before proceeding to the Congo, I had a short briefing period at UN headquarters in New York. There I attended meetings of what was called "the Congo Club", consisting of those officials who advised the Secretary-General, or were deemed to advise him, on that thorny matter. The picture of the condition of the Congo which reached the Congo Club was rather strikingly different from the picture which reached the Congo Advisory Committee. The Advisory Committee saw no cables from or to the field. It was briefed by the Secretary-General, and the briefings invariably suggested that the UN in the field never did anything to which any section of the membership could take exception. The Congo Club, on the other hand, did see the incoming cables from the Congo, though not whatever instructions were going out from headquarters. Even the incoming cables suggested a pattern of more purposeful, less scrupulous, activity than one would have gathered from the briefings of the Advisory Committee.

But after attending a few meetings of the Congo Club, I found that the differences between the Committee and the Club were only in degree, not in kind. In both there was an appearance of consultation without the reality. And the Club was even more remote from reality than the Committee. Members of the Committee were appointed by, and responsible to, member governments. Members of the Club were selected by the Secretary-General, and so unlikely to question versions of events approved by him. They were there in reality to supply to certain groups approved versions of transactions. One of the most important of these groups in the Assembly was the Afro-Asian group, and a high proportion of the membership of the Club was drawn from that group.

A few members of the Club were in Hammarskjold's confidence but these were of less importance than some who were not in the Club at all. Andrew Cordier was not a member of the Club, having "lost the confidence" of the Afro-Asian block through his major role in the destruction of Patrice Lumumba. But the very manner in which he had forfeited the confidence of the Afro-Asians, meant that he retained the entire confidence of the people who always mattered most: the Americans.

Hammarskjold gave me no special briefing before I left for the Congo. He knew I would do my level best to implement the February Resolution. When I tried to do so, both he and I would see what happened then, how strong the opposition was, and how firm our backing would be against the opposition. All that was still to play for.

To Katanga and Back contains an account of my state of mind at the time when I set out for the Congo.

Naturally, I did not come to Katanga entirely without preconceived ideas, with my mind an ideal blank. From the character and arguments of Mr Tshombe's friends abroad, I thought it likely that his regime was indeed – as its critics said – a device for preserving local European, and outside financial, control of this very profitable territory. From what I have said about my general views, it will be understood that I did not find this system particularly congenial. But it would be wrong – and in one sense too flattering to myself – to assume that I came in any crusading spirit. I thought it quite natural that the local Europeans, the Union Miniere and other large interests, should try to hold on to what they had, and not at all surprising that they should have been able to find some local Africans to co-operate with them. The Europeans of Elisabethville, in the circumstances of July 1960, had reacted very much as any community placed in their position would have done and I knew that if I had been born and brought up among them I should have been likely to react in the same way (just as if I had been born a Kikuyu, and poor, I might have joined the Mau Mau). Historical relativism is not a point of view conducive to keeping up a high level of moral indignation. At the same time I felt that it should be possible, rationally, to convince those concerned that what had perhaps served their interests once – the secession of Katanga – could no longer serve them in the new "American-Afro-Asian" political conjuncture, and could only, if persisted in, bring upon them the very disasters they most feared. I knew that the great resources of American diplomacy would now be seriously exerted in this direction and I believed that the resources of British diplomacy – no less great in this area – would also be brought to bear, even if somewhat reluctantly. Against this background – and despite what I knew of the nature and tenacity of the forces supporting "Independent Katanga" – I thought it should be possible for a combined effort, pivoting on Hammarskjold and using the lever of the resolutions, to bring back Katanga into the Republic of the Congo without violence. Not only did I not desire or expect violence but at this moment I did not even take the prospect of violence very seriously, inclining – too schematically – to the belief that the people behind Tshombe had too much at stake to risk disorder.

In short, my state of mind, at the beginning of this most critical phase of my life, was not fanatical, but it was dangerously complacent, not to say smug.

The story of my eventful sojourn in Katanga is set out in length in *To Katanga and Back* and I don't want to cover all that ground again. As soon as I can, I want to "cut to the chase" and get to the "show-down" period of August-September 1961. But first something needs to be said about the three most important figures with whom I was to have dealings during this period.

At the time I arrived in Elisabethville, in mid-June 1961, Tshombe was more or less a prisoner in Leopoldville, where he agreed to end the secession of Katanga. Once back in Katanga, in late June, however, he ignored what he had agreed to in Leopoldville and declared that Katanga would remain independent: "We shall see to it that the Katangese nation shall endure. Let the enemies of Katanga know that they have to do with a people."

The following is my account in *To Katanga and Back*:

"From this time on I saw Tshombe almost every day, sometimes at the CSK building with his ministers, more often in his palace, formerly the Governor's palace – a large suburban villa in front of which groups of his supporters, Lunda tribesmen or white-robed members of the revivalist sect of Apostles, would gather to beat drums, dance and sing. I suspect that this continuous spectacle was organized, like other spontaneous manifestations of African feeling in Elizabethville, by the Minister for Information, Lucas Samalenghe, with the help of French specialists who were used to organizing similar demonstrations of Moslems in Algiers. (A pleasing and not untypical item in the *Echo du Katanga* at this time told of a patriotic Katangese woman who had given birth to triplets whom she had christened Tshombe, Moise; Munongo, Godefroid and – Samalenghe, Lucas). We used to sit in a little, rather over-furnished salon with a French window giving on the lawn: a French window through which Munongo used often to arrive "accidentally" and rather out of breath, when I had been twenty minutes or more with the President. He had, apparently, his sources of information in the palace.

"Tshombe was always hospitable and friendly in manner. He often wore an attractive, rueful but consciously winning smile, like a spoiled boy caught with the jam but knowing that he is not likely to be punished. He had a pleasantly reminiscent vein of conversation: about the shop he used to run at Sandoa; about the Belgians – how they had always hated him, because he, a black, was successful in business – how they had worked against him and caused his three bankruptcies; about his brother who now owned a chain of shops and had nothing to do with politics and how he, Tshombe, envied his brother; about the Leopoldville politicians and what a worthless lot they were, with the exception of Mobutu; about his sufferings and apprehensions in Coquilhatville and Leopoldville – the sufferings seem to have amounted to not much more than the refusal of writing material, but the apprehensions must have been real enough; above all about his health, which he believed to be very bad. While he was talking, a maidservant would come in carrying on a silver tray glasses of champagne and beer! Both of us took beer; I don't know what happened to all the champagne. Tshombe, unlike Munongo, was reasonably abstemious and, like the moderately good Methodist he was, very censorious of the night-club existence of several of the Leopoldville ministers. Indeed the only political theme which he ever discussed voluntarily was the incompetence and irresponsibility of these ministers. Unlike Munongo, he never showed any outward sign of 'Katangese patriotism' – or indeed of any other political feeling. Politics, he conveyed, was the business he happened to be 'in' at present – unlike his more fortunate brother – and its ups and downs were distinctly trying. He made no pretence of being master of the situation in Elisabethville. 'Munongo is a very loyal man,' he said, 'but if I tell him to do something he doesn't like, he simply refuses. He tells me, "You are just a president. You are not a dictator. This is a democracy and as Minister of the Interior I do what I wish."'

"It would be wrong, I think, to regard Tshombe either as simply a tool, or an independent agent. It is certain that he would not have reached the eminence of a 'Head of State' without the support – including at a crucial stage, military support – of local and other Europeans. But it was by no means certain that the same interests which had made him president – in preference to the more eminent and impressive Munongo – now had direct control of him. In a sense it might be said that the more moderate Europeans were prisoners of their own fiction; once it had been proclaimed that there was a Katangese Nation, of which the hero, the symbol and the spokesman was Tshombe, then it became considerably more difficult for local European residents to control Tshombe than it had been when he was a moderately successful grocer. This, in a rather unpredictable way, gave remarkable scope to Munongo and his friends. Tshombe knew he did not have to fear the moderate, or the faint-hearted, Europeans; they could not publicly attack him – or if they did he, and especially Munongo, would have a splendid time defying 'Belgian dictation'. Moderate industrialists could try discreet financial pressure – since the 'State of Katanga' was entirely dependent financially on the great European enterprises – but that too had its risks. One of Munongo's favourite themes, both in public and in private, was the 'scorched earth' policy which Katanga would pursue if it were ever 'betrayed to the Lumumbists'. This programme included blowing up the great hydro-electric station at Le Marinel, and doing such other damage to the highly valuable technological network of the mining area as would take many years to repair. His French friends backed Munongo in this, and also dropped hints about what the 'counter-terrorists of the Main Rouge' had done to industrialists of Milan and the Ruhr who had helped the FLN. In the Katanga situation, remarks of this kind had their impact and the 'moderates' – including, I believe, Tshombe himself – were distinctly impressed. Tshombe had nothing to fear, he believed, from the moderates and little from the UN; he might have much to fear, politically and even physically, from his own right wing (which included, of course, many Belgian civilian advisers as well as Munongo and the French). The more I got to know Tshombe, the more I regarded him as, above all, a sensitive indicator of the actual balance of political forces in Katanga. Personally, he might well have preferred a safe and dignified place, as provincial president, to the glorious and dangerous hazard of leading a secessionist State; if he made no serious move to end the secession, it may have been because he felt the process of ending the secession likely to be even more dangerous than the secession itself. The obscurity of private life often tempted him, as he confessed; his opponents, like his schoolmate Jason Sendwe, believed that he clung to office so tenaciously because he could not make anything like so much money doing anything else. Certainly glory and patriotic emotion – powerful motives with Munongo – seemed to have little sway over Tshombe's astute though limited intelligence. If Munongo resembled a nobleman of the Wars of the Roses, Tshombe brought to mind the more realistic politicians of a somewhat later age. 'Crooked as this man's course was' – wrote Macaulay of the Restoration statesman, Sunderland – 'the law which determined it was simple. His conduct is to be ascribed to the alternate influence of cupidity and fear on a mind highly susceptible of both those passions, and quick-sighted rather than far-sighted.'"

* * *

Godefroid Munongo had features such as one sees on certain African wood-carvings, with long, almost flat cheeks and a heavy pouting under-lip. You could not tell what his eyes were like, because of the famous dark glasses which he invariably wore, and this increased his rather uncanny sculptural effect. Tall and well-built, he carried his head high, with the bearing of one who was conscious of being an aristocrat. He spoke good French in a low, deep voice which came in rapid surges and as he spoke he had the habit of turning his head slowly from side to side, making the light flash from his spectacles. When things went normally, as when I met him first, he used to sit well back in his chair, immobile save for the restlessness of his head and long, well-manicured hands. If warmed by argument, however, he was liable to violent, convulsive movements. Once, a few weeks after I had met him I happened to mention the name of Lumumba in his presence. He raised his right arm with a jerk and then sharply slapped the back of his neck. At first I thought he had been bitten by an insect. Then I realized that his instinctive reaction, which he had barely, at the last moment, brought under control, was to strike the man who mentioned Lumumba's name.

* * *

215

Much more momentous for me than my relations with the two most prominent Katangese was my relation with Mahmoud Khiary, the Tunisian diplomat attached to UN headquarters in Leopoldville. My first contact with Khiary occurred shortly after my first arrival in Leopoldville, and at that time I was far from recognising his political importance. I encountered Khiary without speaking to him at ONUC Headquarters on the sixth floor of a Leopoldville hotel. I recalled in *To Katanga and Back*:

"I remember a big man in a brown suit standing in the middle of Dr Linner's vast office, and I remember Eliot's line coming into my head: 'The silent vertebrate in brown.'

"The vertebrate in question had a bald head, also brown, and a moustache, and was reading a telegram. He handed the telegram back to Dr Linner without a word, and went out. Not only did I have no faint premonition that I had just met a man whose words and actions would transform the future course of my life, but I was hardly conscious of him at all, or only as one would be conscious of a man who came to read the gasmeter. I took in a vague impression of a person accustomed to work with his hands, and must have drawn the subconscious, mandarin-like conclusion that this was not a person who needed to be reckoned with intellectually. When he withdrew without any comment on the important telegram he had read, I dismissed him from my mind, labelled 'EGD'. This was a contemptuous UN term, applied to those rather numerous officials who appear to have been recruited, not so much for any personal merit, as in deference to the Charter principle of 'equitable geographical distribution' – 'we have nobody from Patagonia'. I was, of course, profoundly misinterpreting the situation. The silence was not caused by absence of ideas – very far from it – but by mistrust. He had not come into the room to read a telegram – which he had read already – but to take a look at the man who was going to Elisabethville. This I learned later. Of my impressions at the time, faint and peripheral as they were, I remember no more. I do not even remember, strange as the thought now appears, whether anyone at any time bothered to introduce me to Mahmoud Khiary."

My next meeting with Khiary was in July 1961 when the Katanga situation was already heating up, and Khiary visited Elisabethville. The Speaker of the "Katanga National Assembly" had been threatening the UN with punitive action if I continued my "provocative" policy towards Katanga, and I was warning him against the danger of any such Katangan reaction. Khiary listened with keen interest to this exchange. Again, from *To Katanga and Back*:

"'Is that', asked Mahmoud Khiary, 'the way you talk to the Speaker of the Assembly? You send me the Fougas, I send you the Gurkhas!' (Fougas were Katanga military aircraft. Gurkhas were the most formidable troops in UN service.) 'Is that the language you usually employ around here? In Leopoldville we are used to a quieter kind of diplomacy.'

"His face is not exactly expressionless, but its expression is not easy to read. His brown eyes, more opaque than most people's, were turned inquiringly in my direction. This was something, as I was to find, unusual with him; he was more apt to look into space or at the ground, and his method of obtaining information was seldom the straight question. He had then only just arrived in Elisabethville; I had already had time to note that he was not at all the gasmeter-mender of my Leopoldville imaginings, but a formidable personality. What his political outlook was I had no idea and his Tunisian nationality gave no clear clue. Some Tunisians were, in their own peculiar way, very 'moderate'. I remembered one prominent Tunisian diplomat whom I had met in New York the previous autumn at the time of Lumumba's arrest. 'Why wasn't he killed trying to escape'? asked the Tunisian. 'After all, chaos has its own logic . . . ' In what direction logic might be taking Mr Khiary I could not know, but his question annoyed me.

"It was necessary, I explained stiffly, to react with great firmness. The people who ran Katanga had got the idea that the UN would do no more than make a pretence of applying the resolutions; it was time to convince them that things had changed and that the UN could neither be intimidated nor cajoled into leaving the Katangan status quo intact.

"Khiary smiled. 'Don't let me get in your way,' he said, 'you have work to do.'"

* * *

From that time until after the outbreak of hostilities between the UN and the Tshombe regime, Khiary and I worked as close allies. Nominally, Khiary was only a "special adviser" to Sture Linner, "Officer-in-Charge" in the Congo since the departure of Dayal. But Linner, though personally trusted by Hammarskjold, was a political cipher. Khiary, on the other hand was a politician to his fingertips, and also politically well-connected in a highly relevant way. He was close to Mongi Slim, Prime Minister of Tunisia, the most influential politician in the Afro-Asian group at the UN, and indispensable to Hammarskjold in his pivotally-important dealings with that group. Unlike myself, Khiary travelled frequently between the Congo and New York and had regular access to Hammarskjold. My own dealings with Hammarskjold were now entirely through Khiary, and that is the way Hammarskjold seemed to want it.

* * *

The plans for the operation known as "Rumpunch" had already been drawn up and went into effect toward the end of August, 1961. By then Khiary and I were convinced that negotiations with Tshombe would always remain fruitless, since Tshombe was not his own master. Direct intervention would be necessary. The first form of intervention chosen was the arrest of the Belgian officers who were in charge of "the armed forces of independent Katanga". This operation was co-ordinated, through Khiary, I assume, with the Central Government of the Congo which passed Ordinance No 70 to expel from the territory of the Republic of the Congo – which legally included Katanga – all the non-Congolese officers and mercenaries, etc. This ordinance, in the Secretary-General's view, "gave the UN legal rights within the Congo" – again including Katanga – "corresponding to the [February] resolution". In other words it was taken as legalising the use of force by the UN to expel the mercenaries.

Finding that the UN now meant business, Tshombe capitulated. At one o'clock on August 28 from Radio Katanga, now back under his control, he broadcast a statement, entirely free from complaint or hostility, in which he said that he bowed to the decision of the UN – *"Je m'incline devant l'ONU"* – and that all the foreign officers were dismissed from Katanga service and must leave Katanga.

In retrospect, I can see that this was the great missed opportunity. If the UN could then have deployed an armed contingent at the presidential palace "for the President's protection", Tshombe would have continued to bow to the decisions of the UN and the secession would have been well and truly over. Tshombe's armed guard, when I encountered them that day had taken the news of the expulsion of the Belgian officers very cheerfully indeed, and certainly would not have opposed the "assistance" of a UN contingent. But control of the presidential palace had not been envisaged in the original plan, and the opportunity of a bloodless end to the secession was missed.

As I wrote to Máire MacEntee on the day after Tshombe's acquiescence:

"We're very happy here and probably dangerously cocky and euphoric about our coup on Monday." Too right, as I was very soon to find. But for a day or so we could bask in approval from UN headquarters. The Secretary General cabled:

"Congo Club in congress assembled passed unanimous vote of congratulations gratification and sincere respect for an exceedingly sensitive operation carried through with skill and courage. We hope that results will render your task in other aspects easier and increasingly constructive."

Both Tshombe and the local Belgians were at this stage ready to give up on the secession, as now endangering the interests it had been set up to defend. But the British and the Rhodesians, seeing a looming threat to their cherished Central African Federation, were by no means ready to give up. Predictably, the loudest, clearest and earliest signals came from the Rhodesian leader, Sir Roy Welensky. Within a few days of Rumpunch, Sir Roy said that the high-handed activities of the UN had caused concern among many Katangese and that he was taking dispositions to protect the security of the Rhodesian frontiers. "It is not in the public interest for me to divulge the exact nature of these dispositions, but they will be adequate." He added that he had received an assurance that the British government "would not accept an attempt by the UN to seize Katanga by force".

It was soon clear that Sir Roy's statement was discreetly but firmly supported by the British government, the discretion being dictated by relations with the United States which was known to have backed Rumpunch. I refer to *To Katanga and Back*.

Sir Roy's statement was conveyed to Mr Tshombe by the British and Rhodesian Vice-Consul, Mr David Smith, who was accompanied by Mr Dunnett, the Consul. Mr Dunnett told me afterwards that he said nothing, but just sat there while Mr Smith read Sir Roy's text in French. Nonetheless, Mr Tshombe and his friends seem to have seen in Mr Dunnett's physical presence, mute but moving testimony to the truth of Sir Roy's statement about the assurance he had received from the British government, and also to the reality of the British support for Sir Roy's stand. *L'Echo du Katanga* carried Sir Roy's message prominently on its front page ("Sir Roy Welensky's Encouraging Stand" was the headline) and it also carried on the back page, above a reassuring communique from the Minister of the Interior ("only suspicious cases will be arrested") the following:

"The British Consul conveys his Government's sympathy to the Katanga cause. President Tshombe received the British Consul, accompanied by his Vice-Consul, who came to convey the sympathy of their Governement to the Katangese cause. They declared to the Head of State that their Government was following the situation in Katanga with much attention.

"At the same time another delegate from the British Government, coming from Salisbury, arrived in Elisabethville to take stock of the situation after the departure of the European technicians".

A few days later Sir Roy announced in Salisbury that the Rhodesian federal government was to have field batteries of artillery. "We cannot," he added, "regard our armed forces as being concerned only with internal security." Sir Roy's oratory and armed preparations, and Mr Dunnett's silent sympathy, must have been most heartening to the friends of independent Katanga. "If things go on," wrote *La Libre Belgique* on September 9, "some people consider that Sir Roy Welensky would not hesitate to intervene, with his troops already massed on the Katangan frontier."

In those first days of September the pressures were mounting rapidly from Britain and Rhodesia, but also mounting inside Katanga itself. Munongo's police attacked the Baluba residents of South Katanga, suspected (rightly) of disloyalty to the Katanga regime. Persecuted by Munongo's police, the Balubas took refuge in the vicinity of the UN military camps.

By August 31, there were 700 refugees in our camps; by September 1, 4,000; by September 3, 10,000; by September 5, 20,000; by September 9, 35,000; by September 12, probably more than 45,000; but in reality we had lost count. These were mainly Baluba of Kasai, with a minority of Baluba of Katanga, Tshokwe and other groups. They included among them the African elite of Elisabethville, almost all Kasai Baluba: white-collar workers with good homes who now came to squat on the ground around our camps in conditions of the greatest misery and squalor.

Simultaneously, Munongo's police started organising "spontaneous African demonstrations" against the UN. Ray Moloney of the UPI described aspects of this campaign:

"I watched the Katanga Government mount a deliberate 'hate campaign' against the UN. I saw UN troops being stoned even though they made no attempt to retaliate. The stoning attacks were led by officials of the Katanga Information Service. I listened to Katanga Radio while it claimed that UN Indian troops raped and pillaged their way through the African quarters of Elisabethville."

It should be noted that these actions were not the immediate reaction to the operation of August 28; they came only after Welensky's message. The demonstrations were also directed against the American Consulate. The

British and French consulates were not molested. The untutored and spontaneously indignant natives thereby indicated a surprisingly accurate appreciation of the alignment of the powers.

In the British press, and also in much of the American press, the activities drummed up by the British and Rhodesians and Munongo's police were interpreted as the breakdown of order in Katanga due to the intervention of the UN. And this view of the matter looked plausible, not merely to many outsiders, but also to many of the UN troops, some of whom had adapted only too well to the view of local realities which prevailed among the Europeans of Katanga.

In the circumstances I advocated UN military intervention under paragraphs A.1 and 9 C of the Security Council Resolution of February 21 1961, allowing "all appropriate measures to prevent the occurrence of civil war in the Congo." Khiary secured Hammarskjold's approval for this intevention, although this was later to be disputed. A recent scholarly study – *Britain and the Congo Crisis (1960-1963)* by Professor Alan James (Macmillan Press 1996) – leaves no doubt about the facts, however:

> "At this juncture Linner was absent from the Congo, putting the UN's view of things to Brussels. It was therefore Mahmoud Khiary (standing in for Linner) who took up the correspondence with New York. Khiary was head of ONUC's civilian operations, but had become deeply involved in high political matters. He assured Hammarskjold that the warrants were on the way, and that the instructions to O'Brien were those given in 9C, subject to Hammarskjold's emphasis on the importance of keeping the door open for Tshombe to maintain his legitimate provincial status. Khiary wrote of the necessity of implementing 9C as a whole, and sought authority to do so. But he said, in a phrase which later assumed significance, 'the instructions will be carried out only after agreement with yourselves [sic] at Leo[poldville]' (Hammarskjold was due to arrive there on September 13). Hammarskjold responded by saying: 'we are beyond the point of no return as regards your plans under 9C. You are therefore authorised to pursue the policy'."

(*Britain and the Congo Crisis* pp 102-3. The author sent me a copy of his book with the inscription: "To CCOB – who was, I think, rather hard done by over the Congo . . . ")

I served notice on Tshombe that the actions of his government were likely to cause civil war.

Khiary himself and Vladimir Fabry, ONUC's adviser, brought me the instructions for the operation which was to bear the military codename Morthor – a Hindu word meaning "smash".

In the drawing-room of the UN residence, Villa des Roches, on the afternoon of Monday, September 11, Fabry opened his brief-case and handed me five individual warrants. He was smiling like a Machiavellian Santa Claus. Khiary looked on benevolently. The documents were *mandats d'amener* – warrants for arrest, in the names of Tshombe, Moise; Munongo, Godefroid; Kibwe, Jean-Baptiste; Kimba, Evariste; and Mutaka, Charles. The charges were the same in all five cases: *"Tortures et assassinats."* These warrants were printed forms, with blanks, apparently as used in the former Belgian Congo. There was only a small space for the charge, or *motivation*, and the *mandats* did not say whom these men had tortured or assassinated – presumably Lumumba and his companions, perhaps others also. The document was signed by the head of the central government *parquet* – the attorney-general, roughly speaking – in Leopoldville.

I have not preserved copies of the individual warrants, but I have a copy of a collective warrant in the same five names, which accompanied the individual warrants and ran, in translation, as follows:

"REPUBLIC OF THE CONGO
Pro Justitia
Mandats d'Amener

Article 15 of the code of penal procedure,

We, de Loof Adrien, Officier du Ministere Public pres la Cour d'Appel de Leopoldville:

On foot of the proceedings instituted against:

Tshombe, Moise; Munongo, Godefroid; Kimba, Evariste; Kibwe, Jean; Mutaka-wa-Dilomba –

charged with: Sedition, Murder, Arbitrary Arrests and Bodily Torture, Crimes envisaged in and punishable under Articles 43, 44, 45, 67, 180, 192, 193 of the Penal Code.

Pursuant to the ministerial decrees of 6 September 1961;

Pursuant to the Parliamentary Resolutions of 8 and 9 September 1961;

As there exists against the aforesaid grave evidence of guilt and as there is reason to fear that they may attempt to evade arrest,

Request and require that the aforesaid be arrested and produced before us,

Request all commanders of the armed forces to assist in the carrying out of the present mandate.

Leopoldville, 9th. September 1961
L'Officier du Ministere Public
A. de Loof

(Rubber stamp: Republic
of the Congo. Parquet
General de Leopoldville)"

Clipped to this last document (probably in error since it had no direct bearing on the execution of our task) was a copy of a document on the same headed paper, under the same date, signed by the same official, this time in the capacity of Procureur General *ad interim* and reading as follows:

"Note to Messr s . . .

– *Procureur d'Etat Torfs*
First Substitute Thirriart

Are requested in confirmity with the decision of the Minister of Justice, to place themselves at the disposition of M. Khiary, Agent (*Chargé de Mission*) of the UN at Leopoldville and to obtain all relevant information at the UN Security Office (*le Royal*)."

As regards Tshombe, we were to arrest him only in the last resort. His residence was to be cut off, the entries and exits to it sealed, and then I was to parley with him, making it clear that his only hope lay in co-operating with the United Nations, and in peacefully liquidating the secession of Katanga.

Khiary asked me whether Tshombe would be likely to co-operate. I told him I thought Tshombe would, if he were sure we meant business, and if he felt the danger of being sent to Leopoldville for trial was greater for the moment than the danger of being murdered by Munongo and his friends. He had "bowed before the United Nations" on August 28; he had stopped bowing after Welensky's statement, but he had not been active personally in the anti-UN campaign. He had, indeed, given me the impression of a man who wondered what we were waiting for. If we acted firmly, he would bow again.

Sporadic firing against UN forces broke out, orchestrated by the French officers who had escaped arrest, probably supported by Rhodesian infiltrators who supplied the core of what later became known as "the Katanga resistance".

At half-four on the morning of September 13 while heavy firing continued, the telephone rang. It was Tshombe, very excited. He kept asking "What does it mean? What does it mean?" I told him what the instructions were, and asked him to order his forces not to resist the UN. He said a ceasefire should be ordered on both sides. I said UN forces would cease fire if Katanga forces were prepared to do so. The UN forces must, however, take over the objectives assigned to them; my instructions were categorical (*formelles*) and I had no power to depart from them. While we were talking, fighting was going on unnecessarily. I asked him to end it by an unconditional ceasefire order, and then contact me again. He agreed.

Fifteen minutes later Tshombe rang again. He had sent out an aide, Major Mwamba, to Camp Massart to order the cessation of all resistance to the United Nations. I now asked him to make a statement on the radio declaring the secession of Katanga at an end. He had only one question to ask about this proposition:

"Est-ce que vous me garantissez ma sécurité personnelle? Do you guarantee my personal safety?"

I told him that, assuming he agreed to make the statement I suggested, and was prepared to co-operate with the central government civil representatives who were now on their way, I was empowered to guarantee not only his personal safety but also his retention in office as provincial president. He said he agreed. *Entendu. D'accord.* I asked him to come over to the Villa des Roches – a distance of about half a mile – to settle the details. He said he was afraid of being shot at on the road and asked for a UN escort.

No escort was immediately available. We sent for one, but, knowing there would be a delay, Michel [Tombelaine, my press assistant] said he would take his own car and fetch the President. Tshombe agreed to that; he would wait for Michel. I said that I thought his attitude was wise and statesmanlike and in the best interests both of Katanga and the Congo. I thanked him for it.

"Pas d'quoi. Not at all," he said.

As I put down the phone, Michel grinned. Both of us felt a lightness of heart such as we were not again to experience for quite a long time. Michel drove off to the palace.

At five o'clock Raja sent the following wireless message: "Tshombe has requested all firing to stop. He is ordering own troops to cease fire. If they do so UN troops should stop firing, but they should continue to take objectives with or without firing."

I dictated a draft statement for Tshombe to make on the radio. It was a good text, statesmanlike and wise. Before I had finished it, however, Michel was back, without Tshombe. The guard on the gate – excited by the noise of firing still continuing in the distance – had tried to arrest him and as he escaped had shot at his car. But the really grim news he brought was that not a single UN soldier was to be seen in the neighbourhood of the palace, which we had been assuming to be securely blockaded.

The absence of any UN force in the area was a really grave matter. I do not know the reason for this absence. I know that Katanga headquarters and Sector B had different conceptions regarding it; my belief is that the point about encirclement of the palace got lost in the linguistic and other interstices between the two headquarters. In any case, wherever along the line it had got lost, there was no point in my seeking out the responsible person – and thereby perhaps aggravating certain frictions – because the responsible person was myself. Nobody, so much as myself, appreciated, or could be expected to appreciate, the central and vital political importance of isolating Tshombe. If I had failed to stress this sufficiently, and failed to check exactly what was being done about it – as if it were one among the details of military execution which did not concern me – then I would have to carry the political consequences of these failures. And I did.

By this time, as I learned shortly afterwards, Tshombe had gone over the wall of his palace into the neighbouring grounds of the residence of the British Consul, Denzil Dunnett. Dunnett, probably acting on previous "contingency" instructions drove Tshombe – I believe under a rug in the back of Dunnett's car – the thirty miles or so to the Rhodesian border, where the Rhodesian authorities warmly welcomed him. Tshombe's voice was then heard over the Rhodesian radio, as was to be expected, declaring war on the UN. By this time, Morthor had definitely gone off the rails.

That was how things stood when Hammarskjold arrived in Leopoldville, probably expecting Tshombe's surrender.

On his arrival, Hammarskjold received an early and clear military report as to the action taken on September 13. The following message was signalled at 7.20 pm:

"1920 From HQ Katanga Command Eville to ONUC Leopoldville Info: HQ Sector A Aville, HQ Sector B Eville, HQ Sector C Kamina

Sitrep from 121600 Z to 131600 Z

Firstly for OP Morthor plan as follows. Alpha 1 Dogra Bn Gp with under emd one coy 3/1 AR. task. seize. one. EVILLE post office and Radio installation in vicinity. two. Radio Katanga studio three. Take in UN costody minister of info Samalenghe four. secure air field five custody of arrested personnel. Bravo. 35 Irish battalion GP. task. seize. one. Radio transmitter at college St. Francois, two. take into UN custody Minister of finance Kibwe three seize and est rd bloc railway tunnel. four secure refugee camrp at factory and own line. charlie 12 swed battalion GP with one coy of 3/1 AR task to seize. one. radio transmitter en route de Kilobelobe. two take into UN custody Minister interior Munongo. officers of surete white personnel working and African chiefs. three secure refugee camp. secondly first shot was fired from Belgian Consulate building near post office at 130400 B at Dogras. Thirdly radio Katanga studio and post office captured by Dogra by 130500 b after heavy stiff hand to hand fighting. Both places counter attacked by gendarmerie with their armd cars led mostly by Belgians in civilian clothes. counter-attack repulsed by Dogras and Swedish armed cars. Fourthly due heavy mortar fire and automatic fire from gendarmerie studio completely damaged beyond repairs. Fifthly Irish BN captured transmitter at College St. Francois firmly in our hands. Sixthly Swedish Bn captured radio transmitter Kilobelobe. Seventhly. strong and automatic firing and sniping inside the town continues. Eighthly Irish coy at Jadotville attacked by gendarmerie. attack repulsed reinforcement of one coy and three armd cars sent to Jadotville and coy directed to remain there until further orders. Ninthly Kibwe apprehended. Munongo, Mutaka, Samalenghe and Kimba have disappeared. Tshombe is not traceable at present . . .

* * *

Since Hammarskjold had approved our action in advance, he could have justified it on the only grounds that could justify what we had actually done: that UN action had been taken under the authority of paragraph A1 of the February resolution, which authorised the use of force in civil war situations.

He could have identified the secessionist government of the State of Katanga as a fomentor and wager of civil war both inside north and central Katanga and between Katanga and the rest of the Congo, and as an instigator of inter-tribal hate even in the south Katanga towns. He could have said that, once the force acted under A1, he, as Secretary-General, under the general authority of the resolutions, was bound to co-operate with the central government in installing its legitimate authority in the province.

It is true that such action is plainly contrary to the literal meaning of some parts of some of the resolutions (notably paragraph 4 of the resolution of August 9). But the Secretary-General has to interpret the resolutions as a whole and could hold that, in the event of apparent conflict between parts of them, the latest and most specific resolution, that of February, was the best guide as to his present mandate.

The tragedy is that he took a course which could only be justified by lying. He allowed the world to be given an official version which was so phrased as to conceal the reality of what had happened, making what had been an active intervention by the UN look like a defensive action. The following is the wording of the relevant section of the UN document (S/4940) issued on September 14th, when Hammarskjold was in Leopoldville:

"Paragraph 15: In the early hours of September 13th, the UN forces therefore took security precautions similar to those applied on August 28th. and deemed necessary to prevent inflammatory broadcasts or other threats to the maintenance of law and order, while the UN resumed carrying out its task of apprehending and evacuating foreign military and para-military personnel. At this point, an alert was set since arson was discovered at the UN garage. As the UN troops were proceeding towards the garage premises, fire was opened on them from the building where a number of foreign officers are known to be staying. UN troops were subsequently also resisted and fired at as they were deploying towards key points or while they were guarding installations in the city."

If this is an accurate account of what took place in Elisabethville on the morning of September 13, my name is Titus Oates.

The fighting started in the quite different way set out in this chapter, and had its origin in Katango-European resistance to a planned action by the UN. The historical inaccuracy of S/4940 – which reversing Ridley and Latimer, put out a fire that was never lit – had very important practical implications. It put the UN in every sense, in a false position. False, literally, first and worst of all; false militarily and false politically; false from the point of view of public opinion, for it was meeting the Big Lie of Katanga propaganda with something less than a half-truth. The Big Lie could, I suppose, be met with another Big Lie; it can also be met effectively with the truth, as the BBC showed on many occasions during the Second World War; it cannot be met with evasion, concealment and ambiguity. Friends of the United Nations could only be puzzled, and rendered ineffective, by this official version; enemies of the organization could use it to back their accusations of hypocrisy. The version was false militarily because the UN forces could not be given a clear mission. Finally the version was false politically for the great political objective of the UN was, and necessarily remained, to end the secession of Katanga, and that objective was jeopardized, or at least postponed, by an official version which made it possible for Mr Tshombe at any moment – by simply saying "I accept a ceasefire" – to come back to Elisabethville and re-establish his secessionist state.

It is true that the last paragraph of the document contained indications that the UN action after all did have something to do with ending secession:

> "Paragraph 20: In the afternoon of September 13, the Central Government of the Republic of the Congo dispatched the Commissaire d'Etat for Katanga, Mr ED Bocheley, to assist the provincial authorities in the restoration of law and order. The UN dispatched a team of technical experts to help in the restoration of essential utilities and public services."

Both the Commissaire and the team were dispatched, though the report does not say so, in the same UN plane. Nor does the report mention the decisions of the Central Parliament. Mr Bocheley-Davidson, and his government, thought that his mission was to end the secession. The UN action had been designed solely towards that end, and from that end it was now beginning, murkily and irresolutely, to recede.

I did not see S/4940 until the fighting was over, and I did not imagine that our action would, or could, be explained to the public in anything like this way. My instructions, taken as a whole, had the unmistakeable meaning of ending the secession of Katanga, following the application of A1 (preventing civil war). I saw no point in attempting to pretend that our action had any other character, and I declared that the secession of Katanga was at an end. In my opinion, if the UN had not tried to disguise its own action, but had firmly followed it up, the secession then could have been ended. I do not believe that the military command was of a different opinion. But, in view of the very different decision, or indecision, represented by S/4940, my remarks, and similar remarks on Radio Tombelaine, sounded very bad in Leopoldville. We were severely rebuked. As we had not read S/4940 we could not understand what was now happening, since we did not know what was supposed to have happened already.

The operation had gone wrong, and consequently Hammarskjold was under heavy political pressure to pretend, as he did in S/4940, that it had never been attempted.

Arthur Gavshon, in his valuable book *The Mysterious Death of Dag Hammarskjold* has given a detailed account, clearly based on conversations with eye-witnesses, of Hammarskjold's last days in Leopoldville. Amid much else of interest, he records the crucially important *démarche*, made to Hammarskjold on the evening of September 13 by the British Ambassador, Derek Riches, on instructions from Lord Home:

"The Ambassador began to read with care a compelling passage in his instructions, Hammarskjold's aides leant forward to listen more intently. The sense of what they heard amounted to just this:

"Her Majesty's Government was serving notice, with the greatest emphasis at its command, that Britain would have to consider withdrawing all support from ONUC's missions unless:

1: Hammarskjold could provide an acceptable explanation for what had happened in Katanga; or

2: Hammarskjold could provide an assurance that the fighting would swiftly be ended.

That night, after discussions following the departure of Ambassador Riches between Hammarskjold and his senior advisers – discussions in which McKeown, Khiary and Fabry favoured reinforcement and a firm line, but were overruled – Hammarskjold, Linner, Khiary, Fabry and some of the others turned to the precise terms of the official report that had to be sent early next day to New York."

The official report, Document S/4940, contained, in paragraph 15, an attempt to find the "acceptable explanation", so insistently demanded by Lord Home.

These were adequate political reasons for adopting what might appear a rather squalid course. But I don't think Hammarskjold would have seen it as at all squalid.

Psychologically, one can only hazard a few guesses. Hammarskjold was a very proud man who had been under intense strain and subjected to violent personal vituperation. He had taken this, from the Soviet side, unflinchingly; but I believe that some of the Western attacks must have hurt more deeply, because they struck a responsive chord in himself. For him, determined action in Katanga, of the Rumpunch-Morthor character, was warranted by international necessities, but I suspect that he may have felt some sense of guilt at the need to disturb the order which we believed reigned there. He was affected, in any case, by the fact of his own past reluctance to disturb that order, and by words which he himself had spoken, a year before, about not interfering in internal affairs, and not using the UN force to influence the outcome of constitutional disputes.

He was involved here in a concealed contradiction. An essential element of his policy, in the early days, was not to use the UN force to end the secession – which was one of the objects for which the Congo government had invited the force in. The Afro-Asian governments had criticised this severely, and ultimately carried the February Resolution which, as they interpreted it, provided a means, in effect, of using force to end the secession. And Hammarskjold had bound himself to seek their guidance on how to apply the Resolution. This contradiction may have led him to seek consistency with previous words at the expense of consistency with present action. This might have cost him less of a struggle than it would have cost anyone who delighted less in ambiguity. The successful wielder of ambiguity has a certain high imperiousness in his attitude to facts and inclines to a magician-like confidence in the overmastering power of language. This confidence is unfortunately contagious.

* * *

At midnight on September 16, Mr Dunnett told me that Tshombe was prepared to meet me at Bancroft, Northern Rhodesia. I cabled to Leopoldville for instructions, adding a recommendation that I should not go to Rhodesia, since to do so might be tantamount to accepting something resembling the arbitration of Sir Roy Welensky. I had already made it clear to Tshombe, through Mr Dunnett, that I was prepared to meet him without escort anywhere in Katanga.

Hammarskjold took off from Leopoldville on September 17 for Ndola, Northern Rhodesia, where Tshombe and Lord Alport, British High Commissioner in Rhodesia, awaited him. As the world knows the plane crashed near Ndola and all aboard, including Hammarskjold, were killed.

It was asserted at the time by some of those who were waiting for Hammarskjold at Ndola that his plane, when seemingly about to land, turned and made off in the direction from which it had come. Those who made this claim had a certain interest in doing so, since it had the effect of distancing them from the disaster. However, an independent writer seems to attach some credence to the story:

Arthur Gavshon asks, "How would Hammarskjold have reacted if at the last moment he had learnt from Fabry – Khiary's collaborator – just how the UN action in Katanga had come to be ordered? Is it conceivable that the Secretary-General may have felt a need to talk to O'Brien – who had asked to be taken along to Ndola – before seeing Tshombe?" (*The Mysterious Death of Dag Hammarskjold*, p. 238).

It remains conceivable, certainly; if I no longer felt it to be probable it was because I had been reluctantly driven to the conclusion that Hammarskjold knew as much as he wanted to know about what had happened in Elisabethville. In any case we now know, as a result of Alan James's research, to which I have referred, that Hammarskjold had been fully briefed in advance. Nothing that Fabry could have said, would have lessened the force of the British diplomatic representations: the diplomatic propellant towards Ndola.

Subsequently there were three Commissions of Enquiry into the Ndola crash. The first was a Rhodesian enquiry whose verdict was already contained in its terms of reference: it was an enquiry "into the accident at Ndola" and it concluded that the crash was indeed an accident.

I am not at all suggesting that either the Rhodesians or the British government were guilty of any foul play, in the sense of having caused the crash. It was simply not in their interest to do so since Hammarskjold, at this moment in time, was doing exactly what Britain and Rhodesia wanted him to do. He was on his way to make peace with Tshombe; necessarily, in the circumstances, largely on Tshombe's terms.

But it is important that the Rhodesians were first on the scene of the crash. If they found any evidence of foul play at that scene, it was in their interest to hush up that evidence. The two later commissions were looking at a scene which the Rhodesians had had the opportunity to tidy up. So the fact that the other commissions did not find conclusive evidence of foul play does not establish that no such evidence ever existed. In fact both the UN enquiry and the Swedish enquiry did not find conclusive evidence either way. It might have been an accident, it might have been foul play. Who could tell?

I don't know about the Swedish enquiry but anyone who knew the UN could have predicted the UN report's finding. Western countries were afraid of a "foul play" verdict which might possibly tend to incriminate some of them. Afro-Asian countries, on the other hand, would not accept an "accident" verdict exonerating the defenders of Katanga. So the UN Secretariat, needing to soothe both major constituencies within the General Assembly, temporised. Nobody who had come to understand the Secretariat would have expected it to do anything else.

However, about a year after the three basically unsatisfactory "official accounts" a much more substantial account, purporting to be first hand, by people who claimed to have organised an attempt to kidnap Hammarskjold, in the course of which attempt he was accidentally killed, was published.

The account was contained in a book called *Notre Guerre au Katanga* by Commandant Faulques and two other Frenchmen. Faulques and his colleagues had been members of the *Organization de l'Armée Secrète*, the French right-wing group set up in France and Algeria to organize armed attacks on de Gaulle and his associates once their intention to disengage from Algeria had become clear. Shortly after the "Independent State of Katanga" had been established under Belgian protection in August 1960, de Gaulle convened some of the officers whom he knew to be in the OAS, to offer them an alternative: they could remain in France and continue to work with the OAS. In that case, they would be dismissed from the army and tried before military courts. De Gaulle could and would ensure that they would be convicted. They would then be dismissed from the army with ignominy, would face long jail sentences and forfeit their pension rights.

Alternatively: they could retire from the army, and volunteer to "defend the white man's role in Africa" by joining the Katanga Defence Forces, for which the controllers of the Tshombe regime were then seeking recruits. If they chose this alternative, they could have an honourable discharge from the French forces, retain their full pension rights and return to France as soon as their period of service in Katanga was over.

An unknown number of French officers, probably no less than fifty, accepted the second alternative and came to Katanga. None of them was caught during Rumpunch and they were at the centre of organizing the resistance to Morthor from the Union Miniere mining towns of Jadotville and Kolwezi. Before Rumpunch, several UN officers had social contacts with them and knew them to cherish a fanatical personal hatred for Hammarskjold whom they believed to have undermined the French Empire in North Africa.

That was the background. The story told in *Notre Guerre au Katanga* was as follows:

When they learned from the press that Hammarskjold was flying to Leopoldville and would fly on to meet Tshombe, these officers, according to their own account, planned a hijacking. They would hijack Hammarskjold's plane after it left Leopoldville and take it to Kolwezi, then fully controlled by the OAS officers, and there would oblige Hammarskjold, at a press conference, to recognise the sovereign independence of Katanga. They named the officer whom they claim to have got on board Hammarskjold's plane: a Belgian called Gheyssels.

There is nothing implausible about the claim that they put him on board. The UN report on the subject acknowledges that Hammarskjold's plane was left unguarded on the tarmac at Leopoldville Airport for more than twenty-four hours and that this represented a high security risk. Nor is it at all unlikely that Gheyssels could have been able to board the plane.

UN berets could easily be obtained on the market in Leopoldville. Wearing such a beret, Gheyssels could easily have "passed". Hammarskjold's party consisted of two groups – those from New York and those from Leopoldville – and neither group knew all of the other. So an unknown face, topped by the right kind of headgear, could easily have passed muster. As the UN report itself acknowledges, Hammarskjold's entourage at this time was alarmingly negligent regarding security.

Up to the take-off from Leopoldville, the Faulques account, whether we accept it or not, is a claim of fact. And it is a highly plausible account. The officers concerned had motive, means and opportunity for such an action.

Motive: personal hatred of Hammarskjold over North Africa, combined with an urge to humiliate him.

Means: the OAS officers had experience in hijacking by air. Their most spectacular achievement of that kind was then quite recent – the successful hijacking of the plane of the Algerian leader, Ben Bella.

Opportunity: this is acknowledged by the UN itself. The opportunity was that unguarded plane.

Up to Hammarskjold's departure from Leopoldville, what we have is what claims to be a factual account, and the claim appears probable. After Hammarskjold's take-off, the French officers, like the rest of us, are left with conjecture. Their conjecture is as follows:

> When the plane was over Eastern Katanga, Gheyssels drew a gun on the pilot and ordered him to proceed to Kolwezi, then controlled by OAS officers. The pilot then, being uncertain what to do, circled the airport (just as members of the British party at Ndola claim to have seen it doing). Then the UN security people tried to overpower Gheyssels and a struggle occurred in the course of which the pilot lost control and the plane crashed.

Almost entirely conjectural, but not improbable.

Notre Guerre au Katanga contains the most internally-plausible account of the course of events that led to Hammarskjold's death that has been presented to the public. And it is a claim made by those who said they were "responsible for putting the hijacker aboard": a *claim*, not an *accusation* made against them by others. In the circumstances I urged that, in the light of weighty new evidence concerning the circumstances of Hammarskjold's crash, the UN enquiry be reopened and Faulques and others be questioned exhaustively. This never happened. *Notre Guerre au Katanga* fell totally flat and has disappeared from "history".

In his life of Hammarskjold, Brian Urquhart treats the claim of the French officers with complete contempt (in a footnote), and it has been ignored by more recent and more impartial writers, such as Alan James. One can see why Western officials – American as well as British – should have wished not to reopen what was for them a politically divisive issue. It is more surprising that the Afro-Asian block should have shown no interest in the subject, as was the case. But it was, I suppose, easy enough to convince them that the words of these virulently racist officers – as undoubtedly they were – ought automatically to be disregarded. So what ought to have been a big story sank without a trace.

* * *

On September 20 at Ndola, Khiary signed a provisional ceasefire agreement, ending the operation which his instructions of September 11 had begun. Tshombe and Munongo returned to Elisabethville. The secession was maintained. Officially, no one had even tried to end it.

10

FAREWELL TO KATANGA
AND TO THE UN

SACHA GUITRY IN HIS FILM ON NAPOLEON PLAYS THE PART OF TALLEYRAND telling his friends, under the restoration, the great story. Having told of the victories of 1805, Ulm and Austerlitz, he is moving on to 1806 when one of his listeners interrupts him. "Eighteen hundred and five?" she asks. "Was that not also the year of Trafalgar?"

"Trafalgar?" says Talleyrand. "Trafalgar? Let the English talk of that; not us. *Que les Anglais en parlent – pas nous!*"

In a similar spirit I shall leave Moise (or his ghost) to tell, in his autobiography, the detailed story of the return of his regime to Elisabethville. This was his apotheosis. In his newspapers and on his radio, his Minister for Information, Samalenghe, compared him to Jesus Christ, crucified and risen again. He was hailed as "Tshombe the Magnanimous". The epithet "magnanimous" seems odd, but in fact it had a propaganda function similar to that, at the earlier stage, of the theory that the UN had broken the beautiful friendship between black and white. The difficulty and its solution may be expressed in dialectical form.

Thesis: Tshombe's forces defeated the forces of the UN

Antithesis: But the forces of the UN are still in Katanga.

Synthesis: How magnanimous Tshombe is!

Militarily, of course, the operation had been a stalemate – indeed, as will be seen in a moment, much nearer a defeat for Tshombe's forces than for the UN – but politically, granted the relative importance of the UN and of Tshombe, it was certainly a victory for what Tshombe represented.

I had thought towards the end of Morthor, after Hammarskjold's death, that I was about to be promptly replaced in circumstances which would have amounted to disgrace. My predecessor in Katanga, M Georges Dumontet, was dispatched to the Congo and the press reported, generally with satisfaction, that he was about to replace me. This was bitter, not only personally – to be replaced by one's predecessor has unflattering implications – but also politically. M Dumontet was known for having "got on well" with the Katangese and particularly with Mr Munongo whom he regarded as being at heart a moderate. His relations with the Katangese had no doubt been appropriate in their time, but to reappoint him now would have been pushing the appeasement of Tshombe to the farthest point yet reached. Some people in Leopoldville – notably Mr Khiary and Mr Adoula – felt the same way; in the event M. Dumontet got no further than that city.

There were in any case some difficulties in the way of removing me. My tenure in Katanga had won me, as well as condemnation in Western Europe, a considerable degree of approval in Afro-Asian countries. This had been symbolized by a message of good wishes and concern for my safety sent by Dr Nkrumah of Ghana – whom I did not then know – to the UN during the fighting in Elisabethville. It would have been difficult to drop me immediately without giving further offence to Afro-Asian opinion, already incensed by the way in which the UN seemed to draw back from what it seemed to have undertaken.

Yet there were two powerful and interconnected reasons why I should be dropped. The first reason was that my version of the nature and purpose of Morthor, as given to the press at the time, was at variance with the UN's official version as presented in S/4940.

The second reason was that the British government infinitely preferred Morthor in its official version to Morthor in its raw state of brute fact, as all too faithfully portrayed by me.

The official version had represented a kind of shrinking back from the realities of Morthor in the direction of the resolution of August 9, 1960, and Sir Patrick Dean's reservation to the UN resolution of February 21, 1961. The British government (with the future of the Central African Federation in mind) wanted the shrinking to go all the way; and it wanted to commit the UN to the doctrine that it was unthinkable to try to end the secession by force. The British government may have had a shrewd suspicion that my indiscreet remarks in Elisabethville were nearer the truth than the Leopoldville version, but that was all the more reason for taking the Leopoldville version very seriously indeed and for getting me repudiated and removed. This was what Lord Lansdowne had meant when in Leopoldville, he "expressed concern" to Hammarskjold "at certain statements attributed to UN personnel in charge of Katanga operations". Hammarskjold did not disavow me but he could not, in the light of S/4940 and what it represented, altogether avow me either.

After Hammarskjold's death, the pressure continued with persistence, which was logical for I was in Elisabethville still, the incarnate negation of Sir Patrick Dean's reservation. And of course the British government was pressing on what was for the UN a very sensitive nerve. My statement about ending secession was not only contrary to what Sir Patrick had said; it was also contrary to what the UN itself had said it had done. This put any British representative discussing me with any UN official in rather a strong position. The dialogue might be imagined as running something like this:

UK: The UN position is much better understood now of course. What still gives us a lot of trouble, though, are those extraordinary statements of O'Brien's about ending the secession, and arresting ministers, and so on. Did you ever get to the bottom of that?

UN: Well, you know, a lot of reports coming out of Katanga at that time were pretty garbled . . .

UK: There's not much doubt about these ones, I'm afraid. Some of the worst of them are recorded . . . By the way, I suppose I am right in taking it that there's nothing in what the fellow said? I mean, there was no question of using the UN forces to arrest the government – the provincial government – and end the secession, as he called it?

UN: No, of course not. It was just completing the August 28th operation really – you've seen the report.

UK: I entirely accept that, naturally. I should have thought, though, that from the point of view of bringing the UN operation to a successful conclusion – which is what we all want – it's hardly wise to leave O'Brien in such a delicate post. After all he not only has been gravely indiscreet but he seems to have wildly exceeded his instructions. He certainly arrested Vice-President Kibwe – Dunnett is quite clear on that. I don't mind telling you that people in Britain would feel much happier about the UN Katanga operation if it were in other hands.

UN: We've told him to be more careful about what he says to the press . . .

As a result, no doubt, of some such conversations, I received – in, I think, late September or early October – two telegrams from New York stressing the embarrassment which reports of my verbal ending of the secession were still causing the UN. One of them mentioned a British Foreign Office official who had referred to "that dreadful statement". UN headquarters in New York wanted to know, it said, what I had really said.

I now knew the official version of what had happened and I took it, perhaps wrongly, that New York was animated not by a dispassionate intellectual need to know exactly what I had really said, but by a desire to have from me, in order to strengthen its own diplomatic hand, an account of my words which would not be entirely irreconcilable with the official version.

As well as being sick at heart with the failure of Morthor and haunted by the social and political implications of the refugee camp, I was bewildered and depressed by the way in which, from the beginning of Morthor, I had lost the rapport with headquarters which I had believed myself to possess up to then. I was rather childishly anxious to reinstate myself in their good graces; a feat the impossibility of which should have been clear to my mind, had the lucidity of analysis not been rendered turbid by hope.

In this situation and condition I committed the only actions of my Katanga time of which I am ashamed. First of all I referred headquarters to statements which I had indeed made during the fighting but in the later days of it, when it had already been impressed on me, by the telegrams from Leopoldville, that talk about ending secession was frowned on. These statements were naturally more guarded and *nuancé* than my first statements. They were not really much use to New York, however, as they still based the action on paragraph A1 (prevention of civil war) and not on paragraph A2 (mercenaries) which was the basis given in the official version of the officer-in-charge.

I also referred them to an interview I had given Keith Kyle for the BBC. Khiary, who was in Elisabethville at the time, asked whether it was an "orthodox" interview. *C'est catholique, au moins, cet interview-là?* And smiled the smile of a man who knows that all official versions are, have been from the beginning of time and will forever be, worded to deceive the enemy and appease the clamour of the ignorant.

Khiary was also there at a press conference when someone raised the question of what I had said on September 13. I gave an answer based on what I had said, but with some rather fine-spun legalistic qualifications.

They were very felicitous and balanced qualifications. They had only one little defect: I did not make them at the time.

Khiary smiled.

Conscience at this moment, to my surprise, assumed the voice and shape of Mr John Latz. Mr Latz had a large nose, an RAF moustache and small close-set eyes. He kept a laundry in Elisabethville, and was part-time correspondent for the Associated Press. He was a friend of the mercenary, Captain Browne, and had been his host during some of the Captain's frequent but brief visits to Katanga. He was, of course, hostile to the UN. We were short of chairs at our press conference and Mr Latz was sitting on the floor, on my right hand, with his back to the window.

He had been at my earliest press conferences during the fighting – as most of those present had not – and when I had finished this rather carefully-worded exposition, he shook his head.

"That," he said, "is not what you said."

He spoke very quietly, not much above a whisper and in a tone even of some sympathy. That was the worst of it. I found myself unable to reply. Mr Latz had over me at that moment the immense moral authority of the man who is telling the truth over the man who is dodging it. That is why I shall remember all my life exactly where he was sitting on this occasion, and how he looked. As for me, I was sitting tilted back in a swivel-chair and feeling as if I could do with a good cleaning in Mr Latz's laundry.

At this moment I began, dimly and reluctantly, to see the truth; that I could not recover or preserve my self-respect unless I could rip myself away from the sticky clutches of the official version of what had happened on September 13. In fact, as it turned out, the UN saved me the trouble by doing most of the ripping for me. However, it might not have done so, I think, if I had been prepared to take a hint and my reluctance to take a hint had something to do with unwillingness, following six words from Mr Latz, to accommodate myself any more to the necessities imposed by the discrepancy between the official version and the historical reality.

The hint took the form of a letter from a friend in Dublin, written about mid-October. This friend had been informed by FH Boland, who had been in contact with Dr Ralph Bunche, Deputy Secretary General of the UN, that Dr Bunche felt that I might be wise to apply for a transfer from Katanga. I had inevitably lost the confidence of Tshombe – "through no fault" of my own – and that obviously curtailed my usefulness.

It is unwise – how unwise I was soon to find – for an official to disregard a hint of this kind: a hint which is tantamount to a semi-official request.

239

I felt in any case that if the Secretariat wanted to shift me it could do so, making it clear where it was shifting me to. If one is transferred "at one's own request", one can find oneself editing pamphlets or compiling the first draft of the definitive official history. I knew, of course, why it was desired that the request should come from me. The Afro-Asian countries were aware of British pressure and suspicious of it, and would be likely to criticize my transfer as a surrender to the Foreign Office view. The effective answer to this was to produce my own request for a transfer – or, as it eventually turned out, my government's request for my return.

Dr Linner in the course of one of my visits to Leopoldville, had asked whether I would like a transfer from Elisabethville, either to Leopoldville (taking over Khiary's political work) or to New York (possibly as successor to Wieschhoff), I wrote as follows on November 8:

"As I understand it, there are two questions to be decided: how long I should stay in Katanga and where I am to go then.

"As regards the first question, the important thing seems to be that my departure should not take place at a time or in a way which would give Mr Tshombe and his friends the impression that they had scored a victory or that they had some sort of say, or veto, on how the UN should be represented here. Such an impression could only tend to increase their obstinacy and multiply their evasions thus making the UN's task all the more difficult and prolonged.

"I take it as axiomatic that Tshombe will not negotiate seriously until he, and above all his friends, are convinced that the balance of forces is shifting against them. That moment has not yet arrived and Tshombe has therefore no intention at present of negotiating seriously. When the balance does shift – and this moment may now be fairly near – it may be that a fresh representative here might be able to take better advantage of the changed situation. I may add that even on this point I am not altogether convinced, as I think that when Tshombe feels that he needs our help as intermediaries with the Central Government he will not be fussy about the personality with whom he may have to deal. In spite of the press campaign, he knows quite well that there was no element of personal enmity in my dealings with him and I don't believe he feels any personal enmity towards me. The 'O'Brien must go' idea is mainly a British one and, whereas it may be expedient and useful to the UN to yield or appear to yield to their pressure on this matter at the right time, it will be well in my view to wait before doing so for some real proof of the goodwill which they profess in relation to Katanga. I have little doubt that if they wished to apply the necessary pressure they could get Tshombe to go to

Leopoldville. The day after they do so would be an opportune moment to transfer me from here.

"So much for the timing. As regards the place, I would, on consideration, like to go to Leo as political adviser to you (or whatever the title might be, assuming this to be the general idea). This would be on the understanding that Mr Khiary wishes to devote much more of his time to his duties as Chief of Civil Operations, although I know and am very glad of the fact that his great experience and skill will be still available in the political field also.

"As regards New York, if the possibility you mentioned is offered to me I shall take it. I would not, however, wish to go straight from here to New York without a specific assignment nor, in the light of the considerations in the first part of this letter, do I think it desirable that I should be asked to do so."

* * *

It was not of course entirely a matter of cold and abstract calculations. As I was not an IBM machine, personal factors also came in, in the shape of two of the Seven Deadly Sins: Pride and Anger. Pride forbade me to apply for a transfer because that would be accepting defeat. And Anger urged me to carry on the fight against the Independent State of Katanga by any means to hand. Pride and Anger, are of course, good partners who reinforce each other's arguments. And their arguments are not necessarily always unsound.

For many reasons, then, both good and possibly bad, I wanted to stay on in Katanga until such time as the UN should see fit to recall or transfer me, which I knew it would find a little difficult to do. In view of Afro-Asian attitudes it would be difficult to recall me to New York (or transfer me to Leopoldville) except for an important political post – and an important political post was just what those who most wanted to see the last of me in Katanga did not want to see me fill in New York.

On October 31, two important visitors joined me at Les Roches. The first was George Ivan Smith. As I wrote nearer to the time:

"The 'Ivan' is an Australian remnant of Sullivan and that has always formed a bond. I like Australians generally and this Australian in particular and his arrival at this time was a ray of light. George was a very old UN hand who had known Hammarskjold well, and was the principal UN expert in press relations. It was in that capacity he had come, I believe, to see that I made no more 'dreadful statements'. He did this effectively and so nicely that one hardly noticed him doing it. George was tough and wily, with a face like a sunset over a sheep farm: he was a friend of James

Stephens, loved poetry both good and bad, and recited it with a strange plangency; he had an exuberant sense of humour, both personal and catholic, and he was apt to break, on suitable occasions, into a solo dance of his own design: a sort of shuffling saraband with both hands clasped over his head."

"I'm glad," my daughter Kathleen once said to me when I relented after being cross with her, "that you finally got over that old seriousness." A certain amount of old seriousness was in the air in the days after the ceasefire, and George was the man to blow it away.

October 31 was a good day.

My second visitor that day was Máire MacEntee. So great is the impact of the confluence of the political and the personal life that several million people now know that Máire and I loved each other (we still do, as a matter of fact) and it was for that reason that I asked her to spend her holidays in Elisabethville and that she had come. Several people have told me since that this was indiscreet on our part and there is no doubt at all that it was. What impressed me about some of the people who most emphasized the indiscretion, however, was the complacency with which they accepted the implication regarding themselves: that they had never cared enough about anybody or anything to do something indiscreet for the sake of him, her or it.

* * *

The situation in Albertville, and throughout UN-garrisoned North Katanga was a strange one in the days after Morthor. In all these centres the UN had effectively got rid of the foreign officers during Rumpunch and had established complete military predominance during Morthor. In Manono, the gendarmerie had capitulated without firing a shot; in Nyunzu they had fled into the bush and then fled back again, for fear of the Baluba; finally they had placed themselves under UN protection. Only in Albertville where there is a sizeable European population, was there fighting. There, on September 17 a mixed force of gendarmes and Europeans opened fire from the buildings on the hillocks round the UN camp – the hospital, in particular, was turned, Major Padda told us, into "a pukka fortress". Sharp fighting followed in which Major Padda, a hawk-nosed Indian cavalryman, distinguished himself capturing with, as he liked to say, his "lo-onely armoured car", a great number of gendarmerie positions. The gendarmerie then fled and the European population, deprived of any screen, subsided.

Under the ceasefire agreement, the gendarmerie in these places were released from captivity in an exchange of prisoners and got their weapons back. The gendarmerie in Nyunzu, however, did not want their weapons back; they wanted to go home, so we let them go. The inhabitants immediately set up a Balubakat administration which co-operated very well with the UN (Irish) forces. The flag of the Congo now flew over Nyunzu as well as over Kabalo and in many smaller places all along the CFL railway line from Kabalo eastwards towards Lake Tanganyika.

Shortly afterwards Albertville could be added to the list. Tshombe still claimed all of Katanga, but had in fact lost, and never was to regain, authority over all the northern part of the province, which now accepted the authority of the central government. That was satisfying from my point of view. But although I was not aware of it, my time in Katanga was drawing to a close.

When we arrived back from visiting north Katanga Máire wrote to my son, "Conor was summoned to New York with McKeown for the Security Council debate. He is very pleased as it means he will get a hearing at the highest level".

Yes, indeed.

There is a good novel, in an Orwellian vein, by David Karp, called *One*. It is set in the remote future, when universal peace has been firmly established on a psychological basis. Scientists have studied those elements in human character which can lead to subversion, dissension, rebellion and war. There is a great organisation devoted to the surveillance of humanity and to the eradication of such characteristics. The central character is one of the thousands employed by the organisation, to furnish reports on his fellows. The opening of the book finds him setting out for the seat of the organization, having been officially summoned there. He is a cocky fellow and he is confident that he is going to be given some kind of medal for his brilliant reports. In fact his superiors have found, in the tone and language of these reports, the very characteristics – bumptiousness, individualism – against which they are pledged to hold the ramparts of society. The only thing they are in doubt about is whether to liquidate him or give him "a new personality". Finally they decide on the latter course. By various horrifying methods, they eradicate his memory and build up a new one in his brain, with a different name, a different job, a different home-town, a different family. Then he is again required to furnish reports but on new colleagues. At the organisation they read the reports very carefully. The first few seem all right but – there it is again! – in the latest report, a touch of the old bumptiousness, conceit about phrase and judgement. There is no doubt about it now: this time he will be liquidated. He is summoned to headquarters. The last scene of the book finds him in the train, content in the conviction that he is about to be awarded some kind of medal.

He is about, you might say, to get a hearing at the highest level.

Immediately after I arrived in New York with General McKeown, my pleasure at being about to get a hearing at the highest level began to collapse. FH Boland, still head of the Irish mission to the UN, invited General McKeown to dinner, on the night of our arrival.

The other guests were Sir Patrick Dean, Permanent Representative of Great Britain; Mr Charles Ritchie, Permanent Representative of Canada, and Dr Bunche.

"I hope you won't mind my not asking Conor," said Boland to McKeown. "He's not quite the right colour."

Francois Mauriac, writing about the deceitful glosses of Parisian society, says that there is only one sure index of one's rating at any given moment and that is the place assigned to one at table. *Seule, la place a table ne trompe pas.*

By this index it appeared that in Boland's opinion I did not rate a place at all. This was bad, because Boland's opinion was a sound one. As Tshombe was apt to reflect the balance of forces in Elisabethville, so Boland recorded the prevailing wind on the East River. And the wind was blowing from a point somewhere between Mr Charles Ritchie and Sir Patrick Dean.

I turned up my collar.

I had not been at all prepared for such a reception, or rather lack of reception. I did not realize that my colleagues in New York, Boland and Kennedy, had been working quite closely with the British to blacken my character and have me removed. This is documented in Chapter 10 of Alan James's *Britain and the Congo Crisis 1960-1963* (London and New York, 1966). It seems that Boland had recommended to Aiken that I be withdrawn from UN service and recalled to Ireland, but Aiken had refused to recall me. Then Boland suggested to the British that they should go over his own Foreign Minister's head and get the Taoiseach, Seán Lemass, to recall me: "It was recorded that the head of Ireland's Permanent Delegation had suggested to the British 'in confidence' that the 'best way to get rid of O'Brien (whom incidentally they all hate) is somehow to get beyond the Irish Foreign Minister and go to the Prime Minister.'" (Alan James, *Congo Crisis* p.109: quoting FO despatch of November 3, 1961.)

I did not know of this unusual *démarche* during my brief stay in New

York but I couldn't help knowing that my country's permanent mission in New York was now in hostile hands as far as I was concerned.

Meanwhile I listened to the Belgian Prime Minister attacking me in the Security Council. In the Security Council chamber I sat behind the Secretary-General. Mr Thant had greeted me politely and without comment. Dr Bunche's greeting had been friendly but absent-minded. Mr Narasimhan had told me what a strain he had been under in September.

M Spaak was addressing the Security Council. M Spaak, in the flesh, which he is, looks like M Spaak in the photographs, only more so. I looked at M Spaak and thought of M Muller and M Thyssens and even of MM de Vos and Michel. I also thought of our well-fed cat at Les Roches which Francis Nwokedi had christened Spaak and which used to give us so much innocent pleasure: "Down, Spaak, down!" *"Bas les pattes, Spaak!"*

M Spaak, for his part, seemed, at this moment to have little feeling for the days when he and I had been as you might say, fellow-workers in the same field, making our parallel and over-lapping collections of *conseillers occultes*. He was talking about me, but without any touch of nostalgic affection.

M Spaak's speech fell into two parts, easily recognizable by anyone who has ever had anything to do with speeches. There was the statesmanlike bit, for the *New York Times* and the *"Life of Spaak"*, and there was the bit for the home papers. The bit for the home papers was about me. There had been a time when M Spaak had despaired at the task of finding an appropriate epithet for me: I was *l'inqualifiable M O'Brien*. His spirits had recoverd a little, however, and he was now fumbling for the *mot juste*.

What interested me about this was not M Spaak's invective, which I thought rather provincial in style, but what the Secretary-General was going to say in reply.

The delegate for Ceylon, a scholarly-looking man whom I took to be a lama, spoke up in my defence. I thought this very decent of him. I thought it even more decent when I had had a look at the text of the Secretary-General's draft reply.

The draft, which Dr Bunche had written and which he showed me, said nothing specific about me. It said that the Secretary-General was not going to make any defence of the Secretariat because he thought it needed none. The Secretariat did make mistakes, it added, but these mistakes were not caused by a spirit of discrimination against a particular country (Belgium).

This might, perhaps, be called a vindication, I thought, but it could hardly be called a ringing vindication. Having brooded over it for a while,

I passed a note to Dr Bunche. The note said that Spaak had attacked me personally, with the clear implication that I had exceeded my instructions. By not replying specifically on this point, the Secretary-General would seem to confirm this. I set down, lest there be any doubt about it, the instructions which I had received from Khiary.

I thought the note rather worried Dr Bunche. He made some changes in the draft, but I could not grasp their purport. In all essentials the draft remained as it had been. At the end of the debate Mr Thant read it out.

Someone – General Rikhye, I believe, but I am not sure – said to me at this time: "Spaak saved you, you know." What I had been saved from was not clear. The appropriate comment was made by the Herald in *Murder in the Cathedral.*

> *"There are several opinions as to what he meant*
> *But nobody considers it a happy prognostic."*

It seems that, as a result of Spaak's intervention, and Afro-Asian reactions to it, Acting Secretary General U Thant had decided to send me back to Katanga. But then an unexpected incident occurred, upsetting all calculations.

I had come out nominally for consultations in connection with the Security Council proceedings. I had not been told that I was being replaced in Elisabethville, although I knew that this was, or had been, under consideration. Now that the Council meeting was over I had my passage booked back to Elisabethville and sent on a cable to George Ivan Smith to tell him of my impending arrival. Among the inward cables from the Congo, of which copies came to me on the following day (either November 25 or 26), was one from Linner to Bunche referring to this cable and expressing incomprehension. I gathered that Dr Linner had not been expecting me back.

Dr Bunche did not clarify the position at this stage, but he did ask me not to leave just yet as I was needed for further consultations about the refugee camp. What I had to say about the camp in reality was short and simple. If further action was imminent in Katanga, which would be followed by revolutionary changes, then the refugees should stay, in order to return to their homes after the end of the secession. If no such action or changes were likely in the near future then it would be better to transfer the refugees: the Balubakat to North Katanga, the Kasaians to Bakwanga, the rest to Leopoldville. I spelled out these concepts in detail at various meetings of the Congo Club – now presided over by Dr Bunche, without the participation of Mr Thant – over the next few days. There were also other discussions of a political and military character, and while these were important, I did not feel that they were the reason why I was being retained in New York.

Mr Dayal had been recalled for conversations, had been kept on ice, and then left the Secretariat. I was now being kept on ice. I was about to leave the Secretariat.

In a murder, they say, the difficulty is not how to kill the victim but how to dispose of the body.

Administratively I had already been killed. My successor, Brian Urquhart, whom I knew well and liked, was already in Leopoldville. He went to Elisabethville – and to a most memorable reception, soon to be recorded – on November 28. But the body, the physical remains of the administratively defunct O'Brien, was still shuffling zombie-like up and down the long corridor of the 38th floor, being "consulted", rather as the Chinese consult their deceased ancestors.

Fortunately, the problem of the disposal of the body was about to solve itself in a rather dramatic way.

It was, I believe, on the morning of November 27 (it may have been November 28) that Dr Bunche, after the ceremonies of consultation, called me into his office.

Dr Bunche always looked a little rueful; his face is humourous but harassed. On this occasion he looked a bit more than rueful: he looked sad. The name that flashed across my mind was that of a character in Damon Runyan – Regret, the Horse-player. I liked Dr Bunche, as most people did, and I had the feeling that he did not much care for what he had to do.

"Who," he said, "is Miss MacAndrew?"

I set him right about the name, which had become garbled in transmission. (Englishmen often have trouble with Irish names). I told him that I had taken the first steps for a divorce, that Máire and I intended to get married as soon as the divorce was through, and that Máire had come to spend her holiday in Elisabethville on my invitation. When I left Elisabethville, I had thought I should be returning in a few days, and she had stayed to await my return. Since the consultations had become protracted, I had sent her word not to wait for me but to go on home. I did not know whether she had yet left Elisabethville.

Dr Bunche spoke mildly, but somehow definitively:

"I think," he said, "that you have made a mistake."

That, for the very short time-being, was all.

It was not until the evening of November 29 that word of "Senator Dodd's party" reached New York.

We were sitting round the conference table – Dr Bunche, General Rikhye, Mr Gardiner, myself and one or two others. Mr Narasimhan came in with a very long sheet of paper – a telex report.

"This is very bad news," he said.

He passed the message to Dr Bunche who, as he read it, kept saying "My God". Obviously stricken, he passed the report to me.

The report was from Elisabethville. It began by saying that Brian Urquhart, George Ivan Smith and Máire MacEntee of the Irish Foreign Service had set out from Les Roches . . .

The print did not, as people say it does, swim before my eyes. But there seemed suddenly to be an immense amount of print, almost impassable, and holding somewhere in its core some fact which would have to be found and faced, perhaps death.

It was not as bad as that and – since the news was of injury inflicted on two of my friends – I can only hope they will forgive me, in the circumstances, when I say that my first feeling, on finishing the message was one of overpowering relief.

What had actually happened is best told in Máire's own words:

"After Conor had gone to New York I stayed on in the Villa des Roches expecting him back from day to day; Josie and Paddy (Conor's driver, Private Patrick Wall) were there too. George Ivan Smith, who was acting as Conor's deputy, travelled to and fro between Elisabethville and Leopoldville and brought me news of him. In the afternoon of Tuesday, November 28, a little after three o'clock – I had just left Les Roches in the car for Mr Kuitenbrouwer's house, on the edge of the refugee camp, where I took Swahili lessons – a UN car piled with luggage passed us on the road from the airport. I thought it was Conor, and Paddy turned back. It was George Ivan Smith and Brian Urquhart. They brought a message from Conor for me to go to Dublin. There had been strong rumours that Brian was to succeed Conor and I was uneasy and depressed. I arranged to take the first plane next morning.

"I had been invited that evening to a cocktail party at the American Consulate 'in honour of Senator and Mrs Dodd'. I liked the Hoffackers [American Consul and his wife] very much and I had accepted. I thought it might be a slightly sticky occasion and that by going I could be of some help to Mrs Hoffacker, who had arrived in Katanga only a few days before. I felt now that I would rather stay at home and pack for the journey. George and Brian persuaded me to change my mind and come with them.

"It was an exceedingly good party. The drawing-rooms of the American Consulate look out on a courtyard shaded with tall trees and while the guests, very elegant and *mondains,* moved about inside under the bright lights, the 'Apostles' from the president's palace up the road gathered in the dark of the courtyard outside to put on a show for the Senator. They danced and sang, swaying and stamping in and out of the shadows, and women wearing their lovely African dresses – richly coloured cottons, elaborately draped – and complicated, knotted turbans. Watching them were the Senator's motor-cycle escort in the bravura uniform of Tshombe's guard. As the evening moved on, guests drifted out to the dancing and 'Apostles' began to infiltrate towards the buffet through the french windows.

"Most of the UN people I knew were at the party as well as everyone else, practically, who played any avowably important part in the life of Elisabethville – some of the less avowably important too. Tshombe and several of his ministers were pointed out to me and I was introduced to Mr Kimba, 'the Minister of Foreign Affairs', who had great charm.

"The UN officers were not in uniform. I imagine that like myself they came to the party solely out of affection and respect for Lew Hoffacker and did not want to make things more difficult for him by the risk of provoking 'an incident'. Tshombe had made his murderous speech on the Sunday before, just after the news of the Security Council resolution, and there was considerable tension in town. As I was talking to General Raja, a young Indian officer joined us, looking harassed. 'You shouldn't have come, Sir; you're being marked.' Raja was clearly not pleased. I thought the Indians were rather overplaying the military melodrama and put the whole thing out of my mind.

"We left early. George had another party for the Senator to attend, a dinner this time, given by the Mobiloil representative in Elisabethville. (In fact, as we found out later, this gentleman had to go to Leopoldville on business and a cousin of his wife's was acting host). I was going to eat in town with Brian Urquhart and Fitzhugh Greene of the US Information Service, who was covering the Senator's tour. We all got into a UN car, driven by Paddy Wall, intending to drop George first.

"The Mobiloil house is only a few doors away from the suburban residence of General Muke, Commander of the Katangese forces. Paddy knew this was not a healthy area for UN personnel, but his opinion wasn't asked and he didn't volunteer it. As we turned into the avenue, we saw a military truck parked at the side of the road with some soldiers in it and heard them shout, 'Onu! Onu!' We drew up at the gate of the Mobiloil house a few yards farther on and were immediately surrounded by a sullen, aggressive crowd of Africans in camouflage uniforms, very heavily armed. Someone said they were 'paras'.

"They asked for documents. Through the window of the car Paddy handed his UN pass. The man who took it flung it down in the roadway and stamped on it. I heard George Ivan Smith say, 'Easy, Paddy' and saw Paddy visibly control himself. He got quietly out of the car, picked up his pass, put it in his pocket and stood still in the middle of the road with the paras all around him.

"Meanwhile the Senator's hosts had heard the commotion and three or four gentlemen came out of the house. One of them, a big man, had short reddish hair, almost a crew cut, and a bow tie; I had seen him at the American party. They expostulated with the paras who were, it appeared, General Muke's guard. They explained about the dinner party, that Senator Dodd was 'the friend of Katanga', that even President Tshombe might turn up. The 'paras' were not impressed, but, reasonably according to their lights, they agreed that their NCO would go with us into the house and telephone Minister Kimba for confirmation that we were there in good faith. At first they wanted to hold Paddy as a hostage but finally gave way on that and let him come with us.

"As I remember it, the house had a fairly large hall opening into a very large room with french windows, the two rooms forming an L so that not all the drawing-room could be seen from the hall. Perhaps a dozen people were already there, among whom I recognized Mr Dunnett. The Hoffackers and the Senator had not yet arrived. The telephone was on a low table to the left of the hall door; people busied themselves getting Kimba. George went on into the drawing-room as an invited guest and Fitzhugh Greene – as a good USIS-man alert for copy – did likewise. Brian stayed with the group at the telephone and sat, I think, on a low chair near the table. Myself and Paddy sat on a bench opposite the door, feeling a little awkward. The lady of the house came very kindly and offered us drinks.

"The telephoners contacted Kimba and handed the phone to the 'para' corporal (?) who was actually in conversation with him when the action, so to speak, suddenly speeded up. The hall door burst open and six or eight paras exploded into the room, fantastically over-excited and brandishing lethal weapons, sub-machine guns, I think, which they seemed to be constantly loading and unloading, as if to make it quite clear that they really had ammunition. Someone tried to explain about Kimba. The first man in screamed *Je me fous de Kimba* and snatching the phone from his fellow-soldier, dashed it to the floor. I think at the same time a similar group had come through the French windows in the drawing-room, out of sight of the hall, and gone for George Ivan Smith.

"By now Paddy and I were on our feet. I could see Brian Urquhart, his face unrecognizable, covered with blood. In the confusion I had moments of not being sure even that it was Brian and thought, irrationally, that it might be Fitzhugh Greene, although I knew him to be in the other room. Paddy had seen the blow; the para had got Brian on the nose with his skull as he got up from the chair. He seemed to stand swaying as we moved across to him and then to collapse back again. He was saying firmly and politely, *'Il y a erreur, Messieurs, il y a erreur'.* I stood in front of him; the telephoners had been dispersed. I have never spoken French in my life with such an urgency of conviction as I did to those 'paras'. I called them *'mes enfants'*; I even touched one boy on the cheek. I said this was not the way to treat a visitor, that they had hurt the poor gentleman and that soldiers should be ashamed to behave like this. I said, *'Soyez gentils'* – 'Be nice'. I had the impression that under their bluster they were frightened and disconcerted. I was certain that if I could only keep on talking I could win. They weren't used to breaking into Belgian houses; they *were* used to doing as they were told by French-speaking ladies. They were like children, who, having begun to stone a cat, are unable to stop and yet half hoping to be prevented. Paddy stood beside me and held them off; he put aside the barrels of the sten-guns with his arm as they came at us and they didn't persist. I seemed to be thinking on several different levels simultaneously: 'Perhaps I am only making things worse' – the classical argument against interference, especially by women – but I knew I wasn't; 'Here goes our hope of a quiet divorce' – and I knew that was for sure; 'I don't think I could bear it if they smashed my face with one of those things' and I was so frightened that fear was a new dimension. But I kept on talking. Brian's head had fallen forward against my hip from behind and the back of my right arm, all the way down, was covered with blood.

"And in the moment I thought that I might have persuaded them, the worst happened. A third wave crashed in, older and somehow darker men with faces carved in deep wrinkles like gashes, grim, tough and experienced – not at all children. One of them hit me across the face. Paddy and I were simply thrown bodily aside, poor Brian was yanked from his chair and, as he was thrust out the door, George Ivan Smith, heels dug in and fighting every inch, was forced past us from the drawing-room with another battered figure through the door into the garden on a wave of 'paras'. I saw Fitzhugh Greene, volubly protesting, but unharmed, swept out with them – and that was strange because in some way I had thought at intervals that he was the man behind me.

"Someone shut the door and stood against it. A terrible despair, such as I never hope to feel again, flooded over me. I was quite certain I would never see George and Brian alive any more. They would be killed in spite of my trying so hard, perhaps because of it, and I was so desperately tired. My friend with the crew-cut said, 'This is your fault; they were trying to protect you'. Indignation flared in me. I can't remember exactly what I said, but I got my own back. I held out the white skirt of my dress: the front was clean, the back heavily stained with blood, where Brian's head had been. I indicated with some force that what protecting there had been, had been done by me. Mr Dunnett was standing in the entrance to the drawing-room. Paddy was insisting on being allowed to use the phone to call headquarters. Someone said, 'If your Indian friends get here we'll all be killed'. I heard Paddy saying, 'If they don't Mr Smith will be killed.' Someone reported that the para truck had driven off, accompanied by a big car at high speed. Paddy got Indian headquarters and gave the alarm. I also spoke to them. We both had the same impression: the Indians thought it was a joke – in poor taste. It would be hard to blame them.

"The lady of the house was having hysterics, 'I will not sleep another night here with those savages loose. *Franchement je prefere l'Onu!*' Paddy said, 'It's no good waiting here. I'll try to get to the civilian mess and come back with an armoured car'. He went out over the backgarden wall and did just that, only he didn't wait for the armoured car, but came back immediately with a civilian driver and a machine-gun in a Volkswagen, having run the whole distance to the civilian mess where they thought at first he was drunk. Meanwhile the dinner guests were telephoning the police – 'They would come if we sent a car; Muke [head of the Katangan police] – if the animal could talk any known language'.

"A neighbour came in through the garden. He had the strange detachment of people who are no longer shocked by violence. His wife would take the children, it might be safer. All was quiet now outside, he reported; the UN car had been driven off by a white man, *'un blanc'.* A frightened teenager and a sleepy little girl, wrapped in a blanket, were brought downstairs and handed over. *'Proteste pas, mais fous-le-camp, que je te dis.'* We sat and looked at each other. There was a phone call for Mr Dunnett. Rather grudgingly he told us that George and the Belgian banker, the second captive I had seen carried out, were safe in the US Consulate. There was no news of Brian. Mr Dunnett did not say at the time that it was George himself on the phone asking for me – perhaps it did not seem important. The front door opened; it was Paddy and the UN driver. I have never been so glad to see anyone in my life.

"The story of George's rescue has been told elsewhere, but I would like to set it down here now as I heard it from him in the small hours of that morning. It is a heart-warming story to tell.

"The paras had got the three men on to the truck and had ordered them to lie down. Brian and the Belgian banker did so and were savagely bludgeoned. Perhaps it was some atavistic stubbornness which made George an enemy to lying down to be beaten, perhaps it was his Australian upbringing. He got his back against the cab of the truck and fought them off with his feet. A glare of headlight and a roar of motor-cycle engines, and the US Consulate car with its superb escort of Katangese Keystone Cops swept up behind them. Mrs Dodd was heard to exclaim, 'Why, if it isn't that nice Mr Smith!' and Hoffacker was out of the car hurling paras left and right and shouting 'Consul Americain!' – and I should add that he was a thin, rather lightly-built young man. He got George Ivan Smith off that truck and went back for the banker. He was going back for the third time when the paras realized what had hit them and drove off. Crouched on the floor of the big, luxurious car, the Senatorial party with its rescued got the hell out of there. So quickly was it all over, that in the house we did not know it had happened. All we knew was that an unidentified car had driven rapidly away. I never heard what became of the escort.

"At about four o'clock that morning, Brian was released from Camp Massart where he had been held. The negotiations and operations which led up to this are a matter of record and I will not try to re-tell them. Nor will I attempt any interpretation of the night's happenings. I will only add a picture of George Ivan Smith with his face swollen and holding his cracked ribs together with both hands, directing, advising, restraining, imperturbably at the centre of everything until the very moment he fell, and of Brian being brought into Indian HQ and saying wryly, 'A pity it wasn't some other fellow – if they'd killed me what a magnificent *casus belli*'.

"When we got back to Les Roches I couldn't sleep. It was about six in the morning and I sat on the verandah listening to the Ghurka guard going about their breakfast. Banza, one of the Baluba servants, who arrived on his bicycle inperturbably every morning, came up to me. 'Mademoiselle,' he said, 'there is a dead Indian on the road near Tshombe's palace.' Quite cheerfully he went back with the Gurkhas to to show them where. When they got there the body was gone, but there is little doubt that it was the murdered Gurkha driver [a Gurkha driver murdered by Katanga forces].

Later that day I flew in a UN plane to Leopoldville. The Cuban pilot landed too steeply and snapped the blade of the propellor sharp across. It seemed quite an everyday occurrence to me by this time."

* * *

When I had finished reading the dispatch, which Dr Bunche had passed to me, I got off a telegram to Máire to tell her to get out of Katanga immediately.

At the end of the meeting Dr Bunche took me aside and asked me to see to it that Máire left Katanga without delay. I told him of the telegram I had sent, and added that I had sent it because of concern for her personal safety.

Dr Bunche seemed a little surprised about the "personal safety" but quickly agreed. He was by nature a humane man and it is symptomatic of the rather thin air on the 38th floor that the personal impact which such a dispatch might be presumed to make on me did not seem, at first, to have occurred to him. When it did he was, as one would expect, sympathetic.

On the following day – with the Elisabethville story now in the papers – he called me into his office again. Mr Thant had been talking to him about "this business". He seemed upset. Dr Bunche did not know just how upset. He would have known with Dag. Dag would have gone through the roof. But with this new man it was hard to tell.

That was all, for the moment.

Very shortly after this – not more than an hour I believe – Mr Aiken, who was in New York for the Assembly session, asked me to come and see him in his room at the San Carlos Hotel.

Mr Thant, he said, had been in touch with him through Dr Bunche, about Máire's presence in Elisabethville. Mr Thant had asked him to recall me to the Irish Foreign Service. Mr Thant had indicated that, if Mr Aiken did not do so, he, Mr Thant, would call for my resignation. The reason to be given was that I had now shown myself to be so indiscreet as to be unsuitable for further service with the United Nations.

Here perhaps I may insert some reflections on the subject of indiscretion from one who came to be considered an authority on the subject. I say "came to be" because one who, like myself, had worked for twenty years in the civil service of a small country, to the rather apathetic satisfaction of his superior officers, can hardly be considered to have been born indiscreet. Some people have indiscretion thrust on them.

The fact is that indiscretion is a function of public attention, and in my case, was a function of politics. Let us assume that my colleagues in ONUC, without exception, possessed the austerity of a Savonarola and the discretion of a Coolidge. But if, *per impossibile*, one of them had committed such an enormity as I had committed, no one would have given a tinker's damn. They would not have rated four lines in the *News of the World*. My case was different. The spotlight was on me and a section of the British press, in particular, would, on a signal or even without one, give me the full treatment. The mud which they would offer in such profusion would splash over on the United Nations, and any British representative, concerned for the Organisation's good name, would be justified in giving warning of this danger.

I found myself in the jaws of a pincer-movement. Sir Patrick Dean's disciplined divisions had long been doggedly pressing on my right flank and now, on the left, over the brow of the hill, I could hear the noisy vanguard of Lord Beaverbrook's uncouth but formidable columns.

What to do?

I had often quoted with approval Joseph Biggar's pithy saying: "Never resign, Misther, get yerself fired!" Reluctantly I realized that this was not the moment for a rugged Biggar stand. I had failed to take a hint before – that of applying for a transfer – and it had now come to much more than a hint. Something told me that if I tried, at this moment, to make a stand, people might start getting rough. The thing to do now was to extricate myself with all speed, and with the honours of war, from the Dean-Beaverbrook convergence. That meant pulling out of the UN quickly, and coming to rest, at least for a time, on the firm [and still mostly friendly] ground of my own country's service. Operation Antaeus.

I said that in that case, Mr Aiken, if he agreed, had better ask for me back. Mr Aiken was very upset. His attitude towards Máire and myself was paternal – that is to say, affectionate and a shade testy – and, in his undemonstrative and sincere way, he wanted to help. I gave him a letter asking him to ask for my return, and he sent off one, as requested, to Mr Thant. Both letters were, as is usual on these occasions, distinguished for their decorum rather than for their candour. Mr Thant agreed to my release. He also said some kind words [probably designed to be shown to Afro-Asian politicians] about the devotion, ability and courage with which I had served the UN in Katanga. The honours of war, at any rate, were safe.

I saw Dr Bunche, to say good-bye, shortly after Mr Thant's *congé*. Dr Bunche was friendly and more relaxed than he had been before. He seemed to be sorry about the way the break had come, but indicated that my position had in any case become untenable as a result of the uncompromising British attitude towards me.

What had happened to me fell, I think, under the head of what is known as expendability. This is quite a rational doctrine. It asserts that what is sacred are the principles and purposes of an organisation; the men who serve it are expendable. Thus, in my case, the objectives of the UN regarding Katanga remained the same. In attempting to reach these objectives I had aroused the hostility of one major power, Britain, whose co-operation was very desirable for the attainment of these same objectives in the future. It became therefore necessary to get me out of the way. As I failed to take a gentle hint, the hint had to be repeated, less gently.

Il faut faire de la politique, as Mahmoud used to say.

Whatever about the logic of expendability, whose beauty is less clear to the expended than to the expender, I remained strongly in favour of the objectives of the UN and especially of ending the "secessionist activities illegally carried out by the provincial administration of Katanga . . . aided by foreign resources and mercenaries". (Resolution of November 24th)

I remained unconvinced by the theory that this end was most likely to be achieved by patiently seeking the co-operation of the British government, and quietly sand-bagging such officials as were indiscreet enough to incur that government's displeasure. To me it seemed that a more promising line to explore would be that of publicly exposing the British government's support for Tshombe. I knew that they would deny that they supported him, but I felt that in the course of my accusations and their denials, 'support for Tshombe' would come to seem a little more heinous, and therefore a little more difficult, than it had been up to now.

This, I thought, would be objectively a useful activity, and it was also subjectively a congenial one. Those old *conseillers occultes,* Pride and Anger, had a share in my decision and I do not, in retrospect, feel that they gave me bad advice.

One cannot, as a member of the foreign service of a small and friendly country, go around publicly denouncing the British government. To permit oneself that luxury one has to become a private citizen. This I now determined to do.

I rang up Máire on the evening of December 1 in Dublin to tell her that the news of my recall, which had just then reached Dublin, would soon be followed by the news of my resignation. I had prepared a resignation statement.

"That's fine," said Máire. "I resigned this morning."

Máire, on her return, had learned from her father that the Secretariat had officially raised the question of her presence in Elisabethville. Being a woman of spirit she promptly resigned. At the moment of her resignation, she did not know of my recall.

On the morning of the following day, which was a Saturday, I sent Mr Aiken my resignation. I expressed my profound and sincere regret for this break in a long and happy association; I told him that I was making the step irrevocable – he would not, I knew, have been likely to accept my resignation otherwise – by sending at a same time a statement, of a political and controversial character, to the press. I gave the *New York Times* my statement on Saturday morning, December 2.

On the morning my statement appeared in the *New York Times*, stressing the British abstraction of UN policy in the Congo, I rang Frank Aiken, and got his sad and adverse reaction: "The cop's turned robber," he said. I thought I would remind him of his own past. "You weren't always a cop," I said. He paused for a moment and then said to my surprise: "No. That's true." I felt he was basically still on my side, though the best he could do for me was to preserve a public silence on the subject.

The British, naturally, stepped up their attacks on me, and one of my former colleagues helped them with material. Alan James writes concerning British, and some Irish reactions to my attack on the British role in the Congo:

"All this happened to come at a time when Britain was experiencing an uncomfortable degree of isolation over Katanga, so it was all the more painful, and resented accordingly. O'Brien was making a 'determined effort to smear the United Kingdom', the New York Mission said. His remarks were 'slanderous and inaccurate' – and the Mission went in search of some counter-balancing dirt of its own.

Sir Patrick Dean, Britain's Permanent Representative at the UN, reported his findings directly to Sir Roger Stevens, a Deputy Under-Secretary in the Foreign Office. When with the Irish Mission to the UN, O'Brien had, according to one of its members, 'spent practically all his time drinking with the press. He is in any case a heavy drinker and is very far to the left in politics. He is probably not a card-carrying communist, but he ["is" is here excised] may be a Marxist. Moreover, according to our friends in the press, he has always been violently anti-British.' To this was added a tale of his improper use of UN channels to communicate with his girlfriend. 'For what it is worth,' the British delegation had been told that both she and he are 'fluent Russian speakers'."

The member of the Irish mission was, I believe, Eamon Kennedy. Stuff like the above would be too crude for Boland. Alan James goes on:

"It was realised that better ammunition than this might be needed. The African Section of the Foreign Office's Research Department was set to work on a study of 'Dr O'Brien's Accusations Against Great Britain: A resume of the Facts Involved'. In 101 detailed paragraphs it refuted the charges. But there was no rest for the Research Department. O'Brien produced a book-length account of his time in Katanga (*To Katanga and Back*) in which he fluently elaborated upon his damaging remarks. A detailed analysis of the book was called for, and duly supplied – this time in fifty-four paragraphs. The Foreign Secretary had read the book, but nonetheless took the analysis away over a weekend. It was as if O'Brien continued to cast a baleful spell.

"For Britain, O'Brien crystallised everything that she was coming to dislike about the Congo operation, and its operators. He was an official who appeared to have acted out of turn, and with inappropriate flamboyance. He represented an organisation which seemed to be getting too big for its boots. His action was believed to threaten the order which existed in a crucial area of the Congo. And towards this end he was not averse to using force. He had to go, and indeed he went. To that extent, Britain was successful. But even if it was a battle won, the war was well on the way to being lost. For, in one of those ironies which help to give history its fascination, the policy with which O'Brien believed himself to have been supplied but which the UN then disavowed, soon came to receive its more or less open endorsement."

The policy in question was of course the forcible liquidation of the independent state of Katanga. Wholeheartedly backed by the United States this time around, and therefore grudgingly accepted by the British, the intervention was speedily and fully successful.

* * *

I add here a coda. As I wrote earlier I had a dream after reading a book that led me to write a play about Hammarskjold and Lumumba that came to be called *Murderous Angels*. This coda is about the strange and sometimes – in retrospect – amusing happenings that occurred in connection with the productions, or proposed productions, of *Angels* in 1970.

The first offer to produce the play was very prestigious indeed and had me gung-ho for a while. This offer came from the British National Theatre, then under the general direction of Sir Laurence Olivier, and it came to me through the theatre's literary adviser, Ken Tynan. Of course I accepted immediately. Shortly afterwards I was invited to lunch with the National Theatre people: Olivier, Ken Tynan and the proposed director of the play (whose name I have forgotten). Olivier asked the director to outline his ideas for the production of the play. The director began by saying that he proposed that the players should wear masks. This was quite a sensible idea and in fact the best European performance of the play – in Lubeck, East Germany – was given in masks. It was, however, a sensible idea that had no appeal at all to Olivier, who crushed it most memorably. Scowling with the full force of his magnificently mobile features, Olivier asked: "What would a man want a *mask* for [dramatic pause] if he had a *face*?"

That was the high point of the proceedings; from then on it was all downhill. Olivier asked me some questions about the script but it soon appeared there was only one point – marginal to my mind – that was worrying Olivier. He said that the script seemed to suggest that Hammarskjold was homosexual. I agreed that that was so. I thought he was probably not actively homosexual, but his leanings were in that direction and he was jealous of women who attracted male attention. At one of my last meetings with him – in New York, before I left for Katanga – he had flown into a rage because there was a large picture of Jacqueline Kennedy on the front page. The attention the media were paying to "that woman" was, he thought, preposterous. His normally pale face turned red and his voice shook. This was the only time I had ever seen him manifest emotion about anything.

Olivier then asked some other questions, but I sensed that the important one had come and gone. Then Olivier said, apparently casually, that he was thinking of asking Sir John Gielgud to play the part of Hammarskjold. I said, sincerely, that Gielgud would be splendid in the part. Olivier agreed but with a distinct lack of enthusiasm. I already sensed that something was wrong and had a hunch about what it was.

I soon had word from the National Theatre that they were very sorry but they could not, after all, produce *Angels*. They had been advised that they could be successfully sued for libel if they did. I protested against this decision. Who, after all, was going to sue? Hammarskjold and Lumumba were both dead. Tshombe and Munungo were most unlikely to sue in a British court, and equally unlikely to win if they did. All the other characters of any importance were fictional. These arguments were well-based, as the sequel showed. The play was subsequently produced in Los Angeles, New York, Paris, Berlin, Lubeck and Dublin (on stage and on radio) and nobody in any of those places even threatened a suit.

The National Theatre ignored my arguments and reiterated their decision. The case was closed.

The real trouble was certainly never libel. I think the real trouble was the suggestion that Hammarskjold had been a homosexual. I believe that

Olivier had been primarily interested in *Angels* as a possible vehicle for Gielgud, who certainly *was* a homosexual. Homosexual conduct was then still a penal offence, so most homosexuals, including Gielgud, remained in the closet. Playing a homosexual Hammarskjold might impair the secrecy of the closet.

I can understand the reasons for the decision, though of course I deeply regret the decision itself and the lost opportunity that it represented. But at least I carried away with me, and shall treasure to my dying day the memory of Laurence Olivier's expression as he pronounced the words: 'What would a man want a *mask* for, if he had a *face*?"

* * *

The first professional performance of *Angels* was also much the most successful. It was directed by Gordon Davidson and ran at the Mark Taper Forum in Los Angeles from February 5 through March 22 of 1970. The star of the show was Lou Gossett, who put in an electrifying performance as Lumumba. He had extraordinary long arms with which he made vast and well-timed gestures with hypnotic effect. For the rest it was, under Gordon's skilled and painstaking direction, a thoroughly professional production.

After the modest but real success in Los Angeles, I looked forward with confidence to the productions booked for New York, and later in Paris and Berlin. Unfortunately the confidence was altogether misplaced in all three instances.

It was in New York that things first went badly wrong. New York was "politically correct" in those days in quite a big way and *Angels* was felt to be politically incorrect, twice over. White liberals, an influential section of the New York theatre audience, cherished the memory of Hammarskjold, and I was felt to have insulted the memory unforgiveably.

That was bad enough, but black reactions were even more damaging. Not that blacks were all that significant a part of theatre audiences, but negative reactions from politicised blacks had a paralyzing impact on the black players and therefore, indirectly, also on the white ones. Politicised blacks in those days objected to *any* white person writing about black people. Only blacks should write about black people. They particularly objected to my portrayal of Lumumba, although it was a favourable portrayal. But any portrayal of Lumumba had to be *entirely* favourable. He had to be seen as flawless in all particulars, and he was not allowed to have a white mistress. In short, both Lumumba and Hammarskjold had become ikons, for black and white audiences respectively.

Under these pressures, the players began to disintegrate at the New York rehearsals. The disintegration began at the top with Lou Gossett playing Lumumba. The black politicians, working on Gossett, had made him feel guilty of betraying his own people by playing the part I had written. I watched with horror, in the rehearsals as those splendid gestures grew more contracted, and a would-be respectable woodenness, in general, replaced the old spontaneity. The same sort of things pervaded the other performances in various ways. In short *Angels* in New York was a total disaster and was rightly taken off after only two days.

* * *

The offer from Joan Littlewood came, I believe, in the interval between the successful production in Los Angeles and the crash in New York, so I was still on something of a high when the Littlewood offer came in. This was unfortunate.

Littlewood said that the Theatre National Populaire de Paris had agreed to stage *Murderous Angels* in its *Grande Salle*, if she would agree to direct it.

This interested me strangely. The Theatre National Populaire de Paris is one of the great theatres in the world. Its enormous *Grande Salle* was also the meeting-place of the second General Assembly of the United Nations. So, an ideal setting for a presentation of *Murderous Angels*, so it seemed to me.

There was, however, a rather large snag. Littlewood stipulated that, if she was to direct the production – which was apparently the prime condition for acceptance by the TNP – she must have complete discretion to edit, and where necessary amend, the text just as she thought fit. From the moment I accepted this conditional offer of hers, she and not I would be in full control of whatever would eventually appear on the stage of the TNP.

In an evil hour I accepted this condition. I was seduced by the glamour of the *Grande Salle* and by its historic association with the UN. I had seen and admired a lively presentation of Littlewood's satirical play about the First World War, *Oh! What a Lovely War*. I realized that what she produced would be rather remote from what I had written. But I thought it would be successful, in its own way, and draw favourable attention to my work. I turned out to be wrong on both counts.

The experience of "collaboration" with Joan Littlewood was one of the most unpleasant experiences of my life. She belonged, by this time, to the hard left, and I was for her one of those whom Lenin called "useful idiots". Her version of *Murderous Angels* would be straight propaganda and nothing else. The text would be edited ruthlessly to meet that project, and indeed totally recast, with almost all of my own lines thrown out the window.

I first realized the dimensions of the editorial horror that was engulfing me when she told me that Wole Soyinka was playing Lumumba, and had total freedom to rewrite the part to suit himself and his views. For starters he had eliminated altogether the part of Madame Rose, Lumumba's white mistress in the play. I knew from painful New York experience precisely what that implied. The black hero could not be seen to be in love with a white chick. That elimination meant that the part would be rewritten to meet the rigorous standards of the black version of "politically correct." Wole Soyinka was a talented writer and perhaps actor but while rewriting Lumumba's part and then playing it, his talent would be entirely on hold.

And this proved to be the case, when I had the dreadful experience of watching Soyinka play in Littlewood's version of *Murderous Angels*. The Littlewood-Soyinka version of my Lumumba came on and preached incessantly, with a dignified air, every black-left-wing platitude in the book. The other parts were also rewritten to similar specifications, but that hardly mattered. Lumumba is the heart of the play I had written and when the heart was eliminated the play died. Whatever talent Littlewood had evinced in *Oh! What a Lovely War* seemed to have died of a surfeit of political correctitude. The audience was thoroughly bored and faintly puzzled. About half of them left in the interval following the first curtain. The first night was also the last. Such notices as appeared were deservedly terrible.

Since the Littlewood version was so awful I had to be glad it was a flop but even so the flop was painful. It was a flop that could not have happened without my fatuous consent.

There was only one element of consolation: a review that appeared in (I think) *Le Nouvel Observateur*. The review was entitled "The art of making a play say what it does not want to say". *L'Art de faire dire a une piece ce qu'elle ne veut pas dire*. Exactly so.

* * *

The last major production of *Angels* was in Berlin at the Schillertheater. It had some striking features in common with the Paris production. It was played in a prestigious setting. And it was a total flop, running for just one night.

In other respects, however, the experiences were very different. The Berlin director, Paryla, was scrupulously respectful of my text and intentions. His troubles had set in with the casting, and derived from liberal intentions. Like prohibition in America his version of *Angels* was "an experiment noble in purpose", which crashed.

Paryla invited me to Berlin for the dress rehearsal. He warned me not to expect too much and I didn't. All the same I was shocked by the extent of the dramatic disaster when I saw it on the stage. Paryla knew I was shocked and was right to be. We had dinner afterwards and he was prepared to answer my questions.

"The people playing the black parts," I said. "They are almost unintelligible most of the time. How come?"

"That," said Paryla, "is where our troubles began. You see, in Germany, there are no black actors. There are blacks who are singers, dancers, musicians. But no black actors. So I had to decide what to do. Were we to have *white* actors, in black face or wearing masks, playing the black parts? I felt that to proceed in that way would be lacking in integrity and in respect for black people. So we decided we would do the best we could with the black musicians, even if their German wasn't up to much."

"Well that certainly accounts for the *black* players," I said. "But the white players aren't much better, even if they are more intelligible. Why are *they* so bad?"

"That," said Paryla, "is an unintended result of the first decision, regarding the black parts. We had recruited some excellent white players. But when these found that they were expected to play along with blacks, who were not players at all, they all resigned."

"This was not," added Paryla rather anxiously, "a result of racist ill-feeling. These white actors would have had no objection to playing opposite blacks who were actors. But they felt that if they played opposite blacks who were not actors, their professional standing would suffer, which indeed would have been the case. So we had to go downmarket in order to replace them. We recruited white actors who were unemployed, almost always for good reasons."

We contemplated the depressing general picture for a moment in silence. Then I said: "All right, I can see why the black and white actors, generally, are not up to snuff. But how about the player who plays Hammarskjold? I have never seen so bad a performance on any stage. The man can hardly speak, and seems paralyzed with fright."

Paryla said, with a little smile: "For that you would need to understand our Germanic character, and our preoccupation with *status*. This man is quite well known in our cinema. He usually plays the part of a stormtrooper, in movies about the Nazi period. But – and this is the important part – the Nazis he plays are *not Nazis of the first rank*. They are just commonplace thugs. So when a German player of that status is called upon to play the part of a person of high rank, like a Secretary-General, he becomes paralyzed with guilt, so that he can hardly speak, you see."

I could see indeed. I could also see that Paryla's misfortunes all stemmed from one high-minded mistake over the black parts. I felt a great respect and affection for Paryla as a person, though I could only mourn the consequences, for *Angels*, of what I regarded as his quixotic original decision.

* * *

Those were the big ones: one good, three bad. There were a couple of modest successes: a production in masks in Lubeck, and a performance on Irish radio, which was brilliantly edited and acted. The play was better suited to radio rather than live theatre: for one thing the problems about black and white players can be ignored for radio. I would hope that RTE might revive their production of *Angels* after my death.

11

DIVORCE AND REMARRIAGE

AFTER MY RESIGNATION, AS WELL AS MÁIRE'S, FROM THE IRISH FOREIGN
Service there was a personal problem to be cleared up, which for the
moment had to take precedence of political ones. The problem concerned
our intention to marry – in my case to remarry. I made that intention
public, immediately after our concomitant resignations. In a statement I
explained that Christine and I were about to divorce, by mutual consent,
with agreed arrangements for the support of the children. As soon as the
divorce had gone through, Máire and I would be married. I did not at that
moment go into the rather thorny questions of what kind of marriage this
would be, or what kind of recognition it might receive.

My public statement did a lot to clear the air as far as Máire's parents
were concerned. Our resignations, and speculations about the reasons for
the same, had been filling both the British and Irish newspapers at the time,
with even quite a lot in the American newspapers, though for a shorter
time. Before leaving New York, I gave a press conference at my hotel, with
a large attendance. The journalist last to leave was an elderly photographer
who was burdened with heavy equipment. Feeling the gap a bit awkward, I
said to him, "I'll be glad when something else takes this off the front page".
The photographer looked at me with scorn.

"No, mister," he said, "you won't be glad. They never are. Good night."

One of the journalists, more enterprising than the rest, had managed to filch from a drawer in my desk a document containing the details of our divorce settlement which his newspaper published on the following day. Actually, this suited me quite well, as the publication of the facts killed off speculation on the subject, which would have been likely to be much more damaging.

Arrived back in Dublin, I made my way to Máire's parents' home in Leeson Park, Dublin. Máire's mother, Margaret, met me at the front door with a broad smile. "Well, Conor," she said, "you've led us a nice dance!" It was evident that, in her case at least, there was no trace of resentment. Indeed in some ways she had enjoyed all the excitement, and especially coping with the press. She told me about it later. When a London newspaper rang and enquired whether she had seen a story they had run about Máire and me, Margaret replied: "Of course not. I never read the British newspapers." As she spoke she had before her a large pile of British newspapers, having read every word of every story they contained about us – which was quite a lot of words at that time.

I thought for a moment that Máire's father's reaction might be different, though I should have known from Margaret's relaxed manner that this would not be the case. In the past indeed, Seán MacEntee had strongly disapproved of me (understandably enough) because of my close connection with Seán MacBride. In his eagerness to discredit MacBride, MacEntee had spread the word that I was a communist, or at any rate a fellow-traveller. Seán had long been a rough and rather unscrupulous political polemicist. On one occasion, when Seán had made aspersions in the Dáil against members of the Clann na Poblachta party, one of those members, Captain Cowan, put a question to the Ceann Comhairle (Speaker of the Dáil). "Is it in order," he asked, "to call the deputy a sewer-rat?" "Certainly not!" said the Ceann Comhairle. Captain Cowan replied sweetly: "Thank you very much, Ceann Comhairle. The sewer-rats will be greatly relieved to hear of that ruling."

Seán himself was highly amused by this intervention.

In the brief period between Máire's resignation from the public service and my public statement, her father had been severe with her, making her feel that she was in disgrace. But my public statement, ending the phase of rumour and innuendo, cleared the air, as Seán himself acknowledged. So Seán now welcomed me as his future son-in-law. He did so altogether without reservations. The past divisions between us were now a closed book. We soon became firm friends and so remained, without any cloud ever, for the rest of his life.

That part was all extremely satisfactory, but there was still tricky going ahead. The divorce was the relatively easy bit. I consulted my friend and legal adviser, Alexis FitzGerald, a good Catholic, and also a humane and civilized person. He advised me, briefly and gently, against getting divorced, but finding me altogether determined on this point, he advised me on the least messy way of attaining my objective. At that time, a divorce in Britain or even in the United States would still have been messy. The best available was a Mexican divorce, which would be immediately available, on production of statements by both parties jointly declaring *assoluta incompatibilidad* between them, and proof of agreed arrangements for the support of the children. The arrangements for the support of the children had already been made and neither Christine nor I had by now any difficulty in acknowledging that our relationship had indeed become one of *assoluta incompatibilidad.* Accordingly, I travelled to Juarez, Mexico, and there obtained the required divorce.

That was the easy bit. The question of remarriage was much trickier. Neither Máire nor myself wanted to cut ourselves off permanently from Ireland, yet my first marriage was not dissoluble under Irish law. Divorce did not become legally available in Ireland until thirty-two years later, in 1997. Rather a long wait. But there was a possible and effective way out. For me it was a hypocritical way and otherwise distasteful, but I took it, as preferable to the alternatives. And I realized that I had in reality taken the decision when I publicly announced my intention to remarry without any qualification. Seán and Margaret undoubtedly understood, by that, a marriage which would be generally regarded as valid in Ireland, even though nothing attainable there was literally valid in civil law. What was attainable was a Catholic marriage, since my first marriage, not being a Catholic one, was not recognized by the Church. My remarriage in a Catholic church would still not be recognized by the state, but in what was still an overwhelmingly Catholic Republic of Ireland, what the state was supposed to think about a marriage mattered much less – even to the state itself – than what the Catholic Church thought about it. The path to a Catholic marriage was clearly open, if I chose to take it. If I refused to take it and offered instead a remarriage in (say) Mexico City – which would be regarded by neither Church nor state in Ireland as valid – Máire's parents would be likely to regard me as having gone back on my pledged word to marry their daughter, and the happy relationship which now existed between the four of us would be broken up. This consequence seemed to me so horrible as far to outweigh the evil of vitally opportune hypocrisy. So I gulped and decided on a Catholic marriage.

The ugliest downside to all this was what I might be taken as saying about my three children. Whatever I might do, the children remained legitimate under Irish law. My remarriage – which would *not* be legitimate under Irish law – could not change their legal status, nor of course did I wish in the least for it to do so. I was glad that they still enjoyed the protection of the civil law. But I knew the Church from which I was accepting remarriage did not accept their legitimacy, nor did I publicly challenge what I knew was their interpretation (though they did not publicize it), since I needed our remarriage to be seen as valid. My children understood the bind I was in. They forgave me and they love me still. But it was a difficult passage, and I was glad when we left it behind. What was good was that absolutely nobody was nasty to us about any of this: neither the Catholics nor the anti-Catholics. Owen, who on past form might have been expected to be rough on my hypocrisy, as he could quite legitimately have been, spoke nary a word along those lines and was most welcoming to Máire. So on the whole I came through that difficult and rather ignominious passage in a somewhat less bedraggled condition than might have been expected.

Máire points out to me that her feelings were different from mine and much simpler. She was proud and glad to marry me and proud and glad to do so in a Catholic church.

* * *

The Catholic Church in Ireland had agreed to our remarriage, but it did not wish the marriage to take place in Ireland. To do so would have shown the Church either as acting in breach of the civil law, or condoning a breach of the same. So it was arranged between the Archdiocese of Dublin and the Archdiocese of New York that the marriage should take place in New York City. Interestingly enough, our previous run-ins with the Archdiocese of New York, over the China vote, did not cause any difficulty. Memories are shorter in New York than elsewhere and that little dispute belonged in a past already felt to be remote.

We travelled to New York for the wedding, but there was a delay. New York could do nothing without a formal Letter of Consent from the Archdiocese of Dublin, and for some reason the Letter took quite a long time to arrive. In the meantime we stayed with Jewish friends, Edward and Vicky Solomons, in their very pleasant home in northern Long Island.

Edward Solomons was a nephew of Bethel Solomons, the gynaecologist who had brought me into the world. Like Bethel – the leading gynaecologist in Dublin in his day – Edward was also an eminent gynaecologist, but he found his professional path, in an independent Ireland, a lot less smooth than his uncle's path had been under the British Raj. The reason was that the Catholic Church, while it had been able to exert considerable and steadily increasing influence within the old United Kingdom of Great Britain and Ireland, became much more powerful, and indeed formidable in an independent Irish state, for about the first forty years of that independence. In certain areas the Church could now wield virtually untrammelled power. One such area was the education of Catholics. Another was medicine, and in particular gynaecology, where the Church was determined to see that the legal prohibition of abortion was rigidly enforced in Ireland. The Church was determined to limit, and if possible terminate, the presence of non-Catholics, and especially Jews, in gynaecological teaching and practice. Catholic doctors – a large majority of the profession – could see advantages in co-operating with this policy. So Solomons found subtle obstructions in his professional career such as his uncle had never known. Realizing this, Edward – though he liked Ireland, and was never bitter about his experience there – decided to make his career elsewhere. He had become a senior gynaecologist at Maimonides Hospital in New York, and he and his family flourished happily there.

I had met Edward through my cousin Owen who had been a contemporary and close friend of his at Trinity College – they were both gifted amateur boxers. When I got to know Edward, while he was still in Dublin, I found that – like Roger Greene and myself – we shared a taste for practical jokes. On one occasion I went as his guest to the annual dinner of the Fellows of the Royal College of Physicians in Dublin. He lent me his Fellow's gown, a splendidly colourful affair, so that I was able to mingle with the crowd in the guise of a Fellow. In that capacity I expounded wildly heterodox views on questions of medical ethics, causing satisfactory quantities of scandal and alarm. Satisfactory to Edward and me, that is.

I found the secular Jewish atmosphere of Edward and Vicky's home very congenial in those weeks. I had been a bit oppressed by the necessity to prepare for participation in a sacrament of a religion in which I did not believe. So it was nice to be among secular friends, who yet understood – out of their own Irish experience – the need for my pretence of conformity.

We were married on January 9, 1962. My biographer, Don Akenson, states that the ceremony was performed by my wife's uncle, Cardinal Browne. I don't know where Don got this story from but it was certainly not from me, and it is not true. The ceremony was performed by Father Donal O'Callaghan (quite a strong Irish nationalist, and a close friend of Frank Aiken's, who must have been disconcerted by my subsequent evolution into a unionist). Among the guests was Ralph Bunche. I was pleased and a bit surprised that he accepted my invitation. He was still a senior serving member of the UN Secretariat and – though my book was still to come – I had already publicly stated that the Secretariat's official version of Morthor was untrue. In any case he came, and I was glad he did.

* * *

We went back to Ireland to live in my old home in Howth, Christine having gone to live elsewhere. My stance on the Congo, having been violently denounced in Britain, was quite popular in Ireland. It was particularly popular among a section of the population whose esteem I would later forfeit, totally and forever: Irish republicans. I received a letter from Dan Breen, the man who fired the first shot in the Irish "Troubles" in 1919, and who wrote the book *My Fight for Irish Freedom*. Dan wrote: "I don't know you but from the kind of things the British are saying about you, you must have done something right."

When it came out, *To Katanga and Back* was quite well received. The political context had changed significantly since the period of my resignation. The Americans had started again to apply serious pressure to Tshombe's Katanga and Britain – having more or less given up on plans for the Central African Federation – was not about to engage again in the hazardous business of trying to undermine a policy supported by the Americans. So, in this calmer atmosphere, most of the reviews were quite acceptable. There was one exception, one vehemently hostile anonymous review in the *Times Literary Supplement*. The reviewer described my account of Morthor as "preposterous" and "a ludicrously thin story". I knew the writer was Brian Urquhart, and I knew Urquhart knew my story was true. I started legal proceedings but was advised that, in view of my still-lingering anti-British reputation at this time, I did not stand much chance of success before a British jury. So, when the TLS agreed to publish a reply from me identifying the author of the review as "a serving member of the United Nations Secretariat". I agreed to settle for that. The agreement to publish that statement without contradiction established that the statement was in fact true. Later, in his biography of Hammarskjold, Urquhart did not repeat his claim that I had been lying, and indeed implicitly accepted the truth of my version.

At about this time Máire's Uncle David, Father Michael Browne in religion, was created a Cardinal by John XXIII. This was kind and generous of the new Pope as Michael Browne had been a very conservative theologian and a devoted admirer of Pius XII. Seán and Margaret had been invited to accompany President de Valera to the ceremony in Rome. Margaret, who was not in good health at the time, was anxious that at least one of her children would come with them. As it happened the only one free to travel was Máire, and it was assumed that I myself would not want to go and that, as we have been such a short time married, she would not want to go without me. Somewhat to my own surprise I volunteered immediately to escort my parents-in-law, and we set out as a party of four. This, as I learnt later, caused some embarrassment among my former colleagues as Máire and I had been struck off the list of suitable invitees to public occasions. In one of the first of his many kindnesses towards us, Mr de Valera had us restored at once to this list and included in all the official invitations for the occasion, which combined a lot of family warmth with some splendid spectacle and enabled us afterwards to enjoy a short Italian holiday on our own.

A year or so later, on our way home from Africa, of which more shortly, we stayed with the new Cardinal in his rooms in St Peter's Colonnade looking out on the Square. This was the suite in which Galilleo Galillei was held during his trial by the Holy Office, and there we had the surreal experience of seeing the space-probe, Mariner I, approaching Mars! Our host could not have been kinder to me, apart from a tendency to translate Latin inscriptions for me, which I could not hurt his feelings by telling him was unnecessary. Once, walking in the Borghese Gardens, he spoke about Cardinal Borgia and I brought up the subject of Lucretia. His comment was characteristic; "Poor Lucretia," he said, "she wasn't the worst . . . " then after a pause, "Anyway, she was his mother." I was glad to have known him.

12

"BIG MAN, WHY NO 'YES'?"

WHILE I WAS FINISHING *TO KATANGA AND BACK* I RECEIVED A TELEGRAM FROM the office of Kwame Nkrumah, President of Ghana, inviting me to be vice-chancellor (that is, academic and administrative head) of the newly-established University of Ghana. Nkrumah himself was chancellor, which within the British and British-inspired academic system is supposed to be a purely dignified and decorative office. The University of Ghana was replacing the old University College of the Gold Coast which had the reputation of being the soundest and most advanced academic institution – as well as the wealthiest – in tropical Africa.

Nkrumah was not altogether unknown to me. In mid-September 1961 when UN headquarters in Elisabethville was under fire, mainly from mercenaries and local Belgians, the president of Ghana, Osagyefo Dr Kwame Nkrumah, addressed to UN headquarters a message of concern for my personal safety.

When this message was transmitted to me by Dr Bunche I was particularly grateful to Dr Nkrumah because I knew that messages of a very different character about me were reaching UN headquarters from other governments at that time.

I had met Dr Nkrumah briefly before this on two occasions. The first time was in May 1960 when he made an important address in Dublin in which he stated that if South Africa, having become a republic, was allowed to remain in the Commonwealth, Ghana would leave: a statement which was generally and rightly regarded as a prelude to South Africa's exclusion from the Commonwealth. The second time was in New York in September 1960 when he addressed the Secretary-General's Advisory Committee on the Congo, on which I was representing Ireland at that time. I was impressed by his analysis of the Congo situation – an analysis which led me to reconsider my own approach to this question, hitherto largely conditioned by the atmosphere on the East River – and also by the patience and good humour with which he replied to some very aggressive questioning.

I was, however, not at first at all disposed to accept Nkrumah's offer. I knew that Nkrumah, although he had first attained power in genuinely free elections, was at least potentially a dictator and that his respect for academic freedom would be at best a doubtful quantity. So soon after Katanga, I was not disposed to involve myself again in another unpredictable and possibly messy situation. So I wrote back civilly declining, thinking that would be the end of the matter.

But it wasn't. Nkrumah's reply followed immediately, inviting my wife and myself to visit Accra as his guests. While there I could visit the university, talk with the senior members of the staff and hear their views. Then I could make up my mind, finally. I discussed the matter with Máire and found that we both liked the idea.

When we arrived in Ghana, Nkrumah was most kind and hospitable, but then we expected he would be, at the time and in the circumstances. The decisive factor turned out to be that my reception at the university was strongly positive. The people I met believed that academic freedom might indeed need to be defended and that I was probably in a better position to defend it than anyone else. My Katanga record protected me against any suspicion that I was an agent of British imperialism.

That was how the matter looked to me at the time and it was broadly right. There was another factor at work in my favour, however, of which I learned only later. This was that university people feared that if they did not accept me they would get Geoffrey Bing, who as Nkrumah's Attorney-General, had drafted the University of Ghana Act, and had been one of Nkrumah's closest advisers. Geoffrey had been an MP on the extreme left of the British Labour Party, and was generally regarded as a fellow-traveller with the communists. It was not, however, his supposed ties with the communists that worried the dons, but his real ties with Nkrumah. They feared that, in any crisis, Geoffrey would help Nkrumah to impose his will on the university.

In so believing, the dons were neither altogether right nor altogether wrong. Geoffrey was a clever and complex person. He had genuinely liberal inclinations, but he also believed that if you were clever enough – as he was – you could in practice reconcile liberalism with communism. This would indeed have made him a very dangerous head of a university. But there was never any real likelihood that he would have been appointed. Virtually everybody in Ghana had come to detest Geoffrey, seeing him as devious (which he was) and his most assiduous enemies were on the Ghanaian left, which was also hostile to the university itself.

I believe it was Geoffrey who recommended me for the post of vice-chancellor, when he found he could not have it for himself. I think he had formed the impression, from the shriller attacks on me in the British press, that I was much further to the left than I actually was; that I would rely on his advice, and that in fact he could run the university through me. He was to be disappointed, but the outcome that disappointed him was partly the result of his own ambition and the fear that it inspired.

In the circumstances, seeing the strong support for me within the university, Máire and I decided that I should accept: a decision that neither of us ever regretted. Foreseeing that some deterioration in relations with the chancellor was likely to ensue if academic freedom did come under pressure, I stipulated that my tenure would be limited to three years. It lasted the full length, to the general surprise of most people in Ghana, whether friend or foe. I took up the appointment in February 1962.

* * *

The University of Ghana was lavishly built and equipped, the most sumptuous university in Africa. Ghana by the end of World War Two had acquired very large financial resources, mainly due to temporarily unrequited exports of cocoa during the war. The buildings were lavish all right, but not particularly well-designed. An architectural journal described the university buildings as "a romantic failure in the grand manner". As I had noticed earlier in the Congo – and particularly in Leopoldville – European architects designing buildings for tropical Africa had a tendency to think more about how a building would look in photographs circulated in Europe than in how they might suit the people who had to live and/or work there in a tropical climate. The vice-chancellor's lodge where we were to live for the next three years was a case in point. It was all set out around a large, roofless patio. This was no doubt very suitable for a Mediterranean climate, but it was grotesquely unsuited for a tropical one. The vertical sun at noon beat down on the patio, not only making that area uninhabitable, but splashing great waves of heat through all the rest of the building. So we had to rig up emergency cover, which was rather unsightly, to remedy the effects of the architecture.

That said, the site of the building, as distinct from the building itself, had great advantages. It was right on the top of the only hill in the Accra Plain. The hill wasn't very high – about 400 feet I think – but after six o'clock, when the sun set with tropical regularity, the top of the hill got all the breeze there was, and was a very agreeable place to be. So we used to give parties there quite often in the evenings, in the large open space around the lodge, for academic staff and some senior students.

I remember two parties in particular, in that first year.

The first was proceeding normally when it was interrupted by the arrival of a large number of (uninvited) students, rushing through the large dark area of "bush" outside into the lighted circle around the lodge. They were already in a state of great distress, verging on panic. The news they brought was of the assassination that day of President Kennedy. They clearly all thought of Kennedy as a friend of Africa's and that he had been murdered for that reason, by American racists. Some feared that, in the confusion, racists might come to power in America, with horrible consequences for Africa, and themselves personally. Others feared that Kennedy might have been murdered by a black, and that white racists might come to power in the United States in the general revulsion against that deed. But it was clear that all the students tremendously admired Kennedy, had indeed loved him from a distance, and that they felt an acute sense of loss at his passing in such a terrible manner.

After my own experiences with the Kennedy administration over Katanga I could not feel quite the same way the students did, but I couldn't help being moved by the sincerity and intensity – and somehow the purity – of what they felt.

The second memorable party on the lawn was given for WEG Du Bois, the great veteran of the struggle against racism in the United States, and the institutionalised racism then still prevailing in the south. He had become a communist, apparently because he believed in the sincerity of communist anti-racist professions. During the year or more in which I knew him and talked with him, he never showed any sign of enthusiasm for communism, or interest in it. This may, I think, have been due to his contacts with Russian communists who generally reeked of unavowed but blatant racism.

This was evident even in the Russian diplomatic representation in Accra while I was there. We gave a luncheon party at the lodge for a visiting Russian cultural dignitary and of course the Russian Ambassador to Ghana came along. Ghanaian intellectuals were among the guests and one of them, George Awoonor Williams, had spent some time in Russia and referred, rather discreetly, to some of his experiences there. His remarks were addressed to the Ambassador, who did not, however, reply. Instead the Ambassador turned to my wife and said in a voice which could be heard by the whole table: "He is quite *intelligent*, is he not – that one?" He had an earnest expression as he spoke, and it was clear that he felt he had delivered himself of a liberal sentiment.

Du Bois was to receive an honorary degree from the University of Ghana, one of the first batch of degrees from the new university. The degree should have been conferred by Nkrumah, as chancellor of the university, but at the last moment he cried off. I later learned that left-wing members of his entourage had convinced him that if he came to the university he would be mobbed by the right-wing students (something of which there was no danger whatever). This was an ominous bit of information as it showed the strength of hostility to the university among people close to Nkrumah. In any case, this meant I had the honour of conferring the degree on Du Bois, and enfolding him in the university's handsome new *kente* gown. Du Bois was deeply moved by receiving a degree from an African university. His wife, Shirley Graham, later told me that he took the gown to bed with him that night.

Later, Du Bois liked to come to the university on Saturday evenings to parties to which students were invited. He was a very striking figure in his wheel-chair; still handsome in extreme old age, aristocratic in his bearing, with a face like a Faulkner colonel. He spoke very little but what he said was always to the point. On one evening the students were celebrating the admission, under federal pressure, of a black student, James Meredith, to the University of Mississippi. Du Bois shared in the general rejoicing but then added in his slow creaking voice: "The only thing . . . I can't understand . . . is why *anyone* would want to be admitted to the University of Mississippi." The students remembered that Du Bois had been educated at Harvard, and laughed.

That was light relief. But the other saying of Du Bois which I remember was profoundly serious and I believe left a mark on the lives of most of those who heard it, certainly including myself. The news had then come in that Moise Tshombe had just been made president of the Congo. All those present at the gathering on Legon Hill, including myself, were outraged at the news. One of the students linked Tshombe to the 19th century black educationist, Booker T Washington, still rather widely regarded as the classical traitor to the cause of black freedom. Then Du Bois delivered the longest and most earnest statement I ever heard him make. He said:

"When I was a young man, I once said something like that about Booker T Washington, who was then of course alive and active. An aunt of mine, who had a great influence over me was present. She said 'I hope you never speak like that again about Booker T. Washington. Remember that he bears the marks of the slave-owner's lash on his back and you don't. You and he are both trying to serve the cause of black people in the United States. But you have to serve in very different conditions. You are serving in the north where conditions are relatively easy and blacks can at least vote. He is serving in the south where blacks are effectively disfranchised and often terrorized. He simply can't use the kind of language you do, now. If he did he would be silenced instantly which you are not. He has to set about his work in a more roundabout way than what is open to you. But his object is essentially the same: more education and more freedom for black people. So I hope I never again hear you speak disrespectfully of Booker T Washington.'

"And," concluded Du Bois simply, "I never did."

* * *

The news that Moise Tshombe had become president of the Congo struck me as outrageous, as if Jefferson Davis had become president of the United States shortly after the end of the American Civil War. I first had the word that Tshombe might become president from Kojo Botsio, Nkrumah's Foreign Minister. Botsio was a hugely fat man, indolent and – like all Nkrumah's henchmen – crooked, but cynically intelligent. I told him that I could not believe that anything of the sort was in the pipeline. "I don't know," said Botsio, "but it seems he's started calling himself *Doctor* Tshombe and that always means something." It did. Nkrumah, of course, had always set great store by his honorary doctorate.

Around the same time, I had a related conversation with the Chinese Ambassador in Accra, a very bright person and also cynical, but in a more elevated Chinese manner. After we had played a game of table-tennis, which he won, he asked me what I thought about Tshombe's elevation (by then confirmed) and I told him, with some indignation. The Ambassador smiled and said: "Think of it all as part of one process of political education – theirs, Dr O'Brien, and also *yours* . . ." Quite so.

There was another related conversation, around the same time, with the Ambassador of Israel, Michael Arnon. Israel was contemplating giving military aid to the government of the Congo under Tshombe, and Arnon wanted me to agree that this would be helpful to stabilize development in Central Africa. I indicated that I strongly disagreed, and this did not surprise him. It was clear that he had been acting on instructions, and he did not press me. "All right, Conor," he said. "You know they pay me to say these things. But why should I insist? They don't pay me all that much." He and I became friends.

These interesting and somewhat disturbing developments were outside the sphere of my actual duties in Ghana. But now there occurred a strange little imbroglio which fell naturally within the sphere of those duties. The imbroglio arose from the sudden resignation of the Professor of Physics, Ray Wright. Ray was also my deputy, as pro-vice-chancellor, and I liked him very much, and relied on him. He was a member of the British Labour Party, not as far left as Geoffrey Bing, by any means, but serious about social issues. One morning Ray came to my office in a state of high excitement, and told me that he would have to resign immediately. When I asked him why, he told me he had been sitting on his porch reading, the previous evening, when the light began to fade. He snapped his fingers and called "Steward!" – university servants were called stewards – "Put on the light". "He put the light on . . . but the switch was only six feet from where I sat. Then I realized how deeply I had been corrupted by the post-colonial environment, and that if I was to be capable of leading any kind of decent life I must get out of here right away."

I tried, of course, to dissuade him. Finding him adamant, I asked about a successor. "Well," said Ray, "there is one eminently qualified possible candidate, living right here: better qualified than myself, and better qualified than anyone else we would be likely to attract. That candidate is Alan Nunn May."

We looked at one another in silence for a while. Then Ray said: "I don't suppose the university would wear it." During the war, Alan Nunn May, an atomic scientist, had provided the Soviet Union – then allied to Britain – with classified information which could help them to manufacture atomic weapons. Under British law this was a very serious offence. Charged with the offence, Nunn May immediately admitted what he had done and was sentenced to seven years, which he served in Parkhurst Prison. On May's release, Nkrumah – probably on Geoffrey Bing's advice – invited him to Ghana, where he became what was called "a presidential professor". This meant that he was paid out of state funds, not university funds, and that he was entitled to use the university library and laboratories, but not to teach. Apparently Nkrumah felt that there was no chance that the university would voluntarily appoint him, and that if he were to impose him on the university, this would not only involve trouble there but could also seriously damage relations with Britain.

But, as Nunn May was much the best professor of physics the university could possibly get, I told Ray to advise Nunn May to apply for the post when it was advertised, and that if he was found to be the best qualified candidate, I would do my best to see to it that he was appointed.

When the appointments board for the post was set up by the Academic Board, I agreed to serve as chairman. The two other members most likely to be influential were the Professor of Mathematics and the Professor of Religion. The Professor of Mathematics was an able and decent man, but he was a British Conservative and unlikely to think well of a British candidate who had been convicted of treason to his country. This negative view would be likely to determine the outcome, unless it was outweighed. I had hopes, however, of the Professor of Religion, Christian Baeta, much the weightiest Ghanaian member of the board, and the most eminent scholar and intellectual in the Ghana of his day. He had been president of the World Council of Churches.

When the board met we had seven applications before us. As chairman, I called on each member of the board in turn to declare which candidate was the best qualified, professionally and intellectually, for the post. The Professor of Mathematics said there was also a question of moral suitability. I said that question would only arise if such a question were raised about the moral suitability of the person found to be the best qualified professionally and intellectually. We should not assume in advance that such a question would arise. The Professor of Mathematics smiled a little ruefully, seeing what way the wind was blowing. Each member of the board in turn then affirmed – some a little unwillingly – that Alan Nunn May was the best qualified candidate, professionally and intellectually.

I then asked whether any member of the board saw any objection, on any other ground, to the appointment of Alan Nunn May? The Professor of Mathematics said that he objected on moral grounds, because of Nunn May's conviction for treason. I then said that every member of the board in turn would have an opportunity of setting out his views on that matter, but I thought it would be helpful to the board if the Professor of Religion, more accustomed than any of the rest of us to the examination of ethical issues, would have an opportunity of making known his views. Christian Baeta spoke as follows:

"Alan Nunn May was justly convicted, after his own confession, of a major crime against the laws of his country. He then served a long prison sentence for that crime, and rightly so. But the only question before us is whether his past commission of that offence, for which he was punished, in itself makes him morally unfit to teach the young? I have carefully considered this matter and I don't think it does. We know that he gave this classified information to the Soviet Union because the Soviet Union was then fighting for its existence against Nazi Germany – with which Britain was also at war – and he thought it his moral duty to come to the help of the Soviet Union, even if he had to break the laws of his country and risk imprisonment and disgrace by so doing.

"I think Nunn May's decision was a gravely mistaken one, but I have no doubt that it was sincerely motivated on a high moral plane. I can only hope that if I thought as he did I would have had the courage to act as he did. There is nothing in this man's record that makes him morally unfitted to teach the young. Rather the contrary."

That did it. Alan Nunn May was appointed, without further discussion.

It proved an excellent appointment in every way. In addition to being an eminent scholar, Nunn May proved to be a first-rate teacher. More remarkably, when the heat came on the university later from Nkrumah's government, as I shall relate, Nunn May unhesitatingly supported the university's position against the government and its raucous allies. This showed remarkable courage as well as principled conviction, for had he been expelled from Ghana he would have found it very hard to find another job, in Britain or America or western Europe. It might be thought that the Soviet Union, for whose sake he had endured so much, would have welcomed him to one of its own universities, but this was by no means the case.

After we had become friends Nunn May told me the story:

"After I came out of Parkhurst I expected to be cut by most of my former colleagues and acquaintances. Most did cut me, but several did not. But I was bewildered to find that *all* my *communist* colleagues and acquaintances cut me dead after I had served a sentence for supplying vital information to the Soviet Union. After a little while, I found that my offence was that I had pleaded guilty as charged, thereby embarrassing the Soviet Union. I should have pleaded not guilty, thereby allowing the Soviet Union to accuse the British government of having framed me, while plausibly asserting their own innocence . . . It was an instructive experience."

* * *

In 1962 and throughout 1963 relations between the university and the president and government of Ghana remained at least outwardly untroubled. Quite early on, Nkrumah asked me to draft a speech for him on university matters, which he delivered on February 24,1963. I included a critically important paragraph in the speech which ran:

"We know that the objectives of a university cannot be achieved without scrupulous respect for academic freedom, for without academic freedom there can be no university. Teachers must be free to teach their subjects without any other concern than to convey to their students the truth as faithfully as they know it. Scholars must be free to pursue the truth and to publish the results of their researches without fear, for true scholarship fears nothing. It can even challenge the dead learning which has come to us from the cloistral and monastic schools of the Middle Ages. [That sentence was the only one not drafted by me. It was, I believe, inserted by Geoffrey Bing]. We know that without respect for academic freedom, in this sense, there can be no higher education worthy of the name, and, therefore, no intellectual progress, no flowering of the nation's mind. The genius of the people is stultified. We therefore cherish and shall continue to cherish academic freedom at our universities."

I was glad of the opportunity of getting the president committed – as far as recorded words could commit him – to cherishing academic freedom. I had a hunch that, at some point in the future, when the university might come under pressure from Nkrumah's government, I might need to quote that passage. And after the university did fall under quite heavy pressure from that quarter, I reached for that speech and did quote that passage. With tongue firmly in cheek, in an address to the university on March 14, 1964, I quoted what I called "the spirit of those noble words of our chancellor" and expressed the hope "that that spirit would prevail in all the practical relations between the university and the authorities." It did not exactly "prevail" but neither was it altogether extinguished. All that, however, was still to come.

The Kennedy government had a policy of encouraging and aiding African governments and Ghana, as the first such government established in the 20th century, was high on the list. The Americans underwrote and helped to carry out a major hydraulic enterprise, the Volta River Project, then nearing completion. A consortium of American medical schools was helping to create a new medical school within the University of Ghana. As vice-chancellor, I worked closely and harmoniously with the American team. What with the Volta River Project and the medical school, Ghana appeared to have strong reasons not to rock the boat, capriciously, in its relations with the United States.

Yet as I would soon find, there were quite powerful currents at work under the surface, capable not only of rocking that boat, but of tearing it from its moorings. The first clear intimation I had of such currents at work came in a visit I had from a South African communist physician, Dr Joseph Gillman. I received Dr Gillman at the request of the president's office. Gillman was one of a motley crew of individuals, refugees from a number of African countries, with whose aid Nkrumah hoped to encompass what had become his principal objective: to become president of a future United States of Africa. The refugees became associated with the far-left Ideological Institute at Winneba, and especially with its newspaper *The Spark* (called after Lenin's ISKRA). The whole thing – refugees, Winneba and *Spark* – had nothing to do with the actual realities of life in Ghana, or with Ghana's real interests, but was designed to project throughout Africa a revolutionary image of socialist Ghana.

In any case, Dr Gillman and myself did not get on. I had invited some relevant colleagues in to hear his ideas. He began by telling me that Ghana did not need a medical school, an expensive and unnecessary luxury Ghana could not afford. What Ghana needed was an extensive corps of medical assistants who could be adequately trained in a short time and at little expense. As he developed this theme his voice rose and there were little flecks of foam on his lips.

I said I could see there was a good case for medical assistants, but I couldn't see there was any conflict with the medical school. On the contrary, a medical school could provide the medical assistants with basic training and also with back-up services when they encountered unusual and difficult cases.

At this Dr Gillman became more excited. "While you are talking," he said "people are *dying* out there in the bush!"

"Well," I said, "they don't stop dying while *you* are talking, Dr Gillman."

Shortly after that the meeting ended. But I was left with a chilly feeling that the medical school project might be in some danger if the president was listening to people like that. And maybe not only the medical school.

During this mostly halcyon initial period, I got to know the people I would be working with on a daily basis: the Registrar, Kofi Edzii, a former District Commissioner under British rule, a tower of integrity and common sense, especially under pressure; my official Ghanaian private secretary, Mr Lamptey, a person of intense respectability and professionalism, who probably found the new vice-chancellor distressingly flamboyant, but bore with me cheerfully, and, most fortunately of all, Mrs Ilsa Yardley, who became and remains one our family's dearest friends. Ilsa was a lovely blonde young Englishwoman, originally an Austrian Jewish child refugee; she had worked as secretary to the founders of the magazine *History To-day*. She immediately took over, as well as all her routine office duties, all my literary secretarial work and all my complicated family life. Besides which she enchanted all comers with her wit and charm, as she does to this day. Even more momentously, I acquired a new pro-vice-chancellor, Alex Kwapong, a Ghanaian with a first-class degree in classics from Cambridge. Alex was – and indeed still is – a rather splendid person, tall, handsome, genial, well-spoken with an air of easy self-confidence. To me he was, at first, civil but reserved. He deeply distrusted Nkrumah and the fact that Nkrumah had appointed me put something of a question-mark over me. The question-mark was to be decisively removed in the following year and we then became, and still remain, firm friends.

Soon after Alex's arrival, we both attended as invited guests the ceremony of the opening of Ghana's parliament by President Nkrumah. Visually, the parliament was a rather splendid affair, blending ceremonial derived from Westminster with Ghanaian and specifically Akan symbolism. The members of parliament were all attired in *kente*, traditional, strip-woven, coloured cloth draped like a toga. They looked like Roman senators in glorious technicolour. Rather *late* Roman senators: they were mostly very fat men who looked as if they were having a good time. Not all of them had been elected as supporters of Nkrumah, but by this time they all *were* his supporters. Under African conditions, parliamentary oppositions had a tendency to melt.

Most of the president's address to parliament was about Africa in general. The general theme was the inevitability of African unity once the distinctions cultivated by the imperialists began to disappear as more and more African countries became independent. This was familiar stuff. But then there was a passage near the end which led to an exchange that made me sit up.

The president said he knew there were some members who had money invested abroad, contrary to Ghanaian laws and regulations. He offered an amnesty to the holders of those accounts, provided they repatriated those balances.

At this the assembled parliamentarians burst out laughing and their laughter continued for quite a long time. The president was in no way put out. He simply smiled broadly and said "Tactical!" and then turned to other matters.

After we left I said to Alex that I couldn't understand why the parliamentarians would laugh at what the president said, and the president not seem to be put out by their laughter.

"Don't you understand?" said Alex quietly. "Well, stick around for a while, Conor, and pretty soon you'll understand."

Alex was quite right. When I attended the next opening session of parliament the following year, I heard that identical performance repeated: same offer, same laughter, same presidential smile, same "Tactical!" And I now understood. The performance was for a document designed to be circulated to African governments who would receive it without the accompanying laughter, and comment, and presumably be edified though they would be unlikely to be edified for long when they found that the performance was repeated unchanged with a new deadline, after the first deadline had long elapsed. The reality was that the president also had large deposits abroad, contrary to law, and all his parliamentarians knew this. Hence the laughter of the parliament and the president's indulgent smile.

There were other indications of the deep corruption of the regime. Towards the end of my first year in Ghana I had a call from Jimmy Philips, the secretary of the treasury. Jimmy was one of a number of highly trained and honest Ghanaian senior civil servants whom Nkrumah had inherited and who were increasingly uncomfortable with his regime (all of them were gone before I left). Jimmy told me that he was about to resign, and he wanted me to know why. I think he wanted me to be a witness to the reasons for his resignation *before* the resignation was submitted, because afterwards the government might invent other reasons, discreditable to him.

Jimmy Philips's story was as follows: One of the functions of his department was to allocate to government departments foreign currency for projects judged to be beneficial to Ghana. As a routine operation he had authorized the Department of Agriculture to acquire foreign currency for the acquisition of a dozen tractors. So far so good. But then, within six months, an application came for funds for the acquisition of a second dozen tractors. On a hunch – and knowing the minister principally concerned – Jimmy decided to go down to the Port of Tema, where the tractors would have been delivered. His hunch was that he would find the first tractors were still there, and so they were. They were standing on the quay, rusted in the rains and with their tyres flat. Jimmy went straight to Nkrumah and reported on the situation. Nkrumah expressed concern and sent for the responsible minister, who came immediately. The minister neither acknowledged his misdeed nor denied it, as Jimmy told the story. He simply went on his knees before Nkrumah, clutched Nkrumah's knees and shouted: "If I ever let you down, Osagyefo," (Nkrumah's honorific title, meaning something like "Saviour") "if I ever let you down you may hang me in the public square. Hang me in the public square!"

The president then lifted the minister to his feet, and embraced him in a manner designed to convey absolution. Loyalty was all-important. Honesty was not.

Nkrumah had had great popular support in the beginning but the support was now rapidly falling away, with experience of his regime. There was one apocryphal story current at this time of an old woman who came in from the bush and waited outside Nkrumah's palace at Christansborg for Nkrumah to come out. When he did, she embraced his knees – just as the minister had done – and cried out: "Kwame Nkrumah! Thank God you have come back! Please liberate us from this terrible man, Osagyefo, who is oppressing us all!"

Ghana under Nkrumah had become what the Germans call a *Raubwirtschaft*: an economy of robbers. The top robber was the president, and subordinate robbers were now in charge of every department of state. There were junior robbers *in petto* who coveted control of the university with all those well-paid jobs. We knew these were only looking for a pretext for the assault and we could not know how soon the pretext might present itself, or in what guise.

* * *

The government of Ghana was extremely corrupt but ordinary citizens could be scrupulously honest and unselfishly helpful to people in distress. Two examples – one of each from this period – must suffice.

One day the university bursar came to my office to tell me that a clerk in his office had come to report the offer of a bribe from a contractor. The bribe amounted to a little more than the clerk's annual salary. The clerk's duties had put him in regular touch with the contractor. The works had been completed, to the satisfaction of the university, within the amount appropriated for them. The clerk could have quietly pocketed the proffered sum without the slightest risk of detection. Instead he had handed the money over to the university.

We decided to treat the money as a gift, or extra exchequer receipt, to the university treasury and not to report the matter to the police of a government which was no less crooked than the contractor.

The second episode was a little more complicated, and more personal. I had been at a party and I had been partaking of a drink called *uhuru* ("independence"), consisting of a potent mixture of palm wine and Guinness. My Ghanaian friends and I had drunk many toasts in *uhuru* to friendship between Ghana and Ireland. It was all very pleasant while it lasted. But as I drove myself away, I began to find that I was drunk and also that I had driven in the wrong direction. It was dark by now and I was in a poorly-lit slum district of Accra. So I decided to make a U-turn. Unfortunately the U-turn was poorly executed and one of my front wheels ended up caught firmly in one of the wide and deep storm-drains which are a necessary feature of every tropical city. While I was stuck, a small crowd of Ghanaians gathered around the car. I became a little apprehensive. The apprehension deepened to something approaching panic when one Ghanaian put his hand through the open window and removed the key from the ignition. When I protested, the man who took the key replied: "You are drunk and not fit to be driving." This was so obviously true that I did not contest the verdict, I only asked: "How then can I get home?" The man who had taken the key – who seemed to be accepted as the leading figure – said: "If you like, all of us here can easily lift your car out of the ditch. Then I can drive you back to the university" – he had recognized me – "and my friend will come with me." I agreed, of course, and they drove me back to Legon without further incident. They got out and prepared to walk back to Accra, a distance of about six miles. They politely and proudly declined my offer of a reward. Finally, they did accept a taxi-ride back to their home.

That was all. Those were Good Samaritans indeed and I was lucky to have fallen in with them.

* * *

On January 2, 1964, a soldier made an attempt on Nkrumah's life in Kulungugu, Northern Ghana, and killed one of his security officers. Following this, a state of emergency was declared. The state of emergency coincided with preparations for a referendum making certain controversial changes in the constitution of Ghana. This state of emergency, combined with the mobilization of opinion required for the referendum, led to considerable excitement in the country, and to the adoption in the government-controlled press of increasingly militant and, at times, vituperative language. The press attacked various persons and institutions whom it suspected of disloyalty, and the latter category included the University of Ghana.

It may seem strange that an attempt on the president's life should lead to attacks on the university, which of course had had nothing whatever to do with the attempt. But the attempt did make it possible for those who wished to undermine the independence of the university to go on the offensive. The people concerned, mostly in the Ideological Institute at Winneba together with a few people in the university itself, had their own agenda: a purge at the university would create a vacuum which some of their own number could expect to fill.

The trial for the attack on the president opened in Accra. The fine Italian hand of the Attorney General, Geoffrey Bing, was at once apparent in the orchestrated language of the proceedings, reflecting coaching of the witnesses. For example: a witness had testified that a soldier had opened fire on the president. It was known that, at that point the president, very sensibly, had run like hell and hidden under a table in the house where he was staying. But it wouldn't do to put it like that. So when he was asked: "What did the president do then?" the witness replied decorously: "The president increased the distance between himself and his assailant."

The soldier was convicted – quite justly, I believe – and sentenced to death and hanged. This was, I think, the only execution during the whole of Nkrumah's period in office. He was corrupt, but unlike other African rulers at the time and since, not sanguinary.

Politically the trial of the private soldier was of no consequence. All political interest centred on who had been "behind" the attempt on the president's life. Almost certainly no one had been. The soldier seems to have been crazed, possibly through drugs. But the leftists in Nkrumah's entourage succeeded – with some spiritual assistance, as I shall explain – in convincing him there had been a deep-laid plot in which the CIA were the prime movers and which included the more conservative members of Nkrumah's government, including perhaps the most powerful member of that government after Nkrumah himself: Tawia Adamafio (previously, Tom Adams).

The "CIA plot" theory was transparent nonsense, as far as Ghana was concerned. There had been plenty of real CIA plots in Africa. For instance, the CIA had played a part, though not a central part, in the downfall and murder of Patrice Lumumba in the Congo. But the CIA had had no reason at all to plot the murder of Nkrumah. Nkrumah's Ghana – up to and including the date of the attack – had been perceived as firmly within the American sphere and it had benefited mightily from that perception, principally through American funding of the Volta River Project, but also in other ways, as through American support for the university's medical school.

Why then did the president take the high-risk course of suggesting a CIA involvement, thereby antagonizing the United States? I don't know but

I can hazard a guess. It is known that the president, at various crises in his career, had been in the habit of consulting a priestess and prophetess at the animistic shrine of Larteh on the Akwapim ridge just above the Accra plain. Like other such priestesses and and prophetesses, such as the keepers of the shrine at Delphi in ancient Greece, the keeper of the shrine at Larteh was believed to accept bribes from people for whom she was prepared to supply rewarding prophecies. I believe those in the president's entourage who wished to influence him against the United States bribed the prophetess and she then assured the president that the shot at Kulungugu had been the result of a plot fomented by the CIA. And the president believed her, at least for a time. So it was a time of trouble for the university which was seen as a hotbed of the (non-existent) plot against the president.

In Nkrumah's Ghana, the shrine at Larteh was a much more significant institution – political as well as spiritual – than the parliament of Ghana ever was. On the recommendation of David Brokensha, a South African anthropologist then working at Legon, I had paid a visit to the shrine. I was accompanied by my wife and by my two daughters (the third was yet to come) Fedelma and Kate. The shrine was a product of essentially matrilinear institutions. At the top was the priestess: the level below consisted of five male priests. To gain admission to the priestess, one had first to pass muster with the priests. Having been advised as to how to pass muster we had brought with us a bottle of schnapps. This was accepted by the chief priest, a rather glum individual, like all his colleagues; one gathered that at this particular shrine priests were at a depressed level of the religious hierarchy. The chief priest then poured out a (very small) libation to the tutelary deities accompanied by an invocation. We understood that our request to be admitted was accepted on high.

The passage from the domain of the priests to the presence of the priestess was rather an intimidating one. One passed first through a kind of slaughterhouse where butchers were preparing sheep for sacrifice. Next was an area where several young girls were immobilized, trussed in white garments with white painted faces. These were novices passing through a period of ritual probation. Then we were in the presence of the prophetess herself: an enormous woman – perhaps twenty-five stone – clad all in white and radiating an immense self-confidence. She was surrounded by a small and devoted crowd, apparently of petitioners. She was engaged in some kind of liturgical performance, chanted in Akan, which was not intelligible to us.

My daughters were not favourably impressed. On the way home, Kate wanted to know why we were supposed to be impressed by this stuff when we were not allowed to be impressed by the religion of our own country, which was at least not so awful as what was going on at Larteh? I didn't really have any effective answer to that one. But I did begin to realize that the university was up against some powerful ancient forces, exploited by some equally unscrupulous contemporary ones, and exploiting those in turn.

* * *

The trial of Tawia Adamafio and his companions ended in their acquittal for lack of evidence. The president then removed the Chief Justice, Sir Arku Korsah, for having acquitted them, and ordered a new trial. I was in Europe – on a recruitment drive for the university – when this news broke, and I publicly appealed to the president to reinstate the Chief Justice. Some people at the university – including some who later defended academic freedom when it came under direct attack – thought this was a mistake on my part. My contention, however, was that this decision affected the university directly through its law school. If the law students saw that a Chief Justice could be removed for complying with the law as he understood it, they would be likely to reach the conclusion that the way to success in the legal profession was through servile compliance with the dictates of arbitrary power, which was the reverse of what we were supposed to be teaching them. At the same time I knew that there was something in what my academic critics were saying. I had handed the university's critics close to the president a weapon that could be used against the university. And it was.

The next passage to get through, in this disturbed and disturbing time, was the referendum, in which the predictable victory of "Yes" would make the president unremoveable in law. Propaganda for "Yes" in the Ghanaian press was of course intense, shrill and intimidatory. Propaganda for "No" was, also of course, prohibited. Car owners were required to show "Yes" stickers, and most of them did. As we were driving through Accra one morning a policeman stopped us and asked a pertinent question: "Big Man, why no 'Yes'?" (Big, in Ghana, meant well-off). Before I could answer in a way that might have got me into trouble, my driver, Amate, had the wit to cut in with: "We're on our way to get one", which got us off the hook. The referendum passed, by 95%, as everyone knew that it would.

The press campaign against the university continued to increase in violence. And then it suddenly turned into something worse than just a press campaign.

On January 30, 1964, I received a visit from two high-ranking members of the security forces. They informed me that they had reliable evidence that three senior members of the university, whom they named, were engaged in subversive activities prejudicial to the security of the state and would therefore have to be deported. The persons named included the Professor of Law, WB Harvey and the senior lecturer in Law, RB Seidman (both American citizens); and a person referred to as "Mr Chester," who later turned out to be Professor LH Schuster, a newly appointed member of the School of Administration. I informed the security officers that I could appreciate the fact that people employed by the university did not thereby enjoy any licence to engage in treasonable activities, and if reliable and adequate evidence was forthcoming that any of them had been engaged in such activities, then I would agree that the people concerned must face the consequences of their acts. The security officers stated that they had such evidence but that they could not reveal it to me. I said that I could take no action on the basis of evidence which I was told was available to others but which was not made available to me. I could therefore take no steps for the dismissal of the persons concerned or for any other sanction against them.

I also urged that no action should be taken by the security forces until I had had an opportunity of seeing the president about the matter, as I believed there was grave danger of a miscarriage of justice. I suspected that at least two of those affected, Professor Harvey and Mr Seidman, might be the objects of malicious denunciation; at this point one of the security officers made a gesture which I interpreted as meaning I was on the right track.

The press began to devote more space to attacking the university as a "centre of subversion", and one journal asserted the doctrine that it would be better to have a university with no professors at all than one that harboured subversives. The students returned to the campus at the end of the recess on February 3 and 4, and it soon became clear that there was considerable unrest among them as a result of the recess itself, the detentions, the deportation orders – which had now been issued and were about to take effect – and the press attacks. Reports reached the president that a big student demonstration against the government would be held on February 8, the day on which the deportations were due to take effect. It was clear that there was some danger of matters getting out of hand, with the university becoming a political storm centre and a wide variety of possible results. The most likely of these would, in my opinion, have been the closing down of the university for a prolonged period, the alteration of its constitution in such a way as to deprive it of the degree of autonomy that it enjoyed, and its reopening on a new footing. With the support of the academic body I therefore decided, while continuing my representations on behalf of the members affected by deportation orders, also to do everything possible to prevent any kind of student demonstration, or even retaliation to provocation.

I addressed the students to this effect at 8 a.m. on the morning of February 8, the day when the deportations took effect. I warned the students that in my opinion some of the attacks by extremists in the press and elsewhere were intended to goad the students into some gesture which would be the pretext for remoulding the university and entirely changing its character. I therefore urged that all students who wished to uphold the existing character of the university and academic freedom at the university should in this excited time exert rigid self-control, even in the teeth of severe provocation. I had no sooner finished this address than word reached me that a mass demonstration was on its way to the university. The vanguard arrived between 9:30 and 10 a.m. There were between 2,000 and 3,000 demonstrators of all ages and both sexes, including a number of schoolchildren. They were led by Nathaniel Welbeck, organizing secretary of the Convention People's Party, who had with him other prominent members of the party. Most of the demonstrators were orderly and good-humoured, but a fringe of activists did some damage to property; broke doors and windows of the halls and committed two minor assaults. Subsequently, the damage having been assessed, I sent a bill to the party for £130.14s.6d which was not paid. The object of the demonstration, as was later confirmed to me on good authority, was to overawe the students and prevent, or blunt the effect of, the student demonstration which was anticipated for that day but which never took place as the students, without exception, obeyed the injunctions of the university authorities. If the student demonstration – which had been seriously discussed – had taken place together with the party's demonstration or if the students had responded to provocation, there would have been an obvious risk of serious violence.

Welbeck with his senior followers then occupied Commonwealth Hall, the centre of the university administration. Their popular supporters remained at large in the university grounds. The students remained in their rooms, refusing to be provoked, just as I had asked them. In Commonwealth Hall, Alex Kwapong and I engaged in dialogue with the leaders of the demonstration. Welbeck demanded that the students should be convened to be addressed by himself and his colleagues. I pointed out that we should be happy to offer him facilities to address any students who might want to hear him, in the ordinary way and on an ordinary day. But I could not convene the students to hear him under such circumstances and in the presence of a quite unnecessary mass demonstration. I had advised the students to remain in their rooms, for the preservation of the peace, and that advice stood.

Welbeck then turned to Alex Kwapong and said: "This kind of stuff is all very well for him, he's a foreigner here. But how about *you?* You are a Ghanaian. Is it not your duty to serve Ghana?"

Alex answered with great calm and deliberation. "Yes," he said, "it is my duty to serve Ghana, just as it is yours. But we seem to have different ideas as to how Ghana can best be served. Some of us try to serve Ghana by teaching young Ghanaians, and preparing them for a better and more productive future. Others seem to think they can serve Ghana best by leading gangs of ruffians round the countryside."

The delegation – if that's what it was – erupted at this point, demanding that Alex withdraw the word "ruffians". Alex affected to be surprised and puzzled at their reactions.

"What's wrong with 'ruffians'?" he asked. "It's a well-established word in the English language. You'll find it in Shakespeare."

For some reason the reference to Shakespeare seemed to unnerve the delegation. Perhaps it served as a reminder of their relative cultural deprivation. At any rate they all – led by Welbeck – left Commonwealth Hall and made their way back to Accra to report the failure of their mission.

There was an anti-climactic sequel. Welbeck took us up on the offer to address the students, and nominated one of their number, Kofi Batsa, to deliver the address. I advised the students to attend and listen quietly, which they did, until Batsa stupidly made an insulting reference to my wife. At this my wife and I got up and left, in silence. The entire student body then filed out behind us, also in silence, leaving Kofi Batsa all alone in Commonwealth Hall.

* * *

The attempt at indirect or "spontaneous" intimidation had failed, mainly through Alex Kwapong's cool nerve and air of effortless authority. But a much more formidable assault was now underway. This took the form of a direct personal intervention by the president himself. Not long after the plebiscite, I received a document in a format I had never seen before. The document was headed "Presidential Command" in large letters of bright purple ink. I imagine the stationery had been ordered for use after the plebiscite to exemplify and enforce the president's now limitless authority.

The command ordered me to appoint certain named people to the academic posts which had become vacant as a result of the recent deportations. The most conspicuous person on the list was Ekow Daniels, formerly third man in the hierarchy of the law school, and now the most senior surviving member following the deportation of the two above him on the list.

I prepared a reply, ignoring the new political context implied by the use and salience of "presidential command". I said that I had no authority to go beyond what was contained in the University of Ghana Act, and the university statutes established under that Act. Under these instruments, there were certain prescribed means of filling university vacancies. Only appointments boards, set up under prescribed procedures, had the authority to fill university posts. I did not have the authority to fill such posts myself, or to vary the prescribed system. I would comply with the statutory procedures and advise the chancellor, in due course, of the outcome in each case.

I then notified the academic board of the presidential command and of my draft reply. The board upheld the draft reply by a considerable majority. All the Ghanaian members present – not including Ekow Daniels – approved the draft reply. So did about half the expatriates, including Alan Nunn May. The other half abstained, mostly on the ground that Ghanaian politics was no business of theirs. There were no votes against.

Shortly after the missive to the president was despatched, I had a speaking engagement at University College, Cape Coast, on an unrelated subject (the Congo). While I was speaking, the doors of the lecture-room were pushed open and a number of working-class blacks came in carrying banners. Most of the banners were all-purpose agitprop against the university. But one banner told me who was behind the demo. The banner read: "Why no Ghanaian Professor of Law?"

The demonstrators made a couple of circuits of the lecture-room and then withdrew. But after a very short interval, while I was getting on with my lecture, I could hear loud and angry cries outside and – remembering Congo experiences – braced myself for a second and probably more dangerous incursion. After a short while, however, the noise died down, and I finished my lecture in peace.

Outside, my driver Amate was waiting. He had seen everything that had gone on out there and he told me about it with a broad smile. "There was a man there who had come to see that they carried the placards into the hall. When they came out, they asked him for the money they had been promised for carrying the placards. When he told them he didn't have any money, they beat him with those sticks" – the poles which had supported the placards.

Amate clearly found these developments quite amusing and so, I fear, did I. Amate was an Accra person, and like almost all Accra persons by this time strongly opposed to Nkrumah. The Chinese leader Chou-en-Lai paid an official visit to Accra during this period. As it happened the "political suit" worn by all leading people in the Convention Peoples Party, including Nkrumah, was modelled on the suit worn by everyone important in the Chinese Communist Party. I had been abroad, during Chou-en-Lai's visit, so when I came back I asked Amate how the visit had gone? Amate said: "At first a lot of people came out to look at him. But when they see he is dressed same-like Kwame Nkrumah they all go home."

* * *

We had feared – and more than half expected – that the university's negative response to the "presidential command" would be followed by punitive executive action: perhaps my deportation and the arrest of Alex Kwapong. But neither of these things happened. I heard from a witness in Flagstaff House that the president had said with reference to me: "That bastard wants me to fire him, and that's why I'm not going to do it."

I don't doubt the president did say something of the kind, but I don't think this adequately accounts for the university's immunity after our defiance of the "presidential command". I think the president, knowing of his own unpopularity, now steadily growing in Ghana, was afraid of the consequences to himself of really drastic action against the university. If he could have got us to give in to threats, well and good. But since we had not given in, the actual implementation of the implied threats, against the top level of the university hierarchy, might be hazardous. Although the left-wing Nkrumahists liked to go on about the elitist character of the university, ordinary Ghanaians tended to be proud of the place and not worried about elitism. More important, the officer corps of the army – now the only people who could actually put Nkrumah out, and eventually did so – were proud of the university, and intensely suspicious of its left-wing enemies, who had their own little projects for "reforming" the army also. So

Nkrumah had adequate reasons for not proceeding against the highest levels of the university, and perhaps thereby precipitating his own overthrow.

All the same, things could have gone badly for us if Nkrumah had played his cards a bit more craftily. Around the time Nkrumah had unmistakeably retreated from his attempt to run the university by "presidential command", I ran into a little man at a reception at the British Embassy whom I believed to be the local representative of British Intelligence. "You came out of this smelling like roses," he said, with a faint undercurrent of complaint. "That's because of this nonsense of a presidential command. That is simply not the way to do it. What he should have done was to have you in quietly and explain to you what he wanted you to do and you could have done it, or most of it, with very little fuss. But if you refused, the president need have said no more about it. But a little later there could have been an announcement that you had been suspended pending an investigation into the state of the university finances. They could probably have found some irregularities if they tried hard enough. Even if they didn't they could make them up. Either way you would leave the university with a shadow over your reputation, which you would probably never live down."

He sounded a bit wistful, as if over a lost opportunity. Nkrumah was then defying the Americans, and Britain was no longer in the business of encouraging people who defied the Americans. Otherwise, he could certainly have helped Nkrumah to solve his little difficulty with a minimum of fuss.

I shivered a little, at the mere thought of what might have been. As we took stock of the situation, we could see that some serious, and probably irreparable, damage had already been done to the university. Our law school, in a flourishing condition under Burnett Harvey throughout my first year, had been reduced to irrelevance by the president's personal and arbitrary domination of the Ghanaian legal system. The medical school, of which we had had such high hopes, had to be indefinitely postponed, following the withdrawal of American support once the President had started shouting about imaginary CIA plots.

For the rest, what was left of the university – primarily the Faculties of Arts and Sciences – was in better shape than ever, after the storm which teachers and students had weathered together in harmony. Everybody knew that we had defied the president's assertion of arbitrary power, and that he had then backed away. The Ghanaian press – run by the left-wing of the

Convention People's Party – continued to rail against the university, but we could now afford to laugh at the Ghanaian Press, which was indeed laughable enough.

Sample incident from this period. There was a small earthquake which rocked the university buildings. The Ghana *Evening Press* affected to believe that the earthquake had been caused by a presidential speech. They ran this story on the front page with a banner headline running: "Oh Ye of Little Faith: Do ye not know, have ye not heard? *He Spoke – And The Earth Shook*"

Alex Kwapong and myself – credited with having saved the university – were now extremely popular with the students. I was fortunate in my initials which became the focus of a mild cult. Students, sighting me on the campus would call out "OBI! OBI! This was a reference to my initials, but Obi, in the Twi language is also the word for a chief. This made a pleasant change from the Ghanaian press.

During this period I had another pleasant experience involving the Holy Child Convent School for girls at Cape Coast. The Catholic convents, run by nuns, were the only institutions besides the university which had made a successful sustained resistance to a policy of Nkrumah's. The priests and other male religious had agreed to use the presidential title, Osagyefo, in their prayers for the president and other references to him. They argued that Osagyefo didn't really mean "Saviour", though that was how it was usually translated. The nuns, however – throughout Ghana – thought that Osagyefo *did* mean Saviour, and that to use it to designate Nkrumah was blasphemous. They told Nkrumah that they would never use the term, and if he insisted on their using it, they would close down their schools. The president backed away, just as he had done in our case, and I believe for similar reasons.

The nuns, noting that we had been under a bit of a strain – just as they had – invited my wife and myself to spend a few days with them in their convent. They indicated delicately that they were aware that I was not precisely a model Catholic, but that that would not weaken their welcome. So we spent a very pleasant few days at Cape Coast as guests of the nuns. Several of them were of Irish origin, but a lot less stuffy than Irish nuns in Ireland would have been at this period. I remember a nun reporting to the Reverend Mother that one of the senior pupils – Patience Aidoo – was about to have a baby. The Reverend Mother gave no sign of shock or horror. She simply enquired when the birth was due, as she was concerned about how this might affect Patience's chances in A-levels. I thought this refreshing and we got on very well.

* * *

In any case the three-year period of my contract with the university was about to expire. I had no intention of applying for a renewal and the renewal would certainly not have been accorded if I had asked for it. I delivered my last address to the University on Legon Hill on March 14, 1964. I shall simply quote here what I regard as the core passage in it. Having referred, without going into details, to the university's period of trouble, I went on:

"The values to which we adhere have nothing in common with colonialism or with any other system of oppression, nor have they anything in common with neo-colonialism or any other system of deceit. They are forces of their nature hostile to such systems as colonialism and neo-colonialism, and they have served to bring about the downfall of the first system and the exposure of the second. Respect for truth; intellectual courage in the pursuit of truth; moral courage in the telling of truth: these are the qualities of a real, of a living university. Since the days of Socrates in Greece and Mencius in China these values have been asserted, and have been attacked. None of us, alas, is Socrates or Mencius – and philosophy seems to have fallen on evil days – but no member of an academy can forget, without being unfaithful to his calling, how Socrates lived and how he died. A teacher may, in the eyes of the world, be a rather battered and insignificant sort of person, but he knows, if he is a good teacher – as he so often, almost inexplicably, is – that he carries responsibilities, and must try to live up to examples, which are on the highest plane of human achievement. This is not, as is sometimes suggested, curiously enough, by both colonialists and some of their adversaries, a question of 'introducing European values into Africa'. These are not European values; they are universal values. Mencius taught in China very much in the same spirit as Socrates taught in Greece. They were almost contemporaries. The geographical and cultural gap between them was the widest possible, yet it is clear that they would have understood one another.

"In Europe, and in America, these values have had at least as many enemies as defenders, as the names of Dr Goebbels and Senator McCarthy remind us. This ancient continent of Africa, which gave the world one of its first and richest civilizations, has the right to share in and contribute to the universal intellectual heritage which we associate with the names of Socrates and Mencius. The university has the duty, not only to transmit intact that heritage, but to provide intellectual conditions in which a modern African genius can make his own fresh and unpredictable contribution to the development of the human mind. We are here to provide, in Yeats's phrase:

> . . . *not what they would,*
> *But the right twigs for an eagle's nest.*"

* * *

While preparing to leave Ghana I wrote a short and civil, but not effusive, letter to Nkrumah thanking him for having brought us to Ghana. I told him – which was quite true – how much we had enjoyed our stay. I knew he wished we had enjoyed it a lot less than we had, but I did not touch on that aspect.

I did not expect any reply but Nkrumah wrote by return inviting me to visit him in Christiansborg Castle to take my leave. Nkrumah's office at Christiansborg was an enormous room, rather larger than a doubles tennis court. When you were in favour, Nkrumah would walk halfway down the room, and would sit down with you at a small round table, like sitting round a tree in the forest. As soon as I walked into that room to take my leave, however, I could see this was not going to be that kind of meeting. Nkrumah remained seated at his desk studying papers, or pretending to study them. I walked up and stood opposite him for a moment. When he still did not look up I sat down. Then Nkrumah looked at me and spoke:

"Ah, Dr O'Brien, yes . . . I want to thank you Dr O'Brien . . . for whatever it was you did for the university."

I think he had meant to say something relatively amiable, but when he actually looked at me, he found that this was the best he could do.

I said that the university had been through a difficult time, for reasons which I did not specify. I expressed the hope that the post of vice-chancellor would not be left vacant for too long.

Nkrumah was ready for me on that one. He sat back in his chair. "The post of vice-chancellor of the University of Ghana," he said, "is an important and a delicate one."

I agreed that this was indeed the case. The president went on: "The filling of the post of vice-chancellor is one to which I shall give very careful attention indeed, Dr O'Brien, *this time.*"

Very much Nkrumah's round, it must be said. But also pretty nearly his last round. He never did appoint my successor. The person most hotly tipped to fill the post was the Professor of Philosophy, Willie Abraham, one of the more cautious and distinguished of his sycophants, who would have made a plausible vice-chancellor, and also a flexible one. (The reference to philosophy having fallen on evil days in my speech of March 14 was generally understood as an oblique reference to Willie.) But Nkrumah never did give Willie the substantive appointment: he only made him *acting* vice-chancellor. I think Nkrumah knew that there would be trouble with the students if he appointed Willie to the substantive post, and feared that trouble with the students might ignite more serious trouble with the soldiers. Alex Kwapong was still pro-vice-chancellor when Nkrumah was ousted by military coup, while abroad on a state visit to China, a few months after my departure from Ghana. Alex Kwapong was installed as vice-chancellor by general consent very shortly afterwards.

Alex's first action as vice-chancellor was characteristic. Alex knew that, after the change, Willie Abraham would be likely to be in physical danger from some of the students, and Willie was also well aware of this. So Alex drove Willie down to the police station outside the main gate of the university and asked the police to see to his protection, treat him well and ensure that he had access to all the books and papers he might need. Later, after the excitement at the university had died down, Willie was restored to his position as professor of philosophy at the university.

The conferring – which I attended on Alex Kwapong's invitation – was attended by the officers of the revolutionary council who made up, for the moment, the government of Ghana. Addressing himself to the council in the course of his address at the conferring, the new vice-chancellor said: "It was the custom of sycophants under the Nkrumah regime to pledge what they called their 'unflinching support' to Nkrumah. As head of an institution still governed by law, I am not in a position to make such an unqualified commitment to you. The best I am able to promise you is our *flinching* support."

This was rather daring, but it met with no objection. After the ceremony, by arrangement with Alex, I had a meeting with the head of the new regime, the man who had in fact carried out the coup which ended the Nkrumah regime. Colonel Kotoka was a young man of agreeable and modest demeanour. I asked Kotoka when and why he had made up his mind to carry out the coup. His answer was simple and frank:

"Several of us, younger officers, had decided that Nkrumah was ruining Ghana and we had been making plans for a coup. But it was all rather vague and amateurish, and would have been slow in getting off the ground, if it ever did, had it not been for an accident. I kept a little pocket diary, with tentative plans for the coup. It was in a kind of code, but the code was a bit amateurish, and could easily have been deciphered. Then one day, I noticed that my little pocket diary had gone missing. So I said to myself: 'Kotoka my boy, it's you or him now!' Then I took my battalion down to Flagstaff House, and you know the rest."

I did indeed. Kotoka's battalion had met with quite fierce resistance from Kwame's Soviet-trained-and-led Nzima bodyguard. And I think the presence of the Soviet officers on Nkrumah's invitation was high among the reasons why the young officers started talking about a coup. By inviting in Soviet military advisers, Nkrumah was implicitly demonstrating that he did not trust his Ghanaian troops. And if you show that you do not trust your own troops, you are thereby ensuring that your troops don't trust *you*. Also, after the rigged referendum that made Nkrumah president for life, there was no way of ending his rule except by military intervention. More and more people among the families and friends of the officers had been asking: "What are you waiting for?"

Even before the Russian-led resistance had been overcome, Kotoka had Nkrumah's wife and four-year old son brought out under flag of truce and put on a plane to Paris where they could and did join Nkrumah on his return from China. A less wise and humane leader than Kotoka would have held the wife and child as hostages for Nkrumah's good behaviour.

Nkrumah and his family went to Guinea as guests of their fellow-left-wing dictator, Sekou Toure, who lavished rather empty honours on them – rather like Louis XIV honouring James II after the latter's ouster from the British throne.

Unfortunately, Kotoka did not last long. He was murdered barely a year after his coup. Most of his successors were less enlightened than he, but on the whole they left the university alone, probably for the same reasons as Nkrumah finally had.

A few years later, I went back to Ghana at Alex's invitation, to receive an honorary degree. Máire was with me and so was our adopted son, Patrick, whose natural father was Ghanaian. Patrick was provided with northern Ghanaian trousers and smock made to his measure and greatly becoming him, and made many friends among the university children.

Many years later in 1998 I was again asked back to Ghana, to take part in the ceremonies for the university's 50th anniversary. Those who invited me had been students at the university during my tenure as vice-chancellor. Unfortunately I was unable to accept the invitation, but I am very glad that it came.

13

NEW YORK UNIVERSITY, 1965-1969

NEAR THE END OF MY FINAL YEAR AT THE UNIVERSITY OF GHANA I RECEIVED a letter from New York University offering me the post of Albert Schweitzer Professor of the Humanities there. It seemed like an answer to prayer (not that I had been praying). This was a tenured post with a comfortable salary, and the right to appoint other scholars as visiting professors or lecturers. I had also the right to nominate my own field of scholarly interest within the broad field of the humanities. I chose "Literature and Politics" but was civilly told that "Politics" wouldn't do. "Politics" had, for various reasons, become a dirty word in polite circles in the United States, which included academic circles. Eventually, we agreed on "Literature and Society".

For the next three and a half years of our lives we were to spend most of our time in Greenwich Village, seat of the NYU campus to which I was attached. We lived and taught in the area where Fifth Avenue joins Washington Square. We had an attractive little house in Washington Mews, across the road from Number One Fifth Avenue and within about fifty yards of the Washington Monument.

All very nice in a number of ways, but there were also certain drawbacks, as we found out rather soon. For one thing we were only a couple of blocks from the area known euphemistically as the East Village. The East Village was a huge slum area populated by poor blacks, most of whom were unemployed and many of whom were on drugs. The East Village at this time, with a population of about a million people, had an annual murder rate several times that of the whole of the British Isles in absolute terms. Conditions in the East Village didn't often directly impinge on the relatively – and often absolutely – affluent life of the Village proper. But one was always darkly aware of the sinister conditions, a couple of blocks away, as part of the background to one's own comfortable life. Rather like living right up against the Third World. And sometimes – though rarely – a member or members of the criminal population of the Village would wander across to rob and/or murder someone in the Village proper.

There were a few other drawbacks. For one thing, both the air and water in metropolitan New York at this time were heavily polluted. One was advised not to drink water from the taps, but to buy bottled water. The air was always pretty foul, and on occasions became so foul that one was warned to stay indoors with the windows shut, or risk being poisoned. Fortunately for us we were able at the worst – that is, the hottest – season of the year to return to the sparklingly clean air and water of the Hill of Howth.

Most of the time, living in the Village one could forget about the East Village, and the need to be careful about air and water. But no one teaching or learning at an American University in this period was allowed to forget about the war in Vietnam, then just beginning to convulse every major urban campus in America. I shall have more to say about that.

* * *

The building in which I gave my two undergraduate lectures a week – and later also two graduate seminars, jointly with visiting scholars – was rather rundown and made an unfavourable first impression. On my first day there, looking at the notice board I read a notice advertising a "Crash course in Speling", so spelled, and wondered for a while what I had got myself into. But this initial impression was unjust. The notice was a consequence of a well-intentioned but rather haphazard effort to help a relatively small group of students from disadvantaged backgrounds, admitted with poor qualifications. As soon as I met my own students, I found that many of them were very bright indeed, and that almost all of them were eager to learn.

I had also some learning to do on my own account, as I soon found. On the first day of my first class, I called the roll, as was then the practice. In one case, I could only hear the surname of the student concerned. So I called out "Christian name?" as would have been normal at an Irish or English university at this time. To my astonishment this request was followed by a gale of Homeric laughter in which almost all the class appeared to join. Most of my students were Jewish and they were teaching me: "*First* name, please!" Fortunately none of them seem to have held this initial blunder against me.

Another incident around the same time was also instructive, though much more unpleasant. It occurred on a pleasant enough autumn afternoon, when I was attending a Socialist Scholars' Conference at Columbia University. I was due to give a lecture on "Counter-Revolutionary Imperialism". This was based on my view that the then dominant theory of the need for the United States to fight communism wherever it might manifest itself was sucking the United States, contrary to its own interests, into fighting hopelessly destructive wars against poor peasants in Third World countries (Vietnam being the most obvious example, though not the only one).

The main Columbian campus was at Morningside Park, on the edge of Harlem. After lunch I took a walk in the park to read over my notes. When I had last spent much time in New York, nearly four years earlier, it had been safe to walk in the parks in daylight, though already (at that time) not at night. But my information was out of date, as I soon found out. Four black youths of about sixteen ambushed me: two from behind, two from in front. The one who seemed to be their leader sketched a gesture with a knife. As I put up no resistance, he relieved me of what money I had – which was not much – and also of my watch. The four youths then departed, no word having been spoken on either side.

I didn't mind much about the money, but I was attached to my watch and thought it best to report the crime in the hope of getting my watch back. So I rang the nearest police station, and a squad car almost immediately arrived with two officers aboard. One was the driver, who said nothing. The other, who was clearly in charge, did all the talking and seemed at first to be friendly. I told him all I knew about my assailants, which basically was that they were all very young and all black. The police officer didn't seem to be disconcerted at the paucity of information. "Let's go see if we can spot them," he said.

We then drove slowly through Harlem, watching the sidewalks. The sidewalks were crowded with black people; about a quarter of them were young males. The police officer started pointing at the young men and asking: "Is that the one? Is that the one?" When I kept answering "no", he turned nasty. He insinuated that I was a homosexual, looking for a black partner and running into trouble. He implied that he might charge me, if I didn't recognize somebody and charge *him*, pretty quick. I asked him to stop the car and let me out. He seemed to consider whether he could safely ignore this request. Then he complied and I got a taxi home.

Thinking about it afterwards, I had the impression that the policeman had been going through a pretty familiar routine. Many white people, robbed by blacks, would recognise *any black*, roughly corresponding to the description of the robber. So identified and charged, the person identified would be likely to be convicted, and the police books would be cleared, which would be to the benefit of the police officer concerned. My refusal to identify was an irritating hitch, leading to the threat of a homosexual charge. But the threat was not followed through. Making charges without evidence against a fairly prosperous white person would be too risky. But poor young blacks had no effective defence against the system of random charges.

I may perhaps have inferred too much from a single episode. But the policeman had all the air of going through a procedure with which he was very familiar indeed, and which had served him well in the past. I had the impression that both the policeman and most of his white witnesses regarded all young black males as either criminals or potential criminals, so there was really, from that point of view, no question of false identifications. All of them were guilty, existentially.

* * *

The teaching environment at NYU was relatively stable, but beginning to be troubled, both by the repercussions of the deteriorating Vietnam War and by increasing racial tensions due to increasing unwillingness by young blacks to accept the status of second-rate citizens.

Sometimes these two themes interacted, and occasionally in a rather bizarre manner. At one point the student representative body demanded that on a given day all classes should be devoted to a discussion of the Vietnam War. I was at first disposed to resist this. I pointed out that the struggle in Vietnam and writing around that struggle, would be an integral part of my course in "Literature and Society", and I wanted to reach it in my own time and deal with it in my own way. The students pointed out that they wanted to highlight the growing concern about the seemingly endless war and that the best way of highlighting it seemed to be to have as many classes as possible devoted to it on a given day. I could see the force of this, and being in sympathy with the growing opposition to the war, agreed to devote my class on the chosen day to the Vietnam War.

That, however, did not end the matter. Two days before the class was due to take place, the student representatives came to me with a completely different demand, replacing the first one. Instead of devoting my class to the Vietnam War, I was now asked to devote it to the topic of "open admissions", the current demand of black radical students for admission without academic qualifications.

I refused. I had agreed to the first demand because a good case had been made for it, and I would do what I had agreed to do. But I did not agree that students should determine what they would be taught, nor was I in favour of the admission of unqualified students to the university. So, no. And the students accepted the no.

Educationally, the "open admissions" demand made no sense at all in my opinion. It actually exploited the students who were supposed to "benefit" from it, and then let them down in a big way. The universities which had begun to practise open admissions – of which Berkeley was the most notable example – had the unlovable habit of admitting quite large numbers of totally unqualified students, and then turning them out before the final year, just as unqualified as when they first came in. The reason for this was that Berkeley could not confer degrees on unqualified students without undermining the credibility of their own degrees, thereby losing out to competing universities. So let them in as undergraduates, in a big flow of pseudo-liberalism, and then turn them out on the streets before their final year.

Educationally, "open admissions" were a snare and a delusion. But politically, they served a definite purpose, and represented a transit of power within the civil rights movement. In the heroic heyday of that movement, in the 1950s and early 1960s, much of the leadership had been supplied by white liberals, mostly Jewish, and the most conspicuous martyrs of the movement were Jewish.

But by the mid 1960s – around the time of our arrival in New York – there was a growing demand that the black movement should be led by blacks exclusively. Indeed the demand was that the leadership should be in the hands of black males exclusively.

In the heroic period of the movement, black females had played an important role. Rosa Parkes had virtually started the movement by refusing to accept segregation in Alabama, and other black women were also to the fore. But by the middle and late 1960s, leading black male leaders – like Stokely Carmichael – were firmly consigning black females to a role supportive of the black male leadership.

The emerging black leadership of what had once been a cross-racial movement – and still retained some of the trappings of its origins – was quick to see the potential of "open admissions" for the advancement and consolidation of their own power. The whites who had played a leading part in civil rights were mostly people who were educationally qualified. The blacks who wished to replace them were no less intelligent – and sometimes more so – but they had had no opportunity to acquire an adequate education. "Open admissions" was a slogan with mass appeal. But it was educationally unsound. A sound strategy for black education would have begun with primary schools, ensuring that they would be adequately funded, equipped and supplied with competent teachers. Those teachers, in the nature of the case, would mostly be white during the period of development. As soon as the reform of the primary system was well under way, a similar reform at secondary level could begin. Only when this educational sub-structure was well and truly laid, would there be any meaning in talking about higher education for blacks. And once the substantive change was secured, there would be an adequate number of young blacks qualified for admission through the normal channels.

The intelligent young men who were taking over the political leadership of the black community from the mid-1960s on could see all this perfectly well. They knew as well as anyone else that "open admissions" were a nonsense, educationally speaking. But the very fact that they were a nonsense, educationally speaking, was what made sense of them, politically speaking. They had considerable mass appeal, seeming to open a painless path to higher education for poor black children. So to mobilize black support for this demand was easy. Probably more important for the new black leadership was the fact that "open admissions" tended to isolate and divide white people within the old civil rights movement. Being educated themselves, these people could see the yawning fallacies behind the seductive appeal of the slogan. But the choices before them in dealing with the call *for* open admissions were essentially choices between different modes of political suicide: they could oppose it honestly, and forfeit almost all support within the black community, or they could come out for it against their better judgement, thus subordinating themselves slavishly to the new black leadership. Either way the new black leadership emerged as the winner. Which it duly did.

During this period, in the more modish universities – of which Berkeley was one, and New York University was not – a loose but effective alliance emerged between "Black Studies" people and "Women's Studies" people. "Studies" was something of a misnomer in both cases. What was going on, under that label, was propaganda and indoctrination. And the alliance between "Black Studies" and "Women's Studies" was a very curious one. The former was run by black men, exclusively. The latter was run by white women, exclusively. So the loose alliance was one between black men and white women. Throughout the sixties and seventies, black women were left entirely out of the picture, primarily at the insistence of the black men, but with the collusion of the white women. It was not until around 1980 that black *women* began to play a significant role in an educational process which had long been seriously skewed in this area.

The loose alliance between the two "Studies" had also automatically cast white males in the role of the root of *all* evil, responsible for all oppression both of blacks and women. But black women knew differently. They knew that many black men were sexist and many white women were racist. The eventual arrival of black women on the scene brought a new and welcome note of realism and intellectual honesty into the debate over race and gender, as affecting education. But that benign change was still a long way off in the 1960s.

That debate was, on the whole, in a pretty sorry condition, during the period of my stay at New York University in the late sixties. All the same there were some memorable and impressive moments. For me such a moment came at a meeting held at NYU to register indignation after the murder of Martin Luther King. I was among the platform speakers, or rather among those who were scheduled to speak. It was a very strange meeting. The people on the platform were all white, and so was the entire audience, when the meeting opened. But just as the chairman was announcing the prepared agenda, the doors of the hall opened and about sixty black students filed in formally dressed and wearing academic gowns. They took up positions around the space allotted to the speakers. The chairman broke off his own remarks, and looked at the black students. He seemed to expect a spokesman for this group to say something. Nobody did. The group simply stood there: sixty black people looking at a few hundred white people. The silence seemed endless and oppressive. Finally the chairman could stand it no longer, and simply declared the meeting adjourned *sine die*.

What the students were declaring, with that momentous silence, was that the question of what should be done, after the murder of Martin Luther King, was a matter to be determined by blacks, exclusively. Steve Biko, in South Africa, was to deliver a similar message a little later. It seems to be a message that has to be delivered, and maintained for a time, whenever a group which has long been excluded from participating in politics begins to take part in them. And it could not have been more effectively delivered than by the dignified silence of those black students that afternoon at New York University.

*　*　*

Towards the end of my first year at NYU I was approached by a group of my students with a political proposition. These students were all Jewish and also all very bright. They knew that I had written and spoken against the war in Vietnam around the theme of "Counter-Revolutionary Imperialism". But now they wanted me to join with them in breaking the law, to register the seriousness of the issue and of our concern with it. They did not propose any violent action, or any flamboyant gesture, such as the burning of the American flag, as practised at that time by the extreme left of the anti-war movement. What they did propose was a sit-in outside the Induction Center in Manhattan in order to obstruct the progress of recruitment for the war. We would no doubt be arrested and charged with a breach of the peace. We might be jailed for a short time. Whatever happened would signal a stiffening of the resistance, by moderates, to the continuance of the Vietnam War.

They said that they, as American Jews, were influenced by the thought of the failure of most American Jews to protest effectively against the rise of Nazism, and in particular their failure to demand the admission of persecuted German – and later Austrian and Czech – Jews to the United States. They had in mind specifically the failure of most American Jews to protest against the position of the American government at the Evian Conference in 1938. At that conference, the Americans had agreed with the European governments not to relax immigration practices in such a way as to admit any large numbers of European Jews to the countries represented at Evian. The Evian decision, in the year before the outbreak of war, sealed the fate of the Jews of Europe. Remembering that, the Jews who were talking to me were determined not to repeat what they saw as a great moral failure: now, failure to protest against what they all regarded as an unjust war.

308

I asked for time to think about the matter. I thought this might be quite a serious step to take. In verbally protesting against the war, as I had been doing, I was protected by the US Constitution as interpreted by the Supreme Court. But by deliberately breaking the law, I would put myself outside the protection of the law. If I received a jail sentence, my green card – in effect my licence to live and work in the United States – might be withdrawn, and I might have to go home in a hurry and jobless. I didn't care for that prospect. But neither did I think I could live with myself if I turned down the request of my students, which seemed to me to be reasonable and well-motivated. So I agreed and Máire agreed to join me.

The subsequent proceedings were rather anti-climactic. Quite a large number of us did turn up, did sit down, and blocked the entrance to the Induction Center. Then the police, who seemed to have been expecting our protest, sent in a number of patrolmen on horses to disperse us. Many of the demonstrators did disperse at this point: most residents of New York city have little to do with horses and are a bit afraid of them. But we had a fair idea that the horses would not hurt us if we just lay there without moving. So we did, and the horses passed over us. Then the police invited us to disperse, but we remained where we were. A number of patrolmen then moved in to haul us away. Some of us, including me, went limp. The patrolman who was in charge of me gave me a sharp and well-aimed kick on the upper hip-bone. This was unpleasant, but not irrational. The practice of going limp made a lot of hard work for the police, so it made sense to discourage it. And in my case, it did discourage it. I never, in all my life, went limp again.

These proceedings attracted considerable publicity at the time, of which we could not complain, since attracting attention was a large part of the exercise. The kick – for the results of which I was treated at Bellevue Hospital – was part of the news. I received a telegram from my friend Wilton Dillon: "I see you were kicked by a cop. What was his ethnicity?"

The cop's ethnicity, just as Wilton had surmised, was the same as my own.

I spent several hours in jail and was then brought to trial in the local district court. The presiding judge was black, which I felt to be a point in my favour. There was no major difference between the physical events as described by the police and as described by me, except that the police neither corroborated nor disputed my story about being kicked. The judge then asked me whether I wished to say anything before he passed sentence.

I said I was charged with a breach of the peace. "But I had not gone to the Induction Center to breach the peace. I had gone there to protest a breach of the peace being carried out by the government of the United States in Vietnam . . . "

At this point the judge interrupted me. "Dr O'Brien," he said, "I was about to dismiss the case against you, but I might change my mind if you don't stop talking."

I stopped talking right there, and the case was duly dismissed.

My arrest and injury had been reported in the press, and Mayor Lindsay of New York wrote me a letter of sympathy and good wishes about the injury. I thought this very decent of him in the circumstances.

I half expected that my Jewish students would come to me with a proposal that we should renew our illegal protest. It would have been logical to do so. After all, the war against which we had protested was continuing and even expanding. I was resigned to renewed protest if the students demanded it. Resigned, but apprehensive: a second breach of the peace might well lead to a jail sentence and withdrawal of my green card. My students, however, did not call for a renewal of the protest. I think they, too, had got a fright and feared the consequences of a renewed protest. I thought of Owen, who would have renewed the protest and gone on protesting, whatever the consequences. But by now I knew I was not Owen. I kept on writing against the war, and joining in lawful protests against it, but I never again broke the law in order to do so.

But other things now came up in Africa, against which I did feel impelled to make a protest which did involve some risk.

* * *

Shortly after the Induction Center episode, I had a visit from Professor Stanley Diamond of the New School, New York. Diamond was a political scientist with a special interest in Africa. He wanted to tell me about the Nigerian civil war which had just begun. He was particularly concerned about the possible fate of the Ibo people of south-east Nigeria who he thought might be threatened with extinction.

I knew what he was talking about because I had paid some visits to Nigeria, at a stage when what became the civil war was already incubating. And I knew the Ibo people of south-eastern Nigeria felt peculiarly threatened by the forces that were making for war. In Ghana our head steward had been an Ibo and a particularly dignified and responsible person.

In the late 19th century, under Governor Lugard, the British had introduced into Nigeria the system known as Indirect Rule. In practice, this mostly meant that the principal peoples of this vast territory were largely left to govern themselves – and also govern some others – subject to the overall supervision of the colonial power. The principal peoples were the Hausa and other Muslims of the north, the Yoruba of the west, and the Ibo of the east. The Hausa and Yoruba had essentially aristocratic polities, which meant that modern education amongst them was essentially the preserve of the upper classes, broadly conceived. But the Ibo were different. Technically, the Ibos were known to anthropologists as an acephalous people. That is, they did not have a dominant, closed caste-system. Careers were open to talents, to a degree unknown to most of Africa.

This condition gave Ibos enormous advantages under the conditions prevailing in most of Africa during the colonial period. Ibos took to modern education to an extent not available to other Nigerians. It soon followed that all the modernized sections of the economy – most notably the railways – were run by Ibos, under the general supervision of the British.

All that was fine, for Ibos, as long as the British Raj endured. But once the Raj was gone, from the 1960s on, there was a price to be paid. Both Muslims and Yoruba resented Ibo successes, and the aggressive manners that often accompanied the successes of the Ibo. During my period at the UN the leading Nigerian diplomat was an eastern Nigerian, widely believed to be an Ibo, Jaja Wachuku. Jaja had in a marked degree those characteristics which other Nigerians resented in Ibos. He had a bumptious, aggressive manner, did not suffer fools gladly, and assumed that most of the people he met were fools. And, as it happened, Jaja had received his higher education in Dublin, at Trinity College.

So the following story was told at the UN in Jaja's day: "Who had the best record, among the colonial powers, for the education of Africans? Well, the French gave a first-rate education to a very small number of Africans. The British gave not quite so good an education to a much larger number of Africans. Those two were about the best. After that came the Portuguese, who gave their African subjects no education at all. But the worst of all were the Irish. They educated Jaja Wachuku." This witty story is almost certainly of British origin. British administrators tended to like the courtly manners of the Yoruba and Hausa aristocrats and to resent the uppity manners of successful Ibos. And the Ibo people were to pay a heavy price for this scale of preferences.

During my trips from Ghana to Nigeria, in the period before the outbreak of the civil war, I had visited Ibadan University in eastern Nigeria. This was in Yoruba territory, but Ibadan was essentially an Ibo university, because Ibos had done much better at the secondary level. Kenneth Dike, the vice-chancellor, was an Ibo. During my visits Dike was clearly tense, and not disposed to candid discussion of the situation. But his wife did discuss it. She was extremely and vocally anxious. She was afraid the Ibos had no future in non-Ibo parts of Nigeria; maybe no future in Nigeria at all. At this time the mass expulsion of Ibos – mainly railway workers and their families – from Northern Nigeria had already started with massive and often lethal use of force to accelerate the flight of the survivors. "We are the Jews of Nigeria," said Mrs Dike.

I thought of the saying of the representatives of the Baluba of Katanga: "We are the Jews of Katanga."

And it was because of this parallel that Stanley Diamond had come to see me. He was Jewish himself and he felt that if he acquiesced in what might become the massacre of the Ibos, he would be re-enacting the betrayal of the European Jews. The similarity with the approach made to me shortly before by my Jewish students, with regard to Vietnam, was extraordinarily close.

I went to Biafra – as the Ibo state called itself – on two occasions and wrote about it. On the first occasion I went with Stanley Diamond. We found Biafra noisy and dangerously excited, with characteristic Ibo ebullience much in evidence and little sign of realization that a very tough war was coming against a much more numerous and better armed, trained and equipped foe. Both the British and the Russians supported the Nigerians – who controlled all the oil – and so did most, though not all, of the African countries, fearing the precedent of tribal disintegration for their own states. But the Biafrans had great faith in the justice of their cause and what that could do for them. Most Ibos were Catholics, and many of their teachers were Irish, who encouraged them with a version of what had happened in Ireland during the Easter Rising of 1916. The Irish rebels had been heavily outnumbered and outgunned, but their cause had prevailed in the end. This "Irish parallel" with the stimulus it gave to the rebels was bitterly remembered by the victorious Nigerians after the war. The religious order primarily concerned was the Holy Ghost Fathers, all of whom were expelled from Nigeria, including former Biafra, after the Nigerian victory. It was said that the Nigerian government had ordered that the Sign of the Cross be amended to run: "In the Name of the Father and of the Son, period."

My second visit to what was still Biafra, but only just, was very near the end of the war. I flew in from Tome in a cargo plane carrying salt. I sat on the salt. We flew mostly over Nigerian territory, and I had some gloomy thoughts about what might happen to me if we had to make an emergency landing. When I did land, it was already clear that Biafra was dying, and that many Biafrans were dying of hunger and related diseases. Biafra capitulated soon afterwards.

We had feared that Nigerian victory would be followed by terrible consequences for the Ibos. This did not happen. I must admit that the victorious Nigerians treated the defeated Ibos with much more magnanimity than I had expected. Yet I think that the widespread international agitation in favour of Biafra had been a fact conducive to the relatively benign outcome. The British government in particular had vigorously denied the prophecies of doom, and so was under pressure to see to it that the prophecies in question were not fulfilled. And the victorious Nigerians, needing continued British support for reconstruction, were in a mood to listen to the British. As Paul Claudel said, *le pire n'est pas toujours le plus sûr*.

* * *

The visits to Biafra were made during university vacations and so did not involve any interruptions to my normal work at New York University. Things at the university had gone on quite pleasantly, in spite of my participation in a deliberate breach of American law over Vietnam. I had more than half-expected that some senior person in the university administration would take me aside to warn me that if there were any repetition of such a breach of the law, and if I were convicted and sent to jail, it would not be possible for me to remain at the university. But no such warning was ever delivered. I suspect the reason for this lay in the volatile conditions of the American campuses at this time in relation to the Vietnam War. Up at Columbia – at the other end of Manhattan from the Village, where NYU was – a number of students were in open revolt, involving physical collisions with the police. Some of our own students went up there to abet the rebels, and some came back with bandaged heads, arms or legs. In these conditions I think the university authorities may have seen our milder little revolt as something of a safety valve. Putting it another way, the university authorities may have considered that, if they attempted to move against any of us, simply for protesting against the Vietnam War, they might have precipitated a student revolt on the scale of Columbia.

In any case, for whatever reason, they let us alone. My memories of what were to be our last months in New York – though we did not yet know this – are mostly pleasant ones. We had two disinguished and highly agreeable visitors at our home in Washington Mews during this period. One was the poet Robert Lowell. The other was Senator Eugene McCarthy.

Robert Lowell – known to his friends as "Cal" – was a victim throughout much of his life of manic-depressive attacks, and it was in the early onset of one of these attacks that he came to visit us. My first father-in-law, Alec Foster, also suffered from manic depression and I knew, from experience with him, that in an *early* phase of manic depression, the victim can be exceedingly good company. He came to our house – and was most welcome there – to talk and drink and read poetry. Especially read poetry. I remember one marathon session during which Lowell and I read the whole of Virgil's *Aeneid* in Latin, reading it book about. For the first four books, one of us read the text of the book, while the other listened. After book four the one who was supposed to be listening would fall asleep. When the relevant book was finished, the one who had read it would waken up the sleeper, and the former sleeper would start reading, while the former reader went to sleep. In this way we got through the twelve books of the *Aeneid* most companionably and to our mutual satisfaction.

When Eugene McCarthy came around we would also drink whiskey and read poetry, though this time it was Yeats, not Virgil. But the circumstances were more peculiar. McCarthy was at this time a candidate for the presidency of the United States. He was in fact the candidate who had ensured there would be a contest. He had decided to run against Lyndon Baines Johnson, when nobody else felt like challenging the sitting president. LBJ – to almost universal surprise – saw at once that he might be beaten because of the unpopularity of the war, and retired from the race. Then other candidates, beginning with Robert Kennedy, entered the race which McCarthy had started. In the circumstances it seemed extraordinary that, while the campaign was in full swing, McCarthy should elect to spend hours reading Yeats with two people who didn't have votes. I inferred that he didn't really want to win. He had made his point by forcing Johnson out of the race, and establishing the massive unpopularity of the Vietnam War. He couldn't foresee that Nixon would end it by pretending the war had been won and withdrawing the American troops, after which the Vietnamese had no trouble in winning the war. All the same, McCarthy had played an important part in bringing about a result which he could not have foreseen. By forcing Johnson's withdrawal, and establishing the unpopularity of the war, McCarthy had begun the devious train of thought in Nixon's mind that was to end the war.

* * *

Those were the large concerns. But I had also small concerns at this time, much nearer to me. Máire and I knew by now that we would not have natural children of our own. So we had decided to adopt. Our first thought was to adopt an orphan of the war in Vietnam, but we were told that no such adoption would be recognised in the United States nor would any such child be admitted to the United States. So we explored the possibility of adopting a child in America. Since our marriage was Catholic and Máire is a Catholic we made contact with a local Catholic adoption society. A representative of the society called on me. She was a brisk young woman who wasted no time. She said she supposed we wanted to adopt a white child. I said I could make no stipulation with regard to colour. She paused for a moment. Then she said: "You do realize that if you make no such stipulation, you will get a black child?" I said: "Very well." Another pause. Then she said, with a palpable sneer, "Why do you want a black? Is it on the principle that an ocelot might be more fun than a cat?" I stood up, opened the door, and wished her good evening. That was the end of our project of adopting a child in America.

Shortly after that incident we were at home in Ireland for a long vacation. We had lunch one day with Máire's uncle, Monsignor Maurice Browne. I told the story of the lady from the Catholic adoption society. The general idea, I fear, was to demonstrate how beastly Catholics could be. Maurice Browne was not easily fazed, nor was he surprised by my story. In his youth he had worked in a Brooklyn parish and knew the prevailing state of inter-racial relations there, which had not changed much since that time. He just said: "If you are willing to adopt a black child you can do that right here. Go to St Patrick's orphanage on the Navan Road and they can fix you up."

So we went to St Patrick's on the Navan Road, where we were warmly welcomed by the nuns, when they learned we wanted to adopt a black child. There was some delay about seeing children, which puzzled us a bit. We later found that they had a particular candidate in mind. The candidate suffered from infantile eczema, which they feared might put us off. The candidate was Patrick. They need not have worried; we both knew from the first that Providence intended him for us.

Patrick's natural mother was Irish, his father Ghanaian.

The consultant paediatrician, Dr Victoria Coffey, recommended Patrick, saying she would not recommend any child who was not highly intelligent. I didn't quite know how she knew that little Patrick, who was then three months old, was highly intelligent but she was quite right. She was also right about Margaret – partly Zambian, partly Irish – whom we adopted on her recommendation two years later.

My three children, Donal, Fedelma and Kate immediately loved Patrick, and later Margaret, and the happiest of bonds subsists between the five – now alas four – to our great and abiding joy.

We brought Patrick home in triumph, but there was a snag. I was due to return to my teaching duties in New York, but I was told I could not bring Patrick with me. A child fostered with a view to adoption was not allowed to leave the Irish jurisdiction under the age of one year. I could have left Patrick with Máire but I didn't want to do that. An adopted child, having gone through an initial trauma of separation, needs both parents to stick around. I explained the circumstances to the authorities of New York University who were very understanding and granted me a year's leave.

There was a kind of bonus to the refusal of permission to leave the jurisdiction. Máire had appealed to de Valera, then President of Ireland, to use his influence with Frank Aiken to have an exception made in Patrick's case. We were prepared to have Patrick made a ward of court as a guarantee that he would, if necessary, be returned to Ireland immediately. But Dev explained gently that he could not use his office to interfere with the course of the law. He added, however, an invitation to come and see him and bring Patrick, whom his wife would also love to see. He asked that we should come soon: "At our age, it doesn't do to postpone a pleasure." So we brought Patrick to see them, and a photograph of the five of us together is among our most treasured possessions.

In the period of our enforced stay-over in Ireland, I became involved in Irish politics, and took the decision to give up my chair in New York. But that story is for the next chapter.

Conor with daughter Margaret (on knee), then just adopted
at seven months, and Patrick aged three.

Conor with son Patrick, then aged two.

Left to right: CCO'B, President Eamon de Valera, Mrs de Valera, Máire with Patrick then aged three months, just after his adoption.

Left to right: Michael O'Leary, Garret FitzGerald, Richie Ryan amd CCO'B: in protest against Springbok visit, under apartheid regime.

Brendan Halligan, Secretary of the
Irish Labour Party. © *The Irish Times*

Brendan Corish, Leader of the
Irish Labour Party. © *The Irish Times*

Jack Lynch, Taoiseach. © *The Irish Times*

Left to right: Donald Trelford, John Cole, CCO'B, Ian Lindsay-Smith, Ken Obank: senior editorial staff of *The Observer*. © *The Observer*

Lord Barneston, then Chairman of *The Observer*, Lady Barneston and CCO'B, with "Valiant for Truth" Media Award (1979).

CJ Haughey, Taoiseach. © *The Irish Times*

In Ballymurphy for a television programme. A somewhat fraught occasion,
as Sinn Féin-IRA could have disrupted the event.

John Hume: he controlled Northern Ireland policy of
successive Dublin Governments. © *The Irish Times*

Caricature of Conor © 1970 by David Levine

14

IRELAND, OPPOSITION POLITICS

WHILE WE WERE DETAINED IN IRELAND BY CIRCUMSTANCES ARISING FROM Patrick's adoption, I became drawn into Irish politics. I had, while at Trinity College, been an active member of the Irish Labour Party. When I became a civil servant – and so ex-officio "non-political" – my membership of the Labour Party had lapsed. But now, my resignation from the Irish Civil Service freed me to rejoin the Irish Labour Party, if I wished to do so.

At first, I was not at all sure that I did so wish. In 1966, in an article called *The Embers of Easter* – in connection with the celebration of the 50th anniversary of the Easter Rising – I had been severely critical of what I regarded as the excessively cautious policies of the then Labour leaders. I called these leaders "poltroons" – a label that stuck, and which I thought would debar me from being welcomed back into the Labour Party even if that was what I wanted, which I didn't at first think it was.

I soon learned, however, that I would be welcome. The Labour Party had been changing since 1966, and the change in Dublin had verged on the spectacular. The new secretary of the Labour Party, a young graduate called Brendan Halligan, and a young TD from Cork, Michael O'Leary, had acquired a decisive influence over the leader of the Labour Party, Brendan Corish. This influence had been used to swing the party rather sharply to the left. Under Irish conditions, the most relevant and salient feature of a swing to the left was resistence to the political influence of the Catholic Church. Birth control, divorce and abortion were all still totally prohibited in the Republic of Ireland at this time. Abortion was still too hot to touch, but the Labour Party was already beginning to come out in favour of the legalisation both of birth control and divorce. This meant that I, as a divorced man, would no longer be ineligible for nomination as a Labour candidate, and it was made known to me that I could have such a nomination if I was ready to accept it.

For me the idea of being able to represent a constituency in the parliament of Ireland, without accepting the teachings of the Catholic Church or pretending to accept them, had powerful existential attractions. It meant that I would be accepted by my own people for what I really was. It closed a kind of schism in the soul, which had long troubled me more than I had ever consciously acknowledged.

So I decided to accept a nomination to run in the constituency of Dublin North-East in the next general election. If I was elected, this meant giving up my much better-paid, much more secure, and in many ways more agreeable chair at New York University. My son Donal, who was familiar both with American academia and with Irish politics, remonstrated with me. "Why do you have to do this?" he asked me. I didn't feel that I could decently go into the stuff about the schism in my soul, or even put that thought into intelligible words. So I just mumbled something about the interest of "the experience". Donal dealt crushingly with that one. "Paw," he asked, "don't you have enough *experience* already?" I did, of course, but there was a lot more to come.

* * *

Running in Dublin North-East I was challenging the leading Fianna Fáil TD for the constituency, Charles J Haughey. I attacked Mr Haughey over certain dealings in development land and over conflicts of interest, trying to use those to expose the workings of the Fianna Fáil speculator-oriented oligarchy, of which Mr Haughey was the most conspicuous member. In a speech during the campaign I said:

"Mr Haughey apparently considers that the sale by him for about £200,000 of a tract of land in this constituency, which was green belt land when he bought it and is now to be building land, is a purely personal question, of interest only to himself and to a few other gentlemen of means and enterprise, directly involved in the transaction.

"According to Mr Haughey, the people in the constituency had no right to interest themselves in this; the taxpayers who paid heavily to subsidise new buildings were not entitled to question this transaction of the private individual who also happens to be finance minister.

"Now, I am sure that Mr Haughey is quite sincere in his opinion that this is a purely personal matter – that he can hold such an opinion sincerely is a symptom of what is wrong with our society and of how the Fianna Fáil government has become part of what is wrong."

Twenty-eight years later, after the exposure of large-scale corruption on Haughey's part, those words of mine were quoted with approval in the press (Emily O'Reilly in *The Sunday Business Post*, July 13, 1997). But in 1969, what I had to say about Mr Haughey's corrupt dealing did not go down so well with the press. The *Irish Times* attacked me in two separate editorials for dealing in what they described as "the politics of envy". They did not refer to the theme of conflict of interest which was my central theme.

In the election campaign, Fianna Fáil did not advert to conflicts of interest or development land. Instead they concentrated on the communist threat: a threat which was non-existent but politically rewarding when skillfully exploited.

Fianna Fáil attacked the Labour Party as infiltrated by communist intellectuals, of whom I was the reddest and most exotic specimen. Evidence connecting me with communism was not to be had – Fianna Fáil had to do what it could with the fact that I had been heard to advocate diplomatic relations with Cuba. But in fact "communism" is a technical term in the political vocabulary of the Catholic state. Formally, in the late 20th century, you can't be seen to go round demanding to know when your opponent was last at mass, confession or holy communion. This would be sectarian behaviour: unmodern, uncivilized, resembling the goings-on in the North of Ireland. But if there is reason to believe your opponent may be vulnerable in this area, you could at that time hit him just as accurately by calling him a communist. This was a *political* charge, impeccably 20th century in character. (The fact that Senator Joe McCarthy was eventually discredited never made much impact on public opinion in Ireland.) But as well as being a political term, "communist" carried a "religious" message: communists are known to be atheists also. So the question of the opponent's religious faith, or lack of it, comes automatically into the zone of legitimate political discussion. A good Catholic, by definition, cannot be a communist. But a bad Catholic may well be one since he, also by definition, being bad, is capable of anything, so may very well be a communist. So, if you call someone a communist, and have no proof of this, you may discreetly adduce indications establishing a presumption of communism: educated at a Protestant school and university, first marriage ended in divorce. These proofs are not coercive in respect of communism, but communism is really beside the point. The point is to show that your opponent is a bad Catholic, so as to enlist the help of the Church in eliminating him and his associates from public life, to the benefit of yourself and your associates.

I was vulnerable in this area, especially because my first marriage had ended in divorce and I had married again. My second wife, Máire MacEntee, was a Catholic, and our marriage took place in a Catholic Church in New York. My wife's father was a former Minister for Finance and deputy leader in Fianna Fáil governments, and my wife's mother was a sister of the eminent Irish Dominican, Michael Cardinal Browne. It was therefore difficult for Fianna Fáil publicly to give me the full treatment, 1891 style, but they did their best by word of mouth on the door-to-door canvass to exploit "the moral issue".

The Labour Party itself was vulnerable, not only to such tactics directed against certain of its candidates but because it had also fairly recently taken to itself the designation of socialist, and because the distinction between socialist and communist is not clear to all Irish minds, and especially not to all Irish clerical minds, especially when they don't want it to be clear. My wife, shortly after this period, heard a priest in Dingle, Co Kerry, deliver a sermon on "communism and socialism." The priest gave communism the expected treatment. Then he went on to socialism. "Socialism," he said, "is worse than communism. Socialism is a heresy of communism. Socialists are a Protestant variety of communists." Not merely communists, but *Protestant* communists! Not many votes for Labour in Dingle.

So the key to the Fianna Fáil leader, Mr Jack Lynch's campaign, in that June of 1969, was a tour of the convent parlours. Like Captain O'Neill, the Northern Ireland unionist leader, he was photographed with nuns, but unlike Captain O'Neill he knew how to talk to nuns. The press and media were not present for that series of convent chats, but the word came through all the same. A Labour colleague from Munster told me ruefully of a mothers' meeting convened in his constituency by a Reverend Mother on the day before polling day. It was not, said the Reverend Mother to the other mothers, for her to advise them on a political matter. Certainly not! She only wished to remind them of their duty, as Catholic mothers, both to vote and to be very prudent about how to vote. She would give them no advice about which party to vote for. That was not her province. Whatever party they voted for, however, they should be sure that it was a party which could provide stable government and which was free from any tendency to communism. If there was doubt as to whether there might be communists in a certain party, it would be wiser not to vote for that party. That was all!

That was one Reverend Mother to whom Mr Lynch's message had not been addressed in vain.

* * *

The anti-communist element in the campaign didn't cut much ice in Dublin where Labour did quite well and where I was elected second to Mr Haughey in a four-seater constituency. But outside Dublin, as Fianna Fáil had anticipated, the "communist" label hurt and Labour lost some seats. The slogan under which Labour had fought the election – "The Seventies will be Socialist" – had lost most of such plausibility as it had possessed.

At Leinster House, I found myself sharing a room with three other Labour deputies: Noel Browne, Justin Keating and David Thornley. Keating, Thornley and I were newly elected. All four of us were identified in the public mind as left-wing intellectuals. Fianna Fáil people, and also at this time some Fine Gael people, called us "smoked salmon socialists". Feeling rather euphoric about the election results in Dublin, where all four of us had our seats, I hung a poster in our room: *Aithníonn Ciaróg Ciaróg Eile*, meaning "one beetle knows another beetle". This was supposed to be a light-hearted reference to our solidarity. I noticed that none of my colleagues seemed to be amused, but I didn't at first recognise this for the bad sign that it was.

Within about a year, the four of us, for different reasons, were hardly on speaking terms. The first relationship to break down was a triangular one between myself, David Thornley and Noel Browne. Noel and my cousin Owen had been political friends – mainly because of their common hostility to the political influence of the Catholic Church – so that my early relations with Noel had been quite good, though never close. But they did not long survive our common membership of the Irish Labour Parliamentary Party.

321

In general, the Parliamentary Party just after the 1969 elections was not a particularly fraternal collection of people. The rural deputies felt they had lost seats because of what they regarded as the antics of the new Dublin deputies and I'm afraid the new deputies did not put themselves out to conciliate their rural colleagues. But there was only one relationship that was really poisonous: that between Noel Browne and the leader of the party, Brendan Corish. And the poison proceeded entirely from Noel, and not at all from Corish. Corish, as a member of the coalition government at the time of the Mother and Child health controversy, had withheld support from Browne, leaving him in such isolation that he felt he had to resign. Like the Count of Monte Cristo, Noel Browne never forgave those who brought about his downfall but was determined to be revenged. And sitting under Corish's chairmanship in the Parliamentary Party after the 1969 election, Noel exacted that revenge in full measure.

Noel signalled his disdain for his party leader at every meeting of the Parliamentary Party he attended (not very many).

But there was one meeting in which he manifested hatred of Corish in a spectacular manner. He arrived late at this meeting and drew up a chair right beside Corish, thus drawing the attention of everybody in the room to him, as was undoubtedly his intention. Then he addressed Corish – being entirely out of order in doing so – in a very low voice. This again was intentional. Everyone in that room had to be hushed and strain to hear him, and strain they did. He spoke for about five or six minutes, in a savagely hostile review of Corish's career. The high moment came when he said, in a tremulous whisper: "You said, Corish, that if you had to choose between your religion and your country you would choose your religion! You actually said that, Corish! Never forget it!" Then Browne stood up and walked out. The whole thing was like the appearance and disappearance of a vengeful ghost.

Brendan Corish was a devout, though not an ostentatious, Catholic, and the choice he expressed was absolutely normal for a devout and consistent Catholic. Noel Browne's position, on the other hand, was odd, even for him. At the time of his resignation he was at odds not only with Costello and MacBride, but with his own party. The republicans of Clann na Poblachta had been the first to repudiate him. Yet in finding it self-evident that a person should be motivated primarily by nationalist politics, and not by religion, he was expressing a classical republican priority. So there was a tremendous confusion bumping around in there as Browne brooded over his past and present fate.

After a few weeks of fairly close political contact with Browne I had come to regard him as half-mad and dangerous to know. But I tried not to annoy him: I just kept out of his way. Yet I was soon to experience the lash of his displeasure because of an attempt on my part to help him. Browne was brooding at this time, with even greater intensity than usual, over his grievances at the hands of the Catholic Church. He wrote and published a savage polemic against the clergy. The most memorable passage in it was one in which he expressed his opinion, as a psychiatrist, that many Irish priests were homosexuals (if he had said quite a few were child-abusers, he would have been on the right track, as appeared much later). Browne undoubtedly enjoyed letting off steam against the Church for the sake of steam. But I think he had two additional motives. One was to embarrass his party leader, the hated Corish. The other was to provoke his own expulsion from the party, thus earning for himself yet another Martyr's Crown.

Like every other member of the Parliamentary Party, by this time, I would like to have seen the last of Noel Browne. And a motion was in fact put down for the removal of the whip from Browne, by David Thornley. Thornley was an unusually flamboyant Catholic who was known to be supported against Browne by most of the rural deputies, who feared that Browne's performances would endanger their seats. Much as I detested Browne's performances, I didn't want to see him disciplined simply for critizing the Catholic Church, even if in excessive terms. Were this to happen, it would copperfasten what I regarded as the already excessive political power of the Catholic Church. So if the whip were withdrawn from Browne, I faced the detestable prospect of having to resign from the party apparently in support of Browne's position.

I therefore opposed Thornley's motion. I suggested instead that Corish should simply issue a brief statement to the effect that Browne had been expressing a personal opinion which was not that of the Labour Party. The urban deputies liked that idea, so did Corish, and it satisfied most of the rural deputies. So the statement was duly issued. Noel Browne never forgave me for robbing him of his second Martyr's Crown.

Shortly after Corish's statement, Browne and I both attended a meeting of the Dublin regional Council of the Labour Party. The regional council was Browne's turf, not mine. Most Dublin Labour Party members – except for those who were in close political contact with Browne – admired him. Romantic leftists, who abounded in the regional council, hero-worshipped him. Browne gave the council a carefully crafted account of the proceedings in the party. Of this account, I was the villain. I had instigated the party leader to issue an implicit repudiation of his article. This was true enough, but it omitted the fact that the alternative, proposed and probably about to be carried, was the removal of the whip from Browne. I filled in that detail for the meeting. But Browne did not corroborate what he knew to be true. I was, and long remained, an established villain in the eyes of the regional council members, and similar elements in the party at large.

* * *

By this time, the theme of "one beetle knows another beetle", implying cordial relations between the deputies in our room, was in bits. Thornley and Browne were not on speaking terms because Thornley had tried to have Browne expelled from the party. Thornley and I were not on speaking terms because I had foiled his effort to get Browne expelled. Browne and I were not on speaking terms because I had foiled his bid for a second Martyr's Crown. The only two denizens of that little room who were still on speaking terms after the foiled attempt to expel Browne were Justin Keating and myself. And Justin and I were not destined to remain on cordial terms for more than a few months after the Browne-expulsion-bid episode.

The abode of the "beetles" was now distasteful to me. But in the Parliamentary Labour Party as a whole – or indeed in the Labour Party in the country – I was by no means isolated. Corish, as party leader, generally approved of me, especially after I had helped to get him off the hook over Browne. Brendan Halligan, the party secretary, was friendly, though we often differed concerning tactics. And I had two friends in the Parliamentary Party who were at this time very influential in the formation of party policy. These were Michael O'Leary and Frank Cluskey.

Michael O'Leary had great influence with Corish in this period and had used that influence to steer the party in a modernising way. "Modernising" meant, in the context, emancipating the party from clerical influences, supporting the legalisation of contraception and divorce. Naturally I was all in favour of "modernisation". But O'Leary also saw things I didn't yet see. He noticed, soon after I returned to Ireland, that I showed some signs of being attracted to Sinn Féin, then in a left-wing and non-violent phase. Michael knew the score a lot better than I did at that time and he warned me against romanticising them or being drawn in any way into their orbit. "Watch out for Cathleen Ní Houlihan!" he warned me. "If you get too near her, she'll scratch your eyes out!"

I never did get all that near, but still got too near. My eyes remained intact but I shall always bear some traces of the scratches she began to inflict within a few months of Michael's timely warning.

Frank Cluskey was at this time chief whip of the party, and also one of Corish's advisers. He and I first became allied over a dispute involving anti-semitism. Steve Coughlan, Labour Mayor of Limerick, had defended Limerick's record over the anti-semitic riots of 1904 in that city. Frank and I tried to get Coughlan disciplined over that matter. At the party's annual conference I spoke in favour of a motion – moved by Máire Walsh, a young delegate from Northern Ireland – to expel Coughlan for anti-semitic statements. The motion had good support from the Dublin branches, but it had little support in the country and the motion failed overall. But it laid the groundwork for a close alliance between Cluskey and myself which lasted throughout the eight years of my membership of the Dáil.

A great bond between Cluskey and me was that we saw the same sorts of things as funny, but saw them from slightly different angles which tended to heighten one another's perceptions. We often sat beside one another in the Dáil, and sometimes exchanged impressions, especially when – as often – the proceedings got boring. On one occasion I noticed that there was a question on the order paper from David Thornley: "To ask the Minister for Local Government whether he will see to it that a pedestrian-crossing is placed outside Our Lady Help of Christians [Church] on the Navan Road."

I drew Frank's attention to this little item. "Don't you think, Frank," I said, "that David is showing a little lack of faith there? Why can't he see that Our Lady can help Christians to cross the Navan Road without assistance from the Irish Minister for Local Government?" Frank looked very solemn. "You don't get the point, Conor. It's not just the Christians David has to think about. He also has a duty to his Jewish constituents."

* * *

The Northern Ireland question hit the politics of the Republic seriously, for the first time since the early 1920s, on August 12, 1970, when the spectacle of the Bogside resistance filled the television screens. On that day the annual Orange parade on the walls of the city had been stoned by republican demonstrators. The Orange march chased the demonstrators into the Catholic Bogside, but there they met with determined, planned resistance by large numbers of Catholics using petrol bombs as well as stones. Against this resistance the Orangemen were unable to make headway.

When the news of the Derry events reached Belfast, Protestant mobs launched violent attacks on Catholic areas, and there were a few fatalities. In the Republic, nationalist emotions ran high on the Catholic side and the Taoiseach intimated that the Irish government "could not stand idly by". This was widely interpreted as promising military intervention and – as later transpired – some of those within the Lynch government actually did plan military intervention and supported the creation of the organization which later became the Provisional IRA.

Before August 1969, I had been marginally involved with the civil rights movement in the North. As I was spokesman for the Labour Party on Northern Ireland (as well as Foreign Affairs) it was my duty to go North and in doing so I took part in civil rights demonstrations with the approval of my party. Indeed at one point I was nearly drawn into Northern electoral politics. At this period Sinn Féin-IRA were under left-wing control, since the IRA Chief of Staff, Cathal Goulding, relied on the political guidance of an ardent left-wing intellectual, Roy Johnston. In that now remote period, left-wing Irish republicans approved of me, mainly because of my record in the Congo, but also because of my vocal opposition to American policy in Vietnam. The two most prominent left-wing Irish republicans – George Gilmore and Peadar O'Donnell – had publicly endorsed my candidature in the Irish general election. Roy Johnston approved of me. Then four senior republicans from Derry came down to Dublin and invited me to run for mid-Ulster in the coming elections. I was tempted and think I might have accepted. But then a message reached me from Bernadette Devlin, then a rising star in Northern nationalist politics, especially in Derry. The message was: "Tell that man to keep his hands off my seat." Faced with Bernadette's wrath my backers withdrew, and Bernadette's seat was no longer threatened.

In that I was very lucky. The Provisional IRA had yet to emerge. When they did I could not have gone along with them. If I had opposed them as member for nationalist ("civil rights") mid-Ulster they would quickly have made the place too hot to hold me. I might not have survived even physically.

To return to Dublin politics, and specifically Labour Party politics: in the immediate aftermath of the Derry/Belfast crisis of August, 1969, the Parliamentary Labour Party had a meeting to determine our course of action. Labour was then in power in Britain, and it was felt that they might welcome advice from their little sister in Dublin. It was quickly decided that we would send a group on a fact-finding mission to Derry and Belfast and then to London to advise our big sister. I was to lead the London mission.

There was one memorable exchange during that Dublin meeting. David Thornley, who was of a somewhat nervous disposition, did not relish the notion of a trip to Belfast in the disturbed conditions. He didn't speak during most of the discussion. Then he intervened in a characteristically dramatic fashion. He said:

"I think I feel now how Michael Collins felt in 1921."

That being the year Michael Collins signed the Anglo-Irish Treaty.

Cluskey looked at Thornley in disgust. He said:

"Listen, David, if you're not careful you'll find out how fuckin' Michael Collins felt in fuckin 1922."

That being the year that Michael Collins was shot.

Thornley did not join our party.

My main recollection of the Northern leg of our journey was of meeting Bernadette Devlin in Derry. Bernadette was weeping bitterly. She was weeping because Derry women, delighted with the British intervention and the removal of the Protestant threat, were plying the British troops with cups of tea. Bernadette needn't have worried. That brief ecumenical phase was soon replaced by the offensive of the Provisional IRA which she supported.

In London we had a meeting with Lord Chalfont, then Secretary of State for Foreign Affairs. I urged the British government to put an end to the Stormont government, which had abused its power, and to resort to direct rule. If that advice had been taken then, before the Provisional IRA's offensive began, and if direct rule had been resolutely sustained, things might have gone a lot better than they later did. Unfortunately, Stormont was not "prorogued" until two years later, after the Provisionals' offensive had begun. In the circumstances, "prorogation" was widely – indeed almost universally – seen as something achieved by the Provisionals, which gave them great prestige in the nationalist community and helped them to sustain their offensive.

I paid a number of visits to the North during the period 1969-70, the period during which the Provisional IRA was founded and began its offensive. My cousin Owen died during this period, in early June 1970. He had been an open enemy to what he called "the crazy militarism" of the

327

IRA. As I wrote some months after his death: "Owen's influence on my own thinking had always been strong. It seems, if anything, to have increased after his death."

* * *

The emergence of the Provisional IRA in the North had important implications also for the Republic. Here again, it meant that a new pattern of IRA activity fitted better, had better chances of winning both influential and popular support, than the old pattern had. The old IRA had favoured revolutions, North and South, and the Official IRA continued along this line. As very few people in the Republic had any desire for a revolution, this cut these movements off from popular support. This policy – and the Marxist rhetoric associated with it – especially alienated rich patriots both in the Republic and in the United States. By this combination, therefore, the IRA, both in its old and Official forms was insulated, and kept relatively ineffective, or harmless.

The Provisional line, on the other hand, made sense in terms of the dominant ideology in the Republic. They were not, they claimed, out to make trouble in the "Twenty-Six Counties." They rejected Marxist language (though not "socialism") and any political alliance with communists. They were out, they said, to liberate the six north-eastern counties of Ireland, occupied by British forces against the will of the great majority of the Irish people. Most citizens of the Republic were conditioned to think of such a policy as well-founded and laudable. They were not conditioned to think of the Ulster Protestants as an important factor in the question, or to see that the Provisionals' policy pointed ultimately to civil war in Ireland between Catholic and Protestant. People might feel vaguely uneasy about the fanaticism of the Provisionals, but found it hard to answer them. It was, in fact, impossible to answer them in terms of the dominant ideology, because they were the most effective and consistent champions of that ideology. Rich and influential patriots, repelled by the Marxism of the old and Official IRA, had a special welcome for the Provisionals: good Catholics, good Irishmen, no threat to anyone but the British . . . and the unionists.

Two of the most powerful members of Jack Lynch's then Government – Neil Blaney and CJ Haughey – were believed to have been actively involved in the setting up, funding and arming of what became the Provisional IRA. I had lunch on July 2, 1970, with Ruairí Ó Brádaigh, leader of Provisional Sinn Féin, political wing of the Provisional IRA, whose "military operations" were then being prepared, but had not yet begun. I wrote in my diary for that day:

"Lunch in National Gallery with Ruairí Ó Brádaigh. An affable Irregular, strongly rather than heavily built. Refuses wine. Pleasant open face. Smiles a lot. Too much? Believed to be the leader of the Provisionals. Angry at assertions his organisation promotes sectarian violence. They are concerned with defence. Their split with the IRA was not the result of Blaney intrigue, but of rank-and-file exasperation with IRA executives for unpreparedness last summer and for unrealistic policies such as alliance with Communist Party. Has no use for Blaney. Opposes sectarianism, and specifically deplored Blaneyite efforts to end Orange processions in Donegal. Admits his rank-and-file are not so ecumenical; there is 'a fever' among the people. But his organisation is not trying to foment violence; they are trying to control it, so that when it occurs it will not be wholly useless. Himself volunteers the thought that the distinction between 'controlling' and 'fomenting' is a difficult one. If you don't do some fomenting you soon won't be in a position to control. In the St Matthew's fighting the defence was improvised by some of the defence committee, and by 'some of our people.' On both sides, deaths of fighters will be presented as civilian casualties; a question of compensation. I ask him about the burning of the big [Protestant] stores. Is that the official IRA line? He smiles. 'I think that is something that would be more associated with our people.' No real rapprochement between 'officials' and provisionals, he says. Some co-operation in local emergencies. I ask him about contacts in Belfast and Derry. He readily gives me names for Derry: Keenan, Ó Conaill: Doherty's telephone number. For Belfast he gives me no names; his face clouds over. Earlier he had agreed in deploring John Kelly's sectarian press release (per the odious Brady). It looks as if the Belfast provisionals are less under his control than the Derry ones. He asks me some questions about the Congo, parallels, etc. Also: a discussion of rumours (enemy lorries approaching from Ballymena or Angola or whatever). R O'B says he thinks these issue instinctively as a means of maximum rallying of the defending group. We part outside the Merrion Square entrance of Leinster House. 'Take care' I tell him. 'Oh, I will,' says he."

On August 12, 1970, on one of my "information-finding" visits to the North, I had an unpleasant experience in Derry. As I wrote shortly afterwards:

"In the afternoon there was to be an Apprentice Boys rally at St Columb's Park on the outskirts of Derry across the Foyle and remote from the Bogside. This was a substitute – a highly unsatisfactory one from an

Apprentice Boys point of view – for the usual triumphal parade. It was also an important occasion however as it was to be addressed by William Craig, the hard-lining former Minister for Home Affairs, who was then making a bid, supported by the whole unionist right, to be the next Prime Minister in Northern Ireland. We decided to attend this rally.

"This was not quite so imprudent as it might appear. On July 13, 1969, I had walked with the great Orange March in Belfast to Finaghy Field, had been recognized several times and without any unpleasantness. But that had been a happy occasion for the Orangemen: they had held their march with full traditional pomp. The Apprentice Boys, on the other hand, were forced to use maimed rites. No one minds onlookers for triumphs; humiliations are another matter.

"We arrived late at St Columb's Park. It was dark and rainy, adding to the misery of the day. I was wearing a heavy raincoat. I bought some literature from a stall at the entrance to the grounds: two sets of prison messages from Dr Paisley, dating from different periods of incarceration, and a booklet with the title, *The Pope is the Devil.* To keep the booklets from the rain I shoved them inside the front of my white trenchcoat. When we reached the fringe of the crowd of about 5,000, Mr William Craig was speaking. A sign over his head said simply 'Welcome'. At each side of the covered speakers' stand were Union Jacks and the plain crimson flag which is the emblem of the Derry Siege.

"Mr Craig's theme was law and order. The government had failed to maintain law and order and had betrayed Ulster by disarming the Royal Ulster Constabulary and disbanding the B Specials. The RUC must be re-armed – whether they wanted to be rearmed or not – and the Specials reconstituted. There would have to be a new government which would do all this and generally restore order by all means necessary, possibly including 'the use of methods that might make me shudder'.

"A young man who had been behind me stumbled against me, stood beside me and asked me what was inside my coat that made it bulge. I told him books. He asked to see the books and I produced them. The book on top was *The Pope is the Devil.* He looked puzzled, relaxed a little, smiled and said: 'Sorry, I thought you might be the reporter for the *Derry Journal*' – the local Catholic and Irish Nationalist paper.

"Mr Craig reiterated his point about re-forming the B Specials. Most of the audience clapped but a good many did not. Ulster Protestants are an undemonstrative breed. The young man who had bumped against me asked me why I didn't clap. I said I didn't clap because I didn't agree with a lot the speaker had said (by this time I had a fair idea that I was going to get a beating and on the whole preferred being beaten without having clapped to clapping and then getting beaten as well). The young man told me I was to clap. I told him – speaking within the context of the emphasis on law and order – that it was my lawful right to decide whether to clap or not to clap at a public meeting. This was an unsatisfactory reply.

"The substance of Mr Craig's remarks was inflammatory, but his manner and delivery were quiet. He was succeeded by a 'Free Presbyterian' (Paisleyite) minister who said the same sort of thing, but in a scream. The temperature went up. The applause became more frequent and several young men moved in around us clapping frequently and vigorously and nudging us with their elbows as they did so. Then they started kicking our legs quite gently from behind. None of these was an Apprentice Boy.

"We moved away from them in order to leave the ground, slowly. For the moment they did not follow. As we moved away a big man in Apprentice Boys regalia came up. He suggested we should leave the grounds immediately. We said we asked for nothing better and moved away with him. As we were doing so several of the young men who had been jostling us came up and struck us. I got a bloody nose and lip; Séamus MacEntee – Máire's brother who was with me – a lump on the head. The Apprentice Boy told them to go away and was joined by two other Apprentice Boys with the same message. They drew back and we went on with our Apprentice Boys. One of them said it was foolish of us to come. We could not very well disagree, and he did not rub the point in. The other said he believed in defending Ulster but didn't believe in this kind of violence. He pointed out that our assailants were not Apprentice Boys.

"At this point we had got about halfway across a large meadow, following a route that was intended to take us clear of the crowd toward the police ranks. (Police were at the exits of the ground, not on the ground itself.) A large group of young men now came running toward us from behind. They were more purposeful this time. An identification had occurred. They wanted "to get O'Brien". They hit me several times and I fell down, then they started kicking me. An Apprentice Boy said: 'Is it murder ye want?' After a short while they stopped kicking and went away. I was shaken and sore but not badly hurt; Séamus – who had been trying to pull back my main assailants but who had not been attacked by them this time – said that the long wet grass got in the way of their boots.

"We walked away through the long wet grass with the three Apprentice Boys for about a quarter of a mile. At the edge of the meadow we met a Royal Ulster Constabulary man who took us over to a police car. Our Apprentice Boy guides disappeared at this point. As we got into the police car a small crowd – it was near the exit to the grounds and near the end of the meeting – took notice of us and began to shout. One man said: 'Ye didn't get half enough.' There was nothing personal in this anger; our former assailants had not followed and nobody in this crowd recognised me. It was just that I was bleeding from the nose and mouth, I had obviously been beaten up at the Apprentice Boys rally, and was therefore clearly a troublemaker and enemy of Ulster. As the police car drew away the crowd began to hammer with fists and umbrellas on its roof and windows."

Not long after this episode I got a postcard from Omagh: "I see you got a Protestant beating-up in Derry. If you come to Omagh I promise you a Catholic beating-up."

* * *

In June of 1971 I came for the first time to take a definite and distinctive position in relation to what was happening in and around the North. This occurred after the outbreak of the Provisional IRA's military offensive in Northern Ireland in the first half of 1971.

The Irish Transport and General Workers' Union held its annual conference in Galway from June 8 to 11, 1971. As a member of the union and of the Dáil I attended the conference. The Northern question did not dominate the proceedings, but there was one significant resolution calling for the release of all political prisoners. What this meant was well understood by all. A resolution in support of the IRA could not be carried at a meeting of this kind. The respectable middle-aged fathers of families who made up the bulk of the delegates generally disliked violence and, like most citizens of the Republic, had been on the whole repelled and puzzled by the ferocity of the Provisional's campaign. But "release the prisoners" was calculated to touch a reflex formed by Irish history. The boys might be mistaken, but they were ours, and brave, and resembled the patriots of the past, and the least you could do for them was to call for their release. Republicans, influential in the union hierarchy, could therefore confidently expect that a resolution of this kind would be carried unanimously by conference, without question and without discussion. The passage of the resolution could afterwards be invoked by Sinn Féin-IRA as proof that the organised working class was behind the republican movement, of which the advancing edge was the Provisional offensive in the North.

Having been brought up in a release-the-prisoners culture – of which my Aunt Hanna had been a pillar, along with Madame MacBride and

Madame Despard – I did not need to have any of this explained to me. I also understood that with a "release-the-prisoners resolution" the thing to do, if you could not actually support it, was to shut up, and preferably keep out of the way altogether. Republicans will tolerate general condemnations of violence, specific condemnations of particular acts of violence, and even verbal attacks on the IRA. People who talked like that were soft and wishy-washy but not necessarily bad at heart; they were inferior to republicans, but still they were Irishmen of a sort. But to question "release the prisoners" was to refuse the *minimum* republicans expected of all Irishmen, and thus to risk exclusion from the Irish nation, in one way or another.

The previous winter I had been a speaker at a meeting convened to call for the release of Miss Bernadette Devlin. As a result of skilful republican floor-management, the meeting had been converted to one calling for the release of all "political prisoners". I had protested about this to the chairman, but had not made my protest public. I was in politics, and I knew very well what bad politics such a public protest would be.

By June 1971, it was still bad politics, but bad politics into which I felt constrained to plunge. Thinking about the implications of the Provisionals' offensive it seemed to me that failure to question "release the prisoners" now would be a kind of combined connivance and betrayal, rather closely analogous to the policy pursued by Mr Lynch, in relation to "the defence of our people".

The resolution was formally proposed and seconded, without speeches, on the morning of June 11. I then got up and asked what was a political prisoner? If, for example, a man booby-trapped a car, putting children's lives at risk and killing innocent civilians – if that man were tried, sentenced and imprisoned could he then become one of the political prisoners for whose release we were asked to call?

One press report of the conference said I was "shouted down"; another that I was "roundly condemned by conference". Neither of these things happened. My short and almost entirely interrogative speech was heard in complete silence, and applauded at the end by most delegates. Then a series of republican speakers, mostly ex-prisoners or internees, took the stand and made the air ring with the names of the patriot dead. None of the speeches answered my questions. All of them denounced me for asking them. All of them were also applauded by most delegates, and very loudly indeed by a minority.

I had not consulted Brendan Corish before I made the case against "release the prisoners". I knew I should have done so, because my intervention was potentially embarrassing for him, both politically and financially. It would be unpopular with a large section of the party, and the hostility of the ITGWU, which paid the electoral expenses of party members who were also members of the union (including myself), could also be financially damaging. Corish, after I had come under attack, got up to speak. I didn't know what he was going to say any more than he had known what I was going to say when I got up to speak. He spoke briefly and calmly. He fully endorsed everything that I had said.

His endorsement meant that I could stick to the line I had adumbrated at Galway, and remain spokesman on Northern Ireland as long as Corish remained leader of the party, as he did throughout the entire period in which I held my Dáil seat. But I was henceforward and have always remained anathema as far as the republican movement was concerned. Within that there were different shades. One of my republican sponsors in the general election, George Gilmore, coldly denounced me. But the other, Peadar O'Donnell, when I met him shortly afterwards, greeted me in a friendly manner. Thanking him, I intimated that this was more than I could have hoped for. "Your fellow republican bishop," I said "has excommunicated me." Peadar laughed. "That's the way we bishops are," he said. "Some of us excommunicate the sinner, others just pray for him like I'm praying for you."

* * *

That week-end in Galway set me on a course which I have followed for almost all the rest of my life. But there was one very brief but marked exception: in the days immediately following Bloody Sunday in January 1972.

On Sunday, January 30, when an illegal "anti-internment" rally was held in Derry, British paratroops, taking aim and firing, shot dead thirteen young Derrymen, all Catholics.

I wasn't in Derry that day and I don't know "exactly what happened". Even if I had been there I should only know a small part of it. Nor did I expect to learn what happened from the official report – the Widgery Report – published in mid-April. However good the intentions of the Lord Chief Justice of England, who conducted the enquiry, the material with which he had to deal, and the pressures upon him, were such as to induce scepticism about his conclusions. As regards the material, the French have the expression "to lie like an eyewitness", the English the expression "to lie like a trooper". As regards the pressures, an English judge, confronted with the testimony of an Irish eyewitness and a British trooper, may well prefer the testimony of the trooper. And the introduction to the report reflects the fact that a report unacceptable to the army would have been extremely inconvenient.

I shared therefore in the scepticism with which the Catholics of Ireland, received the Widgery report, largely exonerating the paratroops.

But scepticism, accompanied by a mild degree of resentment at "British hypocrisy", was in April, after Widgery. What swept the country (consisting of the above) at the end of January and in early February was a great wave of emotion, compounded of grief, shock, and a sort of astonished incredulous rage against an England which seemed to be acting in the way we often accused her of acting but of which we had not for decades really believed modern England capable. The scenario seemed to have slipped back to 1921, or even earlier. For a few days, people talked and wrote of a national change of mood like that which had set in after the executions of 1916. A Dublin periodical came out with Yeats' words "a terrible beauty" on its front cover. The "thirteen dead men", it seemed, would do what the "sixteen dead men" had done. The bony thumb sharply increased its pressure. Mr. Lynch withdrew our ambassador from London. And Sinn Féin-IRA, and its friends in the press and media, set themselves both to exploit this mood and to convert it into one of settled hatred, appropriate to a war of Ireland against England.

I shared, and still share, the belief that what happened in Derry was murder, in the sense that the troops deliberately shot dead young men who had probably been baiting them in various ways, but who were probably not endangering their lives. This was what seemed to emerge from the reports of the more reliable correspondents present (such as Simon Winchester of *The Guardian*). About this, I shared most of the feelings of those around me. But I also feared, more than most, the exploitation of these killings in order to justify other killings, and in order to involve the territory and people of the Republic also in widening, intensifying violence.

I spent the three days after Bloody Sunday in London, where I saw Harold Wilson, Jeremy Thorpe, and the Home Secretary, Reginald Maudling. I went to report to them on the mood of the people in the

Republic, but it seems to me now, in retrospect, that I was not so much an authority on that mood as an example of it. When I saw Maudling I was running a high temperature and was not making a great deal of sense. It is possible that this was fortunate; I may have made more impact than if I had made more sense, more impact as an exhibit than as an analyst. He knew that I had been saying, both in Ireland and in the international press, that if the British troops were withdrawn under prevailing conditions sectarian civil war would follow. What I had now to say was that I still believed that to be true, but that the continued presence of the troops, after Derry, had also a disaster potential. Not merely would any repetition of Bloody Sunday be likely to involve cross-border retaliation – and inhibit a Dublin government from checking such retaliation – but the actual presence of British troops would act on the Catholic population, after Derry, as a standing justification for the IRA, strengthening their hold on the ghettoes. I therefore urged, not the immediate withdrawal of the troops, but the setting of a date for eventual withdrawal.

When, shortly afterwards, I made public this view, in London and in New York, Erskine Holmes, chairman of the Northern Ireland Labour Party, reproached me with practising, or yielding to, what he called "the politics of the last atrocity". There is substance in this reproach. To a considerable extent I was responding to the prevailing mood of my own community to the point of losing sight of the reactions of the other community, whose sense of being abandoned on the setting of a date for the departure of the troops, might well be at least as dangerous as the feelings of the Catholic community about the continued presence of the troops. To that extent, I was over-reacting. Yet what I said was true, in so far as it concerned the relation of the troops to the Catholic community. It is also true that one cannot work for better relations between the two communities in Ireland while remaining completely impervious to the feelings of one's own community. I am sometimes accused of being impervious to these feelings but I am not.

The day I saw Maudling (Wednesday, February 2) was the day of the funerals of the thirteen in Derry. That evening in Dublin members of the IRA, acting under cover of a large, but mainly peaceful, mass demonstration, burned down the British Embassy in Merrion Square. That night, from London, I rang my wife in Dublin. Máire, having been educated almost entirely among Catholics, is usually closer to "the mood of the people" than I am: not the mood the press and media depict, or the mood republicans declare to exist, but the way (Catholic) people generally are in fact responding. She warned me not to exaggerate the post-Derry response. It wasn't a "1916" swing: no "terrible beauty" was in fact being born. The grief and shock were genuine, so had the resentment against England been, especially at the time I left (Monday), but by now the IRA had over-reached themselves in their exploitation of these feelings. In particular the burning of the embassy had been a mistake from an IRA point of view. People were afraid of lawless violence "coming down here". They didn't want any kind of war with England, even an economic war, from which Ireland would suffer more than England. They knew the burning of the embassy would have to be paid for, in terms of jobs and trade and tourists, and they were not in any such mood of exaltation as would induce them to accept sacrifices.

So I calmed down and reverted to my former view, which has been my view ever since, that, whatever difficulties might attend the presence of British troops in Northern Ireland, their withdrawal would be followed by the far greater disaster of full scale civil war.

* * *

As well as being preoccupied with Northern Ireland during this period, I had also to think about electoral politics in the Republic: not quite a completely separate subject but very nearly so. In the period of euphoric hubris before the general election of 1969, under the slogan "The Seventies will be Socialist", the Labour Party had pledged itself never again to go into coalition, without the prior consent of the party's annual conference. I was among those who believed that the party had no future if it ruled out coalition, and that coalition meant coalition with Fine Gael. I believed that Fianna Fáil, with its close ties with Sinn Féin-IRA and with the sinister and equivocal presence of CJ Haughey, was in an extremely dangerous condition and that the only combination capable of putting it out was a Fine Gael-Labour coalition.

I was fortified in this commitment by the perception that the elements in the Labour Party who were most bitterly opposed to a coalition with Fine Gael were those who sympathized in varying degrees with the Provisional IRA. The leading sympathizer was the unstable David Thornley, whom the Sinn Féin lobbyists flattered absurdly, while laughing at him behind his back.

All this meant that I was entirely happy to be part of a pro-coalition band-wagon in the run-up to the general election of 1973. This won me some new and – I would earlier have thought – unlikely allies. One of these was the Kerry Deputy, Dan Spring, father of Dick Spring, later to be leader of the Labour Party. At the end of the party conference which set the party free to engage in coalition, Dan came up to me and draped an enormous arm round my shoulders. "That was a nice speech you made there, boy," he said, "but that was a nice two busloads of delegates I brought up from Kerry there too, boy."

I took his point. I knew that my nice speech carried a lot less weight in practical politics than two busloads of delegates. I came to have a high regard for Dan Spring. He said little in the Dáil or out of it, but what he said was always to the point. He was the author of a statement which I don't think can ever be surpassed for its combination of brevity and wit, in just three monosyllables. He made it a little later than the period I have just been discussing. We were in government and a leading Fianna Fáiler, Brian Lenihan, was engaged in a filibuster. He was interrupted from the government side and – as a good filibusterer should – he took advantage of the interruption to prolong his time-wasting remarks. He affected to be deeply shocked by the frivolity of the interruption and put on a solemn expression. "This is a very serious and important subject," he said.

Dan Spring, silent up to then, leaned forward and said, in his deep, carrying voice, simply:

"Sit down so!"

Beautiful!

* * *

Things had been going rather well for me, on the whole, in Irish politics up to near the end of my first term in the Dáil. But then there was a hitch which was near to getting me expelled from the party. John Hume's SDLP had just come out with a proposal for joint administration of Northern Ireland by the British and Irish administrations. I thought this was a crazy idea, but I knew it would be very rash, in terms of "Twenty-Six County" politics, to say so. In those terms, it has long been mandatory – and still remains so – to say "me too" to whatever John Hume says. Garret FitzGerald, with whom I was in quite close touch in those days over the formation of the coming coalition, advised me that if I could not actually support joint administration, I should at least be silent about it. But I believed the proposal to be exceedingly dangerous and if I didn't say so I didn't feel I could live with myself. So I publicly attacked the SDLP proposal, and immediately fastened my political seat-belt.

Around the same time, my book *States of Ireland*, mainly devoted to the North, was published. John Hume reviewed it for the *Irish Times* and called it "the best statement of the Ulster unionist case ever written". Looking back on it, over a gap of about a quarter of a century, I can see this was quite a perceptive diagnosis. But at the time it sounded rather like a political death-sentence.

After my attack on joint administration, and the publication of *States of Ireland* followed by John Hume's review, my enemies in the party, led by David Thornley, put down a motion for my expulsion from the party. Looking back on it, I can see that this was a bridge too far. If they had put down a simple vote of censure, this would almost certainly have been carried, and would have precipitated my resignation.

The party met and my resignation was debated. The general feeling of the meeting was against me. Most of those present cared very little about the merits or demerits of joint administration, etc. But they all knew that adverse criticism of anything whatever favoured by John Hume was bad news on the eve of the general election. It might cost any of them votes. So there was quite a run of speeches against me. My friends maintained an awkward silence. I knew most of them felt I had put my foot in it, although most of them respected my motives for so doing. But there was a surprise intervention from Justin Keating, with whom I had been up to this point, on what I took to be friendly terms. Justin was seated not at the table, where he usually was, but right behind me. From that position he said he could not vote for my expulsion, but he appealed to me to resign "in the interests of the party". In my reply to the debate I said: "I've got news for Justin Keating. I'm not going to resign. If he wants to get rid of me he should vote for my expulsion."

I think on the whole Justin's intervention did me good rather than harm. Parliamentarians tend to put derogatory interpretations on one another's motivations. Justin's motive seemed rather obvious to some. A coalition was coming up, and Labour would have a limited number of ministerial seats in a coalition government. Both Justin and I were contenders. If I could be eliminated, Justin's chances would be significantly enhanced. So the old hands interpreted the situation and I don't think they were far wrong. Justin himself probably saw it differently. His mother was a strong republican, like my Aunt Hanna, and he himself was republican enough not to like what I was saying. But he liked it a lot less, in my opinion, when he saw it was to his advantage not to like it at all.

In any case, the motion failed to get a majority after a strong and excellent speech by Corish appealing for party unity. Corish had done his best for me and when the time came round he would put both Justin and myself in the new coalition government.

15

IN GOVERNMENT IN THE REPUBLIC,
1973-1977

AFTER THE ELECTIONS OF 1973, FINE GAEL AND LABOUR BETWEEN THEM
had a majority in the new Dáil. Negotiations for the formation of a
coalition government began immediately. I was at a pub in Coolock called
The Sheaf Of Wheat, thanking my party workers in an appropriate way,
when I received a call from Corish offering me a seat in the new
government as Minister for Posts and Telegraphs (later known as
"Communications"). Corish indicated that within the coalition I would
retain my functions as spokesman for the party on foreign affairs and
Northern Ireland.

I accepted Corish's offer immediately. I was slightly disappointed not to
be offered the post for which I was best qualified, that of Minister for
Foreign Affairs. I can see in retrospect that I was quite wrong to be
disappointed. For me the post of Minister for Foreign Affairs in that
government would have been a fatal trap. John Hume was by now my
deadly enemy, politically speaking, and John had enormous weight in the
politics of the Republic in any matter with a bearing on Northern Ireland.
The only way I could have placated John Hume on becoming Minister for
Foreign Affairs, would have been by immediately reversing my opposition
to joint administration, and then slavishly following the SDLP line as laid

down by John Hume. I could not do that. And as I could not do that, John Hume would have driven me from office, by telling Corish and Cosgrave that if they did not drop me forthwith he would denounce the coalition government as "anti-national". And if he did that the two parliamentary parties would split, the government would fall, and the two component parties would be wiped out at the ensuing general election.

I did not consider any of that when I took on John Hume over joint administration. And the fact that I did not consider it shows how much I had changed from the man who had won two out-of-line promotions from Seán MacBride in the Department of External Affairs, by doing whatever MacBride wanted. If I had still been continuous with that young man in the political conditions of the late 1960s and early 1970 and had coveted the post of Minister for Foreign Affairs, I would have seen immediately that the key to advancement was the cultivation of John Hume. When John came out for joint administration, I would have written "thoughtful" articles praising the wisdom and statesmanship of this policy. So John Hume would have urged my appointment as Minister for Foreign Affairs. So supported, I would have been appointed and I would have been rated a success as Minister. And I would have been ruined, morally and intellectually. But I had never even considered appeasing John Hume, nor had I weighed, even for a moment, the probable cost to my career if I failed to appease him. So I seem to have made some progress, morally and politically, since my MacBride period, and lost some ground in terms of career-oriented political success.

* * *

The new government consisted of five Labour members and ten from Fine Gael. Liam Cosgrave was Taoiseach and Brendan Corish Tanaiste (Deputy Prime Minister). The Labour ministers (besides Corish and myself) were Jimmy Tully, Minister for Local Government; Justin Keating, Minister for Industry and Commerce; and Michael O'Leary, Minister for Labour. The most prominent Fine Gael member, after the Taoiseach, was Garret FitzGerald, Minister for Foreign Affairs.

Corish and Cosgrave worked well together; both were politically cautious, temperamentally equable and personally considerate. In general, most of the members of the two component parties got on well with one another; there was never any clash ranging members of the two parties against one another. Such lines of division as there were ran within each of the component parties. Tully, O'Leary and I all disliked Keating and he also must have disliked us, since he knew what we felt about him. But we kept our mutual dislike under control. As used to be said about the dealings between the Irish and Swedish officers in the Congo: "Relations are correct with a capital K".

The divisions within the Fine Gael contingent were more serious. There, there was a smouldering contest for the future leadership of the party, the challenger being Garret FitzGerald. Just as many of us Labour people did not trust Justin, so many of the Fine Gael people did not trust Garret. And, curiously, a working alliance emerged between Garret and Justin. We believed – and indeed soon thought we knew – that Justin's great objective was a European commissionership. Garret, as Foreign Minister, was the person best placed to win him that objective and so he cultivated Garret, and worked against Cosgrave along with him.

Personally, I liked and trusted both Corish and Cosgrave and was happy to work for both of them (I had of course worked for Cosgrave before, in Foreign Affairs and in the delegation to the United Nations). In a little celebration the two parties had after the victory of the coalition, Cosgrave talked about the sufferings of those who, in Fine Gael's lean years, had deserted the party for Fianna Fáil and were now out again. I told Liam of a New Yorker cartoon which showed two starving half-naked men chained in a dungeon, one of whom is explaining to the other: "I thought they couldn't be licked. So I joined them and somebody else licked them."

Liam had a curious explosive laugh, seldom heard. That story produced an explosion. Not long afterwards, I was to hear another one.

* * *

Shortly after the formation of the new government, the President, Eamon de Valera, invited the members of the government to have dinner at the presidential residence, Áras an Uachtaráin. We were a little surprised to be invited. The President must be presumed to have been chagrined by the defeat of the party founded by him, Fianna Fáil, and he had also an excellent excuse for not inviting people. He was now over ninety and in poor health. But he had invited us, and of course we accepted and attended.

The dinner, as might be expected in the circumstances, was a polite and rather subdued affair. During the dinner de Valera was silent, and we did not expect him to speak at all. However, at the end of the dinner, he did get up to speak. He had difficulty both in getting up and in standing. At this stage of his life his spine was severely bent back, and he was constantly in pain. He had also difficulty in speaking but he spoke clearly though spasmodically.

His opening remarks seemed strangely inauspicious. He said:

"I always opposed . . . the electoral system known as proportional representation . . . because I saw that if persisted in . . . that system must one day lead . . . to coalition government."

At those last words Liam's explosive laugh was heard throughout the banqueting hall. He had a glass of whiskey to his lips at the time, and the whiskey splashed over the table. Dev didn't seem to be aware of this incident. He continued calmly.

"It seems to me . . . that coalition government . . . can only work properly . . . if all its members feel . . . and are guided . . . at all times . . . by a feeling . . . of personal loyalty to their Taoiseach." Then Dev sat down.

Liam didn't laugh at those words. He looked quite moved. So was I moved, and also determined to follow Dev's advice, as I consistently did, throughout the life of the coalition government.

* * *

Very early on in its tenure the new government found itself required to discharge a commitment to introduce a highly contentious piece of legislation. This was the first attempt to repeal those laws of the Republic which prohibited the importation or sale of contraceptives.

The laws in question had been introduced in the early years of the new state. Those were years in which the authority of the Catholic Church was virtually all-powerful in any area in which the Church chose to exert that authority. One such area, and apparently the most important for the Church, was the area of family law.

In the thirty years between the first banning of contraceptives and the first legislative attempt to lift the ban, the authority of the Church had certainly slipped, but the extent to which it had slipped remained open to question. It was already clear – from the pattern of the birth statistics – that young Catholic married people were ignoring the ban. Contraceptives could, in practice, be acquired quite easily by a trip to Belfast. All the same many young Catholics were irritated by the ban, which appeared to criminalise them, and so they seemed ready to vote for repeal. It was quite clear that there was a majority for repeal in Dublin, and other large urban centres, where the authority of the Church already appeared to have seriously waned.

How far it had actually waned was still a matter of controversy. While in opposition I had been present at a well-attended conference in Dublin which addressed that matter. One priest said that the authority of the Church had completely gone among young, urban working-class Catholics. Members of this grouping, he said, never now referred simply to "priests". They always called them "fucking priests". This meant that the authority of the clergy was completely gone, as far as this large section was concerned.

Another priest then intervened. He agreed that many working-class people now referred to "fucking priests". But this did not necessarily imply any alienation from the Church. The same young men would refer to "fucking frying-pans" but that did not imply any alienation from frying-pans.

I thought that a neat debating-point but no more. I thought that twenty years before, a youth who would readily refer to "fucking frying-pans" would never have referred to "fucking priests". The priests were then still surrounded by the kind of numinous halo which would have made such language seem impossibly blasphemous. But now the halo had vanished with negative implications for the future of the Church in the urban areas.

Those who opposed the repeal of the anti-contraception laws appeared to be in a minority in the urban areas, but they appeared to be a majority in rural areas. This did not worry Labour very much, for Labour had few seats, outside urban areas. But it did worry Fine Gael TDs with rural seats to defend, as they prepared to support the repeal of the anti-contraception laws. Fianna Fáil, which had won the 1969 general election with the help of the Church, thought that to fight the repeal of the anti-contraception laws, with even more enthusiastic support from the Church, would put them on a winner again. So they prepared for battle, with relish.

After the decision to repeal the anti-contraception laws had been made public, rural Fine Gael TDs went off to take soundings in their constituencies. They returned with long faces, though also sometimes with amusing stories. One Fine Gael minister, Peter Barry, told us of a conversation with an aunt of his in north Cork. She had said to him: "What's all this about contraceptives, Peter? Didn't all of us come into the world without those things?"

Which was incontrovertible.

* * *

If all the TDs belonging to the government parties voted for repeal, repeal would carry. But it soon appeared that it was doubtful that all government TDs would vote in favour. Ominously, the Taoiseach refused to make any such commitment himself, or to demand such a commitment from others. I in particular pressed the Taoiseach to say which way he personally would vote in the free vote on which he insisted. He refused. It was a personal matter with him; he didn't want to influence anyone else's vote.

Most of my colleagues seemed to feel that the Taoiseach would have to vote in the end with his colleagues. Anything else was inconceivable. Having listened carefully to what the Taoiseach had said, and having got to know him fairly well, I didn't think it inconceivable.

When the vote came round, Liam Cosgrave made for the "No" lobby at a smart pace. Dick Burke, the normally very Catholic Minister for Education, was headed resignedly for the "Yes" lobby, when he saw Liam headed for "No". Dick immediately swung away from the "Yes" direction and joined his leader under "No".

There were enough defections from "Yes" to give "No" a victory on the Second Reading.

There was consternation – even excessive consternation – in the coalition ranks at what was seen by some as our leader's defection. The debate had continued to a late hour and further confabulations went on into the small hours. Michael O'Leary told me of one such confabulation in the small hours of the morning in Leinster House, when the cleaners had already arrived. TDs were eagerly discussing the Taoiseach's decision, some of them attributing this to rather fine-spun motivations. Then one of the cleaners, who had been on all fours scrubbing the committee-room floor while listening to the discussion, suddenly could stand it no longer. She got up on her hunkers and said: "What else could you expect him to do? *Sure wasn't he an altar-boy until he was twenty-four?*"

This was so obviously the truth that the subtle politicians dispersed, without further argument.

There was – though for rather a short time – a lot of murmuring at what was seen by some as Cosgrave's treachery. Garret and Justin were giving "off-the-record" briefings along those lines. I countered their activities by noting that the Taoiseach had not let anyone down or failed to honour any commitment. He had insisted on a free vote, and then made use of the freedom on which he had insisted. Personally I regretted that he had voted as he did and I had voted the other way. But I was not about to complain that he had let me down. He had not let anyone down.

In doing this I was quite conscious that I was acting in the manner which Eamon de Valera had advised in giving unwavering loyalty to the Taoiseach. And I am still glad that I did so.

* * *

As for Liam Cosgrave, he signified his personal trust in me by assigning to me delicate new responsibilities, in addition to those of my ministry. He made me responsible at political level for the Government Information Bureau, and consequently for relations with the press. It was rather remarkable that the leader of much the larger party in the coalition should choose to assign such a sensitive area to a member of the smaller party. But I think Liam Cosgrave had adequate political reasons for acting in this way. He knew that some of his Fine Gael colleagues were biding their time, with the long-term intention of replacing him in the leadership, while not being averse, in the short term, to leaking information intended to bring on him a mild degree of discredit. Most of his colleagues were uncommitted as to the future leadership and some might come to lean against him. There were no more than two of Cosgrave's colleagues, who were known to be unconditionally loyal to him, and for Liam to give either of these such a sensitive post would signal distrust of other colleagues and increase the strains within the party. So it must have seemed logical to look to the other party for a reliable handler of the press. His choice fell on me.

Just at this time, the post of Director of the Government Information Bureau fell vacant, and it became incumbent on me with my new responsibilities to propose a name. While I was pondering this choice, I happened to meet Joan FitzGerald, Garret's wife, at a party and she proposed a name: Muiris MacConghail, whom I knew as one of the most distinguished telecasters in the country, and a first-class mind. I suppose I might have been put off by the fact that his name was proposed by the wife of the most notorious leaker in the cabinet, whose activities the new director would have to police, as far as he could. In the circumstances I might have distrusted Joan's proposal. I knew Joan herself to be perfectly straight, and believed her to be ignorant of what might be called the darker side of her husband's character. And indeed it was one of Garret's strengths that he himself was unaware of any darker side. He lived in the sunny confidence that he was invariably acting for the common good which, by a happy coincidence, often coincided with his own good.

In any case I acted on Joan's recommendation. I recommended Muiris, the government agreed, and he was appointed. We worked closely together throughout the remaining years of the coalition government and became close friends. Our common objective was to see that the coalition did not break up. The two previous coalition governments had come down in pieces, amid bitter recriminations, lending credibility to the Fianna Fáil message that coalitions don't work. We saw – in conformity with de Valera's message – that loyalty of the two parties to their Taoiseach, for the duration of the coalition, was the surest way to come down in one piece. We did come down in one piece, and coalitions soon became, and still remain, the norm in Irish politics.

* * *

Relations with Northern Ireland quickly became for a time, at least ostensibly, the main preoccupation of the government. This was an unusual condition. The main preoccupation of the Republic's politicians is normally with the people who elect them: the adult population of the twenty-six counties. This is quite a healthy condition, democratically speaking, but the Republic's politicians generally feel at least subliminally uncomfortable with it. One of Fianna Fáil's two "national aims" since its foundation has been "the reunification of the national territory", a goal enshrined in the Constitution by de Valera and still maintained. The other parties also cherish the idea of reunification, but more faintly. My own party was now pledged to aim at the amendment of Articles 2 and 3, but was aware that this was a far-off goal.

The reunification idea is always floating around in there somewhere in twenty-six county politics, and it is of course kept alive by IRA activity. But it doesn't become a live issue in the democratic politics of the Republic unless there is some British initiative.

In 1975 the subject came alive through the initiative of the British Tory government, under Ted Heath, which led to the Sunningdale Agreement. I believe that the initial British idea had been simply that there should be a coalition government in Northern Ireland, in which both unionists and nationalists would take part, in proportion to their electoral strength. But John Hume – without whose approval the idea would not have the requisite nationalist support – stipulated that there should be an All-Ireland dimension in the shape of a Council of Ireland, felt to be the precursor of a united Ireland, and cherished for that reason by those who did cherish it.

When the matter came before the cabinet for discussion, I warmly welcomed the idea of a bipartisan government for Northern Ireland. But I thought the Council of Ireland, with the implication of progress towards a united Ireland, might be a bridge too far. On that issue, the unionist population might desert Brian Faulkner, and the Northern coalition government would then collapse. I therefore urged that the idea of a Council of Ireland be re-examined.

I think a reasonable response to my objection might have run more or less as follows: "There may well be some such danger as you suggest. But this deal is what the British government accepts, at John Hume's urging, and the unionists now seem prepared to go along with it. So how can we, the government of Ireland, say that it goes too far in the direction of Irish unity?"

That would have been reasonable, but that was not the answer I got. Garret answered, in a tone of cold superiority such as he had never used to me before, that my information was out of date. Northern Ireland was no longer like that. The Protestant population would accept the Council of Ireland without any difficulty. This I knew was a certitude he had derived from John Hume. The Attorney General, Declan Costello – one of the two most vocally Catholic members of that government – intervened to support Garret. The other members of the government, including my Labour colleagues, remained silent. I was acutely conscious in that moment that I was the only person in that room who was acknowledged not to be a practising Catholic.

My mind went back to an earlier episode, of less political importance, in which the same reflection had been forced upon me. This occurred after the publication of the report of the Public Accounts Committee on misapplication of funds appropriated for the relief of distress in Northern Ireland in 1969, when Jack Lynch's Fianna Fáil government had been in power. The report showed that some of the funds so appropriated had been applied to the purchase of arms for use in Northern Ireland (which were eventually used by the Provos). I thought we should exploit this report against Fianna Fáil. The Minister for Finance, when the moneys were misappropriated was CJ Haughey, now once more a rising star in Fianna Fáil.

The then Minister for Finance, Richie Ryan, smiled thinly and indicated without explanation that he did not propose to do anything about the report. Nobody else around that table had anything to say on the subject. I knew the reason: the funds in question had been solicited by members of the SDLP for the defence of "our people in the North". Our people in the North – except occasionally for certain specialized rhetorical effects – are the Catholics exclusively. The others are non-people or, if people, not ours. Proper Catholics understand all that instinctively, without anyone having to draw a map for them. As a non-Catholic, I couldn't be expected to get the message clearly. But I should realize that I was now among people who got that message, and I should know my place.

I felt, in that room, on those two occasions and later on a few others, as if I was surrounded by a wall of glass, as I was clearly visible to the others, but totally inaudible.

* * *

In spite of that rather glaring handicap of mine, Corish kept me on as Labour Party spokesman on Foreign Affairs and Northern Ireland. He did so against sustained pressure from the SDLP, and I think some pressure also from Garret, through Justin Keating. I would have his support for being spokesman, but not explicit support for what I actually said. If he explicitly backed me up, the SDLP would move to destroy the Labour Party, and could at least inflict great damage. So he would keep me there but not back me up against the SDLP. In retrospect, I fully understand and respect his position but at the time I felt a bit unrequited.

Both Corish and Cosgrave still had quite a lot of time for me, short of risking a suicidal confrontation with John Hume for my sake. Corish nominated me – as Labour Party spokesman on Northern Ireland – to the Irish governmental delegation to the Sunningdale negotiations on future arrangements for Northern Ireland. Cosgrave approved the nomination, so to Sunningdale I went.

I was accompanied by Muiris MacConghail, as responsible for relations with the press at Sunningdale. On that front there was an early hitch, which actually helped to clear the air. Muiris gave a press conference at which the account of our first meeting was slanted to the detriment of the unionists, who were furious. I understood how Muiris had been led to do this. To try to put down unionists came naturally to anyone who had been brought up a nationalist, and it would have been a reflex with me, not long before. But I told Muiris this approach would not serve in the new conditions. The unionists who had approved the broad outline of Sunningdale were in grave danger of being repudiated by their own constituents. Any move we might make against them increased that danger. We were committed, rightly or wrongly, to try to make Sunningdale work, and that clearly meant helping the Faulkner unionists and not making life any more difficult for them than it was already. Muiris fully took the point and we never had any further divergence of view about it.

To Faulkner I publicly acknowledged that the press release had misrepresented the unionist position. I expressed regret for this, and promised that nothing of the kind would occur again. Brian Faulkner was favourably impressed by this move, and from that time on I had a good personal relationship with him.

Faulkner wanted us, before concluding any agreement, to undertake to repeal Articles 2 and 3 of the Republic's Constitution. I told him that my own party was committed in principle to the repeal of these Articles, and I personally was strongly in favour of repeal. But if we were to pledge ourselves at Sunningdale to repeal the Articles we would be unable to redeem our pledge. There would have to be a referendum. Fianna Fáil would fight repeal, pulling out all the nationalist stops, and I had absolutely no doubt that Fianna Fáil, strongly backed by John Hume, would defeat the amendment. Thus any unionists who trusted our promise to repeal – were we so irresponsible as to make such a promise – would be seen by their own followers to have been tricked. Faulkner saw the point and dropped the demand for an undertaking to repeal the Articles.

I had expected some trouble from my own delegation – and from Garret in particular – over my apology to the unionists and subsequent rather cosy relations with Brian Faulkner. But I ran into no such trouble for the duration of the Sunningdale negotiations. I had the impression that Garret had begun to realize that John Hume's assurances were ill-founded and that the Faulkner unionists were in real and serious danger and therefore so was the whole Sunningdale deal.

By this time also, John Hume's colleagues – especially Gerry Fitt, who was officially the leader of his party – were feeling that Hume was driving the unionists too hard. He was holding out for joint control of the RUC by the two governments, which neither Faulkner nor any other unionist could agree to. But Hume's colleagues forced him to drop that demand and eventually, after an all-night sitting, the Sunningdale Agreement was signed, setting up the SDLP-unionist coalition government and – in theory – also the Council of Ireland.

After the signature we had two forlorn meetings with Faulkner and colleagues to discuss the powers to be allocated to the Council of Ireland. The discussions took place in forbidding conditions. Northern Ireland was now paralysed by the loyalist workers' strike – including a strike of the power-workers. This was a protest against the Sunningdale Agreement, of which the most obnoxious feature to unionists was the Council of Ireland. We met Faulkner at Hillsborough, Co Down. But we had been told we could not get there safely by road, because of loyalist anger, and control of the streets in and around Hillsborough. So we travelled there by helicopter. Normally I enjoy travelling by helicopter and there is no better way of seeing the country, but these particular flights were a bit depressing, because of the circumstances which made recourse to helicopters necessary.

After a few weeks the unionist members of the joint executive – finding their own community to have turned against them – all resigned from the executive. With their resignation the whole elaborate apparatus set up at Sunningdale automatically collapsed. And all the unionists who had participated in Sunningdale, and in the joint administration, were to lose their seats at the following general election.

* * *

John Hume had been spectacularly wrong in the assurances he had given about the readiness of the unionist community to accept the Sunningdale Agreement, including the Council of Ireland. But John Hume was in no way discredited in the eyes of public opinion in the Republic by having got it all wrong, and having misled others, including the Dublin government. It soon became – and still remains – the version of these events that is accepted in the Republic that the British Government – by then a Labour one, under Harold Wilson – was to blame for the fall of the joint executive. They were to blame because they had not been prepared to use military force to suppress the loyalist workers' strike. It is not, at first, obvious how a strike can be suppressed by the use of military force. But the nationalist version had an answer to that one. The strike was not a real strike at all. It was entirely the result of intimidation by a handful of fanatical loyalists. If the British had had the nerve to take on these evil men, the workers would have flocked back to work, and the Sunningdale arrangements would have survived and flourished.

For the public, believing in this grotesque version of the facts, John Hume was in no way discredited by having got it all wrong, before and at Sunningdale. On the contrary he was seen as a wise hero, who, on the brink of a historic breakthrough, had been stabbed in the back by the perfidious British. Rather like Owen Roe O'Neill or Parnell, in the folklore version of the fates of these heroes.

For me, the aftermath of Sunningdale, with the setting in of the "British betrayal" myth and the mournful apotheosis of John Hume, was a bleak period; especially as I had a painful personal experience during this period of John Hume's continuing dominance, in all that related to Northern Ireland, over the government of which I was part. There was a conference in Belfast in the aftermath of Sunningdale in which nationalists and unionists took part. There was never any prospect that such a conference, in such circumstances, could result in agreement and – when asked about the matter in a radio interview – I said that I saw no prospect of such an agreement. When my words were published, John Hume immediately got on to Garret, to demand that my words be repudiated. And the government met and duly repudiated them. I was quite alone. All my colleagues, including Garret, knew that what I had said was true. That, however, was altogether irrelevant. The only relevant thing was that if the government did not repudiate me, John Hume might denounce the government. And no government in the Republic that was once denounced by John Hume stood a chance of being re-elected. So the government, with the assent of all my colleagues, duly repudiated what I had said. They did not name me, but everyone who followed Irish politics knew who had said the words repudiated.

So this whole period – in pre-Sunningdale, during Sunningdale itself, and especially post-Sunningdale – was a rather sad one for me. I briefly contemplated resignation but soon decided against it. I was altogether out of tune with my colleagues over Northern Ireland, but I would be even more out of tune in that range of issues with an alternative government based on Fianna Fáil. And as regards the actual governance of the Ireland which elected us, and to which alone we were electorally responsible – the Ireland of twenty-six counties – I was not out of tune with my colleagues. And, looking at the grim alternative of Fianna Fáil I still thought it important that the government I belonged to should serve its full term, thereby demonstrating – for the first time – that a coalition government could last for its full term, and was thus a viable alternative to Fianna Fáil.

Still, there were some funny moments even in this depressing period, though the fun might sometimes remind me of the degree of my isolation. One such moment came during a radio discussion with Dick Burke, then our very Catholic Minister for Education. The subject under discussion was, what characteristics of life in the Republic were off-putting to Ulster Protestants? While we were talking, our discussion was interrupted by a recording of the Angelus: a distinctively Catholic ceremony, broadcast by RTE at twelve noon and six o'clock every day since 1950, when it was introduced at what was then the irresistible behest of Archbishop John Charles McQuaid. While we in the studio were off-air, and listening to the bells, I said to my rather stunned interviewer that what we were listening to was a good example of the kind of thing that many Ulster Protestants found off-putting. When we were back on air the interviewer asked Dick Burke what he thought about what I had said about the Angelus and Ulster Protestants. Dick said sweetly: "I'm afraid I didn't hear what Conor said about the Angelus. I was meditating at the time."

Set and match.

* * *

I was by now altogether out of tune with the government to which I still belonged in all that pertained to the governance of Northern Ireland. But I was not out of tune as regards our actual business, for which we had been elected: the governance of the counties that made up the actual (as distinct from the hypothetical, or immanent) Republic of Ireland. In particular I was in tune with both the leaders of our coalition, Cosgrave and Corish, as regards the chief responsibility of any government: the security of the state in which we lived and whose inhabitants had elected us.

Cosgrave and Corish saw the IRA as the greatest and most abiding threat to that security, and I was in full agreement with them on that point. This was an area in which Cosgrave, in particular, would brook no interference even in the name of the Pope. When the Papal Nuncio – who tended to see the Provos as Catholic holy warriors – asked permission to visit IRA prisoners in Portlaoise (who were allegedly being ill-treated), Cosgrave curtly refused permission, without explanation.

A more exacting test of the determination of the Cosgrave-Corish government came over the kidnapping in Ireland of the Dutch industrialist, Tiede Herrema. Herrema had been kidnapped by a maverick republican group which called on the government to release the IRA prisoners in Portlaoise, in which case Herrema would be released in exchange. There was an implication that if the government failed to comply Herrema would be "executed".

When the government met to consider this republican ultimatum

Cosgrave said simply: "I take it we're all agreed that we don't reply". He then paused for perhaps half a second, leaving time for someone to object, if they were quick about it. I looked at Garret and Justin. I had the impression that they would have liked to object but were a bit afraid. Cosgrave then announced there was no objection and passed to the next business.

In the event, we and Herrema got lucky. The gardaí discovered where Herrema was being held and managed to rescue him and arrest his captors.

At this time, as I had been in receipt of republican threats, I was travelling under police protection, and I had come to be on friendly terms with my Special Branch protectors. On a journey immediately following Herrema's rescue, I asked how the Branch had got wind of where Herrema was being held. One of the detectives smiled and said: "One of the gang had been arrested, and we felt sure he knew where Herrema was. So this man was transferred under Branch escort from a prison in the country to a prison in Dublin, and on the way the car stopped. Then the escort started asking him questions and when at first he refused to answer, they beat the shit out of him. Then he told them where Herrema was."

I refrained from telling this story to Garret or Justin, because I thought it would worry them. It didn't worry me.

* * *

There was only one major piece of legislation for which I was personally responsible under the coalition government. This was the Broadcasting (Amendment) Act of 1975. The circumstances which made this Act necessary were as follows:

Since broadcasting began in the Irish state, broadcasting by the IRA had always been prohibited. But, with a rather typical avoidance of direct reference in matters concerning the IRA, the IRA was not directly referred to in the relevant legislation. Rather the Minister for Posts and Telegraphs was given the power to prohibit the broadcasting of "any matter or any class of matter". The Minister was also given the power to remove any member of the Broadcasting Authority at any time without reason given. In the Fianna Fáil government that immediately preceded ours, the then Minister for Posts and Telegraphs, Gerry Collins, had exercised this last power by dismissing and then replacing all the members of the Broadcasting Authority without reason given.

The parties then making up the opposition – and now making up the government – had protested against Collins's draconian action, and we now had the task of framing and then enacting legislation under which a repetition of the Collins assertion of arbitrary power would be impossible.

In drafting the legislation the principle on which I worked was one of *limited liberalization*. It would be liberal in that it would remove from the hands of any Minister the power of removing the Authority – the power that had been misused by Collins – and vest this in the Oireachtas (Parliament) alone (Dáil and Senate). It would not be liberalised in that the Minister would retain the power to order, by directive, the prohibition of broadcasts on behalf of subversive organisations such as the IRA. The principle involved there was the protection of the security of the democratic state against the broadcasting of subversive propaganda by organisations whose function was to work under the orders of the leadership of a private army for revolutionary purposes.

The government had no difficulty in approving the outline of the legislation, once Cosgrave had given it the nod. Nor did I have much difficulty in getting the measure through the Oireachtas. Fianna Fáil would have liked to block it, but found it hard to find presentable grounds for opposition. They didn't like the transfer of power (the power of removing members of the Broadcasting Authority) from the government to the Oireachtas. But as the Oireachtas was the body that had the measure under consideration and would decide what was to be its fate, it was rather hard to explain to the Oireachtas on what grounds this extension of its own authority was objectionable. So that part of the legislation was allowed to pass without serious objection.

The other important part of the legislation was giving the minister power to name by order certain organizations which would then be prevented from broadcasting. We made no secret of the fact that the first organization to be excluded from broadcasting would be Sinn Féin; and as soon as the legislation was passed, Sinn Féin was in fact named as excluded. Now, Fianna Fáil had always excluded Sinn Féin from broadcasting and in all those years had no thought of actually allowing them to broadcast. But what was profoundly uncongenial to Fianna Fáil was excluding Sinn Féin *by name*. *Silently* excluding Sinn Féin was acceptable and – by that time – normal in the Republic. But excluding Sinn Féin by name was repugnant to Fianna Fáil. Fianna Fáil always regarded itself as part of the republican movement – its name in English is "the Republican Party" – and all Fianna Fáilers know that the other branch of the movement is Sinn Féin-IRA. Many Fianna Fáil people, including many TDs, have strong sentimental ties with their fellow – and more consistent – republicans. So to *name* Sinn Féin as excluded from broadcasting would be profoundly uncongenial to Fianna Fáil.

At the same time it was electorally inconvenient for Fianna Fáil to be seen to oppose the naming of Sinn Féin, thus advertising its peculiar esoteric ties with that revolutionary party. Most voters in the Republic, since 1922, distrust and fear the post-Treaty IRA, and know Sinn Féin to be the IRA's political front. So Fianna Fáil does not like to advertise its emotional and traditional ties with Sinn Féin. It is a matter which Fianna Fáil people keep quiet about, except when they are among themselves, singing patriotic songs and drinking strong waters late at night. For the rest it is mostly a matter of silent nods and winks, like so much else in the Fianna Fáil culture of the late 20th century.

These things being so, Fianna Fáil grumbled rather incoherently and offered no serious opposition to the Broadcasting Bill, which passed easily.

The Broadcasting Act (1975) is still in force, but the order banning Sinn Féin was revoked, as part of the growing acceptability of Sinn Féin as a result of the Hume-Adams rapprochement in the early 1990s. But the power to reimpose the ban remains, under the Act, and the ban itself could be reimposed in the event of a further breakdown – or further breakdowns – of the IRA ceasefire.

* * *

By 1976, the Coalition government, approaching its full term, was facing a general election. The omens were not good. The period when we were in office had included, in the Middle East, the Yom Kippur War, which the Arab oil-producing countries had seized on as a pretext for a huge and profitable hike in the price of oil, with high consequential increases in the cost of living in every European country. All the European parties which were in power at the time of Yom Kippur and its immediate economic impact were driven from office at the next ensuing general election, and we were to be no exception to this rule.

That was the forbidding, basic, actual situation. But to make sure of its victory, Fianna Fáil in opposition announced the most reckless economic programme ever offered during an Irish election, including the abolition of rates and huge reductions of taxes all round. This audacious programme bore all the marks of the mind of CJ Haughey, now again the rising star of Fianna Fáil and soon about to succeed Jack Lynch in the leadership. The consequences of Fianna Fáil's promises, and delivery on most of them, were to cripple the country economically for many years.

We made no attempt to compete with Fianna Fáil in promises. The coalition's Minister for Finance, Richie Ryan, was a totally honest and highly competent minister who had done as well as could be done in the daunting post-Yom-Kipper situation. We fought the election on our record which has generally been regarded, in historical retrospect, as about as good as it could be in the circumstances. But retrospect availed us nothing. Fianna Fáil won that election by the largest majority in its history.

When a few years had gone by, we were to have some consolation for our defeat. Fianna Fáil, after their great victory, never again won an overall majority in a general election. Coalition government became the norm in the Republic. We felt that our government, being the first coalition in the history of the Republic to serve its full term and leave office without any resignations or public recriminations between its members, had played a modest but significant part in bringing about that satisfactory outcome.

In that general election, I lost my seat. Both Sinn Féin and Fianna Fáil claimed that my defeat was due to my "anti-national" outlook and behaviour. These factors may perhaps have played a part in my defeat, but if so it was a very small one. Few strong nationalists vote for either Labour or Fine Gael. Almost all of them vote for either Fianna Fáil or Sinn Féin, mostly, of course, Fianna Fáil. And the most "republican" member of our government – Justin Keating – also lost his seat in that election. Both losses were mainly due to the general slide away from the coalition by people who found Fianna Fáil's promises irresistible.

There were however some special features in my case which damaged me somewhat. Fianna Fáil's dirty tricks department – controlled by Charlie Haughey's brother, Jock – was believed to have carried out a filthy smear campaign, through anonymous lying posters, against myself and my family. I don't think that campaign did me much harm, since very few people can have believed it. What did hurt was Fianna Fáil's regular and perfectly legitimate exploitation of the unsatisfactory state of the Irish telephone situation, for which I, as Minister for Posts and Telegraphs, bore full responsibility before the electorate.

Actually I was quite proud of the manner in which I had discharged my responsibility in that matter. Very early on in the tenure of our government, I had approached Richie Ryan and proposed a huge increase in investment in the telephone system, which had been underfinanced for a great many years. Richie saw the general economic need for rescuing the telephone system and backed me fully. Between us we secured a greater total increase in telephone investment during our four years in office than all the actual investment that had occurred in all the previous years since the foundation of the state.

But this achievement didn't do either of us any electoral good. The benign effects of capital investment were not felt for some years after the initial investment, and the condition of the Irish telephone service remained almost as unsatisfactory when we came up for re-election as it had been when we took office.

Fianna Fáil's open and legitimate exploitation of this public issue was very cleverly conducted and subliminally linked to my unorthodox position on the national question. On every doorstep in my constituency, the Fianna Fáil canvasser would ask whether the constituent was satisfied with the telephone service? Most constituents would declare that they were far from satisfied. The canvasser would then say:

"I'm sorry to hear that. You know that the Minister responsible for telephones is your Deputy, Conor Cruise O'Brien? You'd think he'd have done something about the telephones in the four years he has been in office. But he seems to be mainly interested in Northern Ireland."

Nothing about my position on Northern Ireland being "anti-national". That would have put some voters off. This was a neat and well-conducted campaign and it must certainly have cost me a fair number of votes.

* * *

In the immediate aftermath of the election I felt sore and depressed. By way of a consolation prize I ran for the Senate, and was elected head of the poll for my alma mater, Trinity College. I soon became Editor-in-Chief of *The Observer* in London, but I thought I could arrange to be present when the Senate debated Northern Ireland. But Fianna Fáil frustrated that idea. Being now in full control of the order of business in the Senate, as in the Dáil, they would simply change the order of business whenever I came back so that Northern Ireland was never discussed in the Senate in my presence.

In the same period, I had the unpleasant experience of being forced out of the Labour Party by my old friend, Frank Cluskey. I had spoken about Northern Ireland, on my usual lines, at Oxford, and the speech had been reported in the press. Cluskey – who was now leader of the party following Corish's resignation and had also assumed the role of spokesman on Northern Ireland – summoned me to his presence. He told me that, henceforward, I would have to clear any statements I would make on Northern Ireland with him as party spokesman. If not, the whip would be removed from me. Cluskey was clearly influenced by claims that the defeat of the coalition had been partly due to my unpopular position on Northern Ireland. I didn't believe that but he did, which was what mattered now.

I told him that rather than submit speeches for clearance, I would resign the Labour Party whip, which I duly did. And he knew me well enough to know that that is what I would do. I was told that he said of me at the time, "I have him by the short and curlies," and that sounds like him. I resigned the Labour whip and shortly afterwards also my useless seat in the Senate.

I regretted my break with Cluskey, but there were no hard feelings on either side. Some years afterwards he made a friendly contribution to a televised discussion about what my political role had been. And I have always been glad – and am happy to record the fact, now that he is dead – to have known him, enjoyed his marvellous company, and learned from him.

I was now out of politics altogether, except as an independent commentator on them, essentially responsible to nobody except my readers. I was unhappy during the transition, but felt much happier when it was complete than I had ever felt during the political years.

All the same I was never sorry that I had gone into Irish politics and had the four years in opposition and the four years in office. I had learned quite a lot since the time when I had told Donal I was going into politics "for the experience". I am not sorry about the rich accumulation of experience I acquired in my political years. If you write about politics, as I regularly do, it is well to know what the stuff feels like from the inside, unpleasant as that experience must sometimes be.

16

EDITOR-IN-CHIEF OF
THE OBSERVER

EVER SINCE MY RESIGNATION FROM THE UN AND THE IRISH FOREIGN
service, *The Observer* – a liberal British Sunday newspaper – then edited by
David Astor and owned by an Astor family trust, had taken a benevolent
interest in me. Knowing that Prime Minister Nehru of India approved of
me and accepted that I was anti-colonial, Astor wrote to Nehru to say that
he would like to send me to Nagaland in north-east India, to report on the
situation there for *The Observer*. The Nagas were then attempting to secede
from India and the Indian army was trying to crush their revolt, with a fair
measure of success. For the Indian government, the situation in Nagaland
was extremely sensitive because of its close resemblance to the even more
dangerous situation in Kashmir, Nehru's birthplace, which he was
determined to keep as part of India, apparently against the will of most of
its population.

Nehru wrote back in terms complimentary to me, but withholding
permission for me to visit Nagaland. It was the time of the monsoon, he
said, which would make it inconvenient for me to travel. The monsoon,
predictably, ended, but permission was never forthcoming. Astor, however,
seems to have taken the refusal as a kind of backhanded compliment to my
objectivity, and I became a fairly regular contributor to the paper. One

contribution, written from America, caused a good deal of controversy. It concerned the use by Western powers of mercenaries to rescue some missionaries in Zaire. In the course of the rescue operations several hundred Africans were reported to have been killed. My article was headed "Mercy and Mercenaries" and questioned the ethical implications of the decision to send in the mercenaries, who were known throughout Africa for what was either their reckless disregard for African lives or actual pleasure in hunting and killing Africans.

In any case I continued to write for *The Observer* from America and then from Ireland, during my period in opposition there. While I was in government in Ireland I was no longer in a position to write for the paper, but after my electoral defeat, I signalled that I was again available to contribute. At my own suggestion I was sent to southern Africa to investigate the situation in what were then known as "the front-line states" – South Africa's African neighbours – and also on South Africa itself, where strict apartheid still prevailed, but under steadily increasing international pressure which was already beginning to undermine the rand.

Of that trip my two most vivid impressions are of attending the inquest on Steve Biko in Johannesburg, and – in sharp contrast – a dinner with Sir Roy Welensky in what was then still Salisbury, Rhodesia.

The Biko inquest was an extremely chilling affair, in a peculiarly Afrikaner style of the period. The judge and the witnesses – all Afrikaners – were all stolid and quietly-spoken with the air of men going through a tiresome but necessary routine. Everybody knew that Biko had been beaten to death, by the police who held him, and the proceedings were about denying that anything of the kind had ever happened. Biko, while in custody had fallen and so killed himself. The police so testified and the magistrate so concluded. If nobody believed the story, so what?

I wrote a piece about this which I think was one of the best I have ever written, but unfortunately it never appeared, because the issue of the paper for which I wrote it never appeared. Those were the days of last-minute frivolous strikes by the print workers and my piece was a victim of just such a strike. Rupert Murdoch's move to Wapping, with its shattering effect on the power of the print unions, had yet to come.

My tour of the "front-line states" naturally attracted some attention from the governments of those states, and people who were close to those governments. In what was still Salisbury, Rhodesia (soon to be Harare) I had a call from Sir Roy Welensky, the former prime minister, now in retirement. Sir Roy invited me to dinner and I was happy to accept. When wars are well and truly over, persons who have been on opposite sides in those wars generally welcome an opportunity to meet and compare notes about what the views from the two sides had been while the wars in question were on.

I found Sir Roy a genial host and an amiable companion since there was nothing for us to fight about any more. There was, however, something I wanted to find out from him. It was the Rhodesian police who had found the wreckage of Hammarskjold's plane after the crash at Ndola. The police had had the motive, the means and the opportunity to tidy away anything that might contradict the "accident" theory (embodied in the terms of reference of the Rhodesian enquiry). If the retrospective account of the French fascist officers were true, then there was something that needed to be tidied away in the interests of the accident theory: the body of the Belgian hijacker, Gheyssels. If the account were true there would have been one body more than the Rhodesians reported. Trying to sound as casual as I could, I asked the question: "How many bodies were found in the wreckage?" Welensky didn't answer immediately but I thought his demeanour changed to something warier. Then he relaxed, the expression changing again to the merely mischievous. "How many bodies?" he repeated. "I'm not sure, Conor. How many should there have been? Twelve? Thirteen?"

I thought that reply was an implicit confirmation of the French report. But I couldn't get beyond that tenuous "implicit". I asked whether I could see the report – meaning the original one, for the Rhodesian government, before it could have been tidied up, for the edification of the profane. Sir Roy said that it was among his papers for the period which were in the Bodleian Library, which would show me anything I wanted to see. When I later applied to the Bodleian, permission was refused. But I am pretty sure, in any case, that an inspection of the papers would have revealed nothing relevant. If the original report was as I suppose it to have been, it would have been destroyed as soon as the ostensible version was ready.

* * *

When I came home to Howth after my African journey, feeling tired out, I found a message that Lord Goodman wanted me to ring him immediately. Arnold Goodman was the most prominent "Mr Fixit" in the Britain of the day: a very eminent lawyer with a finger in many pies, especially business, politics and journalism. For a person who was out of a job, as was the case with me, a call from Lord Goodman was not to be sneezed at. When I called him he asked me to come to London immediately for a conference at his apartment in Portland Street, on business connected with *The Observer*.

I flew to London and went straight to the house on Portland Street. When I pressed the bell of what I took to be the door of his flat, the door was opened by a lady in pearls and a twin-set. The lady looked at me without enthusiasm. "You," she diagnosed, "must be someone for Lord Goodman." I took her to be a high Tory, who considered Arnold Goodman to be fast and left-wing and that I looked the kind of person who would be a friend of his. In any case she told me in which flat to find him.

In Goodman's sitting-room I found four men: Goodman himself, David Astor, whom I knew already, and two Americans whom I had not met: Robert O Anderson, chairman of Atlantic Oil, the American trust which now owned *The Observer*, and Thornton Bradshaw, president of Atlantic (chairman being senior to president in the American system). Anderson indicated that they wanted me to assume responsibility for editorial policy at *The Observer*. I realized that this proposition must have come originally from David Astor, the only one of the four who knew me. Naturally, I was gratified by this mark of David's confidence in me. But I had also to think of the actual editor, Donald Trelford. I told the Americans that I would first have to meet Donald, and assure myself that he willingly accepted my appointment. This was agreed to. I then told them that (subject to Donald's agreement) I was willing to accept the appointment on the assumption that, as editor-in-chief, I would be in full and final control of editorial policy. This also was agreed to, but as I later realized, the stipulation was quite unrealistic. No one is ever in full control of something that someone else owns, even if the someone else has formally agreed to relinquish control.

I learned later that, after the meeting, Anderson said to Bradshaw that I sounded as if I might be difficult to deal with. Bradshaw replied that if I weren't a bit difficult to deal with I couldn't be the kind of person that they needed. Anderson acquiesced in that proposition, for the time being.

* * *

Donald Trelford came to see me in Dublin and had lunch with me. He told me he would be happy to accept me as editor-in-chief, and to work with me. He regarded his role in journalism as that of a craftsman. Questions of high policy, as in the taking of editorial lines, he was happy to leave to someone else. I learned later that the more hard-boiled *Observer* journalists were in the habit of referring to the paper's editorial columns as "the rubbish-tip" and that was in substance also Donald's view of the matter, although expressed much less abrasively.

There were several others who were not pleased with the decision, as I soon found out. The most candid of the objectors was an old acquaintance of mine, John Cole. John and I saw eye to eye over Northern Ireland although we came from different backgrounds, he being an Ulster Protestant and devoted to the union. John being a hot-tempered man, and also a candid one, told me at once that I ought not to have accepted the post of editor-in-chief, putting me at the head of a body of professional journalists when I was not a professional journalist myself.

I could have said that it was essentially David Astor who had chosen me to fill this position and that David Astor was not himself a professional journalist and yet had done more to shape the character of the paper than anyone else. I didn't say any of that, I didn't argue with him at all. I just told him that I had accepted the position when it had been offered to me on the sole condition that Donald Trelford, the editor, was prepared to accept me as editor-in-chief. When Donald signalled his acceptance I felt free to take what I was offered and had done so. I hoped and believed that John and I would co-operate in running a great newspaper in which we both thoroughly believed and for which we had both been chosen by David Astor.

John departed, still fuming a bit, but I knew him well enough to know that he would calm down when he had thought about it a bit. He calmed down almost immediately and he and I soon became not merely good colleagues, in cordial intellectual co-operation, but also close friends.

Around the same time I had a brief run-in with the only American member of the board other than the co-proprietors. This was Douglas Cater. Cater was quite a distinguished American journalist who had written well about American politics. He was now resident in London and could have been quite a useful member of the board if he had stuck to that function. However, in the early months of the new proprietorship, he had come to see himself as a sort of political overseer: editor-in-chief in fact, minus the title. So my appointment came as a blow to him. David Astor brought me to see him immediately after my appointment and Cater did not conceal his displeasure, though he was rather vague about the reasons for it. David assured me that his opposition would not count for much. Cater's rather heavy-handed interference on the editorial side was greatly resented by Donald Trelford and most of the editorial staff and was – I think – quite high among the reasons why they all acquiesced in my appointment. They expected me to bring Cater's editorial communications to an end, and I did. I told him that I, as now the senior member of the board with direct editorial responsibilities, would always be interested to hear his views on editorial matters and would take account of these. But I did not think that he, as a member of the board with no specific editorial responsibilities, should communicate directly with members of the editorial staff, as he had been doing. If he continued to do so I would put the propriety of his continued editorial interventions on the agenda of the next-following meeting of the board of the paper for a decision. Cater, when he had thought about the matter, accepted this philosophically and gave us no more trouble on the editorial side.

The objections from Cole and from Cater were only passing ones and were left behind early. But there was another set of objections which was much more formidable, deep-laid and dangerous. These were the objections of Kenneth Harris, who soon became – and remained for the period of our combined service on the paper – a poisonous presence in my professional life.

Harris was not in my opinion – or that of most of his colleagues – a particularly distinguished journalist. His contributions were rather infrequent and consisted mostly of interviews with distinguished people. This genre is not greatly esteemed by writers and I am afraid we missed the point. Harris was not looking for the esteem of his colleagues. Harris was looking for power, and his journalism was entirely oriented in that direction. His interviews were subtle exercises in flattery, designed to show the interviewee in such a light as he would wish to be seen in. In this way he attracted to himself a fairly significant clientele, consisting in part of people whose careers he had helped and in part of people who hoped he might be induced to help their careers.

Harris's subjects were primarily drawn from the British upper-class, mainly people fairly prominent in business and industry. But these were people whom wealthy American visitors to London tended to seek out, and through these connections, which he cultivated skilfully, Harris began to acquire a rich American clientele also.

None of these connections did Harris any particular good, as long as David Astor was securely in control of *The Observer*. It was only when David began to lose control that Harris, through the American connections he had cultivated, became a significant – even a pivotal – figure.

* * *

Here the story has to be told of the train of events which had resulted in the decline of *The Observer's* economic position and which was to lead in consequence to David Astor's eventual departure from the proprietorship and editorship, to the acquisition of the paper by Atlantic Richfield, to the emergence of Harris as a grey eminence and – by a kind of eddy among these currents – to my own appointment as editor-in-chief.

The beginning of the decline in *The Observer's* fortunes can be precisely dated. It dates from November 1956, the period of the attack by Britain, France and Israel on Egypt and the occupation of the Suez Canal by these powers. Most of the British press was broadly supportive of the Suez intervention, at least initially. But David Astor, from the beginning, took *The Observer* on a strongly anti-Suez course – more anti-Suez I believe than any other British newspaper. He rightly rejected and exposed Eden's cover-story, that the British and French had intervened only in order to "separate the combatants" – Israel and Egypt – and so restore peace in the region. At the time, being at the United Nations, receiving the press reports, I greatly admired the stand that *The Observer* was taking under Astor's leadership, and was drawn to Astor and *The Observer* in a way that led me to write for them later.

Even many of those who did not agree with him praised Astor's courage. And even he must have shivered a little when he took note of that praise. I have noted that prudent people, both in politics and journalism, are apt to say to someone that some course is "courageous" with a little pursing of the lips, which means: "You are making a fool of yourself. This is going to cost you." And *The Observer* never indeed recovered from the cost of David Astor's politically wise and personally courageous stand on Suez.

When I went to work on *The Observer* more than twenty years later, I used to hear – from the gossip in places like El Vino's in Fleet Street – that *The Observer's* decline had really nothing to do with Suez. Its circulation at the time had been maintained. I put this point of view to Roger Harrison, now managing director, who had been around at the time. He said the point was technically correct, but profoundly misleading. The *number* of people buying the newspaper each week remained much the same as before, but the make-up of the readership had changed. Old readers had dropped away and young readers had been attracted in their place. The young readers were less affluent than the old and *The Observer* had become significantly less attractive to advertisers. *The Observer* started losing money then, and was still losing money when I joined it and also after I left it. Up to Suez *The Observer* and *The Sunday Times* had been running neck-and-neck. Beginning with the immediate aftermath of Suez, *The Sunday Times* began to dominate the up-market section for which both newspapers catered and *The Sunday Times* has held that dominant position ever since.

* * *

Year after year, from Suez on, *The Observer* continued to lose money, not at a great rate but steadily. The deficit each year had been made up for years by the Astor family trust. But a time came when the trustees of the fund decided that the drain on it must stop. David then stepped down as editor, and Donald Trelford took his place. But a new proprietor had to be found, ready to foot the bills until the paper's finances were righted, if they ever were.

This is where Harris came in, through the relations with rich people which he had carefully cultivated and, it must be said, also through his insight into certain kinds of human motivation. One of the rich people whom Harris cultivated was Robert O Anderson. On Anderson's visits to London, Harris flattered him and showed him the bright lights, taking him to places like Annabel's with young women as fellow guests.

Harris was shrewd enough to see how Anderson might become interested in acquiring *The Observer*. Anderson's ruthless business methods had earned him a rather unsavoury reputation both in America and internationally. Harris convinced Anderson that by acquiring *The Observer* he could do a lot to improve his image. Astor had earned for the paper a reputation for integrity. In earning that reputation he had set that newspaper on its loss-making course. That gave Anderson the opportunity to step in, accept the losses, and save *The Observer* in the hope that if he did so, some of the newspaper's reputation for high-mindedness would rub off on him.

As the reader will have noticed, I am not an admirer of Kenneth Harris. But I have to concede that this particular operation was brilliantly conceived and brilliantly conducted. The very characteristics which had caused the paper to run at a loss were adduced as reasons why an unscrupulous millionaire should accept the burden of the loss, in hope that the high-mindedness which had caused the loss would somehow repair the reputation of the person accepting it.

There is a mediaeval hymn about the Incarnation and the Resurrection, two lines of which run as follows:

> *Et medelam ferret inde*
> *Hostis unde laeserat*

Roughly translated: "And take a cure from the very quarter from which the enemy had done the damage." So the brilliance of Harris had converted the damage done over Suez into the cure of the redeeming millionaire!

* * *

So Kenneth Harris saved *The Observer*. And I must admit that he was poorly rewarded for so signal a service. True, he had now a seat on the board. But a seat on a board is not of much use to you unless you carry weight with your colleagues and this Harris never did. Indeed it was, ironically, in the nature of his operation that he should be relegated into obscurity. The whole idea was to cause Robert O Anderson to become associated, if only indirectly, with high-mindedness. A central feature of the whole operation from Anderson's point of view, during the first two years, were the annual Astor-Goodman dinners, in which Robert O Anderson could be heard to extol Astor and Goodman in the hope that something of their savoury reputation might adhere to Anderson, who felt in need of something of the kind.

But the logic of the operation which Harris had devised and Anderson accepted positively required that Harris be kept off stage. If you want the spotlight to rest on people like Astor and Goodman, then you don't want a person like Harris to be seen at all. Harris might be exceedingly useful in brokering back-room deals, but he wasn't the kind of person with whom anyone with regard to their own reputation would wish to be seen in public. So the inner logic of the operation which Harris had master-minded required the disappearance of the mastermind.

As was once said of a ruthless but compromising Moroccan warlord by those to whom he had been useful: "El Glaoui is a dagger which, once used, must be thrown away."

The point at which Harris must have realized he was, if not being thrown away, at least relegated to perhaps temporary obscurity was when I was appointed editor-in-chief. This was an appointment which Harris could reasonably think he had earned by brokering the deal that had saved the paper. Yet again the inner logic of the deal he had brokered excluded him from consideration. The inner logic required Anderson to defer to David Astor, the principal source of the required sanctification. And if Astor recommended me and not Harris as editor-in-chief, then I would be editor-in-chief.

Harris naturally resented my appointment and – rather surprisingly – he allowed his resentment to show. Knowing the crucial role he had played in bringing about the Atlantic Oil deal, I would have wished to be on reasonably good terms with him, if that were feasible, but it wasn't. We had two dinners together. At the first he was faintly menacing. At the second he was openly bullying, or tried to be, and then there were no more dinners. Then, when at David Astor's suggestion I started writing a regular weekly column for the paper, Harris came to me with a face of thunder. I had written a piece about military coups in Africa. Harris was at his most pompous and pretentious. He had my article in his hand and he brandished it in my face. "This," he pronounced, "is Not in Accordance with the National Mood". The capitals were audible. I laughed in his face and we never spoke to one another again.

* * *

On *The Observer*, throughout my years there I was socially most comfortable at boardroom level. I was soon on close and friendly terms with the chairman, Lord Barnetson, with Astor and Goodman and with Thornton Bradshaw, normally the representative of the proprietors at the board meetings since Anderson seldom attended. Relations with the principal proprietor were a little strained, but no more, from early on. He had invited me to spend Christmas with him in New York. I refused, explaining that I liked to spend Christmas each year with my family in Howth. I sensed something patronizing in the form of his invitation, and the role of courtier did not appeal to me. But Anderson put up with me by reason of my holy backing. I was safe as long as the Astor-Goodman dinners continued. But no longer. Harris sensed this and bided his time, maintaining his cordial social relations with Anderson, centering on Annabel's.

As I began to understand how things worked in and around *The Observer* I discovered that the two managing directors, Roger Harrison and Brian Nicholson, while personally friendly enough, did not approve of my role as editor-in-chief. This was because they knew that I was the choice of

David Astor. To them I represented the continuance of David's high-minded but stubbornly unprofitable policy.

Newspaper people generally accept that newspapers have a triple role: to inform, to instruct and to entertain. But different newspaper people assign different priorities within the triple role to the functions which make it up. Astor would have agreed with the managing directors – and most other journalists – in putting information first. But concerning the remaining functions, Astor and the managing directors sharply diverged in their evaluation. Astor put instruction as a close second to information, with entertainment a rather poor third. The managing directors put entertainment second with instruction a bad third. Entertainment generated readership, and therefore attracted advertisers. Instruction put readers off and therefore deterred advertisers.

The managing directors knew that I was Astor's choice because Astor realised that I was committed to Astor's policy. So though they liked me personally, and enjoyed my writing, they saw my being editor-in-chief as the continuation of the fatal Astor albatross. They knew that if another international crisis arose, closely comparable to Suez, I would try to be worthy of Astor's example over the original Suez. That is, I would analyze the situation as I saw it to be, and give the advice I thought to be sound in relation to that situation without any regard at all to the consequences for circulation and advertising. This might be all very fine, intellectually and morally, but a second dose of that sort of stuff could kill off the paper.

What would Harrison and Nicholson have advised over Suez? Understandably, they would have advised journalistic fudging, in harmony with governmental fudging. Don't challenge the original official line about "separating the combatants", and then don't challenge secondary and even more transparent official lines that the object of separating the combatants had been achieved. And they would give the corresponding advice in any future crisis. They knew I would not – indeed could not – take that advice and I was therefore actually a force adverse to the recovery of the paper's profitability and potentially a threat to its very survival. So, whatever they might feel about me personally, they were quietly but implacably opposed to my continuance as editor-in-chief.

I was now in an uncomfortable position with regard to management. I was totally committed to the Astor legacy, had been appointed because of my past commitment to that legacy, and could not honourably retreat from that position while remaining editor-in chief. At the same time, I had begun to understand how solidly based the management objections to the

Astorian heritage were. Another harsh dose of Astorian integrity could indeed kill off the paper. I began to wonder whether I wanted to stick around and wait for Suez Mark-Two in which my Astorian commitment might prove terminal as far as *The Observer* was concerned.

* * *

I began to realize that my position was a very peculiar one. On the one hand I had enormous *latent* power which I could exercise in a political crisis. Yet it was probable that that power could only be used in a manner suicidal to the newspaper. And in relation to the normal daily running of the paper I had almost no power at all. This again was an Astorian heritage. The paper was run editorially on what were called "collegiate" lines. That is to say that various members of the editorial staff controlled policy in certain given areas, which were left to them by the editor and therefore by the editor-in-chief. Thus Colin Legum controlled policy towards Africa. A small group of journalists controlled policy towards the Middle East. Comment on British political affairs was mainly controlled by John Cole. This was the Astorian system, and as I had been appointed by Astor I didn't feel entitled to dismantle it. If I intervened at all it could only be by argument with the policy-framers, and I didn't win the arguments often or to any great extent.

The main area which I knew something about and on which I felt uncomfortable with the *Observer* line, was the Middle East. Robert Stephens was the leader over this area, supported by Colin Legum. Both of them were committed to the "territory for peace" theory: that is that Israel could and should get peace with the Arabs by surrendering territory to them. From my own UN experience, I didn't find this theory credible. I thought Israel could indeed surrender territory but I doubted very much whether Israel would get in return anything that could properly be described as peace. Israel could get peace of sorts with the particular Arabs who signed up for the deal. But other Arabs who did not sign up for the deal would continue to engage in terrorism, and the Arabs who did sign up would be likely to collude with the terrorists, partly out of fear of those fearsome people and partly out of a sneaking sympathy with them.

Robert Stephens listened to me politely, but suggested that my information was out of date. Peace was indeed obtainable if territory was yielded. I was reminded of a similar argument I had had with Garret FitzGerald over Sunningdale. In any case David Astor, who had appointed Stephens, was a known enthusiast for the peace process. If I tried to overrule or shift Stephens just for his commitment to the peace process I would be running into a hornets' nest and the hornets would be my former allies headed by the man to whom I owed my appointment. So I didn't move Stephens. I just determined that, after I left *The Observer*, an event which I began to foresee, I would go to the Middle East, assess the situation there, and write a book about it, which I eventually did.

There was, however, another area on which I was acknowledged to have a certain expertise of my own, and on which my judgement was generally backed up by John Cole, who also had a certain expertise of his own. This area was Northern Ireland. Much of the comment about Northern Ireland in *The Observer* was at this time supplied by Mary Holland. Mary Holland was, and is, an able journalist but her coverage of Northern Ireland seemed to us to give too favourable a view of activities sponsored by "the republican movement", meaning Sinn Féin-IRA. She published one article celebrating the character and achievements of "the blanket women" – relatives of Provisional IRA prisoners who organised demonstrations intended to generate sympathy for the Provos. I wrote to her about this and we had a somewhat acrimonious correspondence. She stuck to her guns and I told Donald Trelford that I had no confidence in the objectivity of her coverage of Northern Ireland. John Cole agreed. Donald Trelford acquiesced, for the moment as he generally did if the opposition appeared adequately motivated. Mary Holland was "out" of *The Observer* as long as I was still there but after I had retired as editor-in-chief Donald quietly restored her. This did not at all surprise me.

* * *

In any case, I was also getting uncomfortable at *The Observer* for family reasons. Patrick and Margaret were doing well at school in Dublin and we didn't want to move them. This meant that I spent half the week in Dublin and half in London, thus being away from the children for more time than was desirable. In the summer holidays Máire and the children came over and enjoyed living on the houseboat I had on the Thames at Chelsea Reaches. Those were good times. But when I was alone on the houseboat in the winter months things were a bit bleak especially as during the storms of January and February along the river the plumbing on the houseboat repeatedly stopped working. So all-in-all the editor-in-chief was not quite as happy as his exalted title might suggest he ought to be.

Still, there were compensations. I enjoyed writing my weekly column, once I got the hang of it, and earned a couple of awards. And I enjoyed travelling and writing about travelling. I remember in particular one trip to the Horn of Africa – Ethiopia and Somalia – with the *Observer* photographer, Tony McGrath, an agreeable and resourceful ocompanion.

This was the period of Colonel Mengistu's "Marxist" regime in Ethiopia. I found that Marxism, by the time it reached the Amharic Highlands, took on rather eccentric forms. There were no pictures of Lenin or Stalin or any other Russians to be seen in Addis Ababa. The Russians who had formerly supported Ethiopia had now switched their support to Ethiopia's enemy Somalia. So Mengistu was now arrayed against his former Russian connections and destroyed their icons of Lenin and Stalin. But everywhere there were huge pictures of what were supposed to be Marx and Engels. Their Ethiopian portraits showed them with very full and well-shaped beards: their eyes were black and absolutely round: their skins were chocolate colour. In fact they were cast precisely in the image of the Coptic saints of traditional Ethiopian iconography.

When we had an interview with Mengistu we found another striking example of the adaptation of Marxism to local conditions. Mengistu's own discourse was impeccably modern and left-wing. He talked like one who could speak the language but whose heart was not in what he said. But while he was talking I could hear a dry coughing sound coming through an open window. I recognised the sound for I had heard it in other parts of Africa. What was coughing just outside Mengistu's office was a lion.

As we were leaving, Tony tried to get a picture of the lion chained up outside the office but was prevented by the guards. I could understand why. The lion, as symbol of sovereignty, was instantly recognisable as such by the local people. They saw the Lion of Judah. But, for exactly the same reason the lion, if photographed, would be incompatible with the modern progressive image that Mengistu wanted to project to the outside world. So the lion had to be there but was not to be photographed.

Mengistu was a bore. But his enemy Siad Barre, the dictator of the Somalis, was not a bore. He was a burly, breezy man with a good command of English. When I met him he disconcerted me by saying immediately: "You like Ethiopia, don't you?" Before I could answer he rolled his eyes and said in an affected falsetto: "Ah, the highlands . . . !"

And it is true that, like every other European visitor I found the Ethiopian mountains physically attractive, and low-lying Somalia repulsive. An early 20th century Somalian ruler, threatened by the British, had said in a striking phrase: "If you come here you will find only three things: thorn-trees, sand and blood." And that is pretty much how it still is.

I had one moment of excitement during my Somalian trip. This was a time when there was speculation that the Kremlin might back up its ally in the region, Somalia, by sending in troops to Somalia to support an invasion of Ethiopia. As we travelled along a Somali road, near the coast, we were overtaken by a number of heavy lorries of obviously military character. I asked my Somali interpreter travelling with me about the lorries. I understood him to reply, in a surprisingly casual voice: "Those are the Russians."

For a moment I had dreams of journalistic glory: that I had the luck to be on the spot to witness the first commitment of Russian troops to the war in the Horn of Africa! Further enquiry dissipated these dreams. The lorries were on a routine mission in which they engaged every month. For "Russians" read "rations".

Too bad.

* * *

The East African journey was on the whole a happy one. Another journey around the same time turned into a near-nightmare, for a time. This was a journey to Kyoto, Japan. I had been invited there, to take part in a symposium by Alex Kwapong, my old Ghanaian friend, who was then vice-chancellor of the United Nations University in Japan. I had just arrived in Kyoto and gone to sleep after the long journey when Alex woke me up. He was the bearer of a telegram which read simply: "Your wife and children have been involved in a car accident. Your children are alive."

I was so distressed by the telegram, hitting me when I was travel-weary, that I was almost helpless. Alex took charge and soon found that the telegram had been garbled. Máire and the children were all alive. The children had been slightly injured but Máire had been seriously injured. Enlisting the aid of the Irish Embassy, Alex got me on a plane to Dublin without delay and drove me to the airport. He also gave me greatly-needed moral support as I set out on my journey. I was lucky indeed to have such a friend on the spot in that grim time.

Máire recovered very well from terrible injuries, but it would take many months for the recovery to be complete. In the circumstances the withdrawal from my responsibilities as editor-in-chief which I had been contemplating would have to be speeded up. So I approached Lord

Barnetson and Thornton Bradshaw with a proposition to which I knew they would be sympathetic. This was that I would retire from the position of editor-in-chief but continue to write a regular column for the paper. As such contributions were then tax-free under Irish law my net earnings would not be greatly less than they had been as editor-in-chief. And I would be able to work at home, be with my family, and not have to worry any longer about editorial responsibilities and the time-bomb of the Astorian heritage.

The deal was worked out and about to take effect when a crisis occurred which would in any case have resulted in my departure as editor-in-chief, but probably under much less favourable conditions than those which I had already received.

The crisis followed the British general election of 1979 in which Margaret Thatcher was running for the first time. She was running against James Callaghan. So what was *The Observer* to do? Donald Trelford, rather characteristically, thought we should take no editorial position. But John Cole who, within the Astorian system normally controlled our commenting on British elections in accordance with our corporate tradition, was for Jim Callaghan. Personally I would have voted for Margaret Thatcher if I had a vote but I didn't. I thought that, in the logic of the Astorian tradition I should defer to John Cole, thus in effect delegating to him the plenary powers which I had secured on my appointment. I also thought that to be guided by John Cole on this issue might lead to a showdown with the owners, testing those plenary editorial powers.

So I wrote to Thornton Bradshaw telling him that *The Observer* was about to throw its editorial support to James Callaghan. Thornton Bradshaw wrote back pleading with me not to act in this way. He implied, but did not say, that Anderson – who alone had real power over the paper, which he owned – would be very annoyed indeed if this happened, and would speedily find a way of manifesting his displeasure. This I fully realised, but I was determined to do my Astorian duty for the short remainder of my period as editor-in-chief. I therefore wrote back that I must exercise the power entrusted to me in the manner that I had indicated.

So *The Observer* came out for Callaghan, its advice was not heeded by the electorate and Margaret Thatcher became prime minister.

The Observer's advice had no impact on the election but it did have considerable impact on *The Observer* itself. Robert O Anderson travelled to London for an emergency meeting of the board, at which of course he took the chair. Without referring to differences of opinion over the election, he said he would not be in a position to attend board meetings for the future. He wanted Kenneth Harris to preside over all future board meetings with *carte blanche* from him. Though Anderson did not say so explicitly, it seemed to be implied that if this was agreed Harris would then have full control over editorial policy. He would thus be *de facto* editor-in-chief. Astor, Goodman and myself spoke against this proposal and it was defeated at the meeting. It was clear that Anderson had no further use for *The Observer* if it were going to be run in this way. The era of the Astor-Goodman dinners was over.

Shortly after that board meeting Anderson reached an agreement with a tycoon of similar, though not identical motivations: Tiny Rowland. The deal was mainly over oil interests of the two tycoons in South America and in southern Africa. But Rowland asked that *The Observer* be thrown in to the deal, as a sort of makeweight and it was. Rowland didn't want to use *The Observer* to sanitise his image, which was beyond sanitising. But he did want to use direct editorial control over *The Observer* to promote various shady deals of his own, especially in southern Africa, where he had large and dubious interests. So *The Observer's* condition became decidedly worse under Rowland than it had been under Anderson (though it was already rapidly getting worse, towards the end, under Anderson). After the sale to Rowland, Astor and Goodman immediately retired from the board and appealed to the Monopolies Commission against Rowland's acquisition. I did not resign but I joined Astor and Goodman in testifying to the Monopolies Commission. I went into some detail there about Rowland's shady African interests and how these were likely to influence his use of *The Observer*.

The Monopolies Commission decided to let Rowland have *The Observer* but subject to the putative control, over editorial policy, of certain independent directors. The "independent directors", as was generally understood, were a fig-leaf. They would have no control over Rowland, but served only to protect the reputations of the respectable members of the Monopolies Commission, who had decided to let Rowland take over *The Observer*.

I had expected Kenneth Harris to be made editor-in-chief – now a vacant post – once Tiny Rowland acquired the paper, but this did not happen. Rowland knew a Harris appointment would be unpopular with the journalists and would tarnish the Rowland acquisition. So Harris – who no doubt played a part in the Anderson-Rowland deal – was rewarded for his services, but not as richly as he probably expected. He became editor of the *Glasgow Herald*, and *The Observer* offices knew him no more.

Harris's departure and my own took place almost simultaneously. In my (often somewhat feverish) imagination I assimilated our joint exit to that of Sherlock Holmes and Professor Moriarty, linked in a mutually-fatal embrace of hate, and falling over the cliff into the Reichenbach Falls.

* * *

Under the pre-Rowland deal with Barnetson and Bradshaw I was still writing for *The Observer* from Ireland after Rowland had taken over. As I had testified to the Monopolies Commission that Rowland was an unsuitable person to own *The Observer*, Rowland when he had acquired the paper decided – naturally enough – that I was an unsuitable person to write for *The Observer*. Trelford – who remained as editor – held out against the proprietorial pressure to sack me for longer than I would have expected: nearly a year, I think. But when a paper is making a loss, as *The Observer* continued to do, and the editor has regularly to ask the proprietor to make good the loss, the editor cannot hold out indefinitely against the proprietor's continuing pressure. So my eventful connection with *The Observer* came to an end.

Trelford and I remained on good terms. Years after the last of the above transactions, he and I both attended an agreeable and instructive meeting of the International Press Institute in Turkey. Trelford was entertaining some American friends to dinner one night and asked me to join them which I happily did. The dinner was at one of the many delightful fish restaurants on the shores of the Bosphorus and we all had a good time. After a while it emerged that both of us had worked for *The Observer*. One of the Americans asked me why I had left? I nodded over at Donald and said: "He fired me." The Americans were quite upset. Why should one of these nice gentlemen have fired the other nice gentleman? The question was put to Donald who replied, calmly and truthfully:

"The proprietor made it clear to me that if I didn't sack Conor he was going to sack me. I thought if he sacked *me*, I might not survive. But I thought that if I sacked Conor he *would* survive, and he has".

17

FREELANCE AND
EXPLORATION OF THEMES

WHEN MY CONNECTION WITH *THE OBSERVER* WAS SEVERED, MY CAREER – such as it had been – came to an end. That is, I never again had a full-time appointment with a duration of more than eighteen months. I did have a series of temporary appointments as a Visiting Professor or Visiting Fellow at a number of American academic institutions: at Dartmouth University, Hanover, New Hampshire: at Williams College, Western Massachusetts; at the University of Pennsylvania, Philadelphia: at the National Humanities Center, North Carolina, and at Fordham University Law School, New York.

Without exception, all these sojourns were very enjoyable and intellectually stimulating, both for my wife and myself. But there was no sense of deep involvement with the institutions concerned; no frictions or divergencies. One was a sojourner and no more; there was a pleasant "holiday" feeling about it all. I had a rest from "themes" for a while, and was grateful for the rest.

After my departure from *The Observer* I continued to earn my living mostly by journalism. I wrote sporadically for *The Times* in London and for the *New York Times* as also for the *Atlantic Monthly*. But the main demand for my journalism was in Ireland where I lived. The person responsible for my debut in Irish journalism was Douglas Gageby, the Editor of the *Irish Times*. As it happened, Douglas and I had been – and still were – moving in opposite directions with regard to religion and nationalism. The reader already knows my own relation to these themes in Ireland. Douglas's was the opposite. He had been born into a Protestant family in Belfast, of moderate unionist tendency, I believe. He had become quite a strong Irish nationalist. Douglas and I had known one another for a good many years and didn't much like one another, either personally or ideologically. But I respected Douglas greatly as an editor, and when he invited me to write a regular column for the *Irish Times* I took this as the greatest implicit compliment that had ever been paid to me, professionally. I stipulated that I should be altogether free – apart from the libel laws – to express my own opinions, with no editorial interference. He made the counter-stipulation that I should not attack any of his other contributors. Both stipulations were accepted and observed. I heard from one of Douglas's colleagues that he often swore when he read my copy. He may have sworn, but he always printed it, unchanged, and that was all that mattered.

After I had been writing for the *Irish Times* for some years I received an offer from the *Irish Independent* to switch to them. The *Irish Independent*, at this time, was somewhat down-market of the *Irish Times*, and had a much larger circulation and readership. I believe – though I was never explicitly told – that the offer was inspired by the paper's proprietor, Tony O'Reilly, whose views concerning the influence of Sinn Féin-IRA were closely similar to my own.

I hesitated before accepting the *Independent*'s offer. I was not at all worried about moving a little down-market, and reaching a lot more readers. What worried me was that if I left the *Irish Times* and if the *Independent* then dropped me, I would have nowhere else to go, since the only other Dublin newspaper, the *Irish Press*, with its strongly nationalist traditions and associations, would be closed to me.

So I stipulated that I would have a written contract – which I did not have with the *Irish Times*; that the *Independent*, which was a lot richer than the *Irish Times*, would pay me a lot more money; and that I would be guaranteed exactly the same freedom of expression as I had on the *Irish Times*. All these conditions were accepted and are still being honoured. Most of my journalism is now for the *Irish Independent* and *Sunday Independent*.

* * *

Under the new conditions I had more leisure for writing books, and this was congenial to me. Three of the books I completed in the period 1986 – 1996 were quite strongly thematic in various ways.

In the case of *The Siege: The Story of Israel and Zionism* (1986) the themes were religion and nationalism. The nationalist theme was fervently proclaimed by the Zionists from the beginning of 1882. The religious theme was ostensibly declared to be irrelevant, but was always a powerful *leitmotiv* within the nationalism.

Zionism as a political movement began as a reaction to the return of persecuting anti-semitism in the Russian Empire in the aftermath to the assassination of Tzar Alexander II in March 1881. This early Zionism was politic and vague about its ultimate objective, but Zionists in their private correspondence could be clear as to where they intended to go. In November 1882 Ze'ev Dubnov wrote from Palestine to his brother Simon, the historian as follows:

"My final purpose is to take possession in due course of Palestine and to restore to the Jews the political independence of which they have now been deprived for 2,000 years. Don't laugh, it is not a mirage. The means to achieve this purpose could be the establishment of colonies of farmers in Palestine, the establishment of various kinds of workshops and industry and their gradual expansion – in a word, to seek to put all the land, all the industry, in the hands of the Jews. Furthermore, it will be necessary to teach the young people, and the future young generations, the use of arms (in free and wild Turkey everything can be done) . . . Then there will come that splendid day whose advent was prophesized by Isaiah in his fiery and poetic words of consolation. Then the Jews, if necessary with arms in their hands, will publicly proclaim themselves master of their own, ancient fatherland. It does not matter if that splendid day will only come in fifty years' time or more. A period of fifty years is no more than a moment of time for such an undertaking."

It took sixty-six years for Dubnov's amazing prophecy to be fulfilled.

Most of the early Zionists presented Zionism as a purely secular movement, and most rabbis denounced it as such, but a few rabbis, sympathetic to Zionism saw deeper. Rabbi Abraham Isaac Kook who was to become Chief Rabbi (Ashkenazi) of Palestine under the British Mandate saw Zionism as basically of religious inspiration.

"What Jewish secular nationalists want," wrote Kook, "they do not themselves know: the spirit of Israel is so closely linked to the spirit of God that a Jewish nationalist, no matter how secularist his intention may be, is, despite himself, imbued with the divine spirit even against his own will."

Theodor Herzl, founder of the international Zionist movement entertained Messianic ideas and was seen by his Russian followers as a Messianic figure. Herzl, in the last year of his life, confided that as a boy he had had "a wonderful dream" about Moses and the Messiah: "The Messiah called to Moses: 'It is for this child that I have prayed!' And to me he said: 'Go and declare to the Jews that I shall come soon and perform great works and great deeds for my people and for the whole world.'"

According to Joseph Nedava: "The combination of Moses and Messiah is a recurring theme throughout Herzl's life and should be considered the *élan vital* of his historic mission."

Herzl never allowed any trace of Messianism or mysticism of any kind to appear in his public statements, which are entirely secular. He may have taken to heart a warning he had received from an Austrian Jewish friend, toward the end of 1895, not to "come forward in the role of Messiah"; and the advice from the same friend: "The Messiah must remain a veiled half-hidden figure."

In his own mind Herzl seems to have entertained both the possibility that he might be the Messiah, or a precursor of the Messiah, and other possibilities. He sometimes compared himself with the seventeenth-century false Messiah, Shabbetai Zevi (1626-1676). In Russia, the year before his death, Herzl was to say, "Our people believe that I am the Messiah. I myself do not know this, for I am not a theologian". The last sentence is characteristic of Herzl in its unique combination of irony, awe and exaltation.

Herzl was right about what people believed about him. Belief in Herzl as the Messiah spread with extraordinary speed, among poor Jews, after the publication of *The Jewish State.* Long afterwards, David Ben-Gurion, then aged eighty, recalled that when he was ten years old, in the Shtetl where he lived, "a rumour spread that the Messiah had arrived – a tall handsome man – a 'doctor' no less – Dr Herzl."

David Ben-Gurion, the first prime minister of Israel, saw himself as a secular figure, but some of the most important of his public statements have an unmistakeably sacral ring. In January 1937, under the British Mandate, Ben-Gurion told the British government's Peel Commission that it was the Jews, not the British who held the real mandate for Palestine.

Ben-Gurion's basic argument implied that the commission, its recommendations and the whole British Mandate were ephemeral and insignificant things in comparison with the title deeds of the Jews: "I say on behalf of the Jews that the Bible is our Mandate, the Bible which was written by us, in our own language, in Hebrew in this very country. That is our Mandate. It was only the recognition of this right which was expressed in the Balfour Declaration."

I believe that that conviction, quite as strong among "non-religious" Jews, as among the "religious" kind was basic to the emergence of the state of Israel as an independent state, and still sustains the existence of that beleaguered state.

* * *

Before I started work on *The Siege*, I had been trying to write a book about Edmund Burke, but had got hopelessly stuck. I had been trying to write a chronologically based book but couldn't make any sense out of a life which – Burke being an exceptionally laborious parliamentarian – skipped around without comprehensible sequence at the behest of the parliamentary calendar. So I gave up on Burke and set to work on Israel. Then, while I was working on Israel, I found that two lines of Yeats kept returning to my mind. The two lines were:

American Colonies, Ireland, France and India
Harried, and Burke's great melody against it.

("It": abuse of power)

At first I tried to brush this distracting refrain away like a nagging insect. But then I began to realize that Yeats was telling me how to organize my book: along thematic lines. And I found that once I did so, all the old chronological difficulties dropped away. The thematic approach worked like a charm for me. The book got written at white heat.

And I found out that, once I started to work thematically, philosophical sub-themes began to loom up along with the geographical themes. And when the philosophical sub-themes are clearly seen, the formidable unity and consistency of Burke's thinking begins to become clear. For example on December 1, 1783, speaking on reform in India, Burke said: "I feel an insuperable reluctance in giving my hand to destroy any established institution of government, upon a theory, however plausible it may be."

In that sentence – with, of course, no reference to France – Burke is stating the precise principle on which, seven years later, he will denounce the destroying theorists of the French National Assembly.

Burke's deep understanding of the principles at work, and of the forces behind them, gave him an extraordinary and unparalleled capacity to predict the future course of the French Revolution. For example he was able to predict, in *Reflections on the Revolution in France* the outcome of the Revolution in the emergence of a military despot.

"It is known, that armies have hitherto yielded a very precarious and uncertain obedience to any senate, or popular authority; and they will least of all yield it to an assembly which is to have only a continuance of two years. The officers must totally lose the characteristic disposition of military men, if they see with perfect submission and due admiration, the dominion of pleaders; especially when they find, that they have a new court to pay to an endless succession of those pleaders, whose military policy, and the genius of whose command (if they should have any) must be as uncertain as their duration is transient. In the weakness of one kind of authority, and in the fluctuation of all, the officers of any army will remain for some time mutinous and full of faction, until some popular general, who understands the art of conciliating the soldiery, and who possesses the true spirit of command, shall draw the eyes of all men upon himself. Armies will obey him on his personal account. There is no other way of securing military obedience in this state of things. But the moment in which that event shall happen, the person who really commands the army is your master; the master (that is little) of your king, the master of your assembly, the master of your whole republic."

The seizure of power by Napoleon Bonaparte – the event predicted in this remarkable passage – occurred on 18 Brumaire (9 November) 1799, nine years after the publication of the *Reflections*, and more than two years after the death of the author.

In a similar way Burke predicted the execution of the king – almost precisely two years ahead of the event. He also predicted – eighteen months ahead of the event – the replacement of the original "moderate" leaders of the revolution by a harder and bloodier strain.

"These [moderates] if I conceive rightly of their conduct, are a set of men who approve heartily of the whole new constitution, but wish to lay heavy on [i.e. to distance themselves from] the most atrocious of those crimes, by which this fine constitution of their's has been obtained. But these men naturally are despised by those who have heads to know, and hearts that are able to go through the necessary demands of bold, wicked enterprizes. They are naturally classed below the latter description, and will only be used by them as inferior instruments. They will be only the Fairfaxes of your Cromwells."

The "Cromwells" were Danton and Robespierre.

Finally, while Pitt and the British Government continued to see the French Revolution as normal and manageable, Burke saw it – as early as 1791 – as a huge convulsion in human history, on the scale of the Reformation.

Having noted that England's Glorious Revolution "did not extend beyond its territory" he goes on:

"The present Revolution in France seems to me to be quite of another character and description; and to bear little resemblance or analogy to any of those which have been brought about in Europe, upon principles merely political. *It is a Revolution of doctrine and theoretick dogma* [Burke's italics]. It has a much greater resemblance to those changes which have been made upon religious grounds, in which a spirit of proselytism makes an essential part.

"The last Revolution of doctrine and theory which has happened in Europe, is the Reformation. It is not for my purpose to take any notice here of the merits of that Revolution, but to state one only of its effects.

"That effect was *to introduce other interests into all countries, than those which arose from their locality and natural circumstances* [Burke's italics]. The principle of the Reformation was such, as by it's essence, could not be local or confined to the country in which it had it's origin.

"These principles of internal, as well as external division and coalition, are but just now extinguished. But they who will examine into the true character and genius of some late events, must be satisfied that other sources of faction, combining parties among the inhabitants of different countries into one connexion, are opened, and that from these sources are likely to arise effects full as important as those which had formerly arisen from the jarring interests of the religious sects. The intention of the several actors in the change in France, is not a matter of doubt, it is very openly professed.

"In the modern world, before this time, there has been no instance of this spirit of general political faction, separated from religion, pervading several countries, and forming a principle of union between the partizans in each. But the thing is not less in human nature."

* * *

I first became keenly interested in Jefferson while I was working on Edmund Burke. I read with surprise a reference to Burke in a letter of Jefferson's to Benjamin Vaughan dated May 11, 1791 just after Jefferson had read one of the first copies of Burke's *Reflections on the Revolution in France* to reach the United States.

Jefferson wrote:

"The Revolution of France does not astonish me as much as the Revolution of Mr Burke. I wish I could believe the latter proceeded from as pure motives as the former. But what demonstration could scarcely have established before, less than the hints of Dr Priestley [Dr Joseph Priestley, leading English radical, and a friendly correspondent of Jefferson's] and Mr Paine establish firmly now [sic]. How mortifying that this evidence of the rottenness of his mind must oblige us now to ascribe to wicked motives those actions of his life which wore the mask of virtue and patriotism."

On this, I commented, not long after reading the passage:

"The mode of reasoning here is curious. The 'rottenness' of Burke's mind is deemed to be 'firmly established', beyond the need for argument, by the 'evidence' of his book in its totality (combined with unspecified hints by Priestley and Paine). Then this imputation of 'rottenness', now claimed to be established fact, must 'oblige us' to ascribe everything in Burke's whole life to wicked motives. This is a clear case of the old *Odium theologicum* transferred to a new and nominally secular sphere. The heretic and blasphemer who opposes the French Revolution represents the forces of evil in the universe and is himself totally evil and all the worse for having formerly worn the mask of virtue and patriotism (over the American Revolution). Fortunately, *Rights of Man* is there as a heavenly antidote."

Jefferson goes on,

"We have some names of note here who have apostatized from the true faith: but they are few indeed, and the body of our citizens are pure and unsusceptible of taint in their republicanism. Mr Paine's answer to Burke will be a refreshing shower to their minds."

On first reading that letter of Jefferson's, I thought that Jefferson was yielding to ungovernable emotions. On studying Jefferson more particularly, however, I found that his emotions were eminently governable, and were always governed in such a way as to serve his political ambitions, which he invariably dissimulated. Jefferson was aiming at power, from a power base in Virginia, and from the beginning of the French Revolution he saw that American enthusiasm for that Revolution – very strong among Americans both North and South for the first four years of the French Revolution – was an enormous political asset both for Virginia and for Jefferson. This was an issue which united the (white) South with few exceptions and divided the North along class lines. The propertied classes in the North were doing well out of trade with Britain, and were busy under Alexander Hamilton, Washington's most trusted aide, in laying the bases of America's future prosperity. Hamilton and John Adams were agreed on that point. So Jefferson saw that the French Revolution could be used to undermine Hamilton and Adams. Those were the "names of note" who had apostatized from the true faith, according to Jefferson's letter to Vaughan. As Julian P Boyd, the great editor of the first twenty volumes of Jefferson's correspondence, noted: "The national debate [over Burke, Paine and the French Revolution] fixed John Adams in the public mind, however unjustly, as an advocate of a monarchical form of government in the United States. In consequence Jefferson's stature as a champion of the republican cause had been greatly magnified."

Up to 1793 and into 1794, the card of the French Revolution was a winning card in American politics and Jefferson played it with great aplomb. But in 1793, after the outbreak of war between Britain and France, and Washington's declaration of neutrality – on behalf of an administration in which Jefferson was still Secretary of State – the game became more complicated. Jefferson played the new and less attractive cards he had been dealt, with even greater skill than before. In the new circumstances he adroitly distanced himself from the French cause, as many others were doing at the time, but without losing any of the popularity he had won in the past by espousing that cause. He was a master politician, and eventually rewarded not only with the presidency for himself, but also with – effectively – the nomination of his two successors, Madison and Monroe.

Jefferson was peerless in his achievements as a political leader. Long after his death, he became the hero of a cult which saw him as without flaw, and which doctored the historical record to make him look that way. In particular his record in relation to slavery was doctored to make him look like a modern liberal.

In the first half of the twentieth century, the most important phase affecting the posthumous reputation and civil-religious status of Thomas Jefferson was the New Deal. As Merrill D Peterson puts it: "The Roosevelt administration built a great national temple to Jefferson's memory." The temple is the Jefferson Memorial in Washington, dedicated by President Franklin Delano Roosevelt on the two hundredth anniversary of Jefferson's birth, April 13, 1943. According to an official brochure: "Inscriptions at the memorial were selected by the Thomas Jefferson Memorial commission and were taken from a wide variety of his writings on freedom, slavery, education and government." The section of the inscriptions that deals with freedom and slavery runs as follows:

"God who gave us life gave us liberty. Can the liberties of a nation be secure when we have removed a conviction that these liberties are the gift of God? Indeed I tremble for my country when I reflect that God is just, that his justice cannot sleep forever. Commerce between master and slave is despotism. Nothing is more certainly written in the book of fate than that these people are to be free."

All of this passage, except for the last sentence, is taken from *Notes on the State of Virginia.* The last sentence is taken from Jefferson's *Autobiography.* That sentence, as isolated in the Memorial inscription, deceived the public as to Jefferson's meaning. For the original passage in the *Autobiography* continues: *"Nor is it less certain that the two races, equally free, cannot live in the same government. Native habit, opinion has drawn indelible lines of distinction between them."* (Emphasis added.)

In short, these people are to be free, and then deported to Africa. Jefferson's teaching on that matter is quite clear and often repeated.

Those who edited that inscription on behalf of the Jefferson Memorial Commission must have known what they were doing when they wrenched that resounding sentence from the *Autobiography* out of the context which so drastically qualifies its meaning. The distortion, by suppression, has to be deliberate.

In that inscription on the Jefferson Memorial in Washington, DC the liberal-Jeffersonian lie about Jefferson's position on liberty and slavery assumes, literally, monumental proportions.

The topic of the French Revolution, and the topic of the defence of slavery in Virginia, were linked in Jefferson's mind and in the thrust of his political ascent.

In purely political terms, it is not difficult to reconcile the Jeffersonian commitment to the Cult of the French Revolution (fervent from October 1789 to July 1793 and desultory thereafter) with the defense of the institution of slavery in Virginia and the rest of the South. Virginia felt threatened by the power of the Northern cities, and the real threat – although no more than an implicit one in the 1790s – was to the existence of slavery in the South, after it had disappeared from the North. Virginians did not, in public, explicitly acknowledge that what was felt to be threatened was slavery. To start a national debate on that topic would have been quite contrary to their interests. Yet they needed to defend what they felt to be the liberty of Virginia, and the distinguishing characteristic of Virginian liberty was the liberty of Virginian gentlemen to own slaves.

Slavery was protected by the Constitution, but it was a grudging protection, as far as many in the North were concerned. Some Northern writers were already addressing the South as from a superior moral height. This was intolerable, especially for high-spirited Virginian gentlemen. Yet to answer the Northerners, on their chosen topic of slavery, would be both difficult and risky. What was needed was a *general* topic, one which was, ostensibly, not sectional at all, but which would enable the South to take the high moral ground against the North, and win national support by so doing.

The political genius of Thomas Jefferson – working, I think, instinctively – identified that topic as the Cult of the French Revolution, presented as the legitimate culmination of the American one, together with which it constituted one single holy cause of "liberty". The Cult had the inherent property of putting the Northern leadership on the defensive because it endangered their commercial and financial relations with Britain. Thus the Northerners could plausibly be represented as having defected – "apostatized" in the holy jargon of the Cult – from the American Revolution itself, by reason of their refusal to embrace the French one.

Thus the moral tables were turned. Southerners need no longer listen to Northerners lecturing them about slavery. The Virginians themselves would eliminate slavery in their own good time and in their own way, and how and when they chose to do it was entirely their own affair. The Northerners were talking about slavery only to divert attention from their own corruption, Anglomania, and monarchical inclinations – all evident from their refusal to accept the French Revolution, true heir to the American Revolution and touchstone of the sincerity of the commitment of any American to the principles laid down by Thomas Jefferson in the Declaration of Independence.

So let's not talk about slavery! Let's talk about the French Revolution!

The Cult certainly met a political need, and got the Republican Party off to a flying start. But it also met an emotional need, on the part of the Virginians, so that their commitment to it was heartfelt (up to the summer of 1793) and not just a matter of expediency. Basically the emotional need was the need to feel pure.

The Jacobins, guided by Robespierre and St Just, divided the world into *les purs* and *les corrompus*. In this respect at least the Jeffersonians were true

Jacobins. They were themselves *les purs*. Adams and Hamilton were *les corrompus par excellence*. (Washington, the Virginian who had declined into being an American, had to be watched.)

In a caste society, such as Jefferson's Virginia, the notions of purity and of contamination are of central importance, and heavily fraught. Ideas of moral purity, sexual purity, genetic purity are all there in shadowy interaction, and all threatened with contamination from the omnipresent pariah caste. One reaction to that is the hysterical exaltation of the purity of Southern (white) womanhood. But the question of the purity of the Southern (white) *manhood* remains in the shadows of silence.

There was a lot of shrewd political calculation there, on Jefferson's part. But there was also a manic, mystic side to Jefferson's cult of the French Revolution when that cult was at its most intense.

At the most exalted point of his commitment to the Cult, in January 1793, Jefferson had a vision of the French Revolution as a destroying and redeeming Angel, purifying and liberating humanity through the slaughter of millions.

This was the weirdest passage in Jefferson's writings, the so-called "Adam and Eve" letter to William Short. Jefferson wrote:

"My own affections have been deeply wounded by some of the martyrs of this cause but rather than it should have failed, I would have seen half the earth desolated. Were there but an Adam and Eve, left in every country, and left free, it would be better than it now is."

Let us leave common sense and common humanity behind for a moment and follow Thomas Jeffereson into the wild vision which, however, fleeting its surfacing, was evidently generated by a powerful wish.

I think we can begin to see what the wish is, if we put a very simple question based on Jefferson's supposition. The question is: *What color are the American Adam and Eve?*

There can be only one answer to that, on Jeffersonian assumptions. Adam and Eve have to be white, because Adam and Eve are *free*. There is no room, in Jeffersonian America (or even in the Hemisphere), for free blacks. Adam and Eve are free and white, and therefore all their descendants are free and white. In terms of racist theology, it is a reversal of the Fall. Washed in the blood of the victims of the French Revolution, and other revolutions inspired by it, humanity is born again. Above all America, and even higher above all, Virginia, is born again, washed clean at last from that deep blurred single stain, composed of blackness and of guilt. The French Revolution gives back to America its lost innocence.

A vision; no more and no less. But visions always tell us something. And this one tells us something about the sources of the power of the Cult of the French Revolution, in its heyday, over the emotional life, and the mind, of Thomas Jefferson.

For a long time, through most of the twentieth century, Jefferson's reputation as a thoroughgoing liberal and anti-racist flourished luxuriantly, nourished by many biographers, historians and politicians. It is still defended, but the defence has shown less and less conviction with every passing decade, since the 1960s. If, as we must hope, the United States becomes a full integrated civil society, rejecting all forms of negative racial discrimination, Jefferson's place in history will have to be seen, not as preparing the way for a modern non-racial society, but as attempting to block the way towards that development. At present we are in a mid-way condition. In the 1990s Jefferson is a hero, both to many American liberals, and also to the racist right, including the Oklahoma City bombings both of whose detected perpetrators are on record as being Jeffersonian cultists. If there is a racist revival in America in the next century, Jefferson will be the central hero of that revival.

* * *

The theme of the defence of academic freedom, as central to the full development of human intellectual development, had been of prime importance to me during my years in Ghana. After that – in New York, in Dublin and in London – the theme remained important to me, but was overshadowed by other, more immediate preoccupations. Then suddenly the theme of academic freedom again became of prime importance, because of developments with which I became involved in South Africa.

It all began – without at first any thematic resonance – with an invitation which I received to give a course of lectures at the University of Cape Town, South Africa. The invitation came from David Welsh, then Head of the Political Science Department at the University of Cape Town, with whom I had become friendly during earlier, journalistic, visits to South Africa. David wanted me to give a five-week series of lectures at Cape Town, under his Department's auspices.

I was at first in doubt as to whether to accept. I had complete confidence in David himself, and indeed a lot of confidence in the university. But I wasn't sure how much freedom the university enjoyed in a South Africa still dominated by *apartheid* laws and practices, even though I knew that some of the practices had become a bit relaxed under international pressure.

My son Patrick would be classified as "coloured" if he had been living in South Africa during the *apartheid* period. So I wrote back to David, saying that I could only accept his invitation if he could give me certain assurances about how Patrick would be treated at the university if he accompanied me, were I to accept. I would only accept if David could assure me that, while on the university campus Patrick would not be exposed to any discrimination on racial grounds. I realized that when off-campus, Patrick would be on his own. I just wanted to make sure that no institution, whose invitation I might accept, would discriminate against my son in any way.

David immediately assured me that black or coloured students, or black or coloured visitors, were not subject to any racial discrimination either at the hands of the university authorities or at the hands of the government or anyone else, while on the university campus. I had no hesitation in accepting David's assurances and later, when Patrick and I went to Cape Town, we found that those assurances were fully borne out.

At the stage of my acceptance it did not seem to me that academic freedom was an issue with regard to South Africa. In fact it seemed that the university was defending its freedom, under the pressures of *apartheid*, with a remarkable degree of success.

But then, quite suddenly, in late 1986 when I was due to start lecturing in Cape Town it became clear that academic freedom was indeed under serious, and in part successful, pressure. The pressure was coming, neither from Cape Town University nor even from the South African government, but from members of the African National Congress, with the connivance of academics in British universities.

The ANC had called for an international boycott of the South African universities – regardless of their own internal practices – for as long as the government of South Africa failed to repeal its *apartheid* laws. Up to this time the international boycott had not been rigorously enforced and foreign scholars coming to South African universities to teach had in general not been interfered with.

But then quite suddenly, on the eve of our visit, there was a flagrant international breach of the principles of academic freedom. In early September 1986 an International Congress of Archaeologists was due to be held at Southampton in Britain. In the ordinary course invitations were sent to four leading South African archaeologists. South African archaeology is highly esteemed by archaeologists in other countries, and South African archaeologists had been invited to all previous international conferences on the subject. But in this case the ANC appears to have invoked the international boycott it had proclaimed, and instigated its sympathizers in British academia, and the British archaeological community – the hosts for the conference – actually disinvited the archaeologists who had received and accepted invitations. There was no pretence that the archaeologists in question were themselves racists or partisans of apartheid. They were just disinvited at the ANC's insistence because of the institutions of the country in which they lived.

Because of the principles involved, and because of the distinction of the victimized scholars, the international archaeological community reacted sharply to the British decision (to which many British archaeologists were also opposed). Eventually, professional and international disapproval of the British decision forced a change of venue for the new conference to continental Europe, and the South African archaeologists, having been previously invited and then disinvited were now reinvited, to the new venue.

While the debate over the decision to disinvite the scholars was at its height I wrote a piece about the matter for *The Times* in support of the protest against the disinvitation and against the "academic boycott" in particular. In the course of the article I indicated that I was about to go to South Africa to teach thereby breaking the "academic boycott" which I believed to be altogether wrong, and a breach of the basic principle of the international solidarity of scholars and teachers. This announcement turned out to be quite imprudent, but I cannot say that I regret the imprudence.

* * *

When we travelled to South Africa it seemed at first that my imprudence would not be resented. For the first three weeks my course on "siege societies" – involving a comparison between South Africa, Israel and Northern Ireland – was attended by about 100 students most of whom were white middle-class English-speakers who were as David Welsh told me probably mostly of a generally liberal outlook. My early classes passed off without incident. But then, in the fourth week, organized trouble began. This was shortly after I had made a public statement, accepting the economic boycott, but attacking the academic boycott. Of the latter I said: "its impact on the apartheid regime would be nil, but the inroads it was making on academic freedom and freedom of expression were very serious indeed. These values would be vital to a non-racial South Africa and to other free societies. What was being conducted in South Africa under the banner of an academic boycott seemed to be a sort of creeping form of the Cultural Revolution, which had wrecked the universities of China and which the China of today repudiated with abhorrence."

Posters appeared on campus denouncing my presence and my breach of the academic boycott. Then I was invited to debate the issue with a group of students. Rather naively I was pleased with the idea of the debate. But when I showed up for the debate the man who had invited me, a student called Bolger – of Irish origin and I believe of Sinn Féin sympathies – announced that there would be no debate. Instead, the students would question me. I realized that I had fallen into a trap. But I said that I had been invited to make a statement and, unless allowed to do so, I would leave. After I had made my statement, I was prepared to answer questions. This was agreed to. My statement was heard in silence. The "questions" began. Most of the questions were in fact hostile statements. Sample: "Why did you break the academic boycott? Was it to sneer at the sufferings of the African people?" I coped with this sort of stuff for about half an hour, then got up to leave. I had some difficulty leaving as a group of the most hostile "students" – including I think some outsiders – formed a ring around me – and baited me with further "questions". But after about twenty minutes of this they seemed to tire of the sport and let me go.

That was only the beginning of a concerted, and soon successful, effort to drive me from the campus. Shortly after the fiasco of the debate on October 7, I gave a public lecture at the university on Israel. Most of the audience were members of Cape Town's large Jewish community. But a large black crowd – some of them students and some not – gathered outside the hall, chanting slogans. The vice-chancellor, Dr Stewart Saunders was in the audience and appealed for calm. I finished my lecture and withdrew, together with my audience. As we were leaving the demonstrators surged in through another door. Stewards tried to hold them back, and some of the stewards were assaulted by students wielding thongs.

After that the disruption of my regular lectures began, again with the organized irruption of large crowds of young blacks, and assaults on the stewards. It later emerged that there was a govermental *agent provocateur* element in these disturbances intended to discourage the anti-apartheid liberalism of the UCT campus. Of this element David Welsh has written:

"Another contribution to wrecking the lecture series came from an altogether different quarter: the notorious Security Police. For years before the Security Police had infiltrated student organisations, spied on lecturers and listened in on their classes. They also employed *agents provocateur* to incite students to engage in illegal activities (not difficult in South Africa's circumstances) or to inflame conflict situations (which occurred often), so that the ever-vigilant Security Police could burnish its reputation as essential custodians of the racial order. One Danie Cronje, who took a prominent part in the demonstrations against Conor (including wading into the Campus Control officials with a studded belt), later confessed to his role as a police informer and agent provocateur."

After the disruption of a second lecture, I had a call from the vice-chancellor. Stewart Saunders told me that if I chose to continue with my course, I was free to do so. However, it was his duty to warn me that in the view of the university authorities, there was a risk of very serious disturbances if I did so. People might be seriously injured, even killed. It was up to me. After reflecting on that, I told the vice-chancellor that I would cancel my remaining lectures on campus. I notified my students that I would give one concluding lecture off-campus and would summarize what I would have had to say in the rest of the course, and provide them with a reading-list. The final lecture was well attended. My own students were horrified by the demonstrations and grieved at their success.

Before leaving South Africa, Patrick and I took an enjoyable holiday in the Kruger National Park to recover from our experience of the academic boycott.

Subsequently the university authorities set up a Commission of Enquiry into the events that had led to the premature cancellation of my lectures. As David Welsh has written:

"Thus was born the (du Plessis) Commission of Enquiry into the events which occurred on the campus of the University of Cape Town on 7 and 8 October 1986. Its members were Dr DJ du Plessis (an academic surgeon and a former vice-chancellor of the University of Witwatersrand), Advocate Arthur Chaskelson, SC (a leading public interest barrister, who had defended many accused in political trials) and Advocate Ismail Mahomed, SC (also a prominent defence counsel in many political trials). It is worth mentioning that Chaskelson is now President of the Constitutional Court and Mahomed is Chief Justice of South Africa. Clearly, the latter two members were chosen to ensure that the Commission enjoyed credibility in more radical circles. Even so, NUSAS, the SRC and AZASO declined to be officially represented at the Commission's hearings on the grounds that they had not been consulted about the appointment and terms of reference of the Commission.

"The Commission completed its labours on December 18, 1986 in the middle of the university's long summer vacation. Its report was submitted to the University Council, which met in special session on January 12, 1987. Despite serious criticisms of the report's lack of objectivity, notably by Dr Frank Bradlow, the Council resolved to accept the 'main thrust of the recommendations made by the Commission' and to reaffirm its commitment to upholding the freedom of the university and 'the right of any academic, subject to the normal rights of the heads of departments, faculties and Senate, to invite any person to take part in an academic programme . . . '

"The key phrase in all of this was the 'main thrust of the recommendations'. It enabled the Council to evade passing judgment on some of the Commission's principal findings, which it knew to be incorrect – and several members believed to be seriously biased. If it was a ploy, which I suspected, I was determined not to let it succeed.

"The vice-chancellor declined to give me access to the report until January 20, 1987. When I read it I was appalled. I immediately did two things: resign as head of department and issue a press statement. My press release described the report as: 'one-sided, flawed and shoddy. In major respects, its reading of the evidence is faulty, while crucial pieces are ignored. I resent in particular the Commission's unfairness to Dr O'Brien, whose alleged personality characteristics and motivations are subjected to an analysis to which Dr O'Brien has had no opportunity to reply. The Commission evinces little recognition of his stature as a scholar and it accepts too easily specious evidence which claims that he came to UCT for ulterior, non-academic reasons. Dr O'Brien is a friend of mine, and I take full responsibility for inviting him – yet I was not asked a single question by the Commission about his personality or about the reasons for my inviting him or his accepting. It is perhaps indicative of the Commission's approach [I should have said "provincialism"] that they even spell his name incorrectly [throughout the report he is called "Connor"].'

"It was not until April 21, 1987 that some measure of justice could be done. This was at an extremely rancorous Senate meeting. A relatively uncontroversial motion, proposed by one of the deputy vice-chancellors, John Reid, acknowledged that the invitation had been extended 'for academic reasons only.' The fireworods began when I, seconded by my colleague, Robert Schrire, proposed that the Senate reject those findings of the Commission's report which concerned Conor personally and express to him its apology for any damage that was done to his reputation.

"I made a fiery speech, extracts from which I now quote (at Conor's express request): 'I would have hoped for a motion that rejected this report outright'; 'it is a shoddy effort, unworthy of association with UCT, and incapable of being used as a basis for reconciliation . . . '

I reminded Senate that we are not dealing with some hick from the bogs of Ireland, but a world-class scholar. [I then listed some of Conor's literary achievements.] But even were he a hick, it would not excuse the Commission's handling of him; even less the Council's crass dealing with the issue.

"'The report is a classic case of blaming the victim . . . Hardly less extraordinary – and I might add, unforgivable – is UCT's failure to ensure that Dr O'Brien had received a copy of the report before its release to the Press . . . [I then quoted Conor:] The first I heard about it was on radio and in the newspapers. I feel pretty shabbily treated in not being given a warning, and I'm surprised at such behaviour on the part of a very respectable university. So were many of us [at UCT] . . . '

"'I invited him, and I could have told the Commission exactly why I had done so . . . I certainly had in mind no thought other than giving our students the opportunity to hear one of the great minds of our time. Yet I was not asked about this. It is hardly necessary to add that the Commission ignores completely the [highly favourable] reaction of Dr O'Brien's class to his course and to the debacle whereby it was terminated [which they deplored].

"It is not good enough for the UCT Council to take refuge in the statement that it accepts the "main thrust" of the recommendations. That, frankly, is an evasion which has brought UCT into disrepute. If the Council, for reasons that I find inexplicable, finds it impossible to bring itself to make a formal apology, then it behoves Senate to do so. I, too, wish to heal wounds, but of one thing I am certain: you cannot heal wounds by ignoring the real injustice done to individuals.'

"After lengthy and acrimonious debate a slightly amended version of the motion was accepted by 59 votes to 9, with 22 abstentions. I was delighted to hear from a colleague that after the meeting a senior official of UCT was overheard to say that mine 'was the most disgraceful speech he has ever heard in Senate.' I could not have wished for a better accolade!"

18

MIRI AND PIRI:
A FUSION OF RELIGION AND NATIONALISM IN NORTHERN INDIA

MUCH OF MY JOURNALISM HAS BEEN AND IS HIGHLY THEMATIC, WITH THE themes of religion and nationalism recurring with what some readers may regard as obsessive regularity. I shall leave the theme of religion and nationalism in Ireland, and my own long wrestlings with that theme, to the last chapters of this book. In this chapter I wish to speak of a strange encounter with what I believe to be the most intense fusion of religion and nationalism to exist anywhere: the case of the Sikhs of the Punjab.

India, with over 800 million people, is by far the largest democracy in the world in terms of population, and the second-largest secular state in the world, after China. When India became independent just over forty years ago and undertook to be a secular and democratic state, many people doubted whether it would live up to that commitment. Its experience of democracy under the British Raj was quite limited, and mostly confined to the generation immediately preceding independence. Secularism seemed to be even more improbable than democracy in the Indian context. Most Indians were, and are, firmly attached to a particular religion; relatively few Indians forty years ago could have grasped the nature of a secular state, or understood the need for such a thing. Extreme religious groups of one kind and another denounced the secular state as godless and therefore illegitimate.

The Indian state came into being amid the scenes of communal-religious carnage that accompanied the partition of the subcontinent between mainly Hindu India and entirely Muslim Pakistan. Muhammad Ali Jinnah, the founder of Pakistan, had resolutely rejected the idea of a secular state that could encompass both Hindus and Muslims. In his presidential address to the Muslim League at Lahore in 1940, Jinnah declared: "Islam and Hinduism are not religions in the strict sense of the word, but in fact different and distinct social orders, and it is only a dream that the Hindus and Muslims can ever evolve a common nationality. . . To yoke together two such nations under a single state . . . must lead to a growing discontent and final destruction of any fabric that may be so built up for the government of such a state."

Yet in the event, the fabric of India's secular state proved tougher than that of confessional Pakistan. Pakistan originally consisted of eastern and western sections, connected by a common religion but different in language and culture. The religious bond proved insufficient, and East Pakistan in 1971 seceded and became the independent state of Bangladesh. Secular India, however, has held together. There are now almost as many Muslims in India as there are in Pakistan. Muslims and Hindus in India may perhaps not have "evolved a common nationality", but they – and Sikhs also, so far – have managed to live together, within one state, for more than forty years now, whereas the "common nationality" of the Muslims of Pakistan burst asunder after twenty-four years.

The viability of the secular and democratic system in India is a remarkable phenomenon, and one that has received less attention in the west than it deserves. Yet there have been and continue to be challenges, both internal and external, to India's secular democracy, and to the very existence of an Indian state.

In this chapter I propose to look at one of these challenges – the challenge of Sikh religious nationalism, discreetly backed by Pakistan. The Sikhs are a religious and ethnic group, distinct from both Hindus and Muslims. Most Sikhs live in the prosperous northwest Indian province of the Punjab. From about 1980 on – with considerable moral backing from their less-militant fellows – some Sikhs have been engaged in a sporadic campaign of violence, mainly against the Indian government, but also against Hindus in the Punjab, and sometimes against Sikhs who happen to have offended the militants.

Previous challenges to the Indian state came mainly from poor and marginal regions or sections. These challenges, including those mounted by the Naxalites (Indian-Marxist-Leninists), exploited the grievances of the most disadvantaged. The Sikh challenge is different. The Sikhs are the most dynamic, and among the most prosperous, of all the peoples of India. They are first-rate farmers, soldiers, sportsmen. Thrifty, abstemious, self-reliant, with a well-developed work ethic, the Sikhs have many of the Puritan virtues. The Punjab is the richest of all the provinces of India. It is because of the Punjab that India has not needed to import food, even during periods of prolonged drought. The wealth of the Punjab is partly due to its natural resources, in particular its great rivers. But it is also partly due to the skill and industry of its farming population, the Sikh Jats. Sikhs are also prospering in various employments – mainly to do with transport – in many other parts of India.

So what are the grievances that have driven a section of this prosperous people into revolt? The answer to this question does not exactly lie on the surface. Before attempting to answer it, we shall need to look first at some of the facts on the ground today and then at the history of the Sikhs, and in particular at the evolution among them of a uniquely explicit institutionalized synthesis of religion and politics – a synthesis that has proved profoundly inimical to the secular and democratic state of India.

In 1988 I attended a Sikh political rally, which was also inevitably a Sikh religious rally, at the Guru Nanak stadium, in the Punjab industrial city of Ludhiana. The rally was organized by the main Sikh political party, the United Akali Dal. The UAD is regarded as a constitutional party in India. I thought a term once used in Irish politics might be more appropriate: "a *slightly* constitutional party".

The crowd consisted almost entirely of large, stolid handsome Sikh farmers: Jats. The Jats sat on the ground of the sports field, in silence, facing the platform. That platform was quite a sight. It was religious on one side and political on the other: a fascinating spectacle for someone like myself, curious about the interdependencies of religion and nationalism.

The political side was a conventional political platform, with chairs, a long table, microphones, glasses of water, and political personalities taking turns to speak. All that was on the right-hand side, from the point of view of the audience, or congregation. On the other side – the gospel side, in Christian parlance – was a dais raised about a foot above the level of the regular platform, and covered by a red and gold canopy. Under the canopy was a copy of the Sikh scriptures: the *Granth Sahib*. Three priests in saffron robes kept silent vigil around the *Granth Sahib*.

The presence of the *Granth Sahib* meant that the gathering was a religious ceremony as well as a political occasion. It also meant that the whole platform and the area immediately around it, including the press gallery, was deemed to constitute a sacred place. I was invited to take a seat in the press gallery but declined on finding that in order to enter I would be obliged to cover my head. Somehow I found the idea of a sacred press gallery, though novel and interesting, also faintly nauseating. I stayed out on the field.

But even out on the field the political proceedings had a disturbingly liturgical character. The political resolutions, all of which were carried unanimously, were put to the vote with the sacred formula:

"BOLE SO NIKAL

SAT SRI AKAL"

("Whosoever responds

God is Truth")

The members of the audience, or congregation, signified their approval by raising their right hands and saying,

"SAT SRI AKAL"

("God is Truth")

Rather like ratifying a political proposition with the formula *Et cum spiritu tuo.*

The liturgical method of dealing with political affairs has some disquieting implications under present conditions in the Punjab. The liturgical method assumes consensus, and that in itself might seem harmless enough. But the form that the present consensus of the Sikh people has assumed is somewhat sinister.

In the forty-eight hours that preceded that rally at Ludhiana, seventeen people had been murdered by Sikh terrorists in the Punjab. Most of those murdered on that particular occasion were themselves Sikhs, designated by the terrorists as collaborationists or as delinquent in other respects (failure to pay up on receipt of an extortion note being probably the most frequent type of offence). So not much Sikh consensus there, operationally speaking. But at that large and respectable liturgico-political Sikh rally there *was* consensus. And it was a consensus that worked, smoothly and solemnly, in support of the terrorists.

As the proceedings at Ludhiana were conducted entirely in Punjabi, I was dependent on an interpreter, a young Sikh official of the government of the Punjab (which is to say, under present conditions, the government of India). I asked my interpreter to let me know if anyone referred explicitly to what the Sikh terrorists had been up to in the previous days, and over many months before that. The meeting went on for five hours, with dozens of speeches. During all this time only one speaker – Amrinder Singh, formerly the Maharajah of Patiala, a city in the Punjab – explicitly condemned the taking of innocent lives. Apart from that there was nothing. So much my interpreter told me, but later I learned that what actually happened was worse than that. A resolution implicitly supportive of the terrorists, and probably drafted by them, had been passed unanimously by that large and peaceful-looking gathering with the obligatory ritual formula:

"BOLE SO NIKAL
SAT SRI AKAL"

I had spent the evening before the Ludhiana rally at Amrinder Singh's home – formerly palace – in Patiala. Amrinder Singh is the greatest of Sikh magnates, and enjoys the unusual distinction of being highly respected by both the Sikh community and by the government of India. He retains the confidence of the Sikh community because he resigned from the Congress Party and from various offices after Operation Bluestar, the occupation by the Indian Army of the Golden Temple complex, in June 1984 (after the murder of Mrs Gandhi, by Sikh members of her bodyguard). Amrinder Singh was greatly concerned by the rising influence of the terrorists (euphemistically known as "militants") and by the apparent drift in the direction of some kind of secession by the Sikhs, with the complicity of Pakistan.

Amrinder Singh explained to me that while he would like to see a resolution passed *condemning* terrorism, there was no way of getting such a resolution from a representative gathering of Sikhs, in present conditions. He knew of the draft resolution *supporting* the terrorists, but thought he had succeeded in averting it on the night before the rally. The organising committee had rejected it by four to one. Then, at the rally itself, a member of the platform party had simply put the resolution, and it had been immediately carried, in the ritual manner. The resolution asserted that Sikh survival is now in danger and that therefore (in addition to constitutional measures of opposition) "in a befitting response, the Sikhs have taken recourse to other modes of resistance, thereby keeping alive the traditions, history, and ethos of the Sikh people".

So after Ludhiana, the Sikh terrorists can credibly claim that their armed struggle has been unanimously validated at a representative gathering of the Sikh nation, and has received the blessing of the Sikh religion.

The word *Sikh* means "disciple". The Sikhs are the disciples of ten gurus who flourished from the late 15th to the early 18th century in the Punjab. The teachings of the ten gurus are explained in the *Granth Sahib*, the bible of the Sikhs.

In the time of the gurus the dominant power in Northern India was the Mogul Empire, in which Islam was the official religion. The religion of the gurus grew up in the borderland between Muslim and Hindu territory. The Punjab was part of that borderland. The first guru, Nanak (1469-1539), was originally a Hindu, and many of his followers have regarded themselves as belonging to the Hindu community and as practicing a purified form of the Hindu religion. The teachings of Guru Nanak are monotheistic and egalitarian, and are opposed to idolatry, to the caste system, and to the oppression of women. As the Sikhs increased in number and in influence in the region, the teachings of the later gurus became increasingly political and eventually militaristic. The fifth guru, Arjan (1581-1606), from the moment of his inauguration, directly challenged the legitimacy of the Mogul Empire. Thus challenged, the reigning Mogul Emperor, Jehangir, seized Arjan and tortured him to obtain a recantation. Arjan refused to recant, and died under torture. He thus became the first great martyr of the Sikh religion.

The dying message of Guru Arjan to his son was "My dear son, sit fully armed on the throne and maintain an army to the best of your ability". Arjan's son was the sixth guru, Hargobind (1606-1645). It was Hargobind who made the union of religion and politics a formal and explicit part of the Sikh religion, and also put the religion on a footing of war. Hargobind assumed the title of *Miri Piri Da Malik*, Lord of the Secular and the Spiritual, and wore two swords, corresponding to this concept. Since that day Miri (the secular) has been co-equal in Sikhism with Piri (the spiritual). This concept remained central to the Sikh revolt of the late 1980s. That rally I attended at Ludhiana passed a resolution reaffirming the sixth guru's doctrine of *Miri* and *Piri*, the inseparability of the religious and secular spheres. This doctrine is, of course, incompatible with full participation in the political life of a nation – India – that is committed to the separation of the spheres in question. Opposite the Golden Temple, Hargobind built a new temple, dedicated to the union of *Miri* and *Piri*, and this became known as the *Akal Takht*, the Timeless Throne. It is the *Akal Takht* that is today the spiritual-cum-secular centre of the Sikh revolt against the merely secular Indian state.

The central significance of the *Akal Takht* in the Sikh revolt has been blurred almost out of existence in the western media. For the fairly brief period in 1984 when the Sikh revolt was making the front pages, it was "the Golden Temple" that was the centre of attention. It was "the Golden Temple" that the Sikh religious-political leader San Jarnail Singh Bhindranwale had turned into the headquarters from which he directed his insurrectionary, or terrorist, campaign. And it was "the Golden Temple" that was violated by the Indian army when it decided to destroy Bhindranwale and his headquarters, in the military action known as Operation Bluestar.

But in reality it was in the *Akal Takht* that Bhindranwale made his headquarters, and it was the *Akal Takht* that was reduced to a ruin by the 105-mm guns of Indian army tanks, leaving the bodies of Bhindranwale and his companions in the rubble.

The confusion is understandable, indeed inevitable, because the expression "the Golden Temple" is generally used, by Sikhs as well as others, to refer to the Golden Temple *complex*. The centre of that complex is not just the Golden Temple, however, but the binary system made up of the Golden Temple proper and the *Akal Takht*. The Golden Temple represents the spiritual aspects of the Sikh religion; *Piri*. But the *Akal Takht*, representing both *Miri* and *Piri*, secular power and spiritual power, is the focus of Sikh sacral nationalism. It was for this reason that Bhindranwale made the *Akal Takht* the headquarters of his rebellion. And the spokesman and some of the leaders of the Sikh rebellion of 1987-1988 have operated from offices within the Golden Temple complex, next to the partially restored shell of the *Akal Takht*, in whose name they speak. In May 1988, Indian security forces intervened in a more sophisticated operation than Bluestar, and succeeded, for the moment at any rate, in again ridding the temple complex of an overtly terrorist presence. But outside the temple complex Sikh terrorism continued.

Indira Gandhi was prime minister at the time of Operation Bluestar. Even before that – as early as 1982 – she was being denounced at Sikh rallies as the "acting Mogul King of Delhi". After Operation Bluestar, Indira Gandhi was execrated, not only by Sikh militants but by the great majority of Sikhs, as the arch-persecutor of the Sikh religion, the right of armed rebellion against external authority being regarded by Sikhs, now as in the past, as an integral part of their religion.

On October 31, 1984 Prime Minsiter Indira Gandhi was murdered by two Sikhs belonging to her personal bodyguard. One of her assassins, Beant

Singh, was killed. Beant Singh has now followed Bhindranwale into the martyrology of the Sikh insurgents.

The sixth guru, Hargobind, gave the Sikh religion its explicitly political form and made the Sikhs into a military force. The tenth and last guru, Govind Singh (1675-1708), reaffirmed the political character of the religion and added a major new institution. He also extended Sikh military power and made militarism part of the Sikh religion. Govind Singh "proclaimed that the sword was God and God was the sword".

Govind Singh's personal arms – an impressive collection of late 17th century weaponry – can be seen today at *Anandpur Sahib*, which is, after the Golden Temple complex, the second of the great temples of the Sikh religion. Govind Singh's arsenal should be seen not as a museum annexed to a holy place but as an integral part of the holy place itself, a central object of the cult. Weapons, according to Govind Singh, are *Pirs*: gods.

It was at *Anandpur Sahib* that Govind Singh founded the Khalsa ("the pure"), the sacred military brotherhood of the Sikh lions. *Singh* means "lion", and every baptized male Sikh is called Singh, being a lion of the brotherhood.

The Sikhs still recite as part of their daily Ardas (prayer), at home or in the temple, what is known as the *Srimukh vak*, the blessed word of Govind Singh. The blessed word runs, in Punjabi:

RAJ KAREGA AKI RAHE NE KOI KHWAR HOI DAB MILENGE
BACHE SARAN JO HOI

("The Khalsa shall rule, no refractory shall exist. In humiliation the refractory shall submit and those who seek refuge shall be protected.")

After the death of Govind Singh in 1708, the *Sikh Khalsa* flourished exceedingly for a while, as an efficient and highly motivated armed brotherhood operating in the propitious conditions of the disintegrating Mogul Empire. By the 19th century the dominions of the Sikh Maharajah Ranjit Singh extended over the whole Punjab, a designation that then applied to a large part of northwest India, including territories that are now part of Pakistan. But in 1849, after two hard-fought Anglo-Sikh wars, Britain annexed the Punjab, thus completing its empire on the subcontinent.

The British, impressed by the courage and martial prowess demonstrated by the Sikhs during the Anglo-Sikh wars, took great pains to conciliate the Sikhs and were largely successful during the heyday of the Raj. The British showed respect for the Sikh religion, which was more compatible with Victorian Protestant values than any of the other faiths of

India. Sikh recruits to the British forces were sworn in on the Sikh scriptures, and were actually required, as a condition of their service, to conform to the requirements of the Sikh religion as laid down by Guru Govind Singh as regards personal appearance and behaviour (turban, beard, abstinence from tobacco, and so forth). From early on Sikhs responded to the conciliatory British approach, and they took the British side against fellow Indians, in the great Indian mutiny of 1857. Although Sikhs were never more than two per cent of the population of India, Sikh soldiers amounted to twenty per cent of Britain's Indian army.

The Sikh religion was able to accomodate itself to the British Raj partly because the British authorities had placed their nominees in control of the *Gudwaras* (Sikh temples), including the Golden Temple complex, but also because the Sikhs came to think of themselves less as subjects of the Raj than as partners in it, "favourite sons of the Empress Mother". In such ways the Sikh religious principle of *Raj Karega Khalsa* adapted itself to the realities of the actual British Raj.

The happy symbiosis of the British and the Sikhs did not long survive the impact of the First World War – as disillusioning an experience for the Sikh soldiers as for other survivors everywhere. In the wave of unrest that swept over India in 1919, Hindus, Muslims, and Sikhs appeared for a time to be united in a common cause. For the Sikhs, the most enduring legacy of this period is the recovery of Sikh religious autonomy: the ending, a generation before the coming of Indian independence, of British control over the Sikh *Gurdwaras*, and so over the means of registering Sikh religious and political opinion.

As independence neared, Sikhs – living in the borderlands between the two emergent states of the subcontinent – did not exactly have to choose between India and Pakistan, because Pakistan, being a Muslim confessional state, did not want the Sikhs, whereas secular India offered them equal citizenship. If the Sikhs had refused the Indian offer and insisted on their own state, Khalistan – meaning the state of the *Khalsa*, "the pure", the Sikhs – they would have had to fight alone, greatly outnumbered, against Pakistan, which laid claim to the Punjab, where Muslims were the largest community. So the Sikhs elected to join India, and Muslims and Sikhs fought it out in the Punjab in 1947, through hideous intercommunal massacres which left more than half a million dead and about two million homeless. The old Punjab was partitioned into West Punjab, part of Pakistan, and East Punjab, part of India.

Sikhs seem to have expected to enjoy some kind of autonomous status for themselves as a religious national community within a federal India. Sikh political leaders soon convinced themselves and their followers that they had in fact been promised such a status and then been cheated out of it. Sikhs, though the largest community in East Punjab, were a minority of its total population.

The Indian government was concerned about the Sikh discontent but unable to concede what the Sikhs were actually looking for: autonomy for themselves as a religious community. To yield on that would be to accept the principle of communalism, an acceptance that would lead to the dissolution of India. Still, it was hoped that the Sikhs could be placated by arranging majority status for them, not through a religious criterion but through a linguistic one. The old Punjab had already been partitioned, between Pakistan and India. Now India's Punjab – East Punjab – was itself partitioned, on the basis of a linguistic survey. The northern part, speaking Punjabi, retained the name Punjab. In this new Punjab the Sikhs are a majority. The southern part of the old Punjab became Haryana, a state of Hindus, mostly speaking Hindi.

The government of India hoped that the Sikhs, having acquired majority status in their homeland, would be content. But the Sikhs were not content.

In the heyday of the British Raj their appetite for martial glory had been satisfied by a sense of participation, and an illusion of partnership, in the world's greatest empire. Later, glory was to be found in the struggle *against* the British Raj. The Sikhs claim that ninety per cent of those who fell in India's struggle for independence were Sikhs; of course, the struggle in question, in the rest of India, was designed to be non-violent. But to the Sikhs, brought up in the teachings of the tenth guru, the idea of a non-violent struggle was incomprehensible.

Some commentators suggest that there are more "practical" reasons for Sikh unrest, high unemployment chief among these. But the question of employment – acceptable employment, that is – is inseparable from the question of honour among Sikhs. Working on your own farm is honourable; so is working for the government, especially the defense forces. But working as a factory hand is not honourable, and therefore not acceptable. To industrialise the Punjab, the factory workers have had to be brought in from the outside, from poor provinces such as Orissa and Bihar. In late May 1988 these immigrant Hindu workers became the main targets of Sikh "revenge" killings, following the reoccupation of the Golden Temple complex.

Central to the Sikh unrest has been the excess in the numbers of young male Sikhs over the amount of honourable employment available. To own even a tiny farm is honourable, but sub-division of the farmland appears to have reached its limit. Sikhs are conspicuous in the armed forces of India, but the proportion of Sikhs in the forces is significantly lower than it was under the British. There are Indian officials who would like to increase the number of Sikhs in the armed forces of India; others resist, believing that the Sikhs would be an unreliable element in the armed forces. (There were some mutinies among raw Sikh recruits immediately after Operation Bluestar). What career is open to a young male Sikh who doesn't have a farm of his own and hasn't been able to get a place in the defense forces or any other branch of government service? That question remains unresolved, and in the meantime there are too many young Sikhs who find no suitable outlet within the law for their abundant energies.

In the present generation a number of Sikhs in this category decided to take up arms and fight for Khalistan. Those who made that choice didn't necessarily have to believe that Khalistan is attainable. Whether it is attainable or not, the fight for it remains a thoroughly honourable pursuit, sanctioned by the Sikh religion through the concept of the *Khalsa* (military brotherhood) and by the general value system of the Sikhs.

* * *

On the day after the Ludhiana rally, I went on, along India's Grand Trunk Road, to the holy city of Amritsar, to visit the Golden Temple complex, the holiest shrine of the Sikhs. The road from Chandigarh, the state capital, to Amritsar runs through flat, lush country of summer wheat, ripening at the time, broken by stands of poplar and eucalyptus. There were few military or police vehicles, and no signs of unrest or tension until we reached Amritsar. The holy city was the centre of the troubles, and the killing grounds have been the region between Amritsar and India's borders with Pakistan.

In Amritsar the security forces of the Indian government were much in evidence. They maintained a cordon all around the Golden Temple complex, and the faithful are checked, questioned, and sometimes searched as they go in and out. The faithful obviously disliked this. It is said that attendance at the Golden Temple dropped to no more than a quarter of what it was before the troubles began. Most Sikhs ascribed the decline to the frightening demeanour of the security forces, and that was no doubt a major factor. But it seems probable that there has also been another factor: the frightening character of certain transactions going on within the temple precincts themselves. (These transactions were interrupted by the intervention of the Indian security forces in the temple complex in May 1988. It may, however, be difficult for the security forces to prevent the re-infiltration of the terrorists, as happened after Bluestar. In what follows, I am describing conditions at the temple complex as they were before the May intervention.)

The precincts of the Golden Temple form a splendid spectacle under the gentle sunshine of the north Indian spring. It is a spacious and soberly harmonious ensemble, nobly planned and executed, and well maintained. The grand feature of the complex is the large artificial Holy Lake (or "tank", as it is called.) The Golden Temple itself is an architectural island in the middle of the lake, a fairly small building, as was necessitated by the cost of its precious covering. Around the lake runs an extremely wide marble promenade: the Parikrama. A pier with an ornate gate connects the Parikrama, facing the entrance to the Golden Temple, with the other great temple of the Sikhs: the *Akal Takht*, the Timeless Throne of *Miri* and *Piri*, the sacred architectural symbol of the fusion of religious and political authority in the holy nation of the Sikhs.

At the time of my visit the *Akal Takht* was under restoration after its bombardment in 1984. The restoration of the exterior was almost complete; workers were applying gold leaf to the cupola. But the sanctity of the restored edifice was challenged. The money for the restoration was contributed by the government of India, as part of an effort to promote reconciliation with the Sikhs after 1984. But the Sikh militants hold that restoration from such an unhallowed source is not acceptable. The new edifice will have to be torn down and the *Akal Takht* restored in all its holiness, and this must be accomplished by Sikhs, alone and unaided. Pending that, the idea of the *Akal Takht* remains – irrespective of the present edifice – the animating concept of the entire complex that includes the Golden Temple.

Apart from the shattering of the *Akal Takht*, Operation Bluestar did little damage to the temple complex. My guide made the most of what damage there was, pointing out some pockmarks of shrapnel on the gold integument of the temple in the lake, and the track mark of an Indian Army tank on the marble flooring of the Parikrama. The guide also told me that the Indian army had completely destroyed the temple library, with its ancient sacred manuscripts. "They did it in order to wipe out the culture of the Sikhs," the guide explained.

The religious life of the temple precincts seemed to be going on normally, though with reduced numbers. In the temple kitchens men and women were preparing the Langar, the communal meal that the Sikh religion offers to all who wish to partake. A group of women were dipping a baby in the Holy Lake. It was a cool morning, and the baby cried. The women took it out, wrapped it up, and comforted it.

A peaceful scene. But things had not really returned to normal in the temple precincts. In normal times the temple is a busy place at night, when the main liturgical events of the Sikh religion take place. But people were now afraid to go into the Golden Temple precincts after dark. The hostels of the complex, where all visitors are entitled to stay for three nights free of charge, had become poorly frequented. Visitors had been terrorised by the militants. Women had been abducted, raped and subsequently blackmailed. Dead bodies had been found outside the temple gates. So it was not a place to linger after dark.

On the first morning of my visit there was just one outward sign of the presence of terrorists in the temple complex. The sign took the form of a makeshift net screen, with bits of paper pasted on it, standing on the Parikrama, right at the edge of the Holy Lake, on the *Akal Takht* side. At the top of the screen was a coloured picture of the martial tenth guru, Govind Singh. Below the guru were newspaper pictures of Sikhs recently killed by the Indian security forces. The iconographic message was altogether clear: those whom the Indians call terrorists are martyrs of the Sikh, and honoured in this holy place.

On the following day I went to the temple complex in order to make contact with some of the terrorists, alias militants. I had been tipped off as to how to do this. The first thing was to make contact with the official custodians of the temple complex, the representatives of the statutory elective religious body, the Shiromani Gurdwara Parbandhak Committee. As often in Sikh affairs, there were two representatives, an old man and a young man. The old man had an expression like an American television evangelist, and he had also an abundant snow-white beard. The combination put me in mind of "the King" in *Huckleberry Finn*, as he appears in Kemble's illustrations. The young man looked hard-eyed and street-wise, and I knew he was the man for me.

The old man started off by telling me nostalgically about his recent stay on a health farm in New Mexico. Then with a "back to work" expression, he delivered a monologue on the Sikh religion, stressing the pacific and ecumenical Guru Nanak side, rather than the militarism of Guru Govind

Singh. Then I put my prepared question. Should you, reader, ever visit the Golden Temple complex at Amritsar, and should you have a mind to visit with the terrorists in residence there – supposing they are there at the time – the way to frame your question is as follows:

"Could you put me in touch, please, with some of those who are engaged in voluntary religious service in the temple precincts?"

Kar Seva – translated as "voluntary religious service" – is a technical term of the Sikh religion. It includes such pacific services as preparing the Langar and cleaning the Parikrama. But it also includes military service in the holy cause of the *Khalsa*, the brotherhood of the Sikhs.

My interlocutors knew I was not talking about the Langar cooks. The old man looked at the ceiling, as if contemplating the mystical beauties of the concept of *Kar Seva*. The young man simply said: "Come back tomorrow at nine."

In a bare office, on the edge of the Parikrama, to the side of the *Akal Takht*, I met representatives of the Panthic Committee. *Panth* means "the Sikh community". The Panthic Committee is an ad hoc umbrella body, empowered to issue collective statements on behalf of the five major terrorist bodies (Khalistan Liberation Commandos, Bhindranwale Tigers and so forth) that were then in control of the Golden Temple complex. There was no furniture in the office. On the walls were three pictures: the inevitable Govind Singh, Sant Jarnail Singh Bhindranwale, and an unidentified young Sikh with a submachine gun.

When I came into the office, I thought there was only one person there: a tall soldierly Sikh who didn't look particularly bright. Then I noticed the soldierly man seemed to be deferring to someone else, in a corner of the room, below my original line of sight.

The man who was sitting on the floor in the corner was very thin – indeed, emaciated. He wore a heavy blanket over his shoulders, though the room did not feel cold. He had a black turban and a long blue-black beard. His features were classical, patrician, his eyes deep-sunken. He was about as pale as it is possible to be, and far paler than any Indian I had ever seen. He looked like a man who hadn't got long to live, and who didn't much care how long anyone else got to live either.

The personage was Narvir Singh, the *Jathedar* – "high priest" – of the Temple at Damdama, the fifth holiest of the temples of the Sikhs. Narvir Singh was in the Golden Temple complex by invitation of the terrorists, who drove out the *Jathedar* of the *Akal Takht*, who had opposed their plans. Narvir Singh was one of the principal preachers and promoters of the Holy War.

Our conversation didn't last very long. Narvir Singh is a man of few words, as one could see by looking at him. He spoke in Punjabi, and the soldier translated.

"What are you fighting for?" I asked.

"Khalistan."

"What exactly is Khalistan?"

At a nod from Narvir Singh, the soldier handed me a map, helpfully headed in English "Map of Khalistan". I looked at the map in confusion.

"But this is a map of India!" I said.

"Not all of the present India," Narvir Singh said, in scholarly correction. "It does not include Jammu and Kashmir."

The map of Khalistan, formerly India, minus Jammu and Kashmir, was covered with markings in the Gurmukhi script, the written language of the Sikh scriptures. I had the notations translated for me after I left the Golden Temple complex. There were some important changes in place names. New Delhi was renamed "Tenth Guru City," after the warrior guru, Govind Singh. And the airport at Delhi, now known as Indira Gandhi International Airport, had become Beant Singh International Airport, after Mrs Gandhi's martyred Sikh assassin.

From an Indian point of view, this last change is equivalent to renaming the John F Kennedy International Airport the Lee Harvey Oswald International Airport.

Narvir Singh could see, apparently, that I was having some difficulty in assimilating the proposition that Khalistan is not so much a secessionist project as a project for the annexation of India by the Sikhs, who number less than two percent of the population of the subcontinent. Narvir Singh said something in a very low voice, charged with emotion. The soldier translated: "It is a little boy walking in a room. Soon it will have the whole house."

The project of Khalistan, as expounded to me in the precincts of the Golden Temple by the representatives of the Panthic Committee, appears about as demented as a political project can be. Yet there is some method in the madness. This is reflected in the omission of Jammu and Kashmir. These provinces are claimed by Pakistan, which covertly backs Khalistan. The developing unrest in the northern part of the Punjab, bordering on Jammu and Kashmir, is favourable to Pakistan's hopes of recovering what it regards as its lost provinces, as well as paying off a number of other old scores.

More than anything else, Khalistan is a project for bringing about the destruction of the Indian state in a welter of communal disturbances, of which the Sikhs see themselves as the spearhead. The Punjab Sikhs Lawyers Council speaks in the name of the "human rights of Sikh and other oppressed nations". The Sikhs are looking for allies and have found some. There were Naxalites in the Golden Temple complex before the storming in 1984. At the Sikh rally in Ludhiana there was a sizeable Indian-Muslim contingent, marching behind a green flag with a crescent: another symptom of the Pakistan connection.

Ten years after the date of composition of the above essay on the religious nationalism of the Sikhs, religious nationalism made a great breakthrough in India, at the expense of the secular tradition of the founders of the Indian state.

In March 1998, the Hindu Nationalist Party, the Bharatiya Janata Party, became much the largest party in the Indian parliament and has been able to form a government with allies from some of the smaller parties. Its need for allies who are not Muslim nationalists, may moderate the course of the BJP in the present parliament. But the BJP itself remains fiercely anti-Muslim as appeared in the course of the 1998 elections. Some years ago BJP supporters destroyed a mosque which had been built on the site of a Hindu temple. During the 1998 elections BJP speakers were promising to rebuild the temple on the site where a mosque had stood for more than three centuries.

Non-Hindus throughout India – including the scores of millions of Muslims – are now living in fear of what the BJP may do, especially if it comes back unencumbered by the need for allies after the next elections. The surge in religious nationalism among the Hindus has to stimulate other religious nationalists, including the already intense religious nationalism of the Sikhs.

It is not impossible that the secular Congress Party now led by Sonia Gandhi, may after all revive, and that India may hold back from the brink. But at the moment it looks as if India's days as a secular polity may be drawing to an end, and that the country may be about to enter a period of religious-national wars.

19

"THE PEACE PROCESS"

"HERE BE GHOSTS THAT I HAVE RAISED THIS CHRISTMASTIDE, GHOSTS OF DEAD men that have bequeathed a trust to us living men. Ghosts are troublesome things, as we knew even before Ibsen taught us. There is only one way to appease a ghost. You must do the thing it asks you. The ghosts of a nation sometimes ask very big things and they must be appeased whatever the cost."
— *Patrick Pearse,* "Christmas Day, 1915"

The reference to Ibsen is to the following passage in Ibsen's *Ghosts* (1881): *Mrs Alving:* "I just have to pick up a newspaper, and it's as if I could see the ghosts slipping between the lines."

Pearse's Christmas Day message was penned at a time when he and his friends had already planned the near suicidal insurrection, launched by no coincidence at Easter, 1916.

In the second half of the 20th century, the year in which the Pearsean ghosts walked to the greatest effect and "slipped between the lines" most disturbingly was 1982. In that year, ten members of the IRA, serving prison terms for various violent offences, starved themselves to death. The first to die, inspiring the others, was Bobby Sands, the most conspicuous example in modern Ireland of the lethal fusion between religion and nationalism.

Like Pearse, Sands believed himself to be continuing – in being willing to sacrifice his life for Ireland – the sacrifice of Jesus on the cross. As Pearse did, he saw Ireland as a mystical entity, to die for which – or whom – opened the way for salvation. On receiving his fourteen-year sentence for possession of arms with intent to endanger life, Sands wrote the following lines:

> The beady eyes they peered at me
> The time had come to be,
> To walk the lonely road
> Like that of Calvary.
> And take up the cross of Irishmen
> Who've carried liberty.

In his hagiographical book, *Bobby Sands and the Tragedy of Northern Ireland (1986)*, John Feehan wrote concerning the burial of Bobby Sands:

"In the quiet evening silence of Milltown graveyard it seemed as if the Republican Movement had reached its Calvary with no Resurrection in sight, that Bobby Sands had lost and the overwhelming power of the British empire had won yet another victory."

The author goes on, however, to suggest that the resurrection duly followed in the shape of the boost given to the republican cause by the deaths of the hunger-strikers. The clincher is in the last words of Mr Feehan's sixth and last chapter.

"In the early hours of the morning of 5 May the immortal soul of one of the noblest young Irishmen of the twentieth century came face-to-face with his Fellow Sufferer and Maker. Bobby Sands was dead."

In a review of Feehan's book I commented on the above passage:

"There were other fellow-sufferers, lower-case ones: the thousands who were either killed, maimed or bereaved by the devotees of the Irish Republic in Mr Sands's organisation, the Provisional IRA. Those other dead, however, being the wrong kind, are implicitly excluded from what is seen as a celestial tete-a-tete.

"The effect of elevating anyone prepared to kill and die for the Republic to the status of Jesus Christ, is to annihilate, morally and spiritually, the adversaries of the [Pearsean] Republic, whom the Republican Christ feels impelled to bump off. Those adversaries of Christ are necessarily cast in the role, if not of Antichrist himself, then of the agents, or at best the dupes, of Antichrist. They deserve no mercy, and that is exactly what they get. This is the very essence of Holy War. And Mr. Feehan shows his hero, on his last birthday, receiving with joy an ikon of Catholic Holy War: 'He was thrilled to get a picture of Our Lady from a priest in Kerry who had encouraged him to take arms for his oppressed people.' To wit, the Catholics of Northern Ireland."

* * *

The deaths of the ten hunger-strikers represented a major turning point in the history of Northern Ireland. In the Republic they brought about reactions which were similar to – though weaker than – the reactions which had followed the execution of the leaders of the 1916 Rising. At a series of meetings in Dublin from 1982 on, the British were urged to adopt policies which would avoid the necessity for such tragedies in the future. Three alternative policies were proposed, the strongest being a united Ireland, the weakest "Joint Administration" of Northern Ireland by Britain and the Republic. Scornfully, the then prime minister, Margaret Thatcher, rejected all three proposals with a famous triple negative: "No, no, no."

But the triple "no", final though it sounded, did not halt the nationalist offensive. Instead the offensive took on a more subtle character, so that to many people in Britain – including eventually Margaret Thatcher herself – it no longer appeared to be an offensive at all.

The new demand was much weaker, in form, than the three previous demands. But because it was weaker in form, it was more insidious in practice and much more dangerous to the Union of Great Britain and Northern Ireland than the previous demands had been. The new demand was for nothing more than a recognised consultative status for the government of the Republic in the governance of Northern Ireland. The British government would continue to govern Northern Ireland but they would consult the Irish government about whatever measures they found it necessary to take. They might not take the advice, but they must engage in the consultation.

Garret FitzGerald, then Taoiseach, negotiated the Anglo-Irish Agreement, based on that principle, with Margaret Thatcher. But every informed person knew that the real architect of the modified nationalist claim was John Hume. Only he had the authority to scale down the nationalist demand, and only he had the political genius to see that the scaling down was the key to the advancement of the nationalist cause.

The Anglo-Irish Agreement was signed by FitzGerald and Thatcher at Hillsborough, County Down on November 15, 1985.

After the signature, Garret FitzGerald claimed that the agreement represented "a reconciliation of the two traditions in Ireland" [Protestant and Catholic] and also that it would "weaken the men of violence".

As I pointed out at the time, in a series of articles, both these claims were unfounded, and the first was utterly absurd. The agreement was between the British and one of the two traditions in Northern Ireland. The other tradition had never been consulted while the agreement was in preparation and all unionists were stunned and outraged when they learned of the agreement's existence. They were even more outraged when they found there was nothing they could do about it. They had been able to overthrow the Sunningdale Agreement, because that was an agreement for the actual governance of Northern Ireland through a joint executive which, as it was to be situated in Northern Ireland itself, could be challenged and disrupted locally. But the Hillsborough Agreement, setting up arrangements which were consultative only between the governments in London and Dublin, could not be disrupted or even disturbed by anyone in Northern Ireland. These arrangements were invulnerable and the unionists could only bluster about them. At the time of writing, the Hillsborough agreement is more or less still in place though probably about to be replaced by arrangements even more detestable to many unionists.

Garret's other contention, that the agreement "strengthened the constitutional nationalists as against the men of violence" was also quite unfounded. I watched Gerry Adams on television immediately after the terms of Hillsborough had been made known. Formally, Adams was rejecting the Hillsborough agreement (as falling short of a united Ireland). But his body language carried a very different message. His delight in the unionist discomfiture showed in his wolfish grin and barking laugh. And it was already clear – and soon became clearer – that he appreciated the political skill which John Hume had deployed for the discomfiture of all unionists.

As for Margaret Thatcher, she continued to maintain that the Hillsborough agreement "strengthened the Union" between Great Britain and Northern Ireland. I doubt if she could have found a single person in the entire island of Ireland who agreed with that contention. It is true that the existence of the consultative arrangements with the Republic relieved some of the pressure on British representatives in the United States and provided a stock answer to representations on the subject. But I doubt if that is the whole story behind Mrs Thatcher's uncharacteristic yielding to nationalist blandishments. I think that she – and other members of her party – had been more shaken by the deaths of the hunger-strikers than they themselves may have been consciously aware. They had been used to thinking of the IRA as "common criminals". Criminals they certainly were, under the laws of the state in which they lived – which laws and which state they deliberately rejected. So criminals all right. But common criminals? What common criminals are prepared to fast to death for ideas in which they believe?

As Patrick Pearse had clearly seen, those few people in any country who are prepared to die for something they believe thereby acquire a certain power over the great majority who are not prepared to die for any idea. The willingness of the few to die inspires, among those with a normal fear of death, something like a superstitious dread. And the dread excites a wish to propitiate those who inspire the dread by gradually conceding parts of their demands and then further parts of the same . . .

I believe this dread has been and still remains a powerful impelling factor within what came to be called "the peace process".

* * *

The death-rituals of 1982 were powerful medicine, working for revenge, among young Catholics in Northern Ireland. As we have seen they didn't work that way in the Republic. Yet even in the Republic these rituals, in the whole context of the IRA's armed struggle, had effects that worked in the IRA's favour. At conscious level, what was evoked by all these deaths and the rituals associated with them was a longing for peace. It is not obvious that an armed struggle can be fuelled by a longing for peace, but it does sometimes work that way. Between the wars, for example, the longing for peace in Britain and France helped the Nazis to rearm with impunity. In Ireland, as well as in Britain, the general longing for an end to political violence has become the IRA's greatest asset. Partly, this is a mechanical and general phenomenon. The more you crave for peace, the more you may come to be dependent on the men of violence, who alone can supply you with that which you crave.

But there is also a reason, specific to the Catholic and nationalist context, why the longing for peace helps the IRA. Catholics and nationalists find it hard – indeed, almost impossible – to conceive of a progress towards peace which is not also a progress towards the achievement of the nationalist goal: a united Ireland. This is also, of course, the goal of the IRA. Though most people strongly disapprove of the IRA's *methods*, there is general approval for a peace process designed to attain the same objective through non-violent means. In practice, as far as the unionist population is concerned, the peace process joins forces with the armed struggle, as part of one sustained Catholic-nationalist enterprise, intended to extort Protestant and unionist consent to that which all unionists and almost all Protestants have long rejected: a united Ireland.

In the period 1982-5, the longing for peace, fuelled by the hunger-strike rituals, produced a strong demand for concessions by Britain to the constitutional nationalists. Shaken by the impact of the hunger-strike deaths, particularly in America, the British government felt a need to placate the constitutional nationalists. The result of this convergence of demand and need produced the Anglo-Irish Agreement, the greatest political victory for Catholic nationalism since the abolition (aka "prorogation") of the Stormont Parliament in 1972.

That agreement gave the Dublin government consultative status in the affairs of Northern Ireland, through the Anglo-Irish Intergovernmental Conference. Thus Dublin – and the SDLP, through Dublin – had now a greater share in the governance of Northern Ireland than the unionists had; quite a reversal.

The Anglo-Irish Agreement was preceded and accompanied by a tremendous amount of hype – along the lines articulated by Garrett FitzGerald – about how it would "reconcile the two traditions in Ireland", "end the alienation of the minority" and so "marginalise the men of violence". Nine years' experience of the agreement has revealed these claims for the hokum they always were. But nobody in Ireland cares about that, because nobody in Ireland ever believed those claims in the first place (except perhaps Garret FitzGerald, who has an unusual capacity for kidding himself, perhaps because he is too decent to understand dark forces in history). The reality was, and is, that the Hillsborough agreement represented a breakthrough for Catholic nationalists over Protestant unionists. What remains, as John Hume and his allies and followers understand, is to exploit that breakthrough until the final victory of Catholics and nationalists is attained.

In the wake of that agreement, what has emerged is not anything remotely resembling a reconciliation of the two traditions, but rather a closing of the ranks of one tradition against the other. The "men of violence" on the Catholic and nationalist side instead of being "marginalised" have now become integrated into a pan-Catholic and pan-nationalist consensus, along with the SDLP, the Dublin government and the Catholic Church. This is known as "the peace process", a use of language which is the up-to-date version of the kind of hokum that preceded the Hillsborough agreement and has now been "transcended" (a word dear to Irish nationalist discourse in the late 20th century).

The pan-nationalist peace process, as it emerged in 1993-4, is based on a dialogue, and an agreement or agreements, between Gerry Adams, president of Sinn Féin, and John Hume, leader of the Social Democratic and Labour Party. The existence of an agreement – and there certainly is at least one agreement – between these two Catholic and nationalist leaders is in itself a remarkable phenomenon. Sinn Féin is an organisation pledged to support the IRA's armed struggle, and is in fact controlled by the IRA, of whose Army Council Mr Adams is generally believed to be a member. The Social Democratic and Labour Party is dedicated to peaceful change, and Mr Hume's international celebrity is based to a large extent on his eloquently expressed abhorrence of political violence. So Hume-Adams – or, as the republican side puts it, Adams-Hume – is a bit of a puzzle. It is a puzzle that concerns us, in the context of the present chapter, for Hume-Adams, aka Adams-Hume, is the most conspicuous manifestation of Catholic nationalism in the middle of the last decade of the 20th century.

So what exactly is Hume-Adams? So far as I know, the two leaders have made only one joint statement, which was published in the Irish Sunday newspapers on April 25, 1993. The core of this joint statement is the following: *"We accept that the Irish people as a whole have a right to national self-determination."*

That formula leaves absolutely no room for compromise between Catholics/nationalists and Protestants/unionists in Ireland. It is a classical expression of traditional Catholic republican nationalism, always rejected and resisted by Protestants and unionists. Ireland's "right to national self-determination" is a breakthrough for the ghosts.

If that "right" were to be vindicated, in the present state of public opinion, it would have to be imposed on the Protestants and unionists by force. Yet this formula for civil war is the core of the Hume-Adams peace process. How come?

Part of the answer is that the original joint statement has been overlaid by a Hume-Adams folklore, circulating among moderate nationalists, and apparently allowing room for compromise. Thus the following appeared in a Dublin newspaper in mid-July under the heading "Hume-Adams document".

"The democratic right to self-determination by the people of the island as a whole must be achieved and exercised *with the agreement and consent of the people of Northern Ireland."* (my italics CCO'B). This was in an article by Garret FitzGerald, *The Irish Times* July 16, 1994). Garret got this version from Seamus Mallon. The good faith of both these gentlemen is beyond question, but the document they have been led to accept is spurious.

I shall believe that version when I see it confirmed by Gerry Adams, in which case that confirmation will be followed immediately by the departure of Mr Adams from the presidency of Sinn Féin, and possibly also from this world.

A president of Sinn Féin who would agree to the omission of the key-word "national", before self-determination, would be guilty of the gravest of sins and crimes; national apostasy. Mr Adams in fact, in his frequent public references to "self-determination" *always* prefaces that word with "national" and a conference of the Sinn Féin party (Letterkenny, July 1994) committed itself, as a matter of course, to the "exercise of national self-determination". And if Mr Adams, addressing his party at Letterkenny, had used the formula "with the agreement and consent of the people of Northern Ireland", he would have been beaten to a pulp. The mere words "Northern Ireland" are unspeakable in a republican context and "the people of Northern Ireland" is even worse.

I believe that phoney versions of "Hume-Adams" are part of a general policy of disinformation which led to, and followed, the Downing Street Declaration of December 15, 1993, and continued through the referendum and election campaign of May-June, 1998.

The Downing Street Declaration, with its inclusion of a (hedged) formula concerning Irish self-determination, was supposed to induce a "war-weary" IRA to agree to a "permanent cessation of violence". The Letterkenny Conference of Sinn Féin, after seven (post-Declaration) months of continuous IRA violence – and rising loyalist violence – finally gave a thumbs-down to Downing Street, but reconfirmed its commitment to "the peace process", based on Hume-Adams. It also reaffirmed its commitment to the 1916 Proclamation of the Republic, which is incompatible with any peace except through total victory by nationalists over unionists.

In the context of the present study, what concerns us is what Adams-Hume (as I shall now call it) has to tell us about the current condition of Catholic nationalism in Ireland. And what Adams-Hume has to tell us is not good.

The best hope for peace in Northern Ireland has always been for an agreement between moderate nationalists and moderate unionists, and a common front of both against the men of violence *on both sides*: both the

IRA and the loyalist paramilitaries. Such a consensus could have led to the taking, by both the Dublin and London governments, of the necessary drastic measures – including internment of the paramilitary godfathers – against both sets of terrorists. Terrorism can never be brought to an end except by recourse to such measures.

From its begining in 1970, under the leadership of Gerry Fitt, the SDLP genuinely sought accommodation with the unionists. Gerry Fitt's loathing of the IRA was courageously explicit and amply reciprocated. As long as he and Paddy Devlin were active in the leadership of the SDLP, there could be no question of any kind of partnership with Sinn Féin.

But after John Hume replaced Gerry Fitt in the leadership (1979) there was a change of approach. Though the rhetoric about "agreement between the two traditions" became more fluent than ever, the real objective was now to circumvent the unionists and squeeze them. The Anglo-Irish Agreement (which was above all John Hume's brainchild) was the first major triumph for this policy. The idea there was to go over the heads of the unionists to the British, and get the latter to push the unionists in the direction that they don't want to go: that of a united Ireland ("an agreed Ireland" in Humespeak). John Hume had never abandoned the policy of using the British to squeeze the unionists. But by the late 1980s, with the Anglo-Irish Agreement under his belt, Mr Hume was talking about the need to "transcend" that agreement. The agreement itself had been rejected (formally) by Sinn Féin, but an attempt to "transcend" it, by further movement down the nationalist agenda, was to be the basis for a common front of all nationalists.

Talks between Gerry Adams and John Hume began in the late 1980's but did not immediately lead to any joint declaration. But they began again in earnest in 1992 and led to the Adams-Hume joint statement of April, 1993 (quoted above).

In theory, the Adams-Hume agreement represented a movement in the direction of peace. The reality was the opposite. Any joint declaration between the leader of the SDLP and the president of Sinn Féin would have automatically poisoned relations between the SDLP and all unionists. The self-determination formula adopted by the two leaders amounted to a declaration of war against unionists, and against the existence of Northern Ireland, and that formula also registered a regression on the part of the SDLP. This formula represents *what has always been the policy of Sinn Féin-IRA*. It is the classic republican formula, dictated by the ghosts and irreversible by the living. Hume simply signed on the dotted line. In the pan-nationalist consensus that began to emerge in April, 1993 the dominant partner has been Sinn Féin-IRA.

Those whom Gerry Adams represents have the mandate from the dead, because they are, in the here and now, though latterly, mostly by indirection, doing the bidding of the ghosts and supplying them with the blood they crave. In the Adams-Hume partnership and in their pan-nationalist partnership, which grew out of the former, Gerry Adams is the predominant partner. He is so, because his credentials are superior, emotionally, within the Catholic-nationalist-republican tradition, as expounded (although with some variations) by the Christian Brothers in the 19th century, by Irish Ireland (with its explicitly sectarian input) in the early 20th century, by Yeats and Maud Gonne in *Cathleen Ní Houlihan*, and then by Patrick Pearse, and all the varieties of Irish nationalists of later generations who claim allegiance to Pearse. You can't have Pearse without the ghosts, and you can't appease the ghosts unless you do what they want. We have Pearse's word for that.

* * *

On August 31, 1994, the Provisional IRA announced "a complete cessation of military operations". This was immediately hailed by Dublin politicians and the nationalist media as if it were equivalent (which it obviously is not) to the acceptance of the "permanent cessation of violence" for which the Downing Street Declaration had called. At the same time, the same politicians and commentators hinted that the "permanent cessation" might not be all that permanent if the British government failed to "respond" to it promptly by "peace dividends", meaning large concessions to IRA demands, and further movement down the nationalist agenda. To accelerate these concessions – also urged by the Clinton administration – Sinn Féin immediately started to apply an "unarmed strategy" consisting of street protests, direct action by civilians and civil disobedience. The security forces could not seriously attempt to resist the "unarmed strategy" without "endangering the ceasefire", and thus they risked becoming the helpless butts of mobs of nationalist youths. The unionist population were witnessing a tripartite phenomenon consisting of: increased political pressure against them, on London from Dublin, backed by Washington; a determined and well-supported effort by Sinn Féin to reduce Northern Ireland to anarchy; and, finally, the apparent impotence of the security forces, shown by their failure to control the Sinn Féin mobs.

Since the autumn of 1994 both the IRA and the loyalist paramilitaries have had truces, although the IRA ceasefire was broken off in January 1996 and did not resume until the following year. It is clear that, as far as Sinn Féin-IRA are concerned, what they call "the peace process" has come to consist of periods of "armed conflict", punctuated by periods of truce, in which British and other fears of resumed conflict will be exploited for the extortion of political advantages. From the point of view of Sinn Féin-IRA this is a shrewdly-calculated politico-military strategy. It is welcome to their "troops" because it affords periods of rest, rehabilitation and redeployment. And it gives Sinn Féin opportunities – which they have used brilliantly – to apply and enhance their by-now-formidable political and propaganda skills. Specialised though their operation is, Sinn Féin are now the most skilfully led political organisation in these islands. But they are a political organisation with a difference, for they exist only to carry out the orders of a private army: the IRA. So their skills are noxious to the community since they are deployed in the interests of a private army which has now found ways of orchestrating "war" and "peace", while alternating the two, for the destruction of Northern Ireland.

* * *

Shortly after the conclusion of the Anglo-Irish Agreement, I accepted an invitation from Ian Gow to address the Friends of the Union at Westminster.

Ian Gow had been one of Margaret Thatcher's closest advisers, and the chief architect of her ascent to the leadership of the Tories and then to being prime minister. Ian Gow, however, was also a believer in the United Kingdom of Great Britain and Northern Ireland, and considered that the Anglo-Irish Agreement, if concluded, would be a major step in the direction of the dissolution of the Union. Finding himself unable to dissuade Mrs Thatcher from the conclusion of the agreement, Ian Gow resigned from her government and brought a brilliantly promising political career to a premature conclusion.

I greatly admired Ian Gow for a decision which I think was unique in our time, for a willingness to sacrifice self-interest through a commitment to principle. Most politicians talk as if they are always prepared for such a sacrifice, but to find someone who actually goes and does it is extraordinary, and profoundly edifying.

I admired Ian Gow, and I also liked him very much, which would not necessarily follow. He was a cheerful, unpretentious humorous person, without any of the gloomy self-absorption which sometimes afflicts political martyrs. It was typical of him that, after his resignation, he called his comfortable home "The Dog House".

It did not take me long to accept Ian Gow's invitation to address the Friends of the Union at Westminster. Yet I did not accept without a little shiver. My grandfather, David Sheehy, had worked at Westminster for thirty-three years for the withdrawal of all Ireland from the parliament of the United Kingdom (though preserving the link with the Crown, and a few other links as well). So it felt a bit strange to go to the scene of his labours with a conflicting intent. Furthermore, I didn't feel myself so much to be a Friend of the Union as a friend of the unionist people of Northern Ireland, and a person determined to associate with them in support of their determination not to be pushed in a direction in which they didn't want to go. Those characteristics have been changing and they later took a surprising turn (see following chapter). However, I didn't wish to be pedantic and I accepted "Friend of the Union" as covering my position and that of others respecting the right of the people in question not to be pushed around or conned.

Shortly after I had addressed the Friends of the Union at Westminster, Ian Gow was murdered by the Provisional IRA. He was murdered precisely because he was a Friend of the Union, and an exceptionally able and resourceful one. After that terrible event, I felt more committed than ever, for some years, to being a Friend of the Union.

* * *

I did, however, have some qualms about associating with either of the unionist parties then existing. Both had strong sectarian associations, and habits of sectarian rhetoric. I found all that both uncongenial and compromising to the cause of the Union.

Digression on Sectarianism in Irish Politics: Sectarian feelings have long been, for historical reasons, among the most powerful motive forces in the politics of the island of Ireland. In the twenty-six counties which make up today's Republic of Ireland, sectarianism is no more perceptible than the air one breathes. Ninety-three per cent of the citizens are Catholics, and the small Protestant and Jewish communities which remain accept the version of nationalism offered by the Catholic majority; in the past, rather pressingly offered. Those members of these communities who could not adapt to that version left the jurisdiction. Today, both the Protestant and the Jewish communities are smaller than they once were. As in other countries once ruled by imperial powers, those whose ancestors had been loyal to the imperial power, and who "stayed on", adapted to their new situation and conformed to the political ideology of the majority. Those things being so, there is now very little friction, and only of a vestigial kind, between the majority and the minority in the Republic.

In Northern Ireland, the situation is very different. There, a rather narrow Protestant majority confronts a large Catholic minority. The divide is at present around sixty per cent – forty per cent. The Catholics sense that they are about to win; the Protestants are by now strongly aware of the possibility of defeat. Both sides feel that if Northern Ireland is in fact detached from the present United Kingdom this will not just be a political change. It would also – if imposed on the Protestants – involve massive religious demographic change as was the case when the Irish Free State came into being. The emergence of the Irish Free State was accompanied and followed by large-scale Protestant emigration. Both sides in Northern Ireland today sense that, if Northern Ireland is ever forced to leave the United Kingdom and to become absorbed in the Republic, that absorption would again be followed by massive Protestant emigration, so that in the whole island of Ireland, as in the Republic today, the Protestants who choose to "stay on" would in fact be accepting the political ethos of the Catholic majority. All that would follow if the unity of Ireland were to be imposed on the Protestants. If they were to *choose* unity, that would be another matter (see next chapter).

For Northern Catholics, this generally appears as a normal and satisfactory outcome. To Northern Protestants, on the other hand, it has represented everything they fear most, having to choose between emigration, and absorption into a polity which they have distrusted and feared.

The attitudes of the two communities are symmetrical up to a point. Both are contemplating the same vision of a possible future. One views that possible future with satisfaction; the other with dread. But whether they view that possible future with satisfaction or with dread it is objectively the same possibility they are contemplating.

That much is symmetrical. For adequate historical reasons, the feelings of the two communities towards one another are also symmetrical. Each distrusts and fears the other, to approximately the same degree in both cases. But the professions of eminent representatives of the two traditions with regard to the future are not symmetrical but in contrast. Protestants are apt to voice their negative feelings towards Catholics quite openly and sometimes brutally. Catholics are good at voicing feelings which are basically no less negative, in a putatively ecumenical manner.

The unrivalled maestro in this genre is John Hume. Mr Hume, for many years now has been repeating that all he is looking for is "an agreed Ireland." That sounds very reasonable to people in Britain and the Republic. But unionists in Northern Ireland well know that Hume is not seeking agreement with them; he has always treated everything their representatives say with sovereign contempt. What he is seeking is an agreement, or rather a series of agreements, *with the British Government over the future of Northern Ireland.* Each agreement is to be imposed on the unionists by the British. If the British dig their heels in, a threat of a resumption of IRA attacks on mainland Britain is likely to move them forward.

And the objective of the whole thing for Hume and Sinn Féin-IRA remains the same: a united Ireland, irrespective of the wishes of a majority in Northern Ireland. That is what Mr Hume means by "an agreed Ireland". The objective was set out in that joint statement by Hume and Adams which was published in the newspapers of the Republic on April 25, 1993: *"We accept that the Irish people as a whole have a right to national self-determination."*

When he signed that letter, Hume knew better than anyone else that that "right" was not likely to be recognised by unionists. But what he hopes eventually to achieve is *British* acceptance of that version of an agreed Ireland. It is *British* acceptance that Hume and Adams both aim at, and seem at present to be achieving in stages. Hume relies on the British to squeeze unionists into concession after concession, ending up in a united Ireland. By that time, the term of art, "an agreed Ireland" will no longer be needed.

* * *

I didn't in fact think that the unionists in Northern Ireland were any more bigoted than nationalists. But because for historical reasons unionists' bigotry tended to be unihibitedly expressed, while nationalist bigotry tended to be covered over with layers of pseudo-ecumenical rhetoric, outsiders – British, American and other – tended to find nationalists nicer and more "reasonable" than unionists, a perception which has been greatly to the advantage of the former.

I wouldn't have volunteered my services to either of the unionist parties which existed at the time I became a Friend of the Union, nor did either of them ask me to do so. But a Conservative candidate in a by-election, coming forward as a non-sectarian unionist, did ask for my help. This was Laurence Kennedy. I spoke in his support at a couple of meetings.

Though personally a good candidate, he never really looked like winning. This was not because of the non-sectarian factor, with which most middle-class unionists were – and are – in agreement, but because of the deep resentment felt, at this time, by unionists of all descriptions against the British Tories for what unionists not unreasonably regarded as a Tory betrayal of the Union, when Margaret Thatcher concluded the Anglo-Irish Agreement over the heads of all unionists without even consulting them. So that particular candidate did very well, in the circumstances, by getting 13,000 votes, which were, however, not enough to elect him.

Not long afterwards, in the summer of 1995, a more formidable non-sectarian unionist, with no Thatcherite baggage, Bob McCartney, asked for my help and got it. Bob had opposed the Anglo-Irish Agreement and still opposes the versions of "peace process" which descended from it. So while he had to fight a candidate backed by the Ulster Unionist Party, his credentials were better in the eyes of many unionists in North Down than were those of his opponent.

I found canvassing with Bob McCartney in North Down a most interesting and illuminating and also a heartening experience. Bob is probably the most successful QC in Northern Ireland, but his own family roots are in the working-class area of the Shankill Road, Belfast. He is at ease with people of all classes in Northern Ireland, as very few other politicians are. In the working-class areas people recognize him and come up and chat with him. To my initial surprise, they were usually laughing and joking together. I was surprised because southern Catholics – the community of which I was an aberrant member – generally think of Northern Protestants as a dour, humourless people. Yet here they were joking and laughing like mad. How come?

When I thought about that for a while, the answer was not hard to find. Most southern Catholics, when they talk with Ulster Protestants, try to induce the Protestants to move in a direction in which they have not wanted to go (that of a united Ireland). If you do that with any group of people you are likely to find that your interlocutors seem glum and uncommunicative. In short: if you try to push people around you will find that they will bristle.

Canvassing with Bob McCartney, I was seeing Protestants as they are when they are at ease with themselves. Few people from a southern Catholic background can ever have seen Ulster Protestants under those conditions and I felt quite privileged and happy to have this experience. Also, many of the people I met knew about me, and what I stood for in relation to Northern Ireland, and welcomed me for that. Those – no doubt no less numerous – who knew nothing about me welcomed me as a friend of Bob McCartney's. Either way, I had become, as it were, a member of a family to which I had never expected to belong. It was one of the most welcome surprises of my life.

Bob won that election quite handily and Bob and I have kept in constant touch ever since. Bob and his wife Maureen and Máire and myself soon became close friends. Even apart from politics, we have many interests in common and – no less important – keen and congruent senses of humour. And their friends and close partners – Cedric Wilson and his wife Eva, Paddy Roche and his wife Liz – soon became our friends also. It was quite a contrast with the often stormy patterns at work within the Irish Labour Party, the only political party to which I had ever previously belonged. As this was a belated experience what it brought to mind was Auden's line about Herman Melville: "Towards the end he sailed into an extraordinary mildness."

The mildness was, however, confined to my close political associates. The wider political water was choppy enough, and getting choppier. A year after that by-election – in May, 1966 – Bob asked me to be a member of his group of candidates for the election to the Forum and "the talks on the future of Northern Ireland". Bob's group won enough votes to have three members seated at the Forum and the talks and I was one of the three.

The Forum was a genuine democratic body in which unionists were in a majority, and to whose deliberations the press was freely admitted. But the Forum had no power. The business end of these arrangements, prepared in order to reach a predetermined conclusion, was "the talks on the future of Northern Ireland". Participants in the talks were selected by a curious system of weighted voting and the press was excluded from the scene of the talks. It soon became clear to anyone who paid close attention, as I did, that the talks were designed in such a way as to reach conclusions satisfactory to nationalists and unpalatable to most of those unionists who understood what was going on.

The predetermined element in all this first became unmistakeably evident after a vote on whether to seat Sinn Féin at the talks, while Sinn

Féin's masters, the IRA, still held on to all their weaponry. The three unionist parties – the Ulster Unionists, the Democratic Unionists and my own United Kingdom Unionists – all voted against the seating of Sinn Féin in such conditions. Under the ground rules of the talks – which required cross-community support for any measure to be adopted – the proposal had failed, and the chairman of the talks, the American Senator, George Mitchell, so ruled. That should have been the end of the matter under the rules of procedure.

But it wasn't the end of the matter. The British government, with the support of the Dublin government, immediately proceeded to seat Sinn Féin at the talks, while the IRA retained all their weapons. Because it had already become evident – though in less glaring ways – that the talks were rigged in favour of the nationalist side, the DUP and ourselves had already decided to leave the talks, but our decision to leave took effect only after the seating of Sinn Féin. The UUP, however, stayed on at the talks along with Sinn Féin, while affecting not to talk directly to their new neighbours.

What had up to then been a condition of rumbling dissent between the UUP and the other two unionist parties now became an open rift. The DUP and the UK Unionists denounced the UUP for having betrayed a basic position previously common to all unionists: that of refusing to sit down with Sinn Féin as long as the IRA retains all its weapons.

The alliance of the two smaller unionist parties in opposition to the large unionist party was now a stark fact of political life in Northern Ireland. The UK Unionists were assailed by several commentators, mostly in the Republic, for making common cause with Ian Paisley, well-known for his past sectarian utterances. But the agreement between the DUP and the UKUP has been an alliance mainly for one specific purpose: that of the defence of the Union, for as long as Protestants continue to adhere to the Union. It does, however, also have other important common features: a common rejection of paramilitary alliances, support for the RUC, and opposition to premature releases for persons serving sentences for paramilitary crimes.

Compare those positions with those of the present "Yes" alliance. Through Hume-Adams, the SDLP are in alliance with Sinn Féin, and Sinn Féin is still nothing more than the propaganda arm of the IRA. The UUP cultivates close relations with the political fronts of two loyalist paramilitary groups which – like the IRA – retain all their weapons. None of that, apparently, raises any eyebrows among the people who profess to be so worried about the "sectarian" associations of the DUP.

When I first came into close political contact with Dr Paisley, I had been prepared to encounter some reserve on his part, since my family background is Roman Catholic. But nothing of the sort. I found Dr Paisley personally most friendly, and even genial, on our first meeting, and he has remained so ever since. I suffered a stroke while the Forum and "talks" were still meeting and on my return to the Forum, after my recovery, the address of welcome to me was delivered by Ian Paisley, in a warm and felicitous statement.

Dr Paisley's public oratory is still rather on the exuberant side, but in private political discussions he is invariably calm and shrewd. He has a remarkable capacity for rapid, almost instant elucidation of a new political document, laying bare its inner tendencies, and proposing an appropriate reply. I would rather have Ian Paisley in my corner than I would David Trimble.

* * *

The elections of late June saw significant gains for the DUP-UKU alliance, and significant losses for the UUP. As I write this – shortly after the elections – the UUP are still the largest party, in terms of seats held, but they already face the probability of some early defections. Trimble is about to be elected First Minister with Seamus Mallon as Deputy First Minister. But later – how much later I do not know – Tony Blair will seat Sinn Féin in the assembly and allocate to it two members in the Ministry presided over by Trimble, while Sinn Féin's IRA masters retain all their weaponry.

I don't think any informed person doubts that that is what Blair intends to do, or that he has already notified Sinn Féin of that intention. Otherwise Sinn Féin would not have recommended a "Yes" vote. But right up to the June elections the prime minister was still dissimulating. In the last Commons debate on the subject, the opposition leader, William Hague, asked Blair to confirm that no prisoners could be released before terrorists organisations had substantially decommissioned their weapons. Mr Blair's reply was clear: "The answer to your question is yes, of course." That unequivocal assurance was omitted from the Hansard report of the prime minister's speech. This little transaction was absolutely typical of the routine dishonesty which has accompanied every stage of the "peace process".

What Blair is about to do, in seating Sinn Féin, runs quite contrary to promises which Trimble claims – almost certainly rightly – to have received from Blair on the eve of the Forum referendum.

Faced with that dire outcome, Trimble has really only two choices. He can resign as head of the new executive, and call on his followers on the executive also to resign. In that event the assembly will lose the "cross-community" support which the new arrangements require and the assembly will be dissolved.

Alternatively, Trimble could swallow hard and remain Chief Minister in a Ministry which includes Sinn Féin members, while Sinn Féin's masters retain all their weapons. If that happens, Mr Timble's parliamentary supporters will desert him in droves so that opponents of the programme approved by the two governments will be in solid possession of a comfortable "blocking third".

It seems to follow that irrespective of which of the two possible lines Trimble chooses to follow after the seating of Sinn Féin, the British government will be driven to dissolve the assembly.

However, the British government's policy of seeking to propitiate Sinn Féin will not disappear after the collapse of the assembly. On the contrary, the appeasement of Sinn Féin will be sought with even more fervour than before. The appeasement is dictated by fear that if Sinn Féin is not appeased the IRA will resume its bombing of mainland Britain. In pursuit of appeasement Britain will speedily release all convicts with paramilitary links.

They will then get on with the "reform" of the RUC (Royal Ulster Constabulary) demanded by the IRA. The reform will include, as a minimum, a change in the name of the RUC deleting the adjective "royal". In itself this might seem a small matter. But it is not a small matter since the RUC will know that this change has been made at the behest of the people who have murdered nearly three hundred RUC members over the past quarter of a century. The change will therefore strike a devastating blow at the morale of the RUC. And once the effects of that blow have sunk in, the IRA will be able to resume its campaign with much brighter prospects of significant military success. Followed by a third ceasefire, further blackmail and further concessions. And so on.

It is possible that the second IRA resumption of military operations, following the second ceasefire, would be followed by a massive shift in British public opinion against any further appeasement of Sinn Féin-IRA. This would be similar in kind, though on a much smaller scale, to the shift against any further appeasement of the Nazis which followed on Hitler's violation of the Munich agreement through his annexation of the rump territory left to Czechoslovakia in that agreement. If such a shift in British public opinion over the appeasement of the IRA did occur, it could establish Northern Ireland as part of the United Kingdom more solidly than has been the case over the past twenty years. In that case, continued adherence to the Union would continue to be sound policy for the present unionists, whose core is the Protestant population of Northern Ireland.

But what if a second renewal of "military operations" by the IRA were to be followed by a third ceasefire, accompanied by further blackmail, extorting further concessions?

It is at this point that unionists are likely to consider the only real option which the weak leadership of Ulster unionism, and British connivance with Sinn Féin, have left them: a deal with constitutional nationalists to avert British surrender of Northern Ireland to violent republicanism.

I shall consider those weighty questions further in my final chapter.

20

THE UNION ON THE EVE
OF THE MILLENNIUM

"WE ASK FOR NO SPECIAL RIGHTS BUT WE CLAIM THE SAME RIGHTS FROM THE same government as every other part of the United Kingdom." – Edward Carson

If the principle which Carson, with his massive commonsense, laid down had been followed in practice, Northern Ireland today might be securely part of the United Kingdom. Unfortunately, Carson's principle was set aside. The governing principle of Lloyd George's settlement of 1920-21 was that Britain should be enabled to distance itself from both parts of Ireland, and that Irish affairs should no longer be able to dominate the proceedings of the Parliament of the United Kingdom, as they had been doing sometimes with shattering impact, at intervals since 1881.

Acting on this principle Lloyd George set up parliaments for both parts of Ireland. "Southern Ireland" – later the Irish Free State, still later the Republic of Ireland – with its huge Catholic majority, was virtually a homogeneous polity. But Northern Ireland was not: it was approximately two-thirds Protestant, and one-third Catholic, with a largely inimical pattern in the relations between the two elements. This had two implications for the new Parliament of Northern Ireland. The first was that there would be a permanent Protestant and unionist majority. The second was that that majority would abuse such powers as it had, in its own perceived interests, as against those of the minority. The Parliament had in fact few delegated powers but it abused those it had in relation to jobs, housing and local franchise. The Parliament of the United Kingdom for many years ignored these abuses as irrelevant to its jurisdiction.

The Catholics of Northern Ireland suffered from a justified sense of grievance, and also greatly exaggerated the extent of the same. The ludicrous claim was frequently made that the sufferings of Northern Catholics were equivalent to those of South African blacks under apartheid.

After the Second World War another analogy was perceived which, although still greatly exaggerated, was much closer to the mark, politically speaking. This was an analogy with the conditions of American blacks – still in the 1960s subject to severe discrimination in the Southern States. The analogy caught on. In the perception of British people, Protestants came to appear as oppressors, Catholics as oppressed. In any collision between the two, British public opinion came to favour the Catholics. This shift in perceptions led, after the troubles of 1969-1970, to the deployment of British troops for the restoration of civil order, and then after an interval, to the effective abolition – initially labelled "prorogation" – of Stormont.

But the interval was important, for in the interval the Provisional IRA had emerged and began its campaign of violence. To many in Northern Ireland the collapse of the Stormont regime appeared to be the work of the IRA, and the IRA's political arm – Sinn Féin – cunningly exploited this impression and benefited from it electorally.

Lloyd George's carefully crafted system had broken down, but the mentality behind it – a strong British desire to tiptoe away from Ireland with all its problems – was a strong as ever. And it became stronger still when the IRA repeatedly demonstrated its capacity to attack targets in mainland Britain. To appease the IRA became a principal though never explicitly avowed motivating force in British policy-making in relation to Northern Ireland. This is the fuel of what is misleadingly known as the "peace process".

In their efforts to tiptoe away from Northern Ireland, without quite seeming to do so, the British Government needed some cover from acquiescent unionists. They have had some success with this. A defining moment came, within the talks on the future of Northern Ireland when it was proposed to seat Sinn Féin at the talks, while Sinn Féin's masters, the IRA, insisted in retaining all their weaponry. All three unionist parties – the Official Unionists, the Democratic Unionists and the United Kingdom Unionists – voted against seating Sinn Féin in these circumstances. The rules of the talks required that any proposition must have cross-community support and the Chairman, George Mitchell, then correctly ruled that the proposition had failed.

That, however, was by no means the end of the matter. The British and Irish Governments then met and decided to seat Sinn Féin at the talks anyway, irrespective of the rules of the talks, which were thereby revealed to be a mere facade and sham. The DUP and UKUP had now given up on the talks, knowing them to be a sham. But David Trimble and his followers decided to stay on at the talks, along with Sinn Féin. A great rift had now opened in the ranks of elected unionists, and that rift is still there at the time of writing.

As Bob McCartney wrote recently:

"Ulster Unionism, under the leadership of David Trimble, has acquiesced in a series of concessions that have rendered the cause of the Union well nigh indefensible. The possession of weaponry with which to threaten a soft and complex mainland society has always been a republican card which Unionism could never trump. Moreover, its use or the threat of it could be played time and again. The failure of David Trimble to ensure its removal during negotiations, and before the concessions contained in the Belfast Agreement had been made, was a strategic error of a major kind. It was a mistake that has rendered the defence of the Union increasingly difficult."

Many unionists now see the disintegration of the Union as something already in progress, and are considering what options are now open to them, in these dire circumstances.

One option increasingly considered – and acted on by some – is emigration to Scotland. The flight of those with capital and a strong antipathy to republican triumphalism is a recurring topic of conversation, while many substantial farmers have already established bridgeheads by acquiring farms in Western Scotland. Paradoxically, the flight option is made psychologically more attractive as the prospect of Scottish independence grows, and antipathy to what is seen as English betrayal deepens. It is ironic that the fracture of the Union between England and Scotland may be welcomed by those who once strove might and main to preserve the Union between Northern Ireland and what was once Great Britain. Almost subliminally, the Scottish option has been creeping up upon the unionist middle classes. Scottish universities have been flooded for years with students from Northern Ireland as increasing numbers find a triumphalist republican ethos in Ulster's two universities unacceptable.

While some may choose to go because they can, at least as great a number may choose to remain and resist by force of arms the imposition by Britain of a political settlement: a settlement they view as having been the product of terrorist violence. It would be a mistake to believe that those who chose this option would be confined to the quasi-criminal, though such might provide the detonating factor in a violent civil war, a war in which the most able and deadly protagonists might be those whose previous civic record was of law-abiding industry, but in whom the violation of their rights, as they perceived them, had provoked a mortal rage.

This would be a disastrous development, but unfortunately it is only one of a number of possible disasters beginning to loom up under cover of the peace process. Less than nine months after the hysterical celebration of the alleged arrival of peace through the Good Friday Declaration, came the most lethal outrage in the whole history of Northern Ireland: the Omagh bomb of 15 August 1998. At a lower routine level, and almost ignored, the savage physical attacks euphemistically called "punishment beatings" continue every week, in a condition which John Hume still regularly describes as "peace". These savage acts have been calmly and silently integrated into what is called "the peace process".

The two Governments, with or without the aid of Mr Trimble may succeed in seating Sinn Féin in the Executive of the new Assembly, without the IRA's having agreed to relinquish any arms. But it is clear that a majority of unionists are now resolutely opposed to such a seating, and without adequate unionist support the Assembly and Executive will not be able to function and will have to be dissolved.

But the failure of the arrangements which represented the culmination for the "peace process" will not mean the ending of the British government's wooing of Sinn Féin-IRA. Quite the contrary. Sinn Féin, by reason of their loyalty to "Yes", will be seen as the good guys who need to be rewarded. And Sinn Féin will not be slow to name their reward. In fact they have already named it. The reward is the "reform" – meaning the castration – of the RUC. And the moment when the British government agree to "reform" the RUC, at the bidding of its mortal enemies, will be the moment when it becomes clear that the Union has become a trap for the unionists.

It is at this point that unionists are likely to be forced to consider the only third option which the weak leadership of Ulster unionism has bequeathed to them – a deal with constitutional nationalism to avert British surrender of Northern Ireland to violent republicanism.

As I write this, in the late summer of 1998, consideration of this third option – a deal with constitutional nationalism – has probably not yet directly troubled the consciousness of many unionists. But later this year it is likely to be coming darkly to the fore. When as seems probable at the time of writing the Government of the United Kingdom seats Sinn Féin representatives in the new Executive, contrary to assurances the leader of the largest unionist party believed himself to have received, a defining moment in the history of the Union will have been reached. The British Government will have reached out to conciliate, at unionists' expense, the people who have murdered hundreds of unionists and maimed thousands over the past quarter of a century – simply for being unionists. So some detailed consideration of this third and, for many, what may seem the most viable option, must be undertaken.

So what if unionists come to see the Union itself, as perceived by Whitehall, as a threat? Where then can they go? Many unionists, contemplating that threat, will be reluctant to avert it by attempting secession, aimed at an independent Northern Ireland. Should that be seriously attempted, a savage civil war would follow, ruinous to both communities in Northern Ireland.

So if one rules out continued adherence to a Union which is being used as an instrument of coercion, and the limited choice of flight, and the option of secession, what else is left?

Perhaps only the third option, I think, which is inclusion in a united Ireland: an inclusion negotiated on terms which would safeguard the vital interests of the Protestant community, the community which has supplied the defenders of the Union for over a century.

Many unionists would presently see this as so outlandish a proposition as not to deserve serious consideration. Yet events may show that, in these circumstances, and in the conditions of the late 20th century, no other way to safeguard the vital interests of the Protestant community in Northern Ireland is available.

Within the United Kingdom, the Ulster Protestants, about a million people in a society of more than fifty million, are without political clout. In a united Ireland, with a total population of less than six million, the ex-unionists would be a formidable voting bloc, for whose support other political parties would compete. These ex-unionists would therefore be in a much stronger position, in defending their vital interests, than they are now as despised hangers-on of a population which no longer wants them, and whose government may progressively coerce them.

Of course, the modalities would have to be worked out. But this may not be as difficult a matter as it now appears, if a substantial number of former unionists moved to seek a role in a united Ireland which would safeguard their basic rights and interests. In that regard, the most important thing is that the Republic would accept, *and embody in law*, in advance of a united Ireland, a guarantee that the population of Northern Ireland would have exactly the same rights and privileges – for *all* of them – as they now enjoy in the United Kingdom. Once their franchise was assured, and it was clear that they no longer posed a constitutional threat, those who have been unionists would be much more secure in a united Ireland than they are at present.

There would be a few other important elements which would need to be worked out in advance of any settlement. The most important element would be the future of the RUC, now seriously threatened by the Government of the United Kingdom in its near-desperate urge to appease the IRA and so deflect renewed attacks on mainland Britain.

The RUC and the Garda Síochána have long enjoyed generally cordial relations with one another, since they both share a healthy detestation of the IRA and the loyalist paramilitaries. A fusion of the two police forces, on terms agreed between them could be scheduled for a future date but should not be rushed. For the immediate future, the important thing would be that the RUC should be convinced that the future of their members, now seriously threatened in the UK of the late 20th century, would be secure within an Ireland united by consent.

The advantages for the unionist community of inclusion in a united Ireland, thus emerging from their present perilous dependence on people who no longer appear to want them, would be very great. I shall look later at the question of whether enough unionists can be persuaded of these advantages. But let us now consider the questions of probable attitudes towards such developments, in the event that they should ever take place. Let us look at the probable attitudes of the British and Irish governments, of the SDLP, and then of Sinn Féin-IRA and the loyalist paramilitaries.

The simplest reaction would be that of the British Government, offered a marvellous opportunity for disengagement from Northern Ireland without any further need to propitiate the IRA or to deceive the unionist population. Once assured of a favourable reaction among most Irish nationalists (see below), the British and the wider international community could be relied on to facilitate the transition, economically and politically, and to help the Irish Government to come to terms acceptable to former unionists.

The position of the Dublin Government would be a little more complicated. Officially, any Dublin Government would have to welcome the unionist proposals opening the way to a united Ireland, achieved by peaceful means. But each political party in the Republic would also be aware that the entry into their polity of northern unionists – and also northern nationalists – would change beyond recognition the nature of the setting in which Irish politics henceforward would have to operate.

The transition would be particularly difficult for Fianna Fáil. Officially, of course, the party would have to welcome the achievement at long last of one of its two "national aims", and to pride itself on its contribution to that achievement; without being quite sure in its own mind as to what the nature of that contribution might have been. Rejoicing outwardly, Fianna Fáil would inwardly be deeply uneasy. They would, of course, acquire some new allies: the SDLP, or most of it, would be likely to join them. But members of the largest political grouping in Northern Ireland, the former unionists, would probably ally themselves with any party (except Sinn Féin) other than Fianna Fáil. Sinn Féin would oppose the whole deal, and also any party that accepted it. So, on the whole, the deal would probably lead to a loss of overall support for Fianna Fáil, which might well prove permanent. Yet the deal – a united Ireland achieved by peaceful means – would be so popular with the electorate in the Republic that Fianna Fáil would not dare to oppose it. If they tried to drag their feet – for example over the RUC – they would soon lose ground to Fine Gael and Labour. So Fianna Fáil would go along with the whole deal, and claim they had master-minded it.

In Northern Ireland John Hume could and would plausibly claim that here at last was "the agreed Ireland" for which he had worked so long and so tirelessly. He could not possibly oppose it and might reasonably hope to get the Nobel Prize for his contribution to the happy outcome. Also – as Mr Hume would be the first to notice – the outcome would be a singularly happy one for the SDLP as a political party. The SDLP have been losing ground in recent years to Sinn Féin, especially west of the Bann. But once a formerly unionist bloc moved to accept a united Ireland, and Sinn Féin opposed that move, while the SDLP accepted it, the SDLP would recover all the lost ground and become unquestionably the party of the Catholics of Northern Ireland. Sinn Féin-IRA would be stricken by a deal which would deprive them of their *raison d'etre* within the nationalist community of all Ireland. In a way that distinguishes them from other nationalists, Sinn Féin-IRA basically hate the Ulster unionists and will hate them even more if they become *ex*-unionists, accepted by other nationalists. Sinn Féin wants to impose such terms on the Ulster unionists as will drive most of them from the island of Ireland, and will reduce the small remainder to cringing submission. Sinn Féin-IRA have believed they were – and indeed still believe they are – on the verge of achieving that desirable aim. To be robbed of that achievement at the last moment by a brilliant political breakthrough for the Protestants would be the bitterest blow Sinn Féin-IRA have sustained since the Treaty of 1921. Worse than that indeed. By being robbed of their *raison d'etre*, Sinn Féin could be put out of business for all time.

When I contemplate that brilliant reversal of the thirteen-year-old political hegemony of Sinn Féin-IRA over the unionist population of Northern Ireland the storyteller's version of an exit from enthralment comes vividly to mind: "with one bound our hero was free".

There might be some attempt at armed resistance to the deal, both by the IRA and loyalists, but it would be likely to be brief. Most nationalists would see the IRA fighting against a united Ireland as utterly perverse and ridiculous and most nationalists would, in consequence firmly support the repression by the security forces of any such rising and would support any measures to do so. When loyalists saw that the deal had deprived the IRA of their *raison d'etre*, and put paid to their very existence, loyalist opposition to the deal would also die down.

* * *

The general character of nationalists' reactions to such an overture (if it were to come) from former unionists is relatively easy to predict. The real difficulty about the idea might well be the traumatic character of the turn-around it calls for on the part of a substantial section of people who have been unionists, and have regarded the idea of union with the Republic of Ireland with settled aversion. Yet the fact is that the union with Great Britain, to which unionists still cling, is being steadily undermined by the political parties in Great Britain, with the approval or consent of most of the British people.

Let us assume that "No" unionists, firmly in possession of a blocking third, are able to frustrate the working of an Executive in which Sinn Féin is seated, while the IRA retains all its weapons. The arrangements scheduled in the Good Friday Agreement, subscribed to by the Official Unionists, would collapse, and the two governments would prorogue the Assembly acknowledging the collapse of the whole ambitious project. What then?

I don't think that the unionists should attempt any major political initiative at this stage. They should wait to see what the frustrated coalition, still dominated by Sinn Féin-IRA, gets up to next. In the meantime the victorious "No" unionists should consolidate their power within unionism. They should build on the fact that this is the first political victory scored by unionist political representatives since the collapse of Sunningdale more than twenty years ago.

Sunningdale was brought down by a popular uprising – the strike of the power-workers – to which the then political leadership capitulated retrospectively. But this time the Good Friday Agreement – "Sunningdale for slow learners" as Séamus Mallon defined it, with a dimension of unconscious irony which escaped him – will have been brought down by elected politicians. Those politicians have now the right to claim the leadership of the present unionist community. At this point, they may decide to assume control of their own political destiny and use that leadership to take their community out of a Union which they then clearly perceive has become an instrument of coercion used to propitiate those who seek to destroy their community.

But they should not move in that direction precipitately. They should wait to see what the British Government does after the collapse of the Good Friday arrangements. And they should be preparing for a far-reaching response to what the British Government does, if the interests of their community require such a response.

And what will the British Government do? Putting it simply, I believe the British Government will go on propitiating the IRA – as it has been doing for many years now – in the hope of averting further terrorist attacks on mainland Britain. To that end it will first speed up the projected releases of what are now presented as "political prisoners": that is, persons convicted of murder and other serious crimes, for which they claim political motivation. The releases are now proceeding and unionists can do no more than protest against them. But in protesting against them, unionists would do well already to strike a warning note: that by such actions, the British Government is undermining the Union itself.

The second stage is much more serious. This is the contemplated "reform" of the RUC. The demand for "reform" is coming primarily from Sinn Féin-IRA, but acquiesced in by the SDLP. Sinn Féin-IRA calls for "community policing", meaning in effect that each paramilitary gang would dominate its own patch of turf, so spreading and legitimising "punishment beatings" and so on, creating conditions of anarchy. Sinn Féin-IRA don't expect to get "community policing" – at least not in the near future – but they do expect to get some sort of "reform" of the RUC which will represent movement in that general direction. The climate of opinion in Britain, following the collapse of the Good Friday Agreement, is likely to be propitious to faster movement in that direction than would have been acceptable before. Sinn Féin, loyal to "Yes" to the bitter end, will be seen by many in Britain as more "reasonable" than the "No" voters, presented as wild men. So, when Sinn Féin presses the British on this they will find a lot of "give".

For Sinn Féin's masters, the IRA, this question of "reform" of the RUC is much the most important item in the present political agenda. The RUC have been increasingly effective against the IRA, especially during the IRA's last – and rather brief – resumption of "military operations". So to demoralise the RUC is quite a rational objective from the IRA's point of view. And how better can you demoralise a force than to have it "reformed" at the bidding of those who have murdered hundreds of its members over the past quarter of a century? Once the message of that "reform" sank in among members of the RUC the IRA would be able to resume "military operations" with a greatly enhanced prospect of success. Why should a policeman risk his life in resisting people who seem to have the implicit backing of his own government?

* * *

The moment of truth for the Union is likely to come when the British Government announces its proposals for the "reform" of the RUC. That would be the most opportune moment for unionists to announce, not that they are leaving the Union but that the Union is in the process of leaving *them*. There are already signs that that recognition is beginning to dawn, together with an intimation of where it might lead. Thus after I had written most of the above my eye fell on an article by Ruth Dudley Edwards which opened with the words:

　"'I think I'd rather the British Government told us we had to have a united Ireland,' said an anti-agreement unionist last week. 'At least then we'd be negotiating with democrats in Dublin rather than being abandoned here to fight two sets of Mafiosi.'" (Irish Times, 30 June 1998).

Throughout the past summer, the British Government appeared bent on convincing itself and others that Sinn Féin-IRA are firmly and unconditionally committed to peace. In doing so, the government seemed bent on ignoring clear messages to the contrary coming from Sinn Féin itself. On Thursday August 6 the Northern Secretary, Mo Mowlam said:

> *"I think the war is certainly over for groups that have signed up to an unequivocal ceasefire, and their political representatives are in the talks process. I have accepted that they are acting in good faith and the security advice I get supports that."*

Having reported that fatuous statement, the same *Irish Times* article (by Theresa Judge in Belfast) went on:

> "Her comments followed publication of an article in a Belfast newspaper yesterday in which the Sinn Féin leader, Mr Gerry Adams, said that 'a peaceful transition to a just settlement and an independent and united Ireland' would require 'more than words or word games about whether the war is over'. He added: 'The war will be over when all of those who have engaged in war – and some are still engaging in war – stop; when the British army of occupation, which still maintains a huge military presence in republican areas, begins demilitarising instead of remilitarising; when all of the prisoners are free; when there is justice and equality and when we have a proper policing service.'"

No comment of Mo Mowlan on Gerry Adams's statement appears to have been reported, nor does anyone appear to have asked her how those two statements can be reconciled. No wonder many unionists have been registering deep distrust of the British Government.

If these feelings are beginning to surface now, they will emerge more forcefully *after* Sinn Féin claim their places in the new Executive. Shortly after that, unionist leaders should begin publicly and seriously to question whether commitment to the Union really any longer protects the vital interests of the Protestants of Northern Ireland. And after the publication of the Government's proposals for the "reform" of the RUC, unionists might then consider opening talks with Dublin, with the immediate objective of protecting the RUC, and exploration of the more long-term objective of entering a united Ireland in which the Protestants would be able to protect their own position far more effectively than they can do by remaining in the present Union, listing, as it does, in the direction dictated by Sinn Féin-IRA.

* * *

For a long time unionists have thought of nationalist Ireland as dominated by the Catholic Church, and a political bloc responsive to the Catholic Church. These perceptions were natural enough in the conditions in which unionists first became aware of a serious nationalist threat, in 1886. But they have long ceased to be relevant to any polity which unionists might now join.

The power of the Catholic Church – real in the early days of the threat to the Union – has now ebbed into near insignificance. The Catholic Church would have no influence whatever over those areas of a united Ireland containing a Protestant majority.

Nor is there any longer any one great political bloc dominating the present Republic or capable of dominating a united Ireland. The Republic, for many years now, has been run by coalitions. In a united Ireland, other parties would compete for alliance and transfer of preferences with members representing so important a bloc as would be made up by Northern Protestants. It is likely, for example, that any government in the Republic would, in the new circumstances, uphold the rights of Orangemen to march down the Garvaghy Road as they have long marched unobstructed in Donegal. Above all – as I have argued above – a united Ireland would, in such circumstances, entail the permanent eclipse of the Provisional IRA.

In short, on one view, the government of the United Kingdom may come to represent a serious threat to the Protestants of Northern Ireland.

This analysis or hypothesis offers no contradiction to my friends and present allies who voted "No" in the Referendum. I share their rejection of a process designed to propitiate those who have murdered and maimed them. I simply postulate some of the logical outworkings of a situation in which British policy and the weak leadership of Ulster unionists may have placed them.

As for me, I shall remain a friend and supporter of the Union for so long as that Union offers the means of protecting the vital interests of those friends and allies. If developing events finally make it clear to me that a Union, which mainland Britain increasingly appears not to want, has itself become the agency for the destruction of their rights as a free people, I will lend my voice and energies to the adoption of whatever is the best course for the maintenance of their historic rights and the political destruction of those who would remove such rights from them.

The Union is perhaps a political abstraction which, for unionists, was synonymous with civil and religious liberty. If it should become an instrument for coercion, then those who seek such liberty will always have to seek union with those who have come to share their beliefs.

Perhaps, as we enter a rapidly changing world on the eve of the Millennium, those who fear change should be conscious of the words of a great libertarian, the late Sir Isaiah Berlin:

"Principles are not less sacred because their duration
cannot be guaranteed. Indeed, the very desire for
guarantees that our values are eternal and secure in
some objective Heaven is perhaps only a craving for
the certainties of childhood or the absolute values of
our primitive past. To realise the relative validity of
one's convictions and yet stand for them unflinchingly
is what distinguishes a civilised man from a barbarian.
To demand more than this is perhaps a deep and
incurable metaphysical need: but to allow it to
determine one's practice is a symptom of an equally
deep and more dangerous moral and political immaturity."

INDEX